The
Psychoanalytic
Study
of the Child

VOLUME SIXTY-EIGHT

The Psychoanalytic Study of the Child

VOLUME SIXTY-EIGHT

Yale University Press
New Haven and London
2014

Yale University Press books may be purchased in quantity
for educational, business, or promotional use.
For information, please e-mail sales.press@yale.edu (U.S. office)
or sales@yaleup.co.uk (U.K. office).

Designed by Sally Harris and set in Baskerville type.
Printed in the United States of America.

International standard book number: 978-0-300-20741-5

Library of Congress catalogue card number: 45-11304
A catalogue record for this book is available from the British Library.

This paper meets the requirements of ANSI/NISO Z39.48–1992
(Permanence of Paper).

10 9 8 7 6 5 4 3 2 1

Contents

A NARRATIVE HISTORY
OF *THE PSYCHOANALYTIC*
STUDY OF THE CHILD

Exploring the Dialectical Space

A Brief History of
The Psychoanalytic Study of the Child

SAMUEL ABRAMS, M.D.

Abrams, currently the longest serving editor of The Psychoanalytic Study of the Child, *offers his views of emerging models and themes in the understanding of children, which has characterized* The PSOC *since its inception in 1945. In his view, the first of its published papers, Hartmann and Kris's "The Genetic Approach in Psychoanalysis," set the stage for examining innovative ways to view the growth of the mind in general and the psychological development of children in particular. In his judgment, many of its published papers have highlighted expectable dispositional discontinuities as well as recognizable continuities interacting with a varying and sometimes unexpected set of environment circumstances. That interaction occurs within a dialectical space that contributes its own unique influences. This investigative trend, scattered throughout its nearly seventy-year history, may reflect the recognition for the need for a different foundational theory for our discipline or perhaps a new paradigm altogether.*

Dr. Abrams is Editor of *The Psychoanalytic Study of the Child*; Training and Supervising Child and Adult Analyst, The Institute of Psychoanalytic Education, an affiliate of The New York University Langone School of Medicine; Former Director of The Institute of Psychoanalytic Education; Past Chairman of the Committee on Psychoanalytic Education, American Psychoanalytic Association; and President of The Anna Freud Foundation.

This is a somewhat extended and modified paper originally presented at the Oral History Workshop at the American Psychoanalytic Association's annual meeting, January 17, 2013.

The Psychoanalytic Study of the Child 68, ed. Claudia Lament, Robert A. King, Samuel Abrams, Paul M. Brinich, and Rona Knight (Yale University Press, copyright © 2015 by Claudia Lament, Robert A. King, Samuel Abrams, Paul M. Brinich, and Rona Knight).

INTRODUCTION: THE MODES OF HISTORY

HISTORY IS THE MORE OR LESS RELIABLE RECORD OF THE PAST. HIS-
torians are the guardians of that database and its principal contributors.
In addition, they share the responsibility of establishing and assuring
standards for new petitioners.

The truly hard-nosed scientifically minded historians use the tools of
empirical research to uncover the past. Those tools are continuously
expanded through modern technology. They examine old documents,
review archaeological digs, unravel scrolls, retranslate ancient records,
use X-rays to discern a hidden predecessor behind an acknowledged
masterpiece, and so on. Using such tools lead to Mary Beard's informed
tour of ancient Pompeii (2009) or Charles Royster's *The Fabulous History of the Dismal Swamp Company* (1999), an account of the failings of
some of America's founding fathers as venture capitalists. Astronomers
go one observational step farther than anyone else. They have devised
the means to actually see past events in our solar system in real time!
How remarkable is that? Such empirically based contributions to the
historical archives are the result of investigative discoveries. They yield
highly reliable facts, the way some things actually were.

However, most historians, including populist writers and clinical psychoanalysts, approach the past differently. They are narrative historians
(Abrams, 2011). Narrative historians arrive at findings by creating a
coherent story with a beginning, a middle, and an end. You were se-
duced as a child—Freud explained, functioning as a reconstructing and
explanatory historian—and that caused excessive stimuli to accumulate
since you couldn't rid yourself of libido at that age. Mounting energy
gave rise to symptoms, until catharsis provided suitable discharge of the
accumulated libido and that's why you're well now. There are a lot of
tooth fairies in that bedtime story, but that's how narrative histories are
constructed, and that's how psychoanalysis was born.

Such inventive discourses are influenced by the customary and customarily unconscious features that affect all creative writing. In invent-
ing a narrative, some empirical facts are selected, others are omitted.
Those selected are framed within a setting that includes organization,
plot, ideology, and one or more tropes. While the hard-nosed empiricist
is very mindful of the strict rules that guide her investigative activities,
the narrative historian is often entirely unaware of the many features
that inform the invention of his stories, features that inevitably fictional-
ize the products to a greater or lesser extent. The empirical researchers are true discoverers of the past—as it really was, albeit invariably
colored by their contextualizing their findings within the present. The

narrative historians use inventiveness to try to create the past within a meaningful framework, although some persuade themselves and try to convince others that their creations are of equal validity as those derived directly by the empiricists.

In truth, such histories may be persuasive, plausible, practical, and may even hit the veridical mark once in a while. However, in general, while the empirical researcher wants to simply tell you what she's found out, the narrative historian wants you to believe that what he's created is real and belongs in the archival records. Often, in pursuing that aim, he fails to notice that his constructions of the past are reflections of something about the present. Convinced he is peering through a glass, he is actually staring at a mirror. And what is seen may be a profound awareness of something of great contemporary consequence. Historical narratives can be stealth allegories. Freud's story about the patient's antecedent seductions, for example, betrayed more about the impact and limitations of his technique in the present than it did about earlier pathogenic elements derived from the past. Narrative historians have much to tell us, but often what they tell us is something different than they may have had in mind.

THE PSYCHOANALYTIC STUDY OF THE CHILD

This will be a brief *narrative* history of *The Psychoanalytic Study of the Child*. I will select some events that reside in the records, add one or two personal anecdotes, and contextualize them into a story. A caveat: this storytelling is subject to the same conditions of any other narrative. I believe what I am constructing is more or less likely to have happened, and I may want you to believe it, but it is a story—an invention—and consequently subject to all the limitations of authenticity that are compromised by the tools of invention. Those tools require as much attention and interest as the manifest content and latent allegories they create and convey.

In 1945 *The PSOC* opened for business. And one aim of that business was to create a platform for Anna Freud's works. The psychoanalytic community was already separating itself into two major groups—those bearing the banner of conflict versus those flying the object-relations flag. The power that drives the mind derived from Instincts, claimed the first group; the mind was the result of the power of parenting and of familial and social structures, claimed the second. In the first post–World War II years, Americans had the choice of the classic Freudians on the one hand and Harry Stack Sullivan and some invading Brits on the other.

The Instinct people saw mental development as the *actualizations* of inherent forces by way of objects—people and things in the external surround. In this model, character or symptoms expressed emergent actualizing oral/anal/phallic phases. If you were compulsive, that was an objectified anal-phase derivative. Chic people, well-dressed sophisticates, asserted cheerfully that they were anal. On the other hand, those who were mindful of the value of the stimulus input looked at development as the *internalizations* of the subject-to-subject exchanges. As far as they were concerned, if you were compulsive, you probably had a compulsive mother. Consequently, other chic people regaled their mothers. For the first group, the Oedipus Complex was a result of the deployment of libido and aggression, cathecting parental objects as they were being represented and, therefore, an inevitable conflict arising from within. For the second, the Oedipus Complex was a result of a seductive mother and/or a rivalrous father, a conflict induced from without. In fact, some of them eventually argued, it really wasn't quite right to call it an Oedipus Complex, so the Jocasta Complex and the Laius Complex crawled into the literature (for example, Ross, 1983).

Popular culture reflected and reinforced this division. On the Instinct side, Leslie Nielson, then a handsome young space traveler in the 1956 film *The Forbidden Planet*, recognizes that Walter Pidgeon's "Id" (the named villain in the movie) has become monstrously actualized, threatening the disruption of all it surveys. Pidgeon and his dangerous Id are cleverly erased, and Leslie Nielson lives happily ever after with Pidgeon's daughter, Anne Francis.

On the other hand, in the 1945 movie *Spellbound*, the psychoanalyst Ingrid Bergman accesses a repressed internalized childhood event in her amnesic patient, Gregory Peck. Not only does this make him well, but he is proved innocent of a pending murder charge as well. All this is achieved by her interpreting his dreams in the midst of some spectacular boundary violations.

Anna Freud was hardly unmindful of this division between causative Instincts and causative events, but her work took her to a different place. Her research into "lines of development" was empirically based. She uncovered the *dialectical space* that exists between the actualizations and the internalizations. It proved to be a vast unexplored terrain containing a treasure trove that has still not been fully mined.

For one thing, it became evident that there were many emerging dispositional potentials in addition to instinctual drives that become actualized in the course of growth. There are the consequences of a silent guiding program of progressive hierarchical organizations, variations in progressive/regressive balances, an enhancing capacity for differentiation of the objects and subjects that peopled the child's world, affective variants, cognitive growth, the importance of transformative processes induced by integrations and reorganizations, and the influence of inherent disparities between developing systems. Examinations of these extraordinary and extraordinarily complex features inspired by Ms. Freud have surfaced frequently in the life of *The Psychoanalytic Study of the Child*, sometimes without direct attribution.

Much of what the volumes would become was heralded in the first paper of the first volume in the series. It was titled "The Genetic Approach in Psychoanalysis," by Heinz Hartmann and Ernst Kris (1945). It posed a challenge to the prevailing three metapsychological points of view by adding a new one. The initial three that informed normal and pathological development included forces, the nature of the energies that drove those forces, and the way they became structuralized into larger systems. They were in turn the Dynamic, Economic, and Structural foundation of psychoanalytic metatheory. These proposals leaned on metaphors that imaged dams filling and emptying, military garrisons, and the way these garrisons dealt with transient defeats. Among other things, it was very much in tune with the prevailing principles of Newtonian physics.

The new point of view that Hartmann and Kris added introduced the influences of both antecedent childhood experiences and innovative developmental transformations on the course of growth. The first of these—historical antecedents—was embraced easily by establishment psychoanalysis in both camps, albeit channeled to support their separate aims; the second—the tracking of developmental transformations has not been so readily accepted or worse—it has been so poorly misunderstood as to entirely nullify whatever promise it contained. In addition to promoting therapeutic work, recognition of this inherent feature of developmental transformations with its complex yield of unpredictable outcomes may help pull quantum mechanics into the foundational base of psychoanalytic metathink and thereby further broaden our theories of psychological development.

The original founders of *The PSOC* were all close to Anna Freud and anxious to see her work thrive, especially since it was losing ground to Melanie Klein in the U.K. and elsewhere. Ernst Kris was particularly close and was very much involved in the early organization of the series. Partly because of Ms. Freud's presence and Ernst Kris's proclivities, the editorial board had many women in influential positions. This was especially so in its earliest years—unusual for the 1940s and 1950s in any discipline much less psychoanalysis. Politically, Anna Freud's presence not only lifted the status of women but also legitimized lay clinicians as well. However, her existence proved an annoying distraction for some of the classical analysts of the time. One very prominent clinician told me in a hushed whisper that things had been just fine until Anna Freud came waltzing in with her crew of dancing girls—quite a vivid and illuminating metaphor.

It's difficult to ignore the gender issue wrapped around such a comment. After all, gender bias has been widespread in our psychoanalytic theories from its very outset. Phallic supremacy partnering with masked misogyny continues to slip into our concepts and clinical approaches, although often disguised as something else. One such abiding disguise is mother-blaming, which sometimes becomes outright mother-bashing. Our discipline, by way of persuasive explanatory stories rooted in a misapplied reductionism, has indicted whole groups of women as schizophrenogenic mothers, refrigerator mothers, misattuned mothers, and phallic mothers. And more recently there appears to be an organized lynch mob waiting to hang any woman in the public square suspected of being a "toxic" mother. Understanding the worldwide bias and outright violence against women is a worthy study for historians and almost everyone else, but it is particularly important that psychoanalysts recognize this bias within their own boundaries. Happily, *The Psychoanalytic Study of the Child*—although not entirely innocent of the prejudice—has been less guilty than most other publications.

The amplification of Ms. Freud's contributions and the derivatives they spawned has proceeded in an uneven fashion over the years, periodically marred by confusion or sometimes a determined obstinacy. Nevertheless, the continuation of her work was assured and abetted in *The Psychoanalytic Study of the Child* by an editorial board that never moved very far from Ms. Freud herself. The message was carried by the competence of several editorial leaders, especially Albert Solnit of New Haven and Peter Neubauer of New York, both close associates and collaborators of Ms. Freud. In more recent times those torches have been passed on to Robert King and Claudia Lament.

Even as Anna Freud has become increasingly irrelevant among educators, *The Psychoanalytic Study of the Child* continues as a vehicle for her message that clinical analysis can be enriched by a closer attention to the undiscovered dialectical space between the actualizations and the internalizations. It has always been a bit puzzling that Ms. Freud has been honored by institutionalized analysis by way of her *The Ego and Mechanisms of Defense* (1936), more a relic of an antiquated system than a reflection of any of the revolutionary concepts that regularly punctuated her career.

SUMMARY

For almost seventy years *The PSOC* series has tried to promote analytic work with children, differentiate it from work with adults, and discern how each might enhance the other. It has focused upon longitudinal studies and illustrations of clinical work with children and adults, while trying to explore that otherwise obscure relatively undiscovered terrain of psychological development that exists between the actualized and identified. These interests were inspired by the efforts of Anna Freud and have been maintained and extended by those who were either initially devoted to her personally or subsequently impressed with the astonishing array of clinical and technical possibilities that are contained in her research.

At the outset, I explained that I would be proposing historical findings by way of a narrative of the emerging *Psychoanalytic Study of the Child*. I suggested that you attend to how I construct my story—what kind of thinking and organization dominates my invention, whether there is an inherent plot form that shapes it, what role can be assigned to my own ideological views, and what consequences by the way I have troped my story. What present-day features of psychoanalytic theory and practice are veiled by this or any other historical revelries about the past? If you find yourself examining those factors, I will have conveyed more about the values I think Ms. Freud and *The PSOC* have made available than simply by listing their intentions and achievements.

BIBLIOGRAPHY

ABRAMS, S. (2011). Historiography 101 for Psychoanalysts. *Psychoanalytic Study of the Child* 65:103–128.

BEARD, MARY (2009). *Pompeii: The Life of a Roman Town*. London: Profile Books.

FREUD, ANNA (1936). *The Ego and the Mechanisms of Defence*. New York: International Universities Press.

HARTMANN, H., AND KRIS, E. (1945). The Genetic Approach in Psychoanalysis. *Psychoanalytic Study of the Child* 1: 11–30.

ROSS, J. (1983). Father to the Child. *Psychoanalytic Review* 70:301–320.

ROYSTER, C. (1999). *The Fabulous History of the Dismal Swamp Company*. New York: Vintage Books.

TRANSGENDER CHILDREN

Transgender Children

Conundrums and Controversies— An Introduction to the Section

CLAUDIA LAMENT, Ph.D.

This paper introduces the readership of The Psychoanalytic Study of the Child *to the topic of transgender children, which will be investigated in the papers that follow. A flashpoint in the recent discourse that escorts children who self-describe as gender nonconforming is whether or not to support the practice of the medical suspension of puberty of these children by the administration of hormonal treatment. Relevant up-to-date research findings on this subject will be reviewed here. Despite those advocates and opponents who swarm around both poles, any reliable conclusions as to the long-term safety and psychological effects of puberty suppressants will remain provisional until future studies proffer more definitive answers. While we await further study, the journal sees the necessity to press for dialogue concerning this conundrum.*

Anchoring this section is a clinical paper by Diane Ehrensaft, Ph.D., which documents the psychotherapeutic treatment of a transgender child who was prescribed puberty suppressants. The commentaries that follow and that are briefly summarized in this introduction will accent the psychoanalytic developmental point of view. This will provide the principal framework for the study of this controversy, which underscores the complementary dimensions of linear and nonlinear progressive

Claudia Lament, Ph.D., is a Training and Supervising Analyst at the Institute for Psychoanalytic Education, an affiliate of the New York University Langone School of Medicine. She is Assistant Clinical Professor in the Department of Child and Adolescent Psychiatry, the Child Study Center, New York University Langone Medical Center. She is also Senior Managing Editor of *The Psychoanalytic Study of the Child.*

The Psychoanalytic Study of the Child 68, ed. Claudia Lament, Robert A. King, Samuel Abrams, Paul M. Brinich, and Rona Knight (Yale University Press, copyright © 2015 by Claudia Lament, Robert A. King, Samuel Abrams, Paul M. Brinich, and Rona Knight).

hierarchical growth. In this context, features such as the developmentally normative fluidity of self-structures, including gender role identity, and the evolution of concrete thinking toward metaphoricity and figurative meaning-making in middle childhood and adolescence will be examined and applied to the clinical data. In addition, the argument that the use of puberty suppressants exacts a premature foreclosure on the reorganizing potential of developmental growth, and the proposed effects of the crosscurrents of the sociocultural body politic on these children and on the decision to opt for the suspension of pubertal growth will be explored.

UNDERSTANDING TRANSGENDER CHILDREN HAS EVOKED GREAT IN-terest and perplexity in our contemporary world. A greater number of youths than ever before, which in years past was considered a rara avis, are entering our consulting rooms with presentations within this scope (Spack et al., 2012; Meyer, 2012), whether it be gender dysphoria, gender variance, gender hybrid, gender queer, or gender fluid. Therapeutic and conceptual quandaries such as whether these children should qualify as requiring treatment at all, and if so, what kind and with what aims in mind have been hotly contested. But what has become a flashpoint in recent discourse that escorts this topic is the practice of the medical suspension of puberty by the administration of hormonal treatment (Byne et al., 2012; de Vries et al., 2010; Hewitt et al., 2012; Shumer and Spack, 2013; Giordano, 2008; Zucker et al., 2011). Puberty suppressants arrest temporarily the emergence of secondary sex characteristics; without these, the child's option to transition to the opposite gender would in most instances be closed; should the child eventually opt to transition to the opposite gender, such a transition would be in most instances irreversible (de Vries et al., 2010). The rationale given for this treatment, provided by specialist clinics in Canada, the United States, the United Kingdom, and several European countries (Hewitt et al., 2012) is to allow the transgender child time—up to several years—to explore her preferences and not be coerced by her biological clock to choose which gender she wishes to be (Ehrensaft, this volume; Hembree et al., 2009). Advocates and opponents swarm around both poles, and any reliable conclusions as to their long-term safety and psychological effects will remain provisional until future studies proffer more definitive answers (Byne et al., 2012).

For these reasons, the editorial board of *The Psychoanalytic Study of the Child* is aware of the necessity, if not urgency, to address this topic. In this section, Diane Ehrensaft, Ph.D., the director of Mental Health Child and Adolescent Gender Center and a child gender specialist, anchors the topic with a presentation of a clinical case of a transgender child who was prescribed puberty suppressants. Three psychoanalysts, specialists in child analysis, will offer commentaries on her theoretical and clinical perspectives.

By way of introducing transgenderism to our readership, I will review relevant findings from the recently published report on the treatment of gender identity disorder[1] assembled by the task force of the American Psychiatric Association, as well as other recent studies. I will also highlight the controversies and questions that have emerged from this literature, which illuminate the conundrums that confront parents, physicians, mental health practitioners, and the larger community in assisting these youths as they negotiate their gender identity over the course of those transformative shifts that occur as the child moves forward toward adulthood.

The plethora of theoretical vantage points in psychoanalytic thinking that are in vogue today, inclusive of the discipline of child analysis, may be overwhelming in their applications to a systematic study of any selected topic. Therefore, the position taken in this volume is to narrow the scope of our investigation and target the study of transgender children primarily, though not exclusively, through the lens of the psychoanalytic developmental point of view. I refer to the inclusion of the complementary dimensions of linear and nonlinear progressive hierarchical growth. This is a model of interweaving and interacting domains—the inherent maturational processes, disposition, and the familial and cultural environmental surround—which comprise the formation of a new realm (A. Freud, 1965). The developmental approach is distinctive for its emphasis on the forward movement of growth and the extraordinary discontinuous changes that accompany the nonlinear shifts as children move from one organization to another. Structures and functions undergo fluctuation, fluidity and novel forms: ". . . the confluence of many influential factors steer [the developmental orientation] in one direction or another, defying prediction and any form of determinism" (Auchincloss and Samberg, 2012, p. 58).

Defining Transgender

The task force (Byne et al., 2012) defines the term "transgender" (p. 762) to denote individuals who demonstrate cross-gender identifications,

---

1. To quote Ehrensaft's footnote in this volume: "Although Gender Dysphoria has replaced Gender Identity Disorder in the new Diagnostic Statistical Manual (DSM V), the concept of Gender Identity Disorder as a diagnostic category is still widely in use in many people's thinking."

whether or not they have initiated hormonal treatment that induces transition to the opposite sex. For many child analysts, a sticking point in this definition is that psychoanalytic investigators view some manner of cross-gender identifications across the developmental spectrum as normative: in and of themselves, such identifications are not signposts that denote disturbance. Rather, as Knight states in her commentary, they reflect the expectable disequilibrium of self structures that gives the child the chance to play with different possibilities of gender role identity. As structures remain fluid and discontinuous in growth, so a child's internal sense of her gender identifications mirror that same fluidity.

Consequently, within the parameters of *The Psychoanalytic Study of the Child*'s purpose in examining Ehrensaft's viewpoint and treatment of her child patient, we will use the term "transgender" with particular qualifications. Namely, we define it as reflecting within the child an unyielding discomfort in her biological sex and a profound identification with the gender of the opposite sex (American Psychiatric Association, 2000; World Health Organization, 1992). Persistent and unrelenting cross-gender thoughts and behavior are manifest and undeniable among these children.

PSYCHOTHERAPEUTIC TREATMENT OF TRANSGENDER CHILDREN

Presently, therapy approaches are designed to facilitate the psychological wellness of the transgender child (Byne et al., 2012). However, what that entails is under dispute. The APA task force outlined several avenues, each tutored by differing underlying principles concerning how to bring about that sense of well-being. Should a treatment approach actively encourage the transgender child to adopt the culturally prescribed codes of gender behavior in order to ameliorate ostracization from peers? One approach (Zucker, 1990) espouses this perspective. The assumption underwriting this point of view asserts that positive self-esteem is better regulated and preserved when children are integrated into their social landscape and bond with same-sex cohort. Another paradigm assumes a neutral position in regard to the child's cross-gender behavior. Proponents take a wait-and-see outlook, to allow progressive development to unfurl in its own fashion without interference from outside sources (Ehrensaft, 2011; Hill and Menvielle, 2010; Pleak, 1999). The practice of this perspective is sometimes inclusive of the child's environment, in that parents and the child's community are engaged to minimize and troubleshoot the potential damaging effects of cultural stigmatization. These therapists take the opposite view of the first treatment option, where the transgender child is persuaded to fit in to the community's standards concerning gender conforming behaviors and dress codes. They aver that self-esteem will be enhanced by promoting the child's recognition that her transgender or gender variant preferences may encounter hostile reactions in the outer world. How to strategize and manage these negative forces is a predictable outgrowth of this treatment approach.

Lastly, a third method works against the argument of neutrality. These therapists lean toward or actively affirm the prepubertal child's gender variant desires and offer the provision of assistance to segue the child into gender role transition on a social level; should the transgender desires continue into puberty, this approach would support the option of pubertal suppressant agents (Ehrensaft, 2011; Brill and Pepper, 2008). Proponents in this camp aver that some children will continue on this trajectory through adolescence and into adulthood, so that smoothing their passage at a younger age benefits their overall adjustment.

The opposing argument to this model rests on the empirically derived evidence that most gender variance in children does not persist into adolescence (Davenport, 1986; Green et al., 1987; Wallien and Cohen-Kettenis, 2008; Zuger, 1978). This finding is especially germane to Ehrensaft's treatment and discussion of her patient, Jacqueline/Thomas. A majority of untreated children between the ages of eight and twelve who receive no mental health intervention and present with transgender leanings *desist*, that is, they naturally arrive at a fresh experience of contentment with their natal sex over time, generally by the onset of puberty itself. What tips the scales toward desistance is unclear, but several triggers are hypothesized: the expectable hormonal changes that accompany early puberty, exclusion from peers, and shifts in cognitive development (Wallien and Cohen-Kettenis, 2008). Those children who *persist* in their transgender preference into puberty and adolescence are more likely to continue this tendency into adult life (Zucker, 2008b). No differentiated variables have been reliably identified that would indicate which prepubertal children will persist or desist as adolescent development proceeds (Cohen-Kettenis and Pfäfflin, 2010; Wallien and Cohen-Kettenis, 2008; Zucker, 2007; Zucker and Cohen-Kettenis, 2008).

Thus, actively supporting or encouraging transgender self-states in middle childhood may act as a subtle leverage toward transitioning. Such stimulation, however tactful or nuanced, may interfere with whatever course the child's development might naturally lead her without it (Pleak, 2010). An additional source of disquiet is that once a child makes the transition across the gender divide, reverting back to the natal gender may present difficulties (Steensma et al., 2011). These children struggle with their change of heart when family, peers, and the community have embraced, if not inspirited, their former desires.

ADOLESCENTS WHO IDENTIFY AS TRANSGENDER

The progression for prepubertal youngsters and adolescents who self-identify as transgender is varied and layered with choices concerning the medical options currently available that can suspend puberty and change one's sex, either partially or wholly. That is, transgender individuals may make a definitive decision to become one gender or another, but, as Ehrensaft states in her paper that follows, others create their own version of gender, which may retain characteristics of both sexes. Some adolescents have felt themselves to be transgender since childhood; but unlike these individuals who experience a continuity of transgender identity from one developmental organization to the next, there are those for whom a transgender orientation first appears in early puberty or adolescence proper: the desire to be the opposite sex is a freshly emergent phenomenon with no prior antecedents in childhood (Byne et al., 2012).

At present, there are two studies, one in Toronto, Canada (Zucker et al., 2011), and the other in Amsterdam, The Netherlands (de Vries, Kreukels et al., 2011), that have acquired sufficient data to fulfill an "empirical 'experience base'" (Byne et al., 2012, p. 764) and which throw light on some of the issues that concern these two groups of transgender adolescents. Both sets of data from these clinic settings report consistency in their findings that the management in those adolescents who report transgender feelings from childhood is more straightforward than in those adolescents for whom transgender feelings are first reported in the pubertal or adolescent process proper. This is partially explained by the trend in the latter group to show significant psychological disturbance that is independent of the transgender experience. For example, it is important to differentiate whether or not the emergent transgender feelings in these adolescents are consequential to an incipient psychosis, schizophrenia, autistic spectrum manifestations, trauma, or other disorders that may cause gender disorientation and dysphoria (de Vries et al., 2010). Of equal relevance, the complications in the management of adolescents also pivot on the controversies that abound over the use of puberty suppressants.

ARGUMENTS IN FAVOR OF THE USE OF PUBERTY SUPPRESSANTS

Transgender adolescents do not infrequently experience depressive reactions to the onset of secondary sex characteristics at puberty. In recent years, those whose responses to these biological changes are severe and unabated have been offered the opportunity to medically suspend puberty for several years. Advocates of this approach cite the advantage of allowing the young adolescent a respite from making a decision that may entrap her "in a body that is experienced as alien" (Giordano, 2008, p. 580): a period of time spent on reflection, possible psychotherapy services to aid in introspective curiosity, and an exploration of feelings. Lastly, this time affords the opportunity, if desired, to live *in vita sua* as a person of the opposite gender. These rationales are seen by those who endorse this perspective as a considered approach to the young adolescent's dilemma. In this way, it is reasoned that the youth may be able to test the waters of his imagination and be better equipped to arrive at an informed decision.

A second advantage reported by this group concerns the fact that the secondary sex characteristics of pubertal development, once set in motion, are either relatively permanent or present special problems in reversing, should the young adolescent eventually wish to make a full transition. The repercussions of experiencing undesired pubertal development are significant (Byne et al., 2012). Features such as height and size—and for men who transition to females, voice quality—cannot be modified with cross-sex hormone treatments or even with cross-sex surgery. For females who transition to males, invasive surgeries such as mastectomies may be necessary for a complete bodily transformation. Thus, those who opt for the suspension of puberty will have a smoother transition to a sex change should this be the desired outcome (Giordano, 2008). As mentioned above, confounding this state of affairs is the impossibility of making a definitive determination in advance as to which youngsters will persist or desist over the course of progressive development. Given this uncertainty over prediction, advocates maintain that as puberty suppressants can be stopped should the adolescent wish to discontinue the transitioning process, puberty will proceed "as normal" (Giodarno, 2008; p. 580; Hembree et al., 2009). Finally, proponents offer that transgender children who are denied puberty blockers are reported at high risk of suicide and of sourcing illegal markets for hormones and medications in lieu of carefully monitored medical supervision (Giordano, 2008; Rotondi et al., 2013). Their reasoning asserts that avoiding such calamities overrides the complexities and uncertainties that accompany the decision to provide puberty suppressants, as will be discussed below. From some quarters, then, the cumulative effect of these points has resulted in a favorable reception for the option of offering medically induced puberty suspension.

Arguments Opposed to the Use of Puberty Suppressants

Arguments raised against the use of puberty suppressants point to several areas of concern. While there are no reported adverse short-term physical effects from the use of puberty suppressants, their use is so recent that follow-up studies that track the consequences of long-term effects are not yet possible (Byne et al., 2012). Specifically, questions concerning sex steroid deficiency on bone metabolism in children has not been subject to tracking and assessment over extended periods of time, which would be necessary for determining possible risk factors for osteoporosis. As brain maturation in the adolescent process is significant for its momentous growth, experts have expressed their concern regarding the possibility of unknown cognitive fallout that may attend the suspension of puberty: presently, there is no research available that investigates long-term effects. Similar concerns have been issued regarding the use of puberty suppressants on future reproductive capacities (Giordano, 2007). The "still emerging evidence base" (Hewitt et al., 2012, p. 581) and the necessity for "rigorous assessment . . . along with the stringent auditing and publication of outcomes" (ibid.) cannot be overplayed. It is not surprising, then, that those who oppose the use of puberty suppressants question certain lines of reasoning cited by advocates to avoid what the latter believe to be an even worse consequence, that is, children trolling the black market for hormones, or managing possible suicide risk and depressive episodes (Giordano, 2008). By weighing one set of troubling potential outcomes against the other, those who contest this position question the validity of making such qualitative and subjective determinations as to which outcome would be worse. In the absence of data and follow-up assessments, can one know that offering puberty suppressants would assuredly foreclose on suicidal risks or depression in all cases, particularly if these risk factors interweave or overlap with other disturbances that emanate from independent sources? For instance, the Dutch and Canadian studies and others have suggested some positive outcomes for those children who receive them, in the alleviation of depressive feelings and behavioral difficulties. However, other feeling states remain untouched, such as gender dysphoria, anger, and anxiety (Cohen-Kettenis, Shagen, and Steensma, 2011).

Other detractors opine additional reservations. They believe that transgender trends in both prepubertal and early adolescent youngsters may reflect long-standing unconscious communications between parents and children that may or may not have specific links to gender identity matters. In such cases, they argue that a transgender picture veils a legacy of other problems, but the concrete operational child (Piaget) who is boundaried and constrained by her unsophisticated cognitive and affective capacities may relate her feelings about the world in forms and expressions that amass around various self-states, including gender identity. Within this context, the child's plea for solutions such as puberty blockers, and the threat of suicide if these are not provided may be the literal expressions of preoccupations and emotions that are more accurately conceptualized in figurative terms.

As Knight suggests in this section, latency-aged children whose cognitive and emotional resources are still concrete may believe that sexual arousal toward a member of the same sex implies that their body is the wrong gender; that is, that to ensure their heterosexuality, they assume their gender assignment must be incorrect. Younger children with persistent cross-dressing behaviors have been reported to show difficulties in gender constancy acquisition—the ability to recognize the immutability of gender over time (Zucker, et al., 1999)—which may undergird gender confusion on the cognitive level for some older children.

Opponents from the psychoanalytic developmental camp put forward what is likely to be their principal argument. Does the use of puberty suppressants obfuscate the role played by the pubertal upsurge and the attendant developmental process and how these epigenetic changes inform and influence the transgender child/adolescent's experience of her gendered self? Namely, like the majority of middle childhood–aged transgender children who eventually arrive at a feeling of comfort with their biological sex by preadolescence, might some young adolescents who initially request puberty suppressants also reach a newfound ease with their natal sex if they may experience the naturally occurring hormonal changes and developmental transformations of adolescence?

Skeptics also state their apprehension about a prepubertal child's limited cognitive capacity to fully grasp the current medical and psychological uncertainties that swirl around the use of hormone suppressing agents. Does their use violate ethical considerations and codes that protect a child's rights and welfare, not only within the boundaries of our current knowledge base and data collection, but in the data that will emerge in the future?

Ehrensaft's paper enlivens the current discussion within the mental health community about how to conceptualize the gender nonconforming child by her bold hypothesis that this child "dismisses or resists" the maxim that we must all give up and mourn the sex we never were and will never be. Rather than labeling these children as "developmentally arrested" or having fallen prey to a persistent delusion, she defies these

notions with the proposition that such children, "the ultimate anti-
essentialists" are aware that gender is not dictated by the body only but
by psychical meanings and assemblages as well. For Ehrensaft, through
refusing to relinquish her gender "inclusivity," the transgender child's
gender creativity should be celebrated. Ehrensaft cites conservative societal restrictions as a central foe in the transgender child's quest to
uncover her "true gender." Her focus, in her treatment model True
Gender Self Therapy, centers on buttressing the child's authentic gender self in the hope that the child's less authentic "false gender self"
will be naturally jettisoned. Within this context, Ehrensaft takes the view
that offering the transgender child the opportunity to utilize puberty
suppressants during middle childhood provides her with the space to
experiment with experiencing in real time what she feels is her true
gender self by literally slipping into the shoes of the opposite sex. Her
thesis, escorted by her treatment modality and its theoretical ground-
work, is the subject of the commentaries that follow. Knight, Brinich,
and Weinstein and Wallerstein deliberate on the quandaries inherent in
Ehrensaft's formulations and elucidate other related conundrums that
hopefully will stimulate the readers' own reflections.

Rona Knight expands on the paradigm of nonlinear, progressive
hierarchical development. She brings to this perspective a lively discourse concerning contemporary research models that illuminate the
fluid quality of normal gender role identity over the arc of the human
lifespan. In particular, she proffers high praise to the proponents of
dynamic nonlinear systems theory. Knight's referencing of biological
influences, such as neonatal exposure to varying levels of androgen,
brings the reader to an in-depth appreciation of innate variants that
inflect and inform gender preference and behaviors. Interacting with
the biologically inspired is the sociocultural domain, and she also invites
our attention to research that has pinpointed how environmental influences, such as the overt and covert messages that are sent by parents to
children, influence their gender behaviors and impressions concerning
gender and gender roles.

Knight turns to Ehrensaft's True Gender Self Therapy as it plays
out in the consulting room with Jacqueline/Thomas. She observes
that Ehrensaft's treatment is designed to unearth the concealed or denied gender preference—that of the opposite sex—which challenges
the position of the usual psychoanalytic investigations into the child's
myriad unconscious meanings and narratives concerning sexuality, aggression, selfhood, gender, and even homosexual fantasies, which may
be screened behind the placeholder of transgenderism. Drawing upon
Piaget's categories of cognitive development, Knight shows the signifi-

cant influence of concrete thinking in the middle years and its role in shaping gender experience. Thusly, for her, foregrounding the figurative meanings over the literal desire to be one gender or another is an imperative facet in treatment paradigms that approach this issue and marks a point of departure from Ehrensaft's model that accepts the emphasis on gender as a manifest, literal concern.

In this way, listening to and considering how a child's gender preference may be turned on its head several times over in the years to come is central to the debate about suspending puberty. For Knight, the use of puberty blockers bars the developmental feature of transformations from expression over the critical years of the adolescent process. In this way, nature itself is prohibited from playing its role as the in-habitus assist, guiding the child's movement toward the gender or gender variation she wishes to be.

Paul Brinich's textured discussion informs Ehrensaft's presentation through the lens of progressive developmental transformations within the larger context of our current sociocultural sensibilities. Fast-forwarding into the future realm of the child's natural developmental thrust, that interplay of nature and environmental shaping that accompanies the child's ever-changing shifts into new organizations is subject to the cultural tropes of contemporary life. In our time, Brinich observes, the narrative of gender has been liberated from myopic constraints. Gender is inclusive of a broadening reach of new forms, inflected by the currents of the contemporary sociocultural body politic, as evidenced by those very aforementioned terms at the outset of this introduction: gender variant, gender queer, gender hybrid, gender fluid. Would such novel assemblages of gender have been remotely possible even a decade ago?

Brinich also brings the dimension of nonlinear progressive development in Ehrensaft's coinage of the term "True Gender Self." He sees in it an oxymoron: as development rests, at least in part, on the principle of biologically inspired nonlinear growth, what is true for gender or for any aspect of a child's identity, for that matter, is subject to continuous transformational change. Thus, he poses the question: "Can what is 'true' at age 3, or 13, or 23 become 'false' at 33 or 43 or 53?" Perhaps, Brinich suggests, a more "modest" proposal that accommodates to nature's discontinuous path would entertain the notion of a "currently adaptive" gender self. In that way, the binary code of male or female can be sidestepped away from the tradition-bound mores that locate gender in reductionistic fashion.

Readers will appreciate the steady and scrupulous gaze of Weinstein and Wallerstein's contribution. These authors compose their discussion as a careful reading of Ehrensaft's treatment approach. They sift the definitional paradoxes that hover about True Gender Self Therapy by way of Winnicott's "true self" and Kohut's "mirroring" technique. From this perch, the authors probe the theoretical underpinnings of the therapy, which permits the readership its own agency in considering whether a child's gender experience is " core" and consequently, "immutable" or, on the other hand, a "complex communication from the child that needs to be decoded." The arguments outlined are critical for how a therapy designs its mission statement: is its goal to treat the gender self as an objective truth that requires sparse inquiry, and thus the work must function as a protective carapace from a possibly hostile and stigmatizing environment? Or is its purpose to *promote* inquiry and tap into unconscious meanings that accrue to gender and explore the metaphoricity of the aggregates that have been brought to bear in sculpting that gender self? One position views the external world as the obstacle to the transgender child's well-being; the other considers internally sourced elements as informing gender preference. Traditional pillars of child analysis, such as frequency of sessions, the child's phenomenological experience, and the use of transference are also brought into deliberation vis-à-vis Ehrensaft's model.

Finally, Weinstein and Wallerstein address the issue of puberty suppressants. They cite the importance of bodily and hormonal shifts during pubertal development in their potential to shepherd the reorganization of the personality in adolescence, which goes beyond the issue of gender experience per se. In referencing quantitative and qualitative research studies that also show the remarkable influence of puberty as marking the advent of the young adolescent's first passage into novel and growth-enhancing experiences, such as love relationships, her preoccupation with the uncertainty of identity, or her newly emergent defiance of parental authority. Puberty is a paramount process that informs how gender identifications will re-form toward the close of the developmental process. With these benefits in mind, the authors conclude their commentary with words of caution. Until future research can provide us with reliable predictions as to which prepubertal youngsters will persist or desist in their gender dysphoric feelings, supporting the use of puberty blockers not only inhibits those features of early adolescence that will inflect gender identity in its fluid course, but it will also "foreclose the potentially organizing experience of development" overall.

Perhaps the questions and conundrums so posed are not within the purview of the psychoanalyst's clinical and investigative template. Yet they are weighty problems that cannot be brushed aside as we await further research and study. Until then, it is incumbent upon our child analytic community as stewards of what is developmental in all of its complementary domains to press for continuing dialogue about the transgender child. The papers herewith are an effort to foster these conversations.

REFERENCES

AMERICAN PSYCHIATRIC ASSOCIATION (2000). *Diagnostic and Statistical Manual of Mental Disorders.* 4th ed. Washington, DC: American Psychiatric Publishing.

AUCHINCLOSS, E. L., AND SAMBERG, E. (2012). *Psychoanalytic Terms and Concepts.* New Haven and London: Yale University Press.

BRILL, S., AND PEPPER, R. (2008). *The Transgendered Child: A Handbook for Families and Professionals.* San Francisco, CA: Cleis Press.

BYNE, W., BRADLEY, S. J., COLEMAN, E., EYLER, A. E., GREEN, R., MENVIELLE, E. J., MEYER-BAHLBURG, E. F. L., PLEAK, R. R., TOMPKINS, D. (2012). Report of the American Psychiatric Association Task Force on Treatment of Gender Identity Disorder. *Archives of Sexual Behavior* 41:759–796.

COHEN-KETTENIS, P. T., AND PFÄFFLIN, F. (2010). The DSM diagnostic criteria for gender identity disorder in adolescents and adults. *Archives of Sexual Behavior* 39:499–513.

COHEN-KETTENIS, P. T., SCHAGEN, S. E. E., AND STEENSMA, T. D. (2011). Puberty suppression in a gender-dysphoric adolescent: A 22-year follow-up. *Archives of Sexual Behavior* 40:843–847.

DAVENPORT, C. W. (1986). A follow-up study of 10 feminine boys. *Archives of Sexual Behavior* 15:511–517.

DE VRIES, A. L., KREUKELS, B. P., STEENSMA, T. D., DORELEIJERS, T. A., AND COHEN-KETTENIS, P. T. (2011). Comparing adult and adolescent transsexuals: An MMPI-2 and MMPI-A study. *Psychiatry Research* 186:414–418.

DE VRIES, A. L. C., NOENS, I. L., COHEN-KETTENIS, P. T., VAN BERCKELAER-ONNES, I. A., AND DORELEIJERS, T. A. H. (2010). Autism spectrum disorders in gender dysphoric children and adolescents. *Journal of Autism and Developmental Disorders* 40:930–936.

DE VRIES A., STEENSMA, T. D., COHEN-KETTENIS, P. (2011). Psychiatric comorbidity in gender dysphoric adolescents. *Journal of Child Psychological Psychiatry* 52:1195–1202.

DE VRIES, A. L., STEENSMA, T. D., DORELEIJERS, T. A., AND COHEN-KETTENIS, P. T. (2011). Puberty suppression in adolescents with gender identity disorder: A prospective follow-up study. *Journal of Sexual Medicine* 8:2276–2283.

EHRENSAFT, D. (2011). From gender identity disorder to gender identity creativity: True gender self child therapy. *Journal of Homosexuality* 59:337–356.

FREUD, A. (1965). *Normality and Pathology in Childhood: Assessments of Development.* Vol. 6 of *The Writings of Anna Freud.* New York: International Universities Press.

GIORDANO, S. (2007). Gender atypical organization in children and adolescents: Ethico-legal issues and a proposal for new guidelines. *International Journal of Children's Rights* 15:365–390.

———. (2008). Lives in chiaroscuro. Should we suspend the puberty of children with gender identity disorder? *Journal of Medical Ethics* 34:580–584.

GREEN, R., ROBERTS, C. W., WILLIAMS, K., GOODMAN, M., AND MIXON, A. (1987). Specific cross-gender behaviour in boyhood and later homosexual orientation. *British Journal of Psychiatry* 151:84–88.

HEMBREE, W. C., COHEN-KETTENIS, P., DELEMARRE-VAN DE WAAL, H. A., GOOREN, L. J., MEYER, W. J., III., SPACK, N. P., MONTORI, V. M. (2009). Endocrine treatment of transsexual persons: An Endocrine Society clinical practice guideline. *Journal of Endocrinology and Metabolism* 94:3132–3154.

HEWITT, J. K., PAUL, C., KASLANNAN, P., GOVER, S. R., NEWMAN, L. K., WARNE, G. L. (2012). Hormone treatment of gender identity disorder in a cohort of children and adolescents. *Medical Journal of Australia* 196:578–581.

HILL, D. B., AND MENVIELLE, E. J. (2010). You have to give them a place where they feel protected and safe and loved: The views of parents who have gender variant children and adolescents. *Journal of LGBT Youth* 6:243–271.

MEYER, W. J. (2012). Gender identity disorder: An emerging problem for pediatricians. *Pediatrics* 129 (3): 571–575.

PIAGET, J. (1967). *Six Psychological Studies*. New York: Random House.

PLEAK, R. R. (1999). Ethical issues in diagnosing and treating gender dysphoric children and adolescents. In M. Rottnek, ed., *Sissies and Tomboys: Gender Nonconformity and Homosexual Childhood*, pp. 34–51. New York: New York University Press.

———. (2010). Transgender people. In P. Ruiz and A. Primm, eds., *Disparities in Psychiatric Care: Clinic and Cross-Cultural Perspectives*, pp. 107–115. Philadelphia: Lippincott, William, & Wilkins.

ROTONDI, N. K., BAUER, G. R., SCANLON, K., KAAY, M., TRAVERS, R., AND TRAVERS, A. (2013). Nonprescribed hormone use and self-performed surgeries: "Do-it-yourself" transitions in transgender communities in Ontario, Canada. *American Journal of Public Health* 103 (10): 1830–1836.

SHUMER, D. E., AND SPACK, N. P. (2013). Current management of gender identity disorder in childhood and adolescence: Guidelines, barriers and areas of controversy. *Current Opinion in Endocrinology & Diabetes and Obesity* 20 (2013): 69–73.

SPACK, N. P., EDWARDS-LEEPER, L., FELDMAN, H. A., LEIBOWITZ, S., MANDEL, F., DIAMOND, D. A., AND VANCE, S. R. (2012). Children and adolescents with gender identity disorder referred to a pediatric medical center. *Pediatrics* 129 (3): 418–425.

STEENSMA, T. D., BIEMOND, R., BOER, F. D., AND COHEN-KETTENIS, P. T. (2011). Desisting and persisting gender dysphoria after childhood: A qualitative follow-up study. *Clinical Child Psychology and Psychiatry* 16:499–516.

WALLIEN, M. S., AND COHEN-KETTENIS, P. T. (2008). Psychosexual outcome of gender-dysphoric children. *Journal of the American Academy of Child and Adolescent Psychiatry* 47:1413–1423.

Wallien, M. S. C., Swaab, H., and Cohen-Kettenis, P. T. (2007). Psychiatric comorbidity among children with gender identity disorder. *Journal of the American Academy of Child and Adolescent Psychiatry* 46:1307–1314.

World Health Organization (1992). *The ICD-10 Classification of Mental and Behavioural Disorders.* Geneva: World Health Organization.

Zucker, K. J. (1990). Treatment of gender identity disorder in children. In R. Blanchard and B. W. Steiner, eds., *Clinical Management of Gender Identity Disorders in Children and Adults*, pp. 27–45. Washington, DC: American Psychiatric Press.

Zucker, K. J. (2007). Gender identity disorder in children, adolescents, and adults. In G. O. Gabbard, ed., *Gabbard's Treatments of Psychiatric Disorders.* 4th ed., pp. 2069–2096. Washington, DC: APA Publishing.

Zucker, K. J. (2008a). Children with gender identity disorder: Is there a best practice? *Neuropsychiatrie de l'Enfance et de l'Adolescence* 56:358–364.

Zucker, K. J. (2008b). On the "natural history" of gender identity disorder in children (editorial). *Journal of the American Academy of Child and Adolescent Psychiatry* 47:1361–1363.

Zucker, K. J., Bradley, S. J., Kuksis, M., Pecore, K., Birkenfeld-Adams, A., Doering, R. W., Mitchell, J. N., and Wild, J. (1999). Gender constancy judgments in children with gender identity disorder: Evidence for a developmental lag. *Archives of Sexual Behavior* 28:475–502.

Zucker, K. J., Bradley, S. J., Owen-Anderson, A., Singh, D., Blanchard, R., and Bain, J. (2011). Puberty-blocking hormonal therapy for adolescents with gender identity disorder: A descriptive clinical study. *Journal of Gay & Lesbian Mental Health* 15:58–82.

Zucker, K. J., and Cohen-Kettenis, P. T. (2008). Gender identity disorder in children and adolescents. In D. L. Rowland and L. Incrocci, eds., *Handbook of Sexual and Gender Identity Disorders*, pp. 376–422. Hoboken, NJ: John Wiley and Sons.

Zucker, K. J., Wood, H., Singh, D., and Bradley, S. J. (2012). A developmental, biopsychosocial model for the treatment of children with gender identity disorder. *Journal of Homosexuality* 59:369–397.

Zuger, B. (1978). Effeminate behavior present in boys from childhood: Ten additional years of follow-up. *Comprehensive Psychiatry* 19:363–369.

Listening and Learning from Gender-Nonconforming Children

DIANE EHRENSAFT, Ph.D.

The twenty-first century brings to our clinical doorsteps increasing numbers of children exploring and questioning their gender identities and expressions. This paper begins with a reassessment of the psychoanalytic thinking about gender and then outlines a clinical and developmental model of gender adapted from D. W. Winnicott's concepts of true self, false self, and individual creativity. The underlying premise is that gender nonconformity, when the core psychological issue, is not a sign of pathology but rather a reflection of healthy variations on gender possibilities. Working from that premise, composite clinical material from the author's practice as a psychoanalytic gender specialist is presented of a gender-nonconforming child transitioning from female to male, to demonstrate the psychoanalytic tools applied, including listening, mirroring, play, and interpretation, with the goal of facilitating a child's authentic gender self. Emphasis is placed on learning from the patient, working collaboratively with the family and social environments, and remaining suspended in a state of ambiguity and not-knowing as the child explores and solidifies a True Gender Self.

FOR THOSE OF YOU OLD ENOUGH TO HAVE HAD YOUR CHILDHOOD imbued with Popeye the Sailor Man, you may remember Popeye, in his gravelly voice, belting out this famous line "I yam what I yam an' that's all I yam." Simply, that is the theme of this discussion: our psychoanalytic work with children and their gender involves learning from the child—who I am. I start from the premise that it is not for us to dictate or legislate, but for the children to explain their gender, whether

Diane Ehrensaft, Ph.D., is an Associate Professor in the Department of Pediatrics at the University of California San Francisco, and the Director of Mental Health of the Child and Adolescent Gender Center.

The Psychoanalytic Study of the Child 68, ed. Claudia Lament, Robert A. King, Samuel Abrams, Paul M. Brinich, and Rona Knight (Yale University Press, copyright © 2015 by Claudia Lament, Robert A. King, Samuel Abrams, Paul M. Brinich, and Rona Knight).

it be conforming or nonconforming. I bring you my thinking within the twelve months that a law was signed into effect by Governor Jerry Brown in California that reads as follows: "No mental health provider shall provide minors with therapy intended to change their sexual orientation, including efforts to change behaviors or gender expressions" (California Senate Bill 1172, 2012). Such practice was assessed as harmful and scientifically unsound. California's action, now followed by identical legislative proposals in two other states, matches the *Standards of Care* set forth by the World Professional Association for Transgender Health in 2011: "Treatment aimed at trying to change a person's gender identity and expression to become more congruent with sex assigned at birth has been attempted in the past without success, particularly in the long term. . . . Such treatment is no longer considered ethical" (Coleman et al., 2011, p. 16). This policy statement and legislative action serve as a wake-up call for all of us. It is time to peruse our clinical theories and practices with the aim of fortifying the mental health of children of all genders, ethically and with no harm done.

I situate myself in the school of thinking that conceptualizes gender as fluid rather than dichotomous. In essence, this is an extrapolation of Sigmund Freud's *Three Contributions to the Theory of Sex* (S. Freud, 1962) in which he posited, as articulated later by Anna Freud, that our bisexual tendencies, considered part of the inborn constitution, "endow all individuals with psychological characteristics not only of their own but also of the opposite sex" (A. Freud, 1965, p. 195). Whereas Anna and Sigmund Freud were referring to sexuality and erotic object choice, I am proposing that the same paradigm can be applied to our gender: we are not born binary but rather gender inclusive. Beyond birth, gender development becomes an interplay of nature and nurture. Within this conceptual framework, the variations on gender that unfold over the course of development do not constitute abnormality but rather creative differences. To use Ken Corbett's words, "Genders both in their central and marginal expressions open out into lives that are led through many ways of being and feeling well" (Corbett, 2009, p. 126). Yet, regretfully, to date, children and youth who show up with the marginal expressions may end up in the hands of mental health professionals who will assess their gender transgressions as pathological, their parents' practices as problematic, and hope to cure them of a diagnosed Gender Identity Disorder.[1]

1. Although Gender Dysphoria has replaced Gender Identity Disorder in the new *Diagnostic Statistical Manual* (*DSM V*), the concept of Gender Identity Disorder as a diagnostic category is still widely in use in many people's thinking.

I am neither an essentialist nor a social constructivist concerning gender. To be either at the exclusion of the other would be ignoring the holistic reality of gender as both born and made. Rather, I think of gender dialectically as a tension between body and psyche, body and culture, psyche and culture. When thinking about early gender development, again referring back to our psychoanalytic forbears, we can find this gender paradigm embedded in Anna Freud's writing on internal harmony and mental health. The forces determining healthy development are both internal and external:

> What needs to be integrated with each other at this time are the potentialities inherent in the inherited constitution; the vicissitudes connected with the gradual structuralization of the personality; and the influences emanating from the parental environment which is responsible for the atmosphere in which development occurs. (A. Freud, 1981, p. 111)

Regarding gender development, I would simply extend the statement further to include not just the parental environment but the social and cultural terrain in which any child grows, highlighting again that gender is both an internal and external affair woven together.

To date, I have found no conclusive evidence to tell us the why of gender, although extensive evidence suggests that both nature and nurture have strong hands to play in the process. In the context of treatment, I would propose that our main task is to concentrate more on the *how* of gender, specifically the ways in which an individual puts gender together, either in conformity or transgression of cultural norms and social expectations. In making sense of gender, I embrace the dual concepts of gender identity and gender expression. Gender identity is who I know myself to be as male, female, or other; gender expression encompasses all the ways in which I perform my gender, both for myself and for others. Although similar in meaning to earlier established terms "core gender identity" and "gender (sex) role socialization," the terms "core gender identity" and "gender (sex) role socialization" have been applied to a developmental latticework with a fixed trajectory within the first six years of life. Gender identity and gender expressions, on the other hand, refer to aspects of self that can be established or altered over the course of a lifetime, not just within the earliest years of life, concepts more in line with the model of gender presented here. To borrow from the constructs of D. W. Winnicott (Winnicott, 1971), gender identity is about the "being" of gender, while gender expression is about the "doing" of gender. In my observations and treatment of children and families, it appears that gender identity is far more resistant to environmental intervention or shaping, while gender expressions are more highly influenced by nurture and culture.

Anthropological investigation enlightens us about the myriad ways that both gender identity and gender expressions can vary dramatically from culture to culture and from one historical era to another. Looking within the boundaries of North America, we can discover multiple genders in the Native Americans or First Peoples. The two-spirited, or third or fourth genders, of Native American culture do not live as either boys or girls, men or women, but somewhere in between, holding the spirit of both the male and female within them. They have often been healers, artists, mediators, and leaders and have been recognized among their people for their flexibility and expanded perspectives. They signify the postmodern concept of gender fluidity, except they go back to premodern times. The berdaches, as the two-spirited Native Americans are referred to, have been seen as exhibiting behaviors that were natural and not to be controlled, habits that showed up early in childhood—"It's natural. They were born that way. It is their nature." In the words of Osh-Tisch, a third-gender member of the Crow tribe, "That is my road. . . . I have done it ever since I remember because I wanted to do it" (Roscoe, 1998, p. 27). Since the gender nonconformity was believed to be in the child's nature, Native American parents did not to try to change the child. Instead, they allowed the child to either cross genders or live as both. In India, we find a similar category of a third gender, known as the *hijra*, defined as an individual who is neither man nor woman. The *hijra* do not garner the same universal respect within their own culture as the berdaches do within Native American tribes, and are often relegated to segregated communities, but they do exist as a recognized entity within Indian culture.

Turning to historical shifts in gender sensibilities, I'd like to share a recent experience. On a visit to the Metropolitan Museum of Art exhibit on impressionism and fashion, I came upon a Renoir painting, *Madame Georges Charpentier et ses enfants*, completed in 1878. In the portrait, a mother sits with her two children, Paul, age three, and his older sister, Georgette, age six. Two elderly women stood next to me, gazing at the canvas. One, puzzled, asked the other, "But where's Paul?" Her companion pointed to the child sitting on the settee next to the mother and read to her the caption for the painting, which explained that in the fashion of the times in France, little boys of three did not yet have their hair cut, and were donned in dresses and frills, like their sisters. Indeed, Paul and Georgette were indiscernible from one other, both with long cascading blond curls, dressed in blue satin dresses with lace trim. The first woman just shook her head in disbelief, muttering, "How could they?" European and also American parents of that epoch and into the early twentieth century could and did—in many places, particularly among the upper classes—undifferentiate small boys from girls in dress and appearance; it was the norm of the times and accepted by all as gender appropriate. At the same time that we see the wide variations in gender norms over time and space, anthropological research also tells us that to date we have no identified culture that does not use some form of gender organization—be it binary, multiple, poles, spectrums, or NOS—"not otherwise specified." So I also start from the premise that gender to date is a universal organizing feature of human society; it is a question of how we organize it, in all its complexities, which I am inviting us to reconsider.

In that light, I call on the oft-quoted words of the late Ethel Person regarding the evolution of our psychoanalytic understanding of sexuality and gender: "we would do well to follow Freud's example and supplement the crucial information we glean from the couch with information garnered from the street, as well as from different historical epochs, different cultures, and other academic and scientific disciplines, information that is relevant to fine-tuning our observation and ever-changing theories" (Person, 2005, p. 1278). I would like to extend that quote one step further and take us from the couch to the street to the *playground* and back to the couch, to learn from our youngest children the dramatic shifts presently occurring in the exploration of "Who are the genders in your neighborhood?"

THE GENDER LENS FROM WHICH I SEE

Some of the children in the neighborhood have come out to say that they are not the gender that everyone thinks they are. Those children are the ones who typically make front-page news or TV specials. In that iteration, we are prone to begin thinking in a tripartite, rather than binary, way about gender: you are either boy, girl, or trans, the three new categories of gender. Such thinking is equally as binding and constricting as the binary gender models. A very small percentage of the gender-nonconforming children who present themselves to us *will* be persistent, insistent, and consistent in their declaration that they are not the gender written on their birth certificate, but rather the opposite one, or another one altogether. They typically do not say "I feel like a girl (boy)" but rather "I am a girl (boy)" (Ehrensaft, 2011a, 2011b; Steensma et al., 2013). These declarations often begin as soon as language develops, and may show up even earlier, as when one toddler is videoed tearing the barrettes out of her hair in distress, a distress followed many years later by her transition to male, with the accompanying male hormones to fortify that transition. In addition to gender-label declarations, these children typically express discontent with their gendered bodies and have more intense cross-gender presentations than their nontransgender gender-nonconforming cohort (Steensma et al., 2013). The insistent, persistent, and consistent cross-gender affirmers, a very small minority, are the only children who would be the transgender children in our neighborhood.

The transgender children are to be differentiated from other children who are fine with the gender assignment on their birth certificate but not with the proscriptions and prescriptions of the culture as to how to "do" that gender. Some of this latter group of children will show themselves to be gender fluid, some to be gender hybrids (part boy/part girl), some as gender queer ("I dispense with your categories of gender altogether"), and some later as gay or lesbian.

Evidence of gender nonconformity, whether it be transgender or the other types, often shows up early in childhood, as early as the second year of life. For some children, the gender nonconformity remains in place throughout their lifetime, especially for those who establish a transgender identity. For others, the gender nonconformity may evolve and change over the years or disappear altogether. For yet another group of children, the appearance of gender exploration, gender stress, or transgender affirmation may first show up only in adolescence, often with the onset of puberty and the new evidence of secondary sex characteristics that accompany this stage of development as the trigger. In sum, there is no consistent developmental trajectory, and the main mistake in the past and continuing into the present is to mislabel these developmental progressions as "just a phase." It may be, but most likely it is not. To date, there are no formal epidemiological studies documenting the prevalence and incidence of gender nonconformity in youth, and the estimates that have been put forward are vastly discrepant from one another (Coleman et al., 2011), ranging from 1 in 100 to 1 in 10,000.

What we do know is that gender-nonconforming children are showing up in larger numbers each year at clinics throughout the United States and Western Europe (Spack et al., 2012; Meyer, 2012). With their growing numbers, these children present us with the opportunity to rethink our assumptions, theories, and practices with children who challenge the normative gender grain of our culture. As the gender language used to express themselves may at times be undecipherable to us, it is a timely endeavor to develop the interpretive skills to understand what each of the children is communicating to us about their unique unfolding gender, both in its identity and expressions.

In my own clinical practice and those of my colleagues, which I recently canvassed, of those children who are carefully assessed as transgender and who are allowed to transition to their affirmed gender, we have no documentation of a child who has "desisted" and asked to return to his or her assigned gender. To the contrary, it is typical for us to observe a reduction of symptoms such as anxiety, depression, or oppositional behavior and an upsurge in positive mood, contentment, and well-being when the children are settled into their affirmed gender. This is not to say that the children do not continue to experience anxiety-provoking situations, but rather that they do so with greater aplomb, especially if social supports are in place, both at home and in the community (Ryan et al., 2010; Spack et al., 2012; Travers et al., 2012). As we listen and mirror back what we see in these children, we observe them poignantly finding themselves and consolidating a solid sense of self through their social transition. Within this phenomenon there certainly may be incidences in which children might revert to their assigned gender, and indeed we would expect to see that if we embrace the concept that gender is a lifelong unfolding rather than set at a moment in time in childhood; we simply have not observed such return to the gender on their birth certificates among the children in our own practices.

Having myself now worked with many gender-nonconforming children and their families, I have learned that gender exploration is not child's play, but rather a serious and sometimes urgent endeavor. I have learned that parents may be faced with a problem but are not themselves problematic. I have said in many other venues that if we listen, the children will tell us who they are (Ehrensaft, 2011b; Ehrensaft, 2012; Spiegal, 2008). In a culture that has depended on the bedrock of gender as a stable and labeled part of existence, first situated in the labor and delivery room when the genitals are observed and the gender declared, this statement generates a fair amount of anxiety and misperception. Some assume that in this model we take a moment, listen to the child's gender declarations, take them at face value, and then rubber-stamp the child's affirmed gender, as stated by the child. Nothing could be further from the truth. Like any other process of discovery, gender exploration is a long and careful endeavor, interweaving the conscious and the unconscious, the psychic and the social, the social and the cultural. This is not a one-person operation on the part of the child. Rather, it is a relational process between child and adult, interweaving thoughts and feelings. If a child should come to us as psychotherapists or psychoanalysts, in need of sorting out gender and discovering his or her own unique gender, the tools of the trade are the same as in any other therapeutic endeavor: providing a safe holding environment, fortifying a therapeutic alliance, playing, suspending oneself in a state of not knowing, allowing a place where pain and suffering can be understood and relieved, employing the tools of neutrality, empathy, observation, relationship, and interpretation to enhance self-understanding and a consolidation of a self. In the cases of children who are gender-nonconforming, the focus will be the gender self, and the goal will be not only the consolidation of that self but the building of gender resilience.

Why resilience? The majority of children who need mental health services to address their gender conundrums are suffering not from a psychiatric but a psychosocial problem—"I am what I am" is frequently met with upset, aspersion, rejection, and distress from the outer world. The children are stigmatized. They may feel a cacophony between the gender they know themselves to be and the body that presents itself to both themselves and the world. We hear a common lament from some of the children: "Why did God make a mistake and make me a girl?" "Why can't you put me back inside and make me come out a boy?" Whether it is social aspersion or incongruence between assigned and felt gender, the children, along with their families, will need to build a psychological tool kit to meet up with a world that may not be accepting and/or a gender-assigned body that feels out of synch with the gender messages from the brain.

Before illustrating the clinical model from which I work, let me back up to the concepts that guide me. The concept of the gender binary has been replaced in recent thinking by the concept of a gender spectrum—children place themselves along that spectrum in an infinite combination of gender expressions and gender identity formation. I have extended that idea one step further by proposing a concept of a "gender web": each child will weave together a three-dimensional web that will be his or her individual gender self. Nature and nurture will come together in a combination of chromosomes, hormones, hormone receptors, primary sex characteristics, secondary sex characteristics, brain, mind, socialization, and culture to create an infinite variety of gender combinations. In sum, each child's gender web is a synthesis of nature, nurture, and culture, and involves a complex relationship between the body, the mind, and the surrounding environment. Like fingerprints, no two people's gender webs will be the same. Unlike fingerprints, an individual's gender web can change over the course of a lifetime. In childhood, it is up to the child, not the parent, to spin the gender web. If the parents grab the web's threads from the child, it collapses the opportunity for the child to discover his or her own authentic gender.

Once again, I turn to the work of D. W. Winnicott, who afforded me the opportunity to extend my thinking even further about the child's crafting of the gender web. I have adapted Winnicott's concepts of the true self, false self, and individual creativity to make sense of children's gender unfolding. To review, the true self is the authentic core of an individual, of which the initial kernel is evident at birth, but then immediately interwoven with the social environment, beginning with the primary dyad between parent and child. The false self is composed of the psychological layers developed to envelop the true self, set up to protect the true self from psychic harm and to adapt and conform to environmental expectations. Individual creativity refers to the impulses inside an individual that act to construct the uniqueness of that individual (Winnicott, 1960; 1965; 1971). In the gender adaptation, the True Gender Self begins as the kernel of gender identity that is there from birth, residing most importantly in our brain, mind, and body. Once we are born, and even in utero, the True Gender Self is most definitely shaped and channeled through our experience with the external world, but its center always remains our own personal possession. The False Gender Self is the face a child puts on for the world, based on the expectations of the external environment and the child's interpretations and internalizations of either "appropriate" or adaptive gender behaviors. Gender Creativity is the process of the child weaving together body, brain, mind, psyche, socialization, and culture in an effort to compose an authentic gender self.

Gender Creativity is where Irene Fast's theory of gender development (1984; 1999) comes into play. In her theory, very young children, once aware of gender, embrace gender inclusivity: "I can be all genders." It parallels a developmental stage of magical thinking (Fraiberg, 1959), in which there is a belief in infinite transformational possibilities and subjective logic dictates that if a frog can turn into a prince, surely a girl can turn into a boy and a boy into a girl. With cognitive and emotional advances and navigation of the oedipal phase, a child grows to realize that it is impossible to be both a boy and girl or to trade between the two. A requisite stage of mourning the loss of the gender that the child can never be prepares the child for the acceptance of his or her immutable singular gender and the relational and behavioral accoutrements that accompany that embraced and fixed gender.

The gender-nonconforming child either dismisses or resists that mourning stage and continues to explore the margins of gender with its mix-and-match possibilities. Some might say that these children are suffering from a developmental arrest, fixated at a stage based on delusion and artifice, rather than material reality. I would like to propose the alternative possibility that these children refuse to relinquish the gender inclusivity of their earliest years and have come to realize that gender is not simply dictated by the body but strongly influenced by our psychic constructions. We could say that they are the ultimate anti-essentialists, who challenge us to reconsider that gender can be all-and-any, rather than either-or. In that sense they are able to maintain what so many of us have relinquished in our earliest childhoods as we strived to accommodate to a social world in which gender is defined by what is between our legs rather than what is between our ears. Rather than an arrest, we can recognize the children's persistent gender inclusivity as an accomplishment, one in which they are better able than those who have relinquished gender inclusivity to privilege psyche and social construction over deterministic biological materiality, much to their artistic and creative credit.

This is not to say that these children fail to accomplish the cognitive tasks of differentiation, categorization, and integration that come with the entrance into the preschool and primary school years, but rather that they are not bound by such schematizations when it comes to the emotionally and socially laden issue of gender. In "Trans: Gender in Free Fall," Virginia Goldner poses the question "Is gender invariance necessarily a developmental achievement, another milestone in Piagetian conservation—or is it simply a concession to normativity?" (2011, p. 162). In different terms, she is raising the same consideration I am—perhaps the youngest of our gender transgressors in our culture are resilient and creative enough to cast a very wide gender net, not encumbered by as many years of the social gender prescriptions and proscriptions as their elders are and with the benefit of a cultural loosening of those very dictates and prohibitions over recent years. Rather than gender in free fall, they are living gender in free form, and in their gender inclusivity, inviting us to loosen our own binary bonds and do the same. Goldner acknowledges the new transgender adult mentality: "My body is no longer my destiny. It is now my canvass" (p. 166). For the new gender-nonconforming generation of children, their body never was their destiny—and never will be, as long as they remain in a state of gender inclusivity with the opportunity to paint their own canvas.

A seven-year-old child was brought to me by the parents because both the parents and the child had questions about the child's gender identity. I walked to the waiting room to be greeted by a child in basketball shorts, tank top, and running shoes, looking like any boy on a school playground. The child then entered my office and spun around. Down the child's back cascaded a long blond braid secured at the end with a bright pink bow. The child spun around again, faced me, and explained, "You see, I'm a Gender Prius. A boy in the front. A girl in the back. I'm a hybrid." This child maintained her assigned gender—female—but refused to conform to the binary identificatory category "girl." Further exploration revealed that a commitment to a singular category of either male or female was internalized by this child as both binding and a "not me" experience—each meant that another aspect of self was foreclosed and lost—internally, a relegation to one binary gender box or the other denied the other half of the child's experience and collapsed into nothingness. Within the psyche, this was a child who lived in the middle, neither boy nor girl but both. "Gender Prius" was this child's articulation of self at this particular cross section in time, the child's own narrated gender snapshot at age seven. Where the Gender Creativity will take her over the course of her childhood is yet to be seen. In the meantime, our Gender Prius stands as a fine example of Irene Fast's concept of gender inclusivity sustained by this child with ample fortitude and jouissance well beyond the toddler stage. Her body is not only a canvas; it lends itself up to a three-dimensional gender sculpture.

THINKING THERAPEUTICALLY

Parents will contact a mental health professional when they have concerns about their child's gender behaviors, feelings, stresses, or distresses. It is usually the child who is the initial agent in this process, by signaling to the parent in any number of ways that "who I am" is in contradistinction of who the parents expected that child to be in terms of gender identity or expressions. Yet it is the parents not the child who typically present themselves to the clinician with their concerns. Based on collaborative discussions between the parents and the professional, the child may then enter a therapeutic process to have a room of his or her own to explore and work through confusions, dysphoria, angst, conflicts, fears, or what have you. Alternatively, the child may stay home while the parents continue to meet with a professional to work through their own worries, confusions, angst, conflicts, and fears with an aim of ensuring the child's healthy gender growth. Whether it is the child or the parents who are seen, in the model of therapy that I have dubbed True Gender Self Therapy, the goals remain the same. The developmental goal is the establishment of a child's authentic gender self with the assistance of Gender Creativity, working in the intermediary space between inner and outer. In this endeavor, the hope will be to minimize the necessity for False Gender Self constructions while at the same time recognizing their protective function for the child in a social environment that is not yet ready to accept the child in all the child's gender uniqueness. The therapeutic goal will be to build gender resilience, both the child's and the family's.

The two underlying principles of the therapy practice are: (1) If you want to know a child's gender, ask the child; it is not ours to tell, but the child's to say; (2) Parents have little control over their child's gender identity but significant influence over their child's gender health (Ehrensaft, 2011a, 2011b). Making the unconscious conscious is definitely a key instrument in allowing the child's True Gender Self narrative to unfold, with specific attention to defenses of repression and denial that bury the True Gender Self deeply underground and create a crusty, protective layer at the surface, one that may be able to meet the world adaptively but constricts the child internally, sometimes to the extreme of psychic suffocation. Yet, although I mentioned earlier that all the standard tools of psychological engagement are appropriate to this task, I have found that mirroring, with both its affective and cognitive components of reflecting back to the child in word and action what the therapist sees there, has proved to be a central therapeutic tool in facilitating a child's unfolding of the True Gender Self, accompanied by the reveries and deeply rooted mentalizations embedded in that process. If we want to know how a child identifies, we listen to the child, pay close attention, provide a safe-enough holding environment, mirror, interpret when appropriate, and over time, that child will tell you. From the children I have seen to date, I have discovered that the children will be the experts of their own gender identity, and while gender expressions may vary over time, their gender identity shows more temporal consistency and simply needs to be brought to the surface.

Returning to the goal of building gender resilience, a final objective of True Gender Self Therapy is to facilitate a child's acquisition of a psychological tool kit, so to speak, one that will allow a child to internalize a positive self-identity while recognizing situations in which that identity may be in need of protection from an unwelcome or hostile environment. The specific tools for self-protection should be consciously constructed rather than unconsciously driven; in essence, it is the intentional crafting of an outer rather than inner False Gender Self that is flexible rather than rigid and under the child's conscious control, to be used as needed as a protective cloak. Optimistically, this co-construction will be needed only temporarily, as the therapist, in collaboration with other adults in the child's caretaking world, moves from the couch into the community to build more gender-accepting environments, especially within the child's school, where much of the child's day will be spent. The intent in these efforts is to remove the need for either unconsciously driven false or consciously designed outer gender self constructions while expanding the opportunities for spontaneous Gender Creativity.

True Gender Self developmental and therapeutic goals are in line with Mark Blechner's work on identification of groups who have been labeled psychopathological as a result of prejudice. In this situation it is recognized that an individual may be suffering from social stigma and reaction to unbearable social requirements, rather than psychopathology, and there is acknowledgement that the individual's problems will be cured by changing the person's relationship to society, rather than intrapsychic change. In other words, for the ultimate removal of psychopathology, society itself must change (Blechner, 2009). To facilitate this acknowledgment regarding the psychosocial positioning of gender-nonconforming children, I would propose that we start by substituting Gender Identity Creativity for Gender Identity Disorder as our guiding principle, not for curing gender disease but for promoting gender health, defined as the acquisition of an authentic gender self.

The role of the parents is critical in achieving the developmental and therapeutic goals. In Winnicott's (1965) theory, the parent-infant dyad is primary in setting the stage for the expansion of that early kernel of the true self by mirroring the child, that is, by allowing the child's spontaneous expressions to unfold rather than imposing the parent's will and personality on the child. If environmental impingement trumps facilitation of spontaneous unfolding, the child is denied authenticity and compelled to mold to caretakers' expectations of self. If we apply this concept to gender development, it will be the parents' job to mirror back to the child the gender that child experiences him- or herself to be. If the child's inner sense of gender is different than what the parents are both seeing and responding to, the child may deflate or the child may protest. If given the opportunity to protest, the message is, "Hey, you've got it wrong. I'm not the gender you think I am" or, alternatively, "I can't do gender the way you want me to." If the parents can adjust their reflective mirror, the child finds him or herself in clearer focus. If they cannot, gender begins feeling like the distorted mirrors in a fun house: someone is reflecting back to them a sense of gender that looks nothing like the gender they experience themselves as being. It is not uncommon for a parent to say to a little boy who says he is a girl, "Honey, boys can play with Barbies, too, not just girls. We can buy you a Barbie." In response, it has not been uncommon for the child to protest: "I *know* boys can play with Barbies. That's not what I said—I said I'm a *girl* who wants to play with Barbies." That child is putting out a plea for parental mirroring that feels reflective rather than distorted. That child is also telling the parents, "Please do not be the one who paints the gender portrait of me. Put your brush down and pass back to me my own self-portrait, not of your design, but of mine." To do that, the parent often has to work through the discomfort and angst of one's own gender predicates and also make room for recognition of the child being different from them (Solomon, 2012).

Ken Corbett (2009) identifies the sometimes hyperboled expressions of female gender by gender-nonconforming little boys. Poised between the psychic and the social, the gender-nonconforming boy who cries out, in word and action, "'How loud, how colorful, how bejeweled do I have to be before you will see me?'"(p. 159) is in a state of melancholic suffering in which his gender desires are rebuked and repudiated by those around him. I have certainly seen these extreme states of exaggerated gender performances in children I have worked with, particularly boys, which makes sense, because boys in our culture are policed far more heavily than girls in their gender desires, as evidenced in the APA's *DSM IV-TM* (1994). A boy only has to *prefer* cross-dressing or simulating female attire to qualify for the diagnosis; a girl has to *insist* on it. Whether expressed by a boy or a girl, thinking about these hyperboled gender expressions in relational terms, we observe an outlaw phenomenon in which the protesting children take their "doing gender" to the extreme so that those around them get the point. Yet what happens when that repudiation is replaced by recognition? Referring back to the mirroring concept, when stigma is lowered, social acceptance increased, and parental mirroring adjusted to fit the child who appears before the parents, rather than the one they hope to have, the hyperboled sense of gender seems less in evidence. There is no longer a psychic need to scream for recognition.

Two children who have recently visited the Child and Adolescent Gender Center Clinic at the University of California San Francisco Benioff Children's Hospital are perhaps exemplary of this. It should be noted that both children were screened for chromosomal anomalies that might have accounted for gender-nonconforming presentations, and none existed for either, each being unambiguously XY and XX respectively. Casey is nine. She was assigned a male gender at birth, but over the course of her first eight years expressed repeatedly that she thought she was a girl, not a boy. Between third and fourth grade, her parents allowed her to transition to her affirmed female identity. They were supportive of her transition and worked with her school to facilitate the transition and build in the educational supports Casey might need. The fourth-grader who walked into the Gender Clinic was not bedecked in sparkles, frills, or jewels. She had long cascading curls, wore a flannel shirt, jeans, and hiking boots. Right after her came an eight-year-old boy, Danny. Danny was assigned a female gender at birth, but was insistent from age two on that Danny was a boy, not a girl. Danny's parents are divorced, and Danny's father will only recognize Danny as a girl. Danny's mother has sole physical and legal custody. She has acknowledged Danny's gender desires, and Danny has been living as a boy, except at his father's. The child who walked into the Gender Clinic was not dressed up in army fatigues or striving for a "macho" presentation. He was dressed rather like Casey, in the prevalent unisex uniform of their age cohort, wearing a striped T-shirt, jeans, and navy sneakers. He had a short-cropped haircut. In cultural terms, his presentation was so consistent with normative boy presentation that the pediatric endocrinologist, whose very job was to assess the child's physiological status along the Tanner Stages of puberty, and therefore knowing full well the child's natal sex, upon hearing that Danny suffered from enuresis, began to give the mother a lecture about boys' anatomy that might be contributing to her son's wetting, forgetting completely that this was a female-bodied boy.

Are we seeing here a lower-key, relaxed rather than noisy, almost hysterical presentation of gender when we replace blinding police floodlights with soft lighting and safe landings for the gender nonconforming children who are simply telling us, "I am what I am"? If so, could we attribute these more-tempered presentations in part to a more sensitized process of mirroring and a diminution of impingement on the part of the parents, which might end up being our most important clinical intervention in promoting a child's gender health?

It is right about now where the thought might be brewing "But what about the situations in which gender is a symptom of some other psychic disturbance?" That can certainly happen but far less frequently than most people assume, particularly those who formulate gender-nonconforming presentations or desires in young children as evidence of trauma, attachment disruptions, or disturbed parent-child relations (Coates, Friedman, and Wolfe, 1991). The majority of children who are coming to clinics or individual practitioners to address gender issues do not have histories of attachment disruptions or disturbed parent-child relations, and the most common form of trauma they present is usually a consequence rather than a cause of their gender nonconformity, typically a result of parental or social rejection, harassment, and bullying. Still, the most challenging task as clinicians is to tease out those situations in which gender conundrums' roots are some other deeper psychological disturbance or disruption from situations in which a child is simply trying to get to the root of the authentic gender self in all its complexities. To make matters even more complicated, we have to contemplate the gnawing chicken-and-egg question: How do we know that a child's psychological conflicts, syndromes, or disorders are not the sequelae of being forced to live a gender-inauthentic life rather than of an independent core psychological problem residing in the child?

We do have an ex post facto test at our disposal to answer this question: if the disequilibrium in psychological functioning is a secondary effect of being barred from living an authentic gender life, and the child is given the opportunity to live that life with acceptance and as much sheltering as possible from outside stigma, and the child then gets significantly better and the symptoms subside, gender was most likely the root of the problem, solved by cutting a path to allow the True Gender Self to walk through. This is not an academic exercise. It is an observation reported repeatedly by parents and professionals alike as they watch a child's mental health and well-being improve once the constricting bindings of gender are replaced by a broad band of gender expressions in line with the child's gender desires (Spack et al., 2012).

Lastly, what if there are psychological problems that run parallel to a child's gender conundrums or confusions? Does a "co-morbid" psychiatric disorder preclude a child being able to transition genders or receive interventions such as puberty blockers? I would answer—only if gender nonconformity is considered "morbid," and since I do not operate from a disease model of gender, the other psychological problems are relevant only inasmuch as they are impediments to gender resilience and compromise a child's ability to express the true gender in a potentially gender-unfriendly world. In all cases, the clinical work is the same: using the therapeutic tools outlined earlier to learn from the child what is ticking inside.

FROM THE PLAYGROUND TO THE COUCH: JACQUELINE/THOMAS

We all know that children are more apt to jump on the couch than to lie on it. So using the couch metaphorically, I would like to share some excerpts from a therapy conducted over a four-year period. The techniques employed in this therapy are drawn both from my training as a developmental psychologist and gender specialist along with the tools of the relational, or two-person, psychoanalytic model (Mitchell, 1988), in which a dialogue between patient and therapist and their relational matrix as the therapeutic couple is the means to discovering the child's truth (Spezzano, 1993), in this case, the True Gender Self. As mentioned earlier, whereas bringing the unconscious into consciousness is one cornerstone of the work, the act of mirroring back to the child the child's articulation over time of that child's unique gender web is typically the crux of the therapeutic endeavor. Because the web is a consolidation of nature, nurture, and culture, the collateral work with the child's parent(s) or primary caretakers(s), along with collaboration with other parties active in the child's life, becomes an essential component of the process.

JACQUELINE'S GENDER HISTORY

Jacqueline's mother, Adrian, first contacted me when Jacqueline was nine years old to address her daughter's perceived gender angst.[2] Adrian was a single mother who had conceived her child using a known sperm donor. She gave birth to a daughter and was delighted to have a girl. By age two, her little girl refused to wear dresses and threw away her dolls and pink stuffed animals. She asked for balls, trucks, and action figures. Adrian was able to adapt to the daughter she had with her nonconforming gender expressions, but she became troubled when Jacqueline, still in preschool, began to complain about being a girl, saying maybe she wanted to be a boy sometimes. Throughout grade school, Jacqueline kept her hair cropped short, wore jeans, T-shirts, running shoes, and a baseball cap, with most of her clothes purchased from the boys department. She would only wear pajama bottoms and no tops when she went to bed, and she protested that she could no longer go topless at the community swimming pool, to which Adrian had put a stop when Jacqueline turned seven, explaining to Jacqueline that for girls her age, it was no longer appropriate to appear in public with their chests uncovered.

At age nine, Adrian observed her daughter growing increasingly distraught about and preoccupied with gender conundrums—could she keep living as a tomboy or was she maybe a boy boy? In early consultations, Adrian expressed her own anxieties about Jacqueline's apparent gender dysphoria. As a mother who had for years dreamed of giving birth to a little girl, her deepest hope was that Jacqueline would settle on being a gender-nonconforming girl, maybe a lesbian, rather than a transgender male. She desperately did not want to lose her daughter, but having done her own reading and having talked to other parents of gender-nonconforming children, she was preparing herself to accept whatever was best for Jacqueline rather than what was wished for by her.

2. All names and identifying features of individuals have been changed in this presentation.

In my consultations with Adrian, I learned that Jacqueline had recently been sharing reveries about being a boy and loved it when people took her for one. She had reported a dream to her mother in which she discovered a button inside herself that she could push to turn herself into a boy. Dressed like a boy, she still played mostly with girls and a few "nice" boys. She avoided the loud, rowdy ones. One reason for this was that temperamentally, Jacqueline was a very quiet, shy, slow-to-warm-up child, preferring to fly under the radar screen rather than have attention focused on her. She told her mother she'd like to be a boy, "mostly, kinda." In public, if given a choice, she would go into the single-toilet public restroom marked MEN, but she chose the women's restroom over the men's when there were several stalls rather than one—again, because she loathed drawing attention to herself and thought people might stare.

GENDER CONUNDRUMS IN THE CONSULTATION ROOM

The child I met in therapy closely matched Adrian's description of Jacqueline's personality. Overall, she was extremely shy and a child of few words. Speaking about feelings was particularly difficult for her and engaging in projective play activities, such as drawing, the sand tray, or puppet play, yielded few results and made Jacqueline acutely uncomfortable. This meant that our work went at a very slow pace, with me spending many of our first sessions initiating conversations that allowed her to open up a little at a time and discovering that her limit for engaging in dialogue was about twenty-five minutes, after which she would ask timidly, "Can we play a [board] game now?" breathing a sigh of relief when I assented. So the therapy quickly settled into twenty-five minutes of talk and twenty-five minutes of board games in each session, with Jacqueline taking a seat at my desk and me moving my chair close to her to facilitate more intimate conversation, which Jacqueline readily accepted. Because of Adrian's work schedule and her limited financial resources, Jacqueline and I were only able to meet on a once-a-week basis, which further slowed the forward pace of our work together.

I have learned in my years as a child gender specialist that gender-nonconforming children, even in the most supportive families, have often internalized by a very early age "We don't speak of such things." Thus, as part of my assessment process with a child, I refer to myself as someone who knows about gender things and report to the child a very brief snapshot of what the parent(s) have shared with me about their child's gender nonconformity, and I give the child an opportunity to respond. In Jacqueline's case, I told her that I had learned from her mother that she liked to wear boy clothes (which was also obvious from her gender presentation in my office), be mistaken for a boy, play with both boys and girls, had been wondering with her mom about who she was, and had I gotten that right? Jacqueline did not make eye contact with me but appeared to be listening intently, answering quietly, "Yeah, that's kind of right." My silent interpretation at that time, which I held for later, was that Jacqueline lived in a layered internal world, firm at the core and then covered with doubts. I intuited that she might consciously know more than she was telling and that she might be caught in a conflict with her either conscious or unconscious knowing of her mother's strong wishes for a daughter, tangled up with her own confusion of whether she was one or not. What would she do if the choice were between losing her mother's love and affirming what she might be coming to know about her own gender?

That latter question came to bear over the course of our first year together. Getting to know me better and resonating to my initial observation that in addition to being a person of few words, Jacqueline seemed afraid that if she spoke up she might hurt someone, Jacqueline first expressed that she was fine being a girl as long as people did not expect her to wear dresses and as long as they let her play basketball with the boys, but then she wasn't so sure. She shared with me, in her own tentative language, that she really thought maybe she felt more like a boy but didn't want to lose all her girlfriends, so maybe she should leave it the way it was. In addition to reflecting back to her the girl-boy vacillation that was going on in her head, I wondered with her whether it wasn't just her girlfriends she was worried about losing, but maybe her mother as well. Tears came to her eyes, and she grew silent for some seconds, then mutely nodded her head in the affirmative.

GENDER SUPPORTS: MATERNAL AND MEDICAL

This led me to invite Adrian in for several collateral sessions in which we explored in more depth Adrian's anxieties about Jacqueline opening up further about gender desires and discoveries and the potential loss of a daughter that might ensue. Each of the two members of this relational matrix—mother and daughter—were living in fear of losing each other, and each had to work through their anxieties about this, with Adrian taking the lead to communicate to her child, not just in words but in feelings, that whoever Jacqueline was, her mother would love her. The lack of that parental support can often prove to be the primary obstruction to the child's freedom to creatively explore gender, and I assessed this to be true for Jacqueline, with Adrian expressing her doubts and fears to Jacqueline not overtly but in subtle innuendo. As this parental obstruction was removed through Adrian's own internal work, Jacqueline began to open up and muse more about her gender position, as when she shared with me in one session, "I think I'll still be the same person if I'm a boy instead of a girl, won't I?" I asked her what she thought the answer was, and she began to muse about all the times she had already sat in her room addressing herself as "he" and that nothing seemed to change at all, except that she seemed "kinda happier."

As Adrian did her work to sort out her anxieties about Jacqueline's gender explorations, Jacqueline began to show the first signs of puberty. Having been alerted by parents of other gender-nonconforming children with whom she was in contact, Adrian took it upon herself to become educated about puberty blockers, through reading, Internet research, and consultations with Jacqueline's pediatrician. Adrian was now faced with a dilemma: whether or not to talk to Jacqueline about the possibility of taking puberty blockers as Jacqueline moved into puberty—a medical intervention to stop the flow of a female puberty that might prove to be unwanted, if not traumatic (see Ehrensaft, 2009)—and give Jacqueline more time to explore her gender.

Puberty blockers, also known as GnRH agonists, were originally introduced in the 1970s to stanch the onset of puberty in young children presenting with precocious puberty. Upon stopping the administration of the drug, normal puberty will resume within six months. In the 1990s the clinicians at the first established child gender clinic, located in the Netherlands, began using the GnRH agonists for a new population, puberty-aged youth who were presenting with significant gender dysphoria (Cohen-Kettenis and Pfäfflin, 2003), affording them the opportunity to have more time to explore their gender identity before moving into the puberty of their assigned gender and, alternatively, preventing the onset of an unwanted, potentially traumatic puberty that would match a child's assigned gender but not the child's affirmed gender identity. As in the use of GnRH agonists for precocious puberty, the effects are reversible, if a child decides to proceed in the assigned gender identity rather than change genders. At the same time, if a youth is clear that the affirmed gender is a trans identity, blockers afford that youth the later opportunity, with the aid of cross-sex hormones, to proceed in developing the secondary sex characteristics of their affirmed gender, without the imposition and risks of future medical interventions in adulthood, such as mastectomies, electrolysis, and facial reconstructions to align their physical appearance with their affirmed gender.

Spack et al. (2012) published findings from the GeMS (Gender Management Service) program for youth in Boston that reflect "that psychological functioning improves with medical intervention" (p. 422) for transgender youth, which included both the administration of puberty blockers and, later, when appropriate, cross-sex hormones. From observations of youth in my practice and reports from others, there is no doubt that the availability of hormone blockers has been a tremendous gain for transgender and gender-nonconforming youth. In a follow-up study by members of the Amsterdam clinic, where puberty blockers were first introduced, results corroborated Spack et al.'s findings, indicating that behavioral and emotional problems and depressive symptoms decreased, while general psychological functioning improved significantly subsequent to the administration of puberty blockers for gender dysphoric youth (de Vries et al., 2011). There have been no reports to date of any short- or long-term medical risks of blockers, including negative impact on bone density, which have been many people's concerns (Gooren and Delemarre-van de Waal, 1996; Spack, 2013). It should be noted, though, that extended longitudinal data into middle adulthood are only presently available for children who were administered the drug for precocious puberty; the use with gender-nonconforming youth has been too recent to yet have such long-term longitudinal data. The main problem with hormone blockers in many countries is that they are exorbitantly expensive and, if not covered by medical insurance or government programs, out of reach for any but those with substantial financial means.

Adrian was well aware of the facts about puberty blockers and was also apprised that puberty blockers are most effective if they are administered before the end of Tanner Stage II of puberty, in which the earliest signs of puberty are emerging but no significant physiological puberty changes have occurred. Unfortunately, the fast, ticking biological clock of Jacqueline's emerging puberty was out of synch with Jacqueline's slow progression forward in sorting out her gender questions. Adrian felt torn about intruding on Jacqueline's preadolescent innocence with potentially disruptive information about bodies and secondary sex characteristics and was still working through her own anxiety about Jacqueline possibly exiting girlhood to enter boyhood. Decentering from that anxiety and focusing on Jacqueline's potential needs, Adrian came to terms with the implications of her gender-nonconforming daughter's impending entrance into Tanner Stage II of puberty, when puberty blockers prove most effective. She was able to weigh the potential intrusion against the potential harm done if she failed to provide Jacqueline with information about the possibility of taking puberty blockers when, with the biological clock moving so quickly, it might be "too late" to ward off the negative if not traumatic psychological responses to an unwanted puberty. She imagined Jacqueline later accosting her reproachfully, "If you knew about them, why didn't you tell me in time?" To Adrian, the choice of omission seemed far riskier than the effects of commission, and thus she decided to have a discussion with Jacqueline about the availability of blockers and their effects. We could say her decision was counterphobic in face of her own anxieties, but I assessed it more as Adrian's wish to do what was best for her daughter, as confusing as it was to figure out what that would be.

With professional advice from a pediatric endocrinologist, and after extensive consultation with me, Adrian, first ascertaining that Jacqueline was fully apprised about puberty and the physical changes that come with it for both males and females, spoke to her daughter about the blockers in as sensitive a manner as possible. She explained how puberty blockers worked, how they could buy Jacqueline more time to sort out her gender without the intrusion of body changes, how they were not permanent and she could stop them any time she wanted and go back to have her body change in ways that girls' bodies do, and that puberty blockers could be something she could consider. Adrian reported that at first Jacqueline listened quietly, but then grew fidgety. The more Adrian talked, the more agitated Jacqueline became. This was unusual behavior for Jacqueline, typically a laconic child. She finally looked down to the floor and mumbled to Adrian, "Yeah, maybe I could take that medicine." Then she suddenly leapt up and fled to her bedroom, slamming the door behind her, blurting out, "But girls are nicer than boys." Adrian felt totally deflated and questioned whether she had made a big mistake in bringing up puberty blockers at all. It also opened up hope for her that maybe Jacqueline was going to remain a girl after all.

JACQUELINE AND THE BLOCKER DOCTOR

In my following session with Jacqueline, she was unusually quiet, even for her. She told me about the conversation with her mother about those "blocker things," then tears welled up and she laid her head on the desk. The doubts at the surface and the gender rumblings from below were all coming to a head, and Jacqueline was clearly feeling overwhelmed. In that moment I made a therapeutic decision to say nothing to Jacqueline, but to sit with her quietly and mirror back to her the level of distress she was feeling, along with a wish: "Why couldn't gender just be easier?"

During the following week Jacqueline, upset and worried, approached Adrian. She expressed that she did not want to grow up, she was actually terrified of growing up, and wished she could suspend herself in time and remain a ten-year-old child forever, where she could dress as she liked, present herself as she liked, and not be burdened by the stresses of both changing bodies and shots to actually stop you from changing. She asked Adrian to back off and not talk about puberty blockers anymore, at least for now, which Adrian obliged. Both Adrian and I were left with questions and concerns: Was Jacqueline, usually so taciturn, telling us that girls were nicer and she wanted to be one, which was her mother's wish? Was Jacqueline perhaps a gender-fluid, not a transgender child? Was this simply too much information for Jacqueline to handle as she was trying to pace her own gender explorations in therapy? Catapulted into action by the early appearance of puberty, Adrian chose to take the risk of introducing the topic of puberty blockers too early for where Jacqueline was emotionally in her gender journey, but just in time regarding the physical changes in Jacqueline's body. On balance, it seemed to Adrian a better option than waiting to bring up the availability of puberty blockers too late when Jacqueline was further into puberty, with no time to retreat and think it over for awhile. But was it? Over the subsequent weeks this question hung with me as well as I watched Jacqueline temporarily shut down and not want to think about gender at all.

Then, some weeks after Jacqueline's request for a moratorium on puberty blocker discussions, accompanied by her self-enforced prohibition on any shared dialogues about gender at all, Jacqueline began to slowly open up in the therapy sessions. She had questions she wanted to ask me about how the hormone blockers worked, and she wondered if they would ever come up with a pill because she hated shots and the alternative of a subcutaneous implant seemed even yuckier. I shared with Jacqueline that I first wanted to understand with her what made her want to stop the moratorium about blockers. She told me that she had needed some time to go off and think on her own. I wondered with her how it helped to do this alone rather than with me, and, after some minutes of silence, she was able to tell me that her head was buzzing with too many things at once and she'd needed to turn everything off for awhile, and the only way to do that was to turn me off—and her mom too, but now she was back. I was recalling my own guiding principle that it is not for us to tell, but for the children to say, and I held a concern that too much telling regarding puberty blockers was experienced by Jacqueline as an impingement from which she felt a need to retreat. On the other hand, perhaps the buzzing in her head represented all the gender tensions and conflicts coming to the light of day, which can certainly make a great deal of noise on their way up. Either way, I wanted to return to her question, particularly because Jacqueline asking a question of me was a rare event in our work. Regarding the blockers, I told her that the bad news was that they hadn't yet invented a pill, and interpreted the dilemma of "pain and gain" as she imagined puberty blockers as part of her life.

Jacqueline's mental buzzing began to settle down into cohesive thoughts. She expressed that sometimes she thought it would be better if she were a boy—it would just feel more "right," but only if she could move to a new school and start over. She suggested, at first very tentatively, that maybe she could have an appointment with the "blocker doctor" to find out more about puberty blockers. For the first time, she asked me a direct question about herself and how I thought about her: "Do you think taking blockers would be a good thing for me to do?" I responded that this was a really important question, and the only way to answer the question was to find out more about what *she* had been thinking about it. Jacqueline, who rarely made direct eye contact except when beating me at a board game, slowly looked up and said, "I'm pretty sure I'm a boy." Throughout, my therapeutic provisions for Jacqueline had been primarily in the form of a holding environment, one in which I listened and reflected back what I was hearing, with minimal interpretation and maximum attention to building a therapeutic dialogue toward discovering Jacqueline's True Gender Self. At this point in the treatment, I assessed that we were finally in dialogue with one another and that I could let my silent interpretations begin to speak.

Over the subsequent weeks, Jacqueline, although still shy and somewhat reticent to share what she was thinking, began to open up more, both in her therapy sessions and with her mother; all arrows pointed in the direction of her consolidating a male gender identity. She dropped her tentativeness and made clearer statements: "I know I'm a boy, I was just always afraid to come out and say it." Her fears involved not just the loss of the love of her mother but the loss of the parts of her that she so valued and resided in in her relationships with both her female parent and her female friends—the quietness, the attention to feelings, the collaborative, cooperative spirit among them. At a deep level, she had incorporated the cultural dictum that only girls were allowed those attributes, no boys need apply. Only when she brought these fears to the surface and put them into words in the therapy session was she able to claim a male identity for herself while preserving the gender expressions of her heretofore female self.

Jacqueline repeated her request to make an appointment to see the blocker doctor, and Adrian set forth to schedule appointments with a pediatric endocrinologist who was trained as a gender specialist. Both I and Jacqueline's pediatrician consulted with the endocrinologist, and it was decided that Jacqueline, who was now well into Tanner Stage II of puberty, would start a course of puberty blockers. It was also fortunate that Adrian's place of employment provided insurance that covered the prohibitive cost of the medications and all other gender-related medical interventions, so that the treatment could commence.

JACQUELINE'S TRANSITION TO THOMAS

A few months after starting on puberty blockers, Jacqueline expressed that she was ready to transition to being a boy, at home. She chose the name Thomas for herself and asked her mother and grandmother if they would start using both that name and male pronouns. She was too shy to ask me directly to do the same, so I proactively intervened and asked what name I should be using. Although my training has taught me to wait until the patient brings up material, rather than intruding with the therapist's own agenda—as in my original assessment process in which I introduced gender to break the ice of a potentially prohibitive topic—I felt that Jacqueline might still feel too inhibited to be so bold as to assert a name or pronoun change in my office, so I took the lead and asked what she would like me to do. After a few moments of silence, Jacqueline first muttered, "Oh, I don't know; it doesn't matter," and then a few minutes later, Jacqueline looked down and said quietly, "Well, I guess you can call me Thomas." I explored with her what the name Thomas meant to her, and she reflected that it felt like letting someone come out to play for the first time. It was curious that this child did not choose a new name nearer to the one she had been given at birth, as Jack or even Jacky could have sufficed as a male assignation in closer proximity to who she had always been, but the unconscious need to bring a hidden core male self to the surface and differentiate it from the female outer self, which now felt like a "not me," overrode any desire or need for continuity. So Thomas it was, and Thomas it has been ever since, a Thomas fortified by the mirroring back by both me and Thomas's mother and grandmother that *he* was the child we were now seeing.

During the transition from Jacqueline to Thomas there was one therapeutic moment, seemingly inconsequential, that I think spoke volumes about the positive effects of the introduction of puberty blockers and Jacqueline's subsequent expressed desire to transition to male. Thomas had just returned from a weekend family conference for gender-nonconforming children and youth and their families, accompanied by both his mother and his grandmother. It should be noted that this was the first year that Thomas agreed to attend this annual conference. In the previous two years, Jacqueline had made it very clear that she was not, under any circumstance, going to be forced to go to the conference. This year, as Thomas, he went willingly. Our therapy session following the conference was about to come to a close. Thomas had only cursorily talked about the conference. In the past, this child's consistent mode at the end of every session had been to look down, mumble a barely audible good-bye, and exit. On this particular day, we were about to have a two-week break because I would be taking a vacation. As Thomas got up to leave, he looked right at me with an ear-to-ear smile and announced, with a clear voice and a twinkle in his eye, "Hope you have a great vacation . . . wherever you're going. See you when you get back." I had never seen such self-assurance, and I had never experienced such closeness with Thomas in all our four years of work together. It was as if the Mona Lisa, now transitioned to the Mono Liso, had actually smiled and spoken, and it was at that moment that I recognized the fruits of all of our labor. Releasing the gender conundrums and allowing them to be put into words led to a corrective mirroring experience, so that we found Thomas in translation and could now recognize Thomas as the boy he was. Thomas was definitely coming out, not just about gender but from his protective shell. Discovering a True Gender Self in the context of a protective mirroring relationship, Thomas was also finding the road that would lead him to an authentic, spontaneous, and creative life.

CONCLUSION

Facilitating a child's transition from one gender to another or uncovering a child's true gender fluid self should be done with careful reflection and evaluation, with enough time for exploration and affirmation. Many parents want to be able to look into a crystal ball and be assured of an accurate and permanent gender future for their child before making any major gender decisions. Professionals often share that same urgency to be able to get the child's gender in focus as soon as possible. The problem is that children are moving, evolving organisms who may go through several iterations of self before acquiring their final identities. While their gender history, particularly a long-standing affirmation of a gender they claim to be theirs, is critical information, such histories cannot perfectly or linearly predict the future. Thomas seemed firmly established as a boy at age eleven. He was taking puberty blockers that would allow him to move to hormonal treatments if he continues to affirm himself as male. If adolescence, however, reopens Thomas's earlier questions—"Am I a girl? Am I a boy?"—the most important psychological intervention for Thomas will be exactly what he has been provided with to date: a place to continue to explore his gender to arrive at a True Gender Self.

As clinicians, we will need to train ourselves to live with ambiguity for extended periods of time as a child weaves together an authentic and unique gender web. To make matters more complicated, as Avgi Saketopoulou points out, "treating atypically gendered children at this point in time carries the additional burden of trying to imagine a world that does not yet exist. What does this future that we are asked to envision hold for fluidly gendered kids?" (2011, p. 204). The answer to that question resides in the gender-nonconforming children themselves, as we listen and learn from them.

REFERENCES

AMERICAN PSYCHIATRIC ASSOCIATION (1994). *Diagnostic Criteria from DSM-IV-TM*. Washington, DC: American Psychiatric Association.

BLECHNER, M. (2009). *Sex Changes: Transformations in Society and Psychoanalysis*. New York: Routledge.

CALIFORNIA SENATE BILL NO. 1172, LIEU (2012). Sexual orientation change efforts. Filed with Secretary of State, September 30, 2012.

COATES, S., FRIEDMAN, R.C., AND S. WOLFE (1991). The etiology of boyhood gender identity disorder: A model for integrating temperament, development, and psychodynamics. *Psychoanalytic Dialogues* 1(4): 481–523.

COHEN-KETTENIS, P., AND PFÄFFLIN, F. (2003). *Transgenderism and Intersexuality in Childhood and Adolescence*. Thousand Oaks, CA: Sage Publications.

COLEMAN, E., BOCKTING, W., BOTZER, M., COHEN-KETTENIS, P., DECUYPERE, G., FELDMAN, J., FRASER, L., GREEN, J., KNUDSON, G., MEYER, W. J., MONSTREY, S., ADLER, R. K., BROWN, G. R., DEVOR, A. H., EHRBAR, R., ETTNER, R., EYLER, E., GAROFALO, R., KARASIC, D. H., LEV, A. I., MAYER, G., MEYER-BAHLBURG, H., HALL, B. P., PFÄFFLIN, F., RACHLIN, K., ROBINSON, B., SCHECHTER, L. S., TANGPRICHA, V., VAN TROTSENBURG, M., VITALE, A., WINTER, S., WHITTLE, S., WYLIE, K. R., AND ZUCKER, K. (2011). Standards of care for the health of transsexual, transgender, and gender-nonconforming people. Version 7. *International Journal of Transgenderism* 13:165–232.

CORBETT, K. (2009). *Boyhoods: Rethinking Masculinities*. New Haven, CT: Yale University Press.

DE VRIES, A. L. C., STEENSMA, T. D., DORELEIJERS, T. A. H., COHEN-KETTINIS, P. T. (2011). Puberty suppression in adolescents with gender identity disorder: a prospective follow-up study. *Journal Sex Med* 8:2276–2283.

EHRENSAFT, D. (2009). One pill makes you boy, one pill makes you girl. *International Journal of Applied Psychoanalytic Studies* 6(1): 12–24.

_____. (2011a). Boys will be girls, girls will be boys: Children affect parents as parents affect children in gender nonconformity. *Psychoanalytic Psychology* 28(4): 528–548.

_____. (2011b).*Gender Born, Gender Made: Raising Healthy Gender-Nonconforming Children*. New York: The Experiment.

_____. (2012). From gender identity disorder to gender identity creativity: True gender self therapy. *Journal of Homosexuality* 59:337–356.

FAST, I. (1984). *Gender Identity: A Differentiation Model*. Hillsdale, NJ: Analytic Press.

_____. (1999). Aspects of core gender identity. *Psychoanalytic Dialogues* 9:633–661.

FRAIBERG, S. (1959). *The Magic Years*. New York: Scribners.

FREUD, A. (1965). *Normality and Pathology in Childhood: Assessments of Development*. New York: International Universities Press.

_____. (1981). *Psychoanalytic Psychology of Normal Development*. In *The Writings of Anna Freud,* vol. 8. New York: International Universities Press.

FREUD, S. (1962). *Three Contributions to the Theory of Sex*. New York: E. P. Dutton.

GOLDNER, V. (2011). Trans: Gender in free fall. *Psychoanalytic Dialogues* 21(2): 159–171.

GOOREN, L. J. G., AND DELEMARRE-VAN DE WAAL, H. (1996). The feasibility of endocrine interventions in juvenile transsexuals. *Journal of Psychology and Human Sexuality* 8:69–74.

MEYER, W. J. (2012). Gender identity disorder: An emerging problem for pediatricians. *Pediatrics* 129(3): 571–575.

MITCHELL, S. (1988). *Relational Concepts in Psychoanalysis: An Integration*. Cambridge, MA: Harvard University Press.

PERSON, E. (2005). As the wheel turns: A centennial reflection on Freud's three essays on the theory of sexuality. *Journal of the American Psychoanalytic Association* 53(4): 1257–1282.

ROSCOE, W. (1998). *Changing Ones: Third and Fourth Gender in Native North America*. New York: St. Martin's/Griffin.

RYAN, C., RUSSELL, S. T., HUEBNER, D., DIAZ, R., SANCHEZ, J. (2010). Family acceptance in adolescence and the health of LGBT young adults. *Journal of Child and Adolescent Psychiatric Nursing* 23(4): 205–213.

SAKETOPOULOU, A. (2011). Minding the gap: Intersections between gender, race, and class in work with gender variant children. *Psychoanalytic Dialogues* 21:192–209.

SOLOMON, A. (2012). *Far from the Tree: Parents, Children, and the Search for Identity*. New York: Scribner.

SPACK, N. P. (2013). Management of transgenderism. *Journal of the American Medical Association* 309(5): 478–484.

SPACK, N. P., EDWARDS-LEEPER, L., FELDMAN, H. A., LEIBOWITZ, S., MANDEL, F., DIAMOND, D. A., AND VANCE, S. R. (2012). Children and adolescents with gender identity disorder referred to a pediatric medical center. *Pediatrics* 129(3): 418–425.

SPEZZANO, C. (1993). *Affect in Psychoanalysis: A Clinical Synthesis.* Hillsdale, NJ: Analytic Press.

SPIEGAL, A. (2008). Two families grapple with sons' gender preferences. National Public Radio *All Things Considered*, May 7.

STEENSMA, T. D., McGUIRE, J. K., KREULS, B., BEEKMAN, A., COHEN-KETTENIS, P. (2013). Factors associated with desistence and persistence of childhood gender dysphoria: A quantitative follow-up study. *Journal of the American Academy of Child and Adolescent Psychiatry* 52(6): 582–590.

TRAVERS, R., BAUER, G., PYNE, J., BRADLEY, K., GALE, L., PAPADIMITRIOU, M. (2012). Impact of strong parental support for trans youth. *Trans PULSE*, October 2: 1–5.

WINNICOTT, D.W. (1960). Ego Distortion in Terms of True and False Self. In D.W. Winnicott (1965), *Maturational Processes and the Facilitating Environment* (pp. 140–152). Madison, CT: International Universities Press.

_____. (1965). *Maturational Processes and the Facilitating Environment.* Madison, CT: International Universities Press.

_____. (1971). *Playing and Reality.* London: Tavistock Publications.

Free to Be You and Me

Normal Gender-Role Fluidity— Commentary on Diane Ehrensaft's "Listening and Learning from Gender-Nonconforming Children"

RONA KNIGHT, Ph.D.

This paper suggests that gender role fluidity is a normal self state throughout development. It discusses the nonlinear progression of gender role identity that is constantly fluid and reactive to biological, environmental, and psychological changes. Given the normal fluidity of gender role identity, it argues that giving puberty blockers to young children is against the best interests of the child's development.

"I'm not! And if turning up my hair makes me one, I'll wear it in two tails till I'm twenty," cried Jo, pulling off her net, and shaking down a chestnut mane. "I hate to think I've got to grow up, and be Miss March, and wear long gowns, and look as prim as a China aster! It's bad enough to be a girl, anyway, when I like boys' games and work and manners. I can't get over my disappointment in not being a boy; and it's worse than ever now, for I am dying to go and fight with Papa, and I can only stay at home and knit, like a poky old woman!" [1]

Rona Knight is Assistant Professor in the Departments of Psychiatry and Pediatrics, Boston University School of Medicine, and Training and Supervising Psychoanalyst, Berkshire Psychoanalytic Institute.

The Psychoanalytic Study of the Child 68, ed. Claudia Lament, Robert A. King, Samuel Abrams, Paul M. Brinich, and Rona Knight (Yale University Press, copyright © 2015 by Claudia Lament, Robert A. King, Samuel Abrams, Paul M. Brinich, and Rona Knight).

1. Louisa May Alcott, *Little Women*, Bantam Classic ed. (1868–1869; reissue, New York: Bantam Dell, 2007).

"Pudd'nhead Wilson says Hellfire Hotchkiss is the only genuwyne male man in this town and Thug Carpenter's the only genuwyne female girl, if you leave out sex and just consider the business facts."[2]

FROM THE WRITINGS OF SHAKESPEARE (*TWELFTH NIGHT, MUCH ADO about Nothing*); Mark Twain; Louisa May Alcott; and contemporary characters in literature that include Scout in *To Kill a Mockingbird*; Frankie turning into Francis in *Member of the Wedding*; Pippi Longstocking, who is full of phallic exuberance; and Smidge, the sensitive boy with strong maternal instincts, writers throughout the centuries have articulated the theme of gender role fluidity. Homosexual behavior and role reversal cross-dressing are as old as recorded history (Crompton, 2006).

Given that such feelings and behaviors have existed throughout time, gender fluidity might be considered a normal, classic aspect of human development. In my discussion of Dr. Diane Ehrensaft's paper, "Listening and Learning from Gender-Nonconforming Children," I will show how modern thinking about and research in development support the idea of gender fluidity throughout the life span and discuss some ideas of how this should or should not be treated in children.

A definition of terms is in order before further discussion of this issue. Gender and sexuality are researched, theorized, taught, and used in practice by several different professions and subspecialties within professions, leading to variances in nomenclature. Ehrensaft uses "gender identity" to define knowing the self to be male or female (often referred to as "core gender identity" or "natal sex"), and "gender expression" to mean all the external and internal ways people think about and express their gender identity (often referred to as "gender role identity"). In my discussion, I will use "core gender identity" to mean the biological determination of being a boy or a girl, and "gender role identity" to define the ways children use aspects of male and female gender role and expression in their conscious and unconscious sense of themselves.

Ehrensaft's paper gives us a particular view into the present-day mental health and pediatric discussion and treatment of fluid gender role identity and gender role nonconformance in children. She asks us to think about what is in the best interests of these children regarding the development of their minds, their senses of self, and their bodies when they have a fluid gender role identity or when they insist they are a girl in a boy's body or vice versa.

---

2. Mark Twain, "Hellfire Hotchkiss," 1897, unpublished and unfinished novel until incorporated into *Mark Twain's Satires & Burlesques* (Berkeley, CA: University of California Press, 1966).

While she conceptualizes gender as fluid, her actual practice with children discussed in her paper indicates a conflict between dichotomous and fluid gender identity in children, adolescents, and adults. While she sees the construction of gender expression as a weaving together of the forces of nature and nurture, she also writes that "gender identity [knowing your natal sex] is far more resistant to environmental intervention or shaping." How, then, does one think about the children who from a very early age insistently believe that they are not the gender written on their birth certificate? Ehrensaft labels these children as transgender and describes them as gender dysphoric. While Ehrensaft's theory of True Gender Self Therapy includes listening to the child's gendered sense of self and allows for a more fluid and changing expression of gender, she becomes much more dichotomous when working with children who have gender dysphoria and express a persistent desire to become the opposite sex they feel themselves to be.

Ehrensaft and the endocrinologists working with gender dysphoric children suggest using puberty blockers in middle childhood to give these children a chance to "try on" being seen and existing as the opposite of their core gender identity. Puberty blockers stop an eight- or nine-year-old girl or a ten-to-eleven-year-old boy from producing their body's hormones that would bring into being secondary sex characteristics, as well as the cognitive, biological, and psychological changes that would accompany those pubertal changes. Thus, her paper requires us to think about the psychological and biological effects of puberty blockers and the medical decisions being made by the parents and endocrinologists of the children and adolescents who believe they are not of the natal identity they were born with. Given the wide degree of time from childhood through adolescence to experiment and try on different gender expressions, I think it does a growing child and adolescent more significant harm than good to foreclose this fluid and unfolding process while development is still moving in fast-forward.

To discuss the potential serious psychological impact of this type of focused psychotherapy and the use of puberty blockers on young children, I will first outline how child development is understood by researchers in child development and what we know about children's conscious and unconscious ideas about gender from some of this research. I will then discuss the feminist literature that has been at the forefront of the theoretical discussion of gender and sexuality. Finally, I will use the theoretical, empirical, and clinical literature to discuss Dr. Ehrensaft's model of psychotherapy and what I see as the problem in giving puberty blockers to children with gender dysphoria.

The Developmental Theory of Dynamic Systems

Dynamic systems theory proposes that individual systems—cognition, actions, self states, to name just a few—are influenced by the interplay of biology and environment, producing a complex interaction of systems that are fluid, variable, function driven, flexible, and nonlinear. As new stimuli from either biology or environment are encountered, structures break down and novel, functional, alternative changes in structural systems develop to respond to the incoming stimuli. Changes in one structural system, let's say cognition, can effect changes in other systems, such as self states, causing a cascade of changes within and between systems. In terms of psychological growth, each novel state is progressive, discrete, idiosyncratic, and unpredictable.

This dynamic systems approach to development (Thelen and Smith, 1994; Sander, 2002; Mayes, 2001; Galatzer-Levy, 1995; Tyson, 2002) informs our understanding of human development as well as individual differences in development. Spencer and Perone (2008) point out that the challenge of understanding how a dynamic system change requires looking at multiple time scales to see how attractor states emerge in real time and how they do or do not become more stable to particular situational input throughout development.

Thelen and Smith (1994) were the first researchers to show how infant and toddler cognitive and action development demonstrated dynamic systems theory. Over the past twenty years this theory has been shown in research in motor development (Corbetta and Thelen, 1996), cognitive development (Spencer et al., 2007), socioemotional development (Lewis, Lamey, and Douglas, 1999), and most recently in gender development in normal children between the ages of six and eleven (Knight, 2011). These studies show that development is nonlinear and discontinuous. There are periods of significant disorganization in which structural systems break down and reorganize in transformational ways. New information from the body and the environment is assimilated and accommodated by increasingly complex systems in the mind and the body. Stable configurations of cognitive, biological and emotional systems suddenly become destabilized for no outward apparent reason and shift into periods of fragmentation. As Galatzer-Levy (2004) describes, it is a system constantly on the edge of chaos.

This level of disorganization and reorganization, continuously repeated in biorhythmic systems of increasing complexity, has been found in other living organisms "from the dino-flagellate to the human" (Sander, 2002). Therefore, I think it is safe to say that while the greatest maturational pull forward is from infancy through early adulthood, change and transformation in structures occurs throughout the life span, from the cradle to the grave.

GENDER FLUIDITY IN MIDDLE CHILDHOOD

The middle years of childhood begin with a period of fragmentation—a breakdown in self cohesion—that is followed by a fluid process of change and reorganization that influences self and ego structures, gender role identifications, sexual and aggressive feelings and fantasies, and one's sense of oneself in the world beyond the sphere of the family (Knight, 2011). These periods of disorganization and reorganization suggest a nonlinear development and fluidity in structures that constantly pull development forward in an ever-changing manner.

This disequilibrium of self structures gives the child the opportunity to try on different possibilities of gender role identity, what Ehrensaft calls "gender expression." As structures remain fluid and discontinuous, so a child's internal sense of his or her gender identifications also becomes fluid. Ames et al. (1974), in their study of hundreds of normal children's Rorschach responses, also found gender confusion and either-or gender responses in her middle childhood subjects. My study found that boys and girls make different uses of and have different meanings attached to gender role identity at different ages. Some manifest trends did emerge.

Boys experienced their masculine identity as very aggressive and feared their aggression would get out of control or explode. They used feminine gender identifications to help them manage their aggressive impulses. This may be the boys' identification with their perception of their mothers' relational role and strategies for dealing with aggression. However, they sometimes experienced their femininity as scary and distressing and feared it would lead to them getting hurt. The girls at age eight felt separated and more on their own and developed strong male identifications, sometimes telling Thematic Apperception Test (TAT) stories as though they were a boy. At this age they perceived their fathers as more capable and competent in the outside world, even though all of the girls' mothers worked outside the home. This male identification may be the girls' perception of their fathers as the more competent parent as they continue to develop a more mature sense of personal will, intention, and agency. Following this strong male identification at age eight and nine, the ten- and eleven-year-old girls continued to have fluid gender identifications. This study also found that despite the fact that both parents worked outside the home, parental gender roles and ways of relating to their children remained as traditional as they were in the 1950s and before.

Contemporary gender theorists (Elise, 2000; Benjamin, 1995) have posited that children see fathers as possessing power, agency, activity, and the ability to move into the outside world, while mothers are perceived as lacking those qualities. As the school-aged child moves out in the world of their peers, they continue to identify their mother as tied to the home and thus devalue her strength and power, while fathers are seen as representing the outside world. The girls' test responses in the Knight study (2005, 2011) expressed their conflict of wanting to move into arenas outside the home in their developmental push forward, and the pressure they felt, internally and externally, to remain inside the home in a mothering capacity. Typical of this was one girl's TAT story about her wish to go out and play sports and her concern about disappointing her mother, whom she perceived as wanting her to play with dolls. In the end, she decided to do both.

The gender role fluidity found in these children suggests that this is a *normal process*. As self structures remain fluid in development, so gender identification also remains fluid.

GENDER THEORY

Many writers have proposed that the ability to continually elaborate opposite sex feelings and behavior continues past the oedipal period, through the child's ongoing capacity for flexible cross-gender identifications (Bassin, 1996; Benjamin, 1995; Aron, 1995; Dimen, 1991; Goldner, 1991; and Harris, 1991). Benjamin (1991) suggests that gender role identity is not tied to anatomical difference. She believes that children use male and female identifications to create aspects of their sense of self. In Elise's paper "Gender as Soft Assembly" (2000), she proposes that one's thoughts and feelings about gender are fluid and open to continual changes from internal development in biology and psychology and from external factors that impact one's gender performance and identity. Chodorow (1992) proposes that gender role differentiation is a relational process that starts at birth and continues throughout the life cycle, and that choosing a binary gender representation is a compromise formation. Kirkpatrick (2003) sees gender as resulting from the kaleidoscopic overlapping of many elements that can reinforce, neutralize, or modify gender identifications throughout development. The gender fluidity that I found in the normal children I studied supports these theoretical positions. Very few people in our field today would question the idea that all of us have within us male and female gender identifications with our parents and siblings. I would also suggest that the homosexual play that is typical of children in middle childhood involves the children's ability to take both gender sides in their fantasy play with each other and sets the stage for adolescent and adult sensual and cross-gender empathy.

INFLUENCES ON GENDER ROLE IDENTIFICATION AND PERFORMANCE

Cross-gender identifications with caring figures are one influence on gender role identity and fluidity; the social environment of the growing child is another. Infant and toddler research has shown that boys and girls are treated differently by their parents starting at birth. Mothers encourage boys toward more independent behavior, and girls are encouraged to remain close. Boys are encouraged to control social interchanges more than are girls, who are encouraged to find pleasure in closeness and the interactive regulation of relationships (Olesker, 1984; Biringen, Robinson, and Emde, 1994).

Biological influences also impact gender behavior. Studies looking at neonatal exposure to different levels of androgens have been shown to affect gender play behavior in both boys and girls (Auyeung et al., 2009; Hines et al., 2002; Homburg, 2009). Adrenarche, which occurs between six and eight years of age, is a period in endocrine development when androgens are produced in the body, which leads to the beginning of puberty, and their levels can also affect gender role behavior in children (Finkelstein, VonEye, and Preece, 1994).

DISCUSSION

I have presented developmental theory, my research, aspects of the gender literature, and biological research in this detail because it informs my response to Ehrensaft's paper. Ehrensaft reports a case of a toddler girl in great distress who pulled the barrettes out of her hair and happily transitioned to male in adulthood. This vignette leaves open many questions. What possible androgen exposure in her neonatal period and what early infancy experiences with her family led her to not want to dress like a girl? What was the marital relationship like? What were the parents' conscious and unconscious thoughts and feelings about femininity? What were the siblings relationships like, and how did the parents treat siblings of different genders? There is no information reporting what type of treatment this child and parents received.

While Ehrensaft (2011) discusses her fine therapeutic work helping parents adjust to their child's gender fluidity or normal homosexuality in another paper, what is concerning about the type of treatment she calls True Gender Self Therapy that she is promoting for children who present with extreme gender dysphoria is the degree to which such treatment with these children does not delve into the unconscious thoughts and feelings these children have about their core gender identity and gender role expression. As a child psychoanalyst, I think that these gender dysphoric children need intensive, four-times-a-week psychoanalysis at a very early age and an equally intensive psychotherapy for their parents. Fraiberg, Adelson, and Shapiro's (1975) therapeutic model of working with the child and parents very frequently at a very early age demonstrates how necessary it is to work with the unconscious feelings and defensive behaviors in parents of babies and young children so as not to negatively impact the child's psychological growth and sense of self. Working with a young child in a four-times-a-week child analysis over many years of development allows a child and therapist to understand the many factors that influence unconscious thoughts and feelings, as well as to track changes in those fantasies or conflicts as they develop, co-constructing a self-and-other narrative that provides a child with structure for further development. This process entails mourning body parts wanted or aspects of childhood left behind, which is a normal developmental process of mourning.

Equally troubling is the literal meaning Ehrensaft sometimes proposes as opposed to the many figurative meanings that gender acquires for each gender dysphoric child at each stage of development. In her once-a-week treatment of Jacqueline, the treatment is presented in a very binary either-or way, with no attempt to find out what Jacqueline's life would have been like if she had been allowed to express her gender fluidity and expression on the canvas of the body she was born with. If Ehrensaft believes, as research has shown it to be, that "gender is a lifelong unfolding rather than set at a moment in time in childhood" (Ehrensaft, 2015), then the aim of treatment should be helping a child accept whatever gender they feel like expressing in the body that they have. Typical of a less concrete model of fluid gender expression is the example of the Prius child who looked like both a boy and a girl, so creatively expressing the "and" aspect of gender fluidity rather than the "either-or." The Prius child aptly demonstrates Ehrensaft's idea of a gender spectrum that allows a child to express his or her fluid gender role identity appropriate to the child's level of emotional and cognitive development, and Ehrensaft's work with the parents to allow this expression of gender fluidity.

While Ehrensaft proposes that True Gender Self Therapy involves making the unconscious conscious, it appears to me that she is only interested in uncovering whatever gender seems hidden by repression and denial rather than helping the child to examine his or her feelings and the meaning the child makes of gender, sexuality, aggression, sense of self, self with other, and how all of these intermingle and interweave into narrative structures. As research and developmental theory has shown (A. Freud, 1963; Blos, 1967; Knight, 2011) conscious and unconscious gender role identifications and expressions remain fluid through adolescence and may not show consistency over the wide developmental period from infancy through adolescence. Recent worldwide research has shown that people in their twenties are still in a period of adolescence (Arnett and Eisenberg, 2007), and many of them are still experimenting with their gender role expressions and sexual object choice.

Children before middle adolescence have concreteness to their thinking (Piaget, 1967), which does not seem to be taken into account by gender professionals. Like the children they are treating, endocrinologists and mental health professionals who recommend puberty blockers to children before the onset of puberty assume concrete solutions to what are very deeply embedded and constantly changing concrete senses of self and gender and gender role identifications. To give these young children medicines that will stop their biological growth for many years deprives them of the chance to experience their bodies growing in any age-appropriate way. If anything, keeping them small and young-looking makes them abnormal for their age and prevents them from experiencing all the hormonal effects on their minds and their bodies along with their peers, setting them further apart from the experiences of their peers. I would think puberty blockers might make them feel even more separate and could encourage a false self as they watch their peers grow and develop secondary sex characteristics while they can only pretend. This then becomes a very complicated and layered issue for these children, who might also feel jealous of the peers of their wished-for natal sex, desperate to be like them and change like them, and angry at their parents and doctors who won't give them the hormones that would allow them to develop like everyone else their age and wished for gender.

Research on children diagnosed with Gender Identity Disorder in childhood shows that most GID children ultimately choose same-sex partners in adolescence and young adulthood (Drummond et al., 2008). The outcome research on children who are given puberty blockers is scarce but what *is* known is that many of the children who are given puberty blockers return to a comfort level with their core gender identity in early adolescence (Byne et al., 2012; Wallien and Cohen-Kettenis, 2008), notwithstanding Ehrensaft's report to the contrary. In addition, the peer-reviewed literature (Byne et al., 2012) has shown that it is not possible to *reliably determine* which children will become desisters or per-sisters (Cohen-Kettenis and Pfäfflin, 2010; Wallien and Cohen-Kettenis, 2008; Zucker, 2008). There are no studies that I could find that deeply look at the experiences and underlying feelings the desister children have during the time their development is stopped and *why* they then choose to stop the blockers. In addition, these children are being given body-altering drugs for which no studies of long-term biological effects of these drugs have been completed (Byne et al., 2012).

The finding that many of the gender dysphoric children who are un-happy about their core gender identity choose same-sex partners later in life (Byne et al., 2012) is thought-provoking. Because there are no research studies but only clinical reports about the normal childhood development of gay men and lesbian women, is it not possible that many or most of these children are really expressing their sexual attraction for same-sex children and preferring the play activities of the opposite gender? Louisa May Alcott based her character of Jo in *Little Women* on herself. In an interview she gave to Louise Chandler Moulton (Whiting, 1909), Alcott said, "I am more than half-persuaded that I am a man's soul put by some freak of nature into a woman's body . . . because I have fallen in love with so many pretty girls and never once the least bit with any man." Given (1) the concreteness of children's thinking, (2) the lack of a language for young children to express their homo-sexual desires, and (3) a homophobic society that is unwilling to think about normal homosexual development in young children, homosexual children could arrive at a mental health professional's office with gen-der dysphoria, not understanding that they could *be* their core gender identity *and* have the fantasies, desires, and gender role performance that society doesn't usually accept for their natal sex. These children need a place to express these feelings without being further confused by the suggestion of puberty blockers, which make them have to con-cretely consider their core gender identity during middle childhood, when there is constant disorganization and reorganization going on in their minds and bodies and fluidity in their sense of self.

From infancy through adolescence, development races along on a complex and fast track. Ehrensaft (2011) cautions about moving too quickly in the transgender process, noting an example of a child who quickly changed from being a boy to a girl and subsequently had to be hospitalized and placed in residential psychiatric treatment. This raises the issue of the concretization of gender possibly being used to mask an underlying psychotic process that may take years to uncover, or that may not occur until mid to late adolescence. Given the normal periods of fragmentation and ego disorganization that occur in middle childhood and the unpredictability of nonlinear development, how can a mental health professional definitively determine that there is not an underlying psychotic process being focused through gender (Wallien, Swaab, and Cohen-Kettenis, 2007)?

In middle childhood boys and girls can look alike in their unisex clothes worn by children today. Kids can wear their hair short or long no matter what gender they are. Our culture has reached a point in time where boys can wear a ponytail to school and girls can cut their hair short and wear jeans. As normal children reach the age of around ten years, they begin to feel the changes to their body or know the changes are about to come. Another interesting finding from my research was that neither the boys nor the girls wanted to grow up. Partly this was their wish to remain children and not have to mourn the ending of this phase of their lives, and partly this was their desire to not have their bodies change as they were heading into puberty. The girls expressed unhappiness about their breast development, and the boys did not look forward to puberty. One boy's response sums up the feelings:

RK: Has your body been changing?
Boy: I don't think so.
RK: I mean, you haven't started developing and going into puberty?
Boy: Not yet, thank God.
RK: "Why thank God?"
Boy: I don't want to change yet.
RK: Why not?
Boy: I don't know. I want to be young.

In summary, there are a multitude of conscious and unconscious feelings that effect and are affected by gender and are also expressed through gender that change from year to year due to biology, psychology, and the environment. In my opinion, to interfere with the normal psychological, biological, and sociological development of a child when one cannot be clear about the effects or the short- or long-term outcome of such a massive biological interference (Byne et al., 2012), does significant harm to the child. Children have neither the legal right nor the mature judgment to make such life-changing decisions and must rely on their parents' judgments for them. My concern is that children are dependent on and influenced by the adults around them and often feel the need to be or do what those adults consciously or unconsciously want in order to retain their love and attention. Oftentimes, such adult agendas are not in the best interests of the child.

REFERENCES

ALCOTT, L. M. (1868–1869). *Little Women*. Bantam Classic ed. New York: Bantam Dell, 2007.
AMES, L., METRAUX, R., RODELL, L., WALKER, R. (1974). *Child Rorschach Responses*. New York: Bruner Mazel.
ARNETT, J., AND EISENBERG, N. (2007). Introduction to the special section: Emerging adulthood around the world. *Child Development Perspectives* 1:66–67.
ARON, L. (1995). The internalized primal scene. *Psychoanalytic Dialogues* 5:195–237.
AUYEUNG, B., BARON-COHEN, S., ASHWIN, E., KNICKMEYER, R., TAYLOR, K., HACKETT, G., HINES, M. (2009). Fetal testosterone predicts sexually differentiated childhood behavior in girls and boys. *Psychological Science* 20:144–148.
BALSAM, R. (2001). Integrating male and female elements in a woman's gender identity. *Journal of the American Psychoanalytic Association* 49:1335–1360.
BASSIN, D. (1996). Beyond the he and the she: Toward the reconciliation of masculinity and femininity in the post oedipal female mind. *Journal of the American Psychoanalytic Association* 44S:157–190.
BENJAMIN, J. (1995). Sameness and difference: Toward an "overinclusive" model of gender development. *Psychoanalytic Inquiry* 15:125–142.
_____. (1991). Father and daughter: Identification with difference—a contribution to gender heterodoxy. *Psychoanalytic Dialogues* 1:277–299.
BIRINGEN, Z., ROBINSON, J. L., AND EMDE, R. N. (1994). Mother's style of sensitivity during late infancy: The role of child's gender. *American Journal of Orthopsychiatry* 64:78–90.
BLOS, P. (1967). The second individuation process of adolescence. *Psychoanalytic Study of the Child* 22:162–186.
BYNE, W., BRADLEY, S., COLEMAN, E., EYLER, A., GREEN, R., MENVIELLE, E., MEYER-BAHLBURG, H., PLEAK, R., AND TOMPKINS, D. (2012). Report of the APA task force on treatment of gender identity disorder. *American Journal of Psychiatry* 169:1–35, data supp.
CHODOROW, N. J. (1992). Heterosexuality as a compromise formation: Reflections on the psychoanalytic theory of sexual development. *Psychoanalysis and Contemporary Thought* 15:267–304.
CORBETTA, D., AND THELEN, E. (1996). The developmental origins of two-handed coordination: A dynamic perspective. *Journal of Experimental Psychology: Human Perception and Performance* 22:502–522.
COHEN-KETTENIS, P., AND PFÄFFLIN, F. (2010). The DSM diagnostic criteria for gender identity disorder in adolescents and adults. *Archives of Sexual Behavior* 39:499–513.

CROMPTON, L. (2006). *Homosexuality and Civilization*. Cambridge, MA, and London: Belknap Press / Harvard University Press.

DE VRIES, A., STEENSMA, T. D., AND COHEN-KETTENIS, P. (2011). Psychiatric comorbidity in gender dysphoric adolescents. *Journal of Child Psychological Psychiatry* 52:1195–1202.

DIMEN, M. (1991). Deconstructing difference: Gender, splitting, and transitional space. *Psychoanalytic Dialogues* 1:335–352.

DRUMMOND, K., BRADLEY, S., PETERSON-BADALI, M., ZUCKER, K. (2008). A follow-up study of girls with gender identity disorder. *Developmental Psychology* 44:34–45.

ELISE, D. (2000). Generating gender: Response to Harris. *Studies in Gender and Sexuality* 1:157–165.

——. (2000). Woman and desire: Why women may not want to want. *Studies in Gender and Sexuality* 1:125–145.

——. (2000). Gender as a Soft Assembly: Tomboys' stories. *Studies in Gender and Sexuality* 1:223–250.

EHRENSAFT, D. (2011). Boys will be girls, girls will be boys: Children affect parents as parents affect children in gender nonconformity. *Psychoanalytic Psychology* 28:528–548.

——. (2015). Listening and learning from gender-nonconforming children. *Psychoanalytic Study of the Child* 68 (this volume).

FINKELSTEIN, J., VONEYE, A., PREECE, M. (1994). The relationship between aggressive behavior and puberty in normal adolescents: A longitudinal study. *Journal of Adolescent Health* 15:319–326.

FRAIBERG, S., ADELSON, E., SHAPIRO, V. (1975). Ghosts in the nursery. *Journal of the American Academy of Child Psychiatry* 14:387–421.

FREUD, A. (1963). The concept of developmental lines. *Psychoanalytic Study of the Child* 18:245–265.

GALATZER-LEVY, R. (1995). Psychoanalysis and dynamic systems theory: Prediction and self similarity. *Journal of the American Psychoanalytic Association* 43:1085–1113.

——. (2004). Chaotic possibilities: Toward a new model of development. *International Journal of Psychoanalysis* 85:419–442.

GOLDNER, V. (1991). Toward a critical relational theory of gender. *Psychoanalytic Dialogues* 1:249–272.

HARRIS, A. (1991). Gender as contradiction. *Psychoanalytic Dialogues* 1:197–224.

HINES, M. (2004). *Brain Gender*. Oxford: Oxford University Press.

HINES, M., GOLOMBOK, S., RUST, J., JOHNSTON, K., GOLDING, J. (2002). Testosterone during pregnancy and gender role behavior of preschool children: A longitudinal, population study. *Child Development* 73:1678–1687.

HOMBURG, R. (2009). Androgen circle of polycystic ovary syndrome. *Human Reproduction* 24:528–548.

KIRKPATRICK, M. (2003). The nature and nurture of gender. *Psychoanalytic Inquiry* 23:558–571.

KNIGHT, R. (2005). The process of attachment and autonomy in latency: A longitudinal study of ten children. *Psychoanalytic Study of the Child* 60:178–212.

_____. (2011). Fragmentation, Fluidity, and Transformation: Nonlinear Development in Middle Childhood. *Psychoanalytic Study of the Child* 65:19–47.

LEE, H. (1960). *To Kill a Mockingbird*. Philadelphia: J. B. Lippincott.

LEWIS, M., LAMEY, A., DOUGLAS, L. (1999). A new dynamic systems method for the analysis of early socioemotional development. *Developmental Science* 2:457–475.

LINDGREN, A. (1945). *Pippi Longstocking*. Sweden: Rabén and Sjögren.

_____. (1971). *Kaarlsson-on the-Roof*. New York: Viking.

_____. (1977). *Kaarlsson Flies Again*. London: Methuen Young Books.

MAYES, L. (1999). Clocks, engines, quarks—love, dreams, genes: What makes development happen? *Psychoanalytic Study of the Child* 54:169–192.

_____. (2001). The twin poles of order and chaos. *Psychoanalytic Study of the Child* 56:137–170.

MCCULLER, C. (1946). *Member of the Wedding*. New York: Houghton Mifflin.

OLESKER, W. (1984). Sex differences in 2- and 3-year-olds: Mother-child relations, peer relations, and peer play. *Psychoanalytic Psychology* 1:269–288.

PIAGET, J. (1967). *Six Psychological Studies*. New York: Random House.

ROBINSON, J. L., AND BIRINGEN, Z. (1995). Gender and emerging autonomy in development. *Psychoanalytic Inquiry* 15:60–74.

SANDER, L. (2002). Thinking differently: Principles of process in living systems and the specificity of being known. *Psychoanalytic Dialogues* 12:11–42.

SHAKESPEARE, W. (1623). *Twelfe Night, Or What You Will*. London: First Folio.

_____. (1600). *Much Adoe about Nothing*. London: Quarto.

SPENCER, J., AND PERONE, S. (2008). *Child Development* 79:1639–1647.

SPENCER, J., SIMMERING, V., SCHUTTE, A., SCHONER, G. (2007). What Does Theoretical Neuroscience Have to Offer the Study of Behavioral Development? Insights from a Dynamic Field Theory of Spatial Cognition. In J. M. Plumert and J. P. Spencer, eds., *The Emerging Spatial Mind*, pp. 320–361. New York: Oxford University Press.

SWEETNAM, A. (1996). The changing contexts of gender. *Psychoanalytic Dialogues* 6:437–460.

THELEN, E., SMITH, L. B. (1994). *A Dynamic Systems Approach to the Development of Cognition and Action*. Cambridge, MA: MIT Press.

TWAIN, M. (1897). "Hellfire Hotchkiss," unpublished and unfinished novel incorporated into *Mark Twain's Satires & Burlesques*. Berkeley, CA: University of California Press, 1966.

TYSON, P. (2002). The challenges of psychoanalytic developmental theory. *Journal of the American Psychoanalytic Association* 50:19–52.

WALLIEN, M., AND COHEN-KETTENIS, P. (2008). Psychosexual outcome of gender-dysphoric children. *Journal of the American Academy of Child and Adolescent Psychiatry* 47:1413–1423.

WALLIEN, M. S. C., SWAAB, H., AND COHEN-KETTENIS, P. T. (2007). Psychiatric comorbidity among children with gender identity disorder. *Journal of the American Academy of Child and Adolescent Psychiatry* 46:1307–1314.

WHITING, L. (1909). *Louise Chandler Moulton*. Boston: Harvard University Press.

ZUCKER K. (2008). On the "natural history" of gender identity disorder in children. *Journal of the American Academy of Child and Adolescent Psychiatry* 47:1361–1363.

Discussion of Diane Ehrensaft's "Listening and Learning from Gender-Nonconforming Children"

PAUL M. BRINICH, Ph.D.

My discussion of Diane Ehrensaft's paper begins with some comments that extend her ideas. I suggest that the interaction of nature and nurture in the creation of gender begins before birth and perhaps even before conception. I argue that there are practical limits to the degree to which we can expect sociocultural forces to yield to Ehrensaft's call for a broadened narrative of gender. I then go on to pose some questions: Should children have complete autonomy regarding their bodily development, as Ehrensaft seems to suggest? Does such autonomy extend to areas beyond gender, such as issues of racial identity? And I close with some criticisms, chiefly that gender identity should not be conceptualized as something that is clearly or immutably defined in childhood, but as a component of one's self that constantly interacts with one's biology, psychology, and sociocultural milieu from conception until death. Child and adult psychoanalysts are only beginning to accumulate the data necessary to respond to Ehrensaft's challenging hypotheses.

I ACCEPTED THE INVITATION TO COMMENT ON DR. EHRENSAFT'S PAPER because it introduces us to a topic that rarely has been discussed in the

Dr. Brinich is Clinical Professor (Emeritus), Departments of Psychology and Psychiatry, University of North Carolina at Chapel Hill; Faculty Member and Supervisor, Psychoanalytic Education Center of the Carolinas; and Past President, Association for Child Psychoanalysis.

The Psychoanalytic Study of the Child 68, ed. Claudia Lament, Robert A. King, Samuel Abrams, Paul M. Brinich, and Rona Knight (Yale University Press, copyright © 2015 by Claudia Lament, Robert A. King, Samuel Abrams, Paul M. Brinich, and Rona Knight).

psychoanalytic literature. Children who feel that they "are" a gender
other than that suggested by their external genitalia pose a special challenge to child psychoanalysts—who live, professionally speaking, at the
intersection of body, mind, and culture—as we try to understand how
it is that these children have come to feel that way.

Ehrensaft urges us to approach the topic with open minds. That is
not an easy task; we all are creatures of our own histories and cultures,
and every society has a vested interest in promoting its survival via procreation, an act that generally[1] requires that people be separated into
"male" and "female." As a result, every society has evolved methods
of identifying and segregating the sexes in ways that promote and/or
control fertility.

From time immemorial there have always been some people who do
not fit comfortably into the categories supplied by the society within
which they live. In the case of sex and gender, there are some individuals whose biology does not conform to what is expected (true and
pseudo-hermaphrodites, Turner syndrome, and so on); and there are
many individuals who chafe beneath the constraints of the gender-
linked behavioral patterns prescribed by the society into which they
have been born.

It would be a mistake to view gender-linked behavioral patterns as
immutable or universal; they are neither. One need only consider the
changes in attitudes toward same-sexed marriage that have taken place
over the past decade to see that behaviors that once seemed beyond the
pale are now widely accepted across many countries and cultures. Furthermore, as Ehrensaft points out, some contemporary societies provide
much more room for people whose behavior falls outside the norms for
male and female (for example, the *hijras* of Hindu South Asia) than is
usually found in American or Western European societies.

My response to Ehrensaft's paper falls into three sections. I begin
with a number of comments that extend ideas that she addresses. I then
pose some questions designed to provoke further thought. And I close
with some criticisms that Ehrensaft and her colleagues might wish to
consider as they continue their work.

My comments, questions, and criticisms all are founded in my own
biopsychosocial history. I am no more able to jump over my own shadow
than the next person. This is where Ehrensaft's paper becomes espe-

1. I insert "generally" here because Assisted Reproductive Technology (ART) has challenged the traditional ways of achieving pregnancy, broadening them in ways that only
could be dreamed of a few decades ago. While up to now no one has managed to create
a viable human zygote without using male and female germ cells, even this seemingly im-
passable barrier may be breached in the future.

cially valuable: It shines some light on topics that have been at the center of psychoanalysis since its beginning, but does so from angles that differ significantly from those that were in vogue when I was figuring out how to be a boy, a man, or a child psychoanalyst.

COMMENTS AND EXTENSIONS

From Sigmund Freud's point of view, Dr. Ehrensaft's phrase "gender-nonconforming children" might be seen as almost an oxymoron. Freud's (1905) *Three Essays on the Theory of Sexuality* outline some of the challenges faced by children as they grapple with the different strands of libidinal sexuality that Freud describes. Freud's well-known characterization of children as "polymorphously perverse" (Freud, 1916, p. 209) is itself a reflection on the fact that children have not yet woven the many and various strands of sexuality into something approaching what is normative in adulthood. Young children are especially imaginative and unconstrained in their ideas about sex and gender. Although to a contemporary ear, Freud's use of the term "perverse" has moral overtones, Freud himself used the term in a more neutral way. To him childhood sexuality was "perverse" only in the sense that it does not conform to the social norms that attempt to define and contain sexuality—a task that strains every culture known to man. Freud's emphasis on the innate bisexuality that is part of the human condition, along with his refusal to view homosexuality as pathology (Freud, 1935), suggests that he would be unsurprised by the variations in gendered (or ungendered) behavior that Ehrensaft has observed in the children with whom she works.

Ehrensaft suggests, "It is time to peruse our clinical theories and practices with the aim of fortifying the mental health of children of all genders, ethically and with no harm done" (Ehrensaft, 2015, p. 29). While I agree with Ehrensaft's call for an increased tolerance of differences in gendered behavior, and while I hear in it an echo of Anna Freud's "wide range of 'variations of normality'" (1962, p. 158), I suspect that social realities may force us to accept something less. Just as Goldstein, Freud, and Solnit pointed out how the "best interests of the child" often cannot be realized and must be replaced by the least detrimental alternative (1973, pp. 53–64), it seems likely that we will have to help the children that Ehrensaft sees find their own least detrimental alternatives; there is no available path that leaves "no harm done."

While Ehrensaft writes, "Beyond birth, gender development becomes an interplay of nature and nurture" (Ehrensaft 2015, p. 29). I would push the boundaries of that interaction back farther in time. The development of a gendered identity represents a coming together of nature and nurture that goes back at least as far as the moment of conception. Intrauterine effects on gendered behavior have been demonstrated, and I suspect that with further research it will become clear that both germ cells—the sperm and the egg—are not immune from environmental effects that antedate conception but then go on to be expressed in the zygote that becomes an intrauterine fetus, in the extrauterine infant, and in the growing child.

The narrative of gender in our culture varies in its strength and specificity across time, place, occupation, and other variables. It is worth remembering that both Iris Murdoch and Marilyn Monroe were female in sex and gender; and both William Buckley and Clint Eastwood were male in sex and gender. These contrasting dyads illustrate the huge range in the expression of gendered behavior that was possible in the twentieth century, and it seems certain that that range will expand in the twenty-first.

It's worth noting and remembering that most parents who have had two or more children of the same biological sex can attest to the fact that there is quite a range in how one "is" a boy or a girl. I know of a girl who, as a six-year-old, proclaimed that she was going to be a cowgirl, a ballerina, a tightrope walker, and a nun. Masculine, feminine, bisexual, and asexual all in one go! One might say that this youngster outdid Ehrensaft's "gender Prius. A boy in the front. A girl in the back."

Two psychoanalytic colleagues have challenged my own attitudes, thinking, and feeling about these matters. One was a husband, a father to two children, and a remarkably creative researcher. Some years after his wife died he began a relationship with a man, and they maintained that relationship for nearly two decades until my colleague died. The other psychoanalytic colleague was, like the first, a prolific and generative academic; for many years she was married to a man, but after that marriage ended in divorce, she partnered with a woman whom she then married.

I had known the first, male, colleague while he was still married to his wife and was aware of some of the turmoil created by her illness and death. I was astonished when I later heard of his new relationship with a male partner. I was less astonished when I learned of the second, female, colleague's relationship with a woman, in part perhaps because I had not known the second colleague while she was living with her husband. In both instances, however, I found myself grappling with a question: How is it that a person with an apparently stable gender identity and who has been in a long-standing heterosexual relationship finds him- or herself in a new, homosexual relationship? Is object choice independent of gender identity? Or should we conceptualize gender identity—what Ehrensaft prefers to call the "gender web"—in four dimensions, rather than the three (biopsychosocial) that she suggests? As a developmentalist, I would argue that gender identity (and gendered behavior) should be seen as an intersection of biological, psychological, and sociocultural factors that interact with each other across a fourth dimension of time. My identity, my gender identity, and my (gendered) behavior all exist on a developmental continuum, which is in constant flux. My two colleagues demonstrated, relatively late in their lives, that they were gender nonconforming in some aspects of their behavior. Did this represent some radical rearrangement of their personal biopsychosocial selves? Or was it a less radical but still significant evolution? As a psychoanalyst, I would say that we cannot answer these questions without truly psychoanalytic data. But if I had to put my money on one proposition or the other, I would opt for my evolutionary hypothesis rather than that of a sudden, radical rearrangement.

This leads to Ehrensaft's description of what she calls True Gender Self Therapy (TGST) and its goal of building "gender resilience" in children and their families. While the concept of "gender resilience" makes sense in the context of the paper Ehrensaft has written, it seems clear that the resilience about which she speaks must extend far beyond gender, especially if we agree that gender and its behavioral manifestations are constantly evolving (in both the individual and the social surround). The concept of "True Gender Self" (which I will take up again in the section devoted to criticisms) begs the question: How do we decide what is a "true" gender self? Can what is "true" at age three or thirteen or twenty-three become "false" at thirty-three or forty-three or fifty-three? Perhaps we should replace that "true" gender self with a more modest "currently adaptive" gender self. This would, at the very least, emphasize that these matters are not fixed but continue to evolve as long as we are alive.

QUESTIONS

Ehrensaft writes, "In childhood it is up to the child, not the parent, to spin the gender web." Does that "hands-off" attitude extend to other crucial areas of biopsychosocial development such as toilet training? I very much doubt it. And yet I cannot see a huge gap between the "self" that must grapple with toileting and that which must grapple with questions of gender identity and gendered behavior. Is the true self a poopy self or a clean self? My own answer to that question would be "neither" (or both)—but regardless, children and their families have to come up with something that is currently adaptive; at one age that might involve diapers, at another normal underwear, and then much later diapers once again.

What would Ehrensaft do with a black child, adopted into a white family, who insists that he or she is white? Who refuses to associate with people who share a similar pigmentation? Is the child's true self white, black, or something in between? My guess is that Ehrensaft might argue in favor of some kind of "racial creativity" that evades the usual boundaries of race as defined by the culture within which the child is growing up. Those boundaries would be quite different in Oakland, California; Oslo, Norway; and Johannesburg, South Africa. In each place the child would have to find a series of sequentially adaptive solutions to what it means to be a person with dark pigment in that particular social milieu.

Is Ehrensaft's True Gender Self different in kind from the selves that engage with the challenges of toileting or the socially derived boundaries of race?

CRITICISMS

Writing about her patient Jacqueline/Thomas, Ehrensaft asserts that "the unconscious need to bring a hidden core male self to the surface and differentiate it from the female outer self, which now felt like a 'not me,' overrode any desire or need for continuity." It seems to me that this statement reflects the very kind of binary (either-or) thinking that Ehrensaft has repeatedly criticized in her paper. Likewise, Ehrensaft's suggestion that therapists and parents should mirror a child's "true" gender self without distortion is an ideal that can never be achieved— and at least partly because "true" gender identity is not fixed but is constantly evolving within a social field that also is evolving.

I dislike Ehrensaft's use of the adjective "traumatic" in the context of the use or nonuse of puberty blockers. Is puberty inherently traumatic? I might answer that question in the affirmative; it certainly does have a way of overwhelming previously achieved modes of defense and coping, leaving the pubertal child feeling exquisitely vulnerable from all sides. But I think Ehrensaft actually is using "trauma" in the sense of "stress": She wishes to spare Jacqueline/Thomas the additional stresses that will come if her/his body begins a visible developmental shift toward a normal pubertal female body. Does this qualify as a traumatic experience? Certainly it would be difficult, but unless Jacqueline/Thomas is left without any support, I doubt that such a development would be inherently traumatic in the strict sense of that word.

With Ehrensaft, I would wish that Jacqueline/Thomas and her mother could have the necessary time to consider the available options, without the ticking of the biological clock. But, for better or worse, her/his body did not agree. Nor does our culture: One of its highest priorities is facilitating the procreation that is required for the preservation of the species. Given these two facts—that sexed bodies usually will develop into sexually mature organisms capable of reproduction and that our culture depends upon procreation for its very survival—it seems to me that Ehrensaft's call for gender identity creativity is sailing against some very strong currents.

CLOSING REMARKS

Diane Ehrensaft has addressed a challenging, timely topic in a very thoughtful way. Our control of our own biology is reaching into areas previously thought to be beyond our influence. Meanwhile social mores are evolving in ways that could hardly have been imagined a decade or two ago. This confluence of changes faces psychoanalysts with a host of issues that in the past could have been and were ignored. In much the way that Assisted Reproductive Technology has challenged our ideas of what it means to be a parent (Shapiro, Shapiro, and Paret, 2001), the presence of what Ehrensaft calls "gender-nonconforming children" and the availability of an ever-growing range of medical interventions that can block or divert or modify our sexual capacities faces us with the question of what it means to be male or female . . . or something other than these two. The fact that a person can be, from a biological perspective, one sex while having a gender identity that differs from that biological sex stands as a challenge to the next generation of child and adult psychoanalysts. It seems we have much to learn, and I thank Diane Ehrensaft for beginning the conversation.

REFERENCES

EHRENSAFT, D. (2015) Listening and learning from gender-nonconforming children. *Psychoanalytic Study of the Child* 68 (this volume).

FREUD, ANNA (1962). Assessment of childhood disturbances. *Psychoanalytic Study of the Child* 17:149–158.

FREUD, SIGMUND (1905/1953). Three Essays on the Theory of Sexuality. In J. Strachey, ed., *The Standard Edition of the Complete Psychological Works of Sigmund Freud,* vol. 7, pp. 130–243. London: Hogarth Press.

FREUD, SIGMUND (1916/1961). Introductory Lectures on Psycho-Analysis. In J. Strachey, ed., *The Standard Edition of the Complete Psychological Works of Sigmund Freud*, vol. 15. London: Hogarth Press.

FREUD, SIGMUND (1935/1960). Anonymous (Letter to an American mother). In E. Freud, ed., *The Letters of Sigmund Freud*, pp. 423–424. London: Hogarth Press.

GOLDSTEIN, J., FREUD, A., AND SOLNIT, A. J. (1973). *Beyond the Best Interests of the Child*. New York: Free Press.

SHAPIRO, V. B., SHAPIRO, J. R., AND PARET, I. H. (2001). *Complex Adoption and Assisted Reproductive Technology*. New York: Guilford Press.

If We Listen

Discussion of Diane Ehrensaft's "Listening and Learning from Gender-Nonconforming Children"

LISSA WEINSTEIN, Ph.D., AND HANNAH WALLERSTEIN, M.A.

Given the absence of reliable predictor variables that differentiate between children whose gender dysphoria will desist versus those in whom it will persist into adolescence, child analysis, with its unique capacity to search beyond the manifest content of a patient's desire, potentially offers a venue from which to assess the developmental achievements that might impact a decision to support or question the utilization of puberty blockers to forestall the physical manifestations of gender. An examination of Ehrensaft's True Gender Self Therapy notes an inherent contradiction between her stated view of gender as "an aspect of self that can be altered over the course of a lifetime" and the notion of an unchanging gender self that only needs to be uncovered. The latter position veers toward an essentialist position that neglects the exploration of gender fantasies and defines gender in a manner that necessitates an environmental or medical response.

Lissa Weinstein is Professor, Doctoral Faculty in Clinical Psychology, at the Graduate School and University Center at the City University of New York. Dr. Weinstein has published numerous papers in psychoanalytic theory and film criticism. She received the Margot Marek Book Award from the International Dyslexia Association for her book *Reading David: A Mother and Son's Journey Through the Labyrinth of Dyslexia.*

Hannah Wallerstein is a doctoral student in Clinical Psychology at the City University of New York.

The Psychoanalytic Study of the Child 68, ed. Claudia Lament, Robert A. King, Samuel Abrams, Paul M. Brinich, and Rona Knight (Yale University Press, copyright © 2015 by Claudia Lament, Robert A. King, Samuel Abrams, Paul M. Brinich, and Rona Knight).

WE WOULD LIKE TO THANK DR. EHRENSAFT FOR THE OPPORTUNITY to discuss her thought-provoking paper that brings to the fore the controversial topic of gender dysphoria, one that has been dealt with only summarily in the analytic literature. By introducing the incendiary question of the use of puberty blockers as a treatment to potentially prevent the pain of developing a physical body that does not meet one's internalized image, Dr. Ehrensaft forces us to confront our biases. The paper raises two issues, each of which needs to be examined independently. First, what place does an analytically oriented treatment have in helping a child resolve their gender dysphoria (regardless of the final outcome), and, second, what role should puberty blockers play in the struggle to define one's gender identity, a struggle made potentially, but not necessarily, more problematic by the onset of puberty. At the center of these questions is the ways in which analytic listening must be differentiated from a respectful attention to the child's manifest statements.

Perhaps in no other arena is it as difficult to listen, in Bion's oft-quoted stance, "without memory or desire," than when concerns about gender are raised, even more so in the case of a child where issues of cognitive development, developmentally expected gender fluctuations, and questions of capability to give consent further complicate the field. Phobic and counterphobic responses to the threatening desire to change one's natal body abound. Just how near impossible neutrality remains is clear from the divergent approaches to the treatment of gender dysphoria. These vary in the degree to which they attempt to support (for example, Hill et al., 2010), wait and watch but not suppress (de Vries and Cohen-Kettenis, 2012), or actively discourage (for example, Zucker, 2008a) gender-discordant behaviors, as well as the different modalities utilized (for example, group, individual, parent support, parent-child counseling). The variety of expert opinions are matched only by the lack of randomized treatment outcome studies, obviously methodologically difficult because of the nature of the problem. The current discussion seeks to explore what role child analysis might play in this vociferous conversation, as well as what developmental achievements (standing outside any immediate relation to gender) might impact a clinician's decision to support or question the utilization of puberty blockers in early adolescence.

Dr. Ehrensaft takes a position that actively supports the child in finding his or her "True Gender Identity." From a humanistic standpoint, one could hardly argue with the inherent decency of allowing a child to express feelings that may have been long suppressed or believed to be unacceptable to those the child loved, and this stance is undeniably necessary if one hopes to disentangle the myriad possible factors contributing to such desire. Dr. Ehrensaft's sensitive work with parents, detailed in an earlier paper (Ehrensaft, 2011), shows her to be aware of the multiple, often conflictual determinants of a parent's stance toward their child's gender, and demonstrates her unfailing support for the child's individuality. However, in the context of an analytic/exploratory treatment, to support a child's individuality is importantly *not* to stop asking questions about it.

Early in her paper "Listening and Learning From Gender-Non-conforming Children" Ehrensaft proposes a view of gender identity that seems to allow for continuous questioning, naming gender identity and gender expressions as "aspects of self that can be established or altered over the course of a lifetime, not just within the earliest years of life." Such a view is indeed underscored by research on the trajectories of gender dysphoria in childhood, showing that in a significant proportion of cases, gender dysphoria will not persist into adulthood (for example, Drummond et al., 2008; Wallien and Cohen-Kettenis, 2008) and, additionally, that there is currently no reliable set of predictor variables or screening instruments that can differentiate between children whose gender dysphoria will desist versus those in whom gender dysphoria will persist into adolescence, at which point it seems to remain more permanent (Byne et al., 2012; Dresher and Byne, 2012; Wallien and Cohen-Kettenis, 2008). Only the severity of the early gender dysphoria and the cognitive belief that they were actually the other sex (as opposed to just wishing to be other than their natal gender) differentiated those who persisted in their gender dysphoria. However, these results must be interpreted cautiously, as they may reflect the retrospective reorganization of prior experience after the gender identity was solidified in adolescence.

Yet the treatment Ehrensaft proposes, True Gender Self Therapy, seems at times almost diametrically opposed to the initial framework she espouses. While she aims at "the establishment of a child's authentic gender self with the assistance of Gender Creativity, working in the intermediary space between inner and outer," she later notes, "I have discovered that the children will be the experts of their own gender identity, and while gender expressions may vary over time, their gender identity shows more temporal consistency and simply needs to be brought to the surface." Similarly, she notes that "parents have little or no influence on the child's core feelings that define him or her as gender typical or gender variant. Such core feelings appear immutable" (Menvielle, 2004, quoted in Ehrensaft, 2011, p. 533). If these core feelings are immutable, little remains for therapy except to extract the wooly mammoth from the frozen ice in which society, the negative views of parents, and culture have imprisoned him or her; internal conflict must, by definition, play a secondary role, if any at all.

Ehrensaft bases her idea of the True Gender Self on the work of Winnicott's True Self, yet a rigorous reading of Winnicott raises important questions for her argument. In our reading, the True Self is neither a thing nor a content, but a mode of experience. Although Winnicott certainly connects the True Self to the "spontaneous gesture" and the material "aliveness" of the body, the concept itself is neither, but instead a "theoretical position" from which the former are lived (Winnicott, 1965, p. 148). The idea "does no more than collect together the details of the *experience* of aliveness" (ibid., italics ours). It is presymbolic and prior to identifications (which Winnicott connects both to the False Self and to a later developmental stage). We are not arguing that the True Self is irrelevant to human development past infancy, nor that it is irrelevant to the concept of gender identity. Rather, we contend that its value comes from grappling with its paradoxes: namely, an experience of being really there that is not the emergence of any *thing* that is *there*, and an experience that has everything to do with symbol use, creative expression, and identity, but that can never be found or caught in these products. Such an understanding renders the concept "True Gender Self," and still more the capacity to "find" it, a contradiction in terms.

When the True Gender Self is conceptualized as something that exists from birth and remains relatively unchanging, the notions that children may themselves be ambivalent about their variant gender identity, that the dysphoria is the result of conflict rather than the cause, and that the manifest gender behaviors could serve defenses purposes (against fears emanating from forbidden excitements or competition, the demands of puberty or traumatic experience, for instance) are less likely to be a focus of examination. Similarly, the performative aspects of gender will be seen as emanating from an unempathic environment, which necessitates drama, rather than being a complex communication from the child that needs to be decoded. The problem, so defined, must be located primarily outside of the self, due to some verifiable external reality such as the stigmatization of family or society, against which one builds "a crusty protective layer at the surface, one that may be able to meet the world adaptively but constricts the child internally" (Ehrensaft, 2015, p. 39). Given the supposition that there is something to be found and protected, neutrality quickly morphs into advocacy.

To consider what is lost along the way, we turn to Ehrensaft's treatment and its divergences from an analytic stance. True Gender Self Therapy is sometimes described as an analytic treatment and sometimes an analytically informed treatment (Ehrensaft, 2011). It differs significantly from other analytic treatments of gender dysphoric children reported in the literature (for example, Gilmore, 1995; Lothstein, 1988; Karush, 1993; McDevitt, 1995) in terms of the frequency of sessions, the position of the analyst who is primarily seen in treatment, the importance placed on the understanding of unconscious material, and the exploration of the child's phenomenological experience. In the reported case, Jacqueline/Thomas was seen one time per week, a frequency that not only "slowed the forward pace of our work," as Ehrensaft notes (2015, p. 45), but changed the very nature of the work, making it less likely that the transferential feelings that develop could be experienced as a palpable, and hence interpretable, reality by the child, and increasing the likelihood that these feelings would be expressed in action. In earlier descriptions of True Gender Self Therapy, Ehrensaft (2011) notes that often the work goes on entirely with the parents without the direct participation of the child, highlighting the degree to which the therapeutic role centers on helping the parents mourn the loss of the child that they dreamed they would have in preparation for accepting the child that they do have. The process of finding the child is less clearly articulated but seems to focus on the child's manifest statements.

Although Ehrensaft states in her paper that "gender exploration is a long and careful endeavor, interweaving the conscious and the unconscious, the psychic and the social . . ." (2015, p. 34) there is little exploration of the unconscious in the clinical example given. Typically, the crux of the therapeutic encounter is "the act of mirroring back to the child, the child's articulation over time of that child's unique gender web" (2015, p. 44). Mirroring, a technique most associated with Kohut, offered a systematic way of entering the world of patients who were incapable of what had been defined as an analyzable transference because of early deficits in the development of the self. By echoing and reflecting, and not making premature interpretations, mirroring supported the development of a variety of relatively stable and cohesive self-object transferences (Kohut, 1977). For Kohut, mirroring was a tool in the evocation of transference, allowing a relationship to develop at a point when the patient was able to accept interpretations that offered a different perspective than one already consciously available to him or her. In its intent, it differed from empathic listening. If mirroring is seen as an end in itself, it is difficult to imagine how one can go beyond the manifest material.

In the treatment as reported, almost no information is provided about the development of the transference. (The patient will be referred to as "Jacqueline" and "she" when discussing the treatment prior to her transition to "Thomas" and "he.") We can infer Jacqueline's transferential reactions in behavioral actions, for example, her unwillingness to discuss her feelings and fantasies following the suggestion of puberty blockers with Dr. Ehrensaft, or the fact that she later concealed her chosen name of Thomas. Yet these responses are only summarily explored. We are left with little sense of the process that developed between her and Dr. Ehrensaft, or Dr. Ehrensaft's reveries about Jacqueline. One need only compare the level of detail and the careful examination of meaning and the child's phenomenological experience present in the earlier noted analytic studies of Gilmore (1995) or McDevitt (1995). The unfolding and investigation of the transference, potentially the greatest source of information on the unconscious aspects of the child's gender choices, is virtually absent from the treatment. Nor is it utilized, as in analytic self psychology, (for example, Lothstein, 1988) as a process through which less developed aspects of the self can be realized.

Perhaps in consequence, unconscious determinants of Jacqueline's gender behavior are left unexplored. Jacqueline's statements about her wish to be a boy ("mostly, kinda"), her playing mostly with girls and a few "nice boys," her initial agitated reactions to the first suggestions of puberty blockers ("But girls are nicer than boys"), her worry about the loss a shift will entail ("I think I'll still be the same person if I'm a boy instead of a girl, won't I?"), and her desire not to change her name with Dr. Ehrensaft are at least suggestive of conflict and a wish not to grow up or decide on a gender, rather than a straightforward dissatisfaction with her physical body. Her statements are overtly different from the primarily cognitive declarations that "I am a boy" that characterized the girls who persisted in their gender dysphoria into adolescence (Steensma et al., 2011; Steensma et al., 2013). In those studies, the children who were more extreme in their cross-gendered behavior were the ones most likely to persist. Given Jacqueline's reticence to attend the transgender conferences, it is not clear she falls into the most extreme category. Further, the underlying motives for a wish to be the other gender during childhood emanated from different motives in persisters and desisters. While persisters truly longed for another body, the desisters, lacking a true aversion to their natal body, wanted to have another body in order to fulfill the preferred gender role. At the least, Jacqueline's statements invite exploration as to what it was about a boy that she wanted to be, or an inquiry into what her fantasies were about the lives that boys lead. In addition, no consideration is reported about what the absence of a father meant to Jacqueline or how growing up in a single-parent family might have impacted her sense of gender. If we learn about Jacqueline's gender identity, we do not, as Corbett (2009) urges us to do, learn about her gender fantasies, those organizing and persistent scripts that condense "early identifications, childhood sexual theories and fantasies, experiences, and solutions to important childhood conflicts" (Person, quoted in Corbett).

As gender fantasy is flattened to gender identity, the environment must also take on a one-note position. Dr. Ehrensaft makes an assumption that Jacqueline "lived in a layered internal world, firm at the core and then covered with doubts" (2015, p. 46). The source of the doubt is attributed to her mother and Jacqueline's fear that she will lose her mother's love because of the mother's conscious wish for a girl child. In previous reports of child analyses of gender dysphoric children, from both classical and self psychological perspectives, as well as research studies (for example, Coates, Friedman, and Wolfe, 1991), the mother's fantasy life, her *unconscious* desires about the sex of the child were seen as central. Here, the mother's manifest desires are taken at face value. Her wish to introduce blockers to Jacqueline as potentially motivated by a fear of her child's reprisals go unexamined; there is no mention of aggression in any form.

If Jacqueline/Thomas's doubt is not explored as conflict but instead attributed to her/his environment's conscious wishes, how are we to know that her/his ultimate clarity about the puberty blockers is not what she/he perceives to be the wishes of her/his therapist? As Schwartz (2012) points out in a trenchant discussion of how a clinician's essential beliefs about gender influence the choice of treatment options, Ehrensaft's ideas about the True Gender Self move her closer to an essentialist position, which inevitably brings her to an interpretive process that is "limited in its imaginative range" (p. 472). Gender becomes defined as "a material condition that requires a material response" (p. 465). The danger is in finding in the child's literal statements what the clinician was looking for to begin with.

What child analysis can offer to the debate on the treatment of gender dysphoria is its unique form of listening, possible only in analysis, a situation that allows for and fosters the manifestation of unconscious fantasy in the transference, through the evocation of metaphor in play and words, and the analysis of defense as well as an examination of the analyst's countertransferential responses to the material. It is the opportunity analysis affords to see the multiply layered way that the mind is organized, the admixture of identification and the development of structure, the capacity to separate self from object, and the ability to accept that all bodies involve the limitations of boundaries. The tools of analysis need not, and should not, be used in the service of encouraging a child to accept his or her biological gender, but rather to add an additional lens to the perspective given by the child's (or the parent's) manifest statements. Analysis can help us formulate the right questions. There is no area where true neutrality, always easier in theory than in practice, is more mandatory than in our treatment of gender, where a genuine respect for the child's desire must include the ability to listen and not act. Without attending to their desires as well as their conflicts about those desires, and their apparent statements as well as metaphorical meanings, without allowing the full evocation of the patient's multi-layered and shifting internal world, support can become as constricting as condemnation. Advocacy is an admirable, necessary position, but it is a political position and not an analytic one.

Puberty Blockers

In turning from True Gender Self Therapy to puberty blockers, our question remains the same: Is the use of puberty blockers a neutral, easily reversible intervention that buys the child more time to explore his or her gender, as Dr. Ehrensaft claims?

As noted earlier, without any intervention, a proportion of adolescents will return to their natal gender; the persistence rate is reported as 15.8 percent (Steensma et al., 2011). At the same time, Adams (2007) reports that of the two hundred adolescents treated at Boston's Clinic for Gender Variant Children with puberty blockers and hormones, none chose to return to their natal gender. Given the absence of reliable discriminators, doesn't this at least raise the possibility that the act of taking blockers or the decision to do so may function as an intervention that shifts the child's position vis-à-vis their alternatives? As Anna Freud points out, not only the process, but the timing of development is critical in determining its outcome. Not going through puberty at the same time as one's peers changes the experience. In adolescence, with the developmental decathexis of the parental objects, the peer group is ever more central in defining identity and aiding in the second individuation process. Jacqueline/Thomas felt transitioning would feel more right if she could move to a new school and start over. Thus she would have to leave her peer group, a significant loss. Given the acquisition of a new peer group at a critical time, if she decided to change her mind and stay with her natal gender, returning would be that much more difficult. In fact, Steensma et al. (2011) reported that for some children in their sample, the return from early transitioning in elementary school was accompanied by considerable distress.

The wish to prevent the possible negative consequences for the truly gender dysphoric child that will follow from the further development of a body they believe is wrong is the strong form of the argument for blockers. Yet puberty is for many children a time of disorganization and pain, some of which leads to potential growth and stabilization of identity. The potential to block pubertal development raises the question of the ways in which bodily and hormonal changes potentially aid in the possible reorganization of the personality, not just the assignment of gender. In the quantitative and qualitative studies of desisting and persisting gender dysphoria (Steensma et al., 2011; Steensma et al., 2013), the period between ten and thirteen years of age was seen by both groups as crucial, with the bodily changes accompanying puberty, the experience of falling in love, and sexual attraction all influencing their final gender identification. A first love, a first rejection, the challenges to the parental authority that lead to the object hunger and affect swings of adolescence, the fear and uncertainty of identity that accompany a newly emerging body—should we necessarily "save" people from this? Until we can reliably predict in whom gender dysphoria will persist, the possibility remains that encouraging puberty blockers will foreclose the potentially organizing experience of development.

BIBLIOGRAPHY

ADAMS, C. (2007). Born in a bind: Treating transgender children. *Gay Lesbian Times*, p. 1034.

BYNE, W., BRADLEY, S., COLEMAN, E., EYSLER, A. E., GREEN, R., MENVIELLE, E., MEYER-BAHLBURG, H. F. L., PLEAK, R. R., AND TOMPKINS, D.A. (2012). Report of the American Psychiatric Association Task Force on treatment of gender identity disorder. *Archives of Sexual Behavior* 41:759–796.

COATES, S., FRIEDMAN, R., AND WOLFE, S. (1991). The etiology of gender identity disorder: A model for integrating temperament, development, and psychodynamics. *Psychoanalytic Dialogues* 1:481–523.

CORBETT, K. (2009). *Boyhoods: Rethinking Masculinities*. New Haven, CT: Yale University Press.

DE VRIES, A. L., AND COHEN-KETTENIS, P. T. (2012). Clinical management of gender dysphoria in children and adolescents: The Dutch approach. *Journal of Homosexuality* 59(3): 301–320.

DRESHER, J., AND BYNE, W. (2012). Gender dysphoric / gender variant (GD/GV) children and adolescents: Summarizing what we know and what we have yet to learn. *Journal of Homosexuality* 59:501–510.

DRUMMOND, K. D., BRADLEY, S. J., PETERSON-BADALI, M., AND ZUCKER, K. J. (2008). A follow-up study of girls with gender identity disorder. *Developmental Psychology* 44(1): 34–45.

EHRENSAFT, D. (2009). One pill makes you boy, one pill makes you girl. *International Journal of Applied Psychoanalytic Studies* 6(1):12–24.

_____. (2011). From gender identity disorder to gender identity creativity: True gender self child therapy. *Journal of Homosexuality* 59:337–356.

_____. (2015). Listening and learning from gender-nonconforming children. *Psychoanalytic Study of the Child* 68 (this volume).

GILMORE, K. (1995). Gender identity disorder in a girl: Insights from adoption. *Journal of the American Psychoanalytic Association* 43:39–59.

HILL, D. B., MENVIELLE, E., SICA, K. M., AND JOHNSON, A. (2010). An affirmative intervention for families with gender variant children: Parental ratings of child mental health and gender. *Journal of Marital and Sex Therapy* 36(1): 6–23.

KARUSH, R. (1993). Sam: A child analysis. *Journal of Clinical Psychoanalysis* 2 (1): 43–63.

KOHUT, H. (1977). *The Restoration of the Self.* New York: International Universities Press.

LOTHSTEIN, L. (1988). Self-object failure and gender identity. *Progress in Self Psychology* 3:213–235.

MCDEVITT, J. (1995). A childhood gender identity disorder: Analysis, preoedipal determinants, and therapy in adolescence. *Psychoanalytic Study of the Child* 50:79–105.

SCHWARTZ, D. (2012). Listening to children imagining gender: Observing the inflation of an idea. *Journal of Homosexuality* 59:460–479.

STEENSMA, T. D. (2011). Gender transitioning before puberty? *Archives of Sexual Behavior* 40:649–650.

STEENSMA, T. D., BIEMOND, R., BOER, F. D., AND COHEN-KETTENIS, P. T. (2011). Desisting and persisting gender dysphoria after childhood: A qualitative follow-up study. *Clinical Child Psychology and Psychiatry* 16:499–516.

STEENSMA, T. D., MCGUIRE, J. K., KREUKELS, B. P. C., BEEKMAN, A., AND COHEN-KETTENIS, P. (2013). Factors associated with desistence and persistence of childhood gender dysphoria: A quantitative follow-up study. *Journal of the American Academy of Child and Adolescent Psychiatry* 52(6):582–590.

WALLIEN, M. S., AND COHEN-KETTENIS, P. T. (2008). Psychosexual outcome of gender-dysphoric children. *Journal of the American Academy of Child and Adolescent Psychiatry* 47:1413–1423.

WINNICOTT, D. W. (1965). *Maturational Processes and the Facilitating Environment.* Madison, CT: International Universities Press.

ZUCKER, K. J. (2008a). On the "natural history" of gender identity disorder in children (editorial). *Journal of the American Academy of Child and Adolescent Psychiatry* 47:1361–1363.

_____. (2008b). Children with gender identity disorder: Is there a best practice? *Neuropsychiatrie de l'Enfance et de l'Adolescence* 56:358–364.

ZUCKER, K. J., BRADLEY, S. J., OWEN-ANDERSON, A., KIBBLEWHITE, S. J., WOOD, H., SINGH, D., AND CHOI, K. (2012). Demographics, behavior problems, and psychosexual characteristics of adolescents with gender identity disorder or transvestic fetishism. *Journal of Sex and Marital Therapy* 38:151–189.

BORNSTEIN'S CLASSIC

The "Frankie" Case Revisited

"Frankie" Revisited

Foundational Concepts In Flux—
An Introduction to the Section

SAMUEL ABRAMS, M.D.

The author offers his own historical review of the celebrated "Frankie" case, contextualizing it within political as well as scientific challenges. In addition, he provides an introductory survey of the three contributions that are to follow in the section. Similarities and differences are underscored, as contemporary child analysts revisit this acknowledged "classic" reported more than sixty years ago. In the revisiting and even in one instance where it is surprisingly a first reading, similarities and differences between there-and-then as contrasted with here-and-now reflections prove quite illuminating. There is considerable lauding of the revolutionary nature of the original case on the one hand, along with some open criticisms on the other. Several of the scholars suggest that the technique and the theories of pathogenesis and therapeutic action might well benefit from some selective updating of cognitive stance to the organization of clinical data. In this regard, adding nonlinear thinking to the original reductionism bias gets a strong boost—although that proposal doesn't quite achieve the decisive definition that permits it to flourish.

A FRESH EXAMINATION OF AN EARLIER CHILD ANALYSIS — PARTICULARLY one that enjoys "classic" status—holds much promise. It stimulated some to examine new causative agents—new "whys"—that have been

Dr. Abrams is Editor of *The Psychoanalytic Study of the Child*; Training and Supervising Child and Adult Analyst, The Institute of Psychoanalytic Education, an affiliate of The New York University Langone School of Medicine; Former Director of The Institute of Psychoanalytic Education; Past Chairman of the Committee on Psychoanalytic Education, American Psychoanalytic Association; and President, The Anna Freud Foundation.

The Psychoanalytic Study of the Child 68, ed. Claudia Lament, Robert A. King, Samuel Abrams, Paul M. Brinich, and Rona Knight (Yale University Press, copyright © 2015 by Claudia Lament, Robert A. King, Samuel Abrams, Paul M. Brinich, and Rona Knight).

recognized in the interim. This was what happened when *The Psychoanalytic Study of the Child* published a fresh look on the "Little Hans" saga (Abrams, 2007). A series of alternate explanations were readily provided by a distinguished panel to account for Hans's fear of horses, explanations that ranged well beyond Freud's initial etiologic preoccupations. The 2007 publication revealed wide-ranging divisions over preferred causative agents, not to mention the depth of conviction that escorted each of them. Despite the differences, those who participated seemed to enjoy a certain consensus about the foundational concepts within which their preferred agents operated. While that reexamination of the there-and-then Hans text provided evidence for disputes that reside within the here-and-now discipline, it also revealed what features were left unchallenged. Historical reflections are known to have that uncanny ability to reveal as much of the present as they do of the past.

Berta Bornstein's analysis of "Frankie" was published in 1949 (Bornstein, 1949). Bornstein had been influenced by Sigmund Freud's and Anna Freud's investigations in Vienna. At the time of publication, the Freudians were in a serious struggle with Melanie Klein's brand. One reason for this was that attempts to get child analysis off the ground in Vienna had proved somewhat problematic after Hans. Early on, Hermine Hug-Hellmuth stepped forward to fill the void. She was active in the Vienna Psycho-Analytic Society (for example, Hug-Hellmuth, 1922) and often designated "the first child analyst." An acknowledged scholar, a retired physicist and educator, and an entirely self-taught therapist, she familiarized herself with the prevailing psychoanalytic ideas during her retirement years and then went back to work in her new profession. She was one of the first notable women in psychoanalysis (Balsam, 2003) and may have presented case material as early as 1910—when Anna Freud was only fifteen years old. One of her patients was her nephew. Regrettably, he grew increasingly agitated under her care, became suicidal, and ultimately murdered his aunt/analyst (for example, see Glenn, 1992). This cast a disquieting shadow over the research scene in Vienna. Hug-Hellmuth might also have been the author of the book *A Young Girl's Diary* (Freud, 1919). Freud gave it a glowing introduction, but the book was plagued by the uncertainty of authorship and the possibility that much of it was fictitious (Guirao, 2012). Hug-Hellmuth, whatever her talents might have been, was somewhat of a compromised representative of the work that was being generated in Vienna.

By contrast, at the time, Melanie Klein was feverishly working in Berlin, following a period of psychoanalytic training in Budapest. She churned out one child analytic case after the other—Grete, Rita, Inge, Ernst, Erna, Peter, Ruth, Trude, not to mention clinical efforts with her three children Erich aka Fritz, Hans aka Felix, and Melitta aka Lisa (Frank, 2009). Klein extended her understanding of psychopathology into earlier times, reset the clock on the seminal period within the first year of life, proposed more-archaic instinctually determined pathogenic wishes as well as more-primitive defenses against them, and substituted nodal "positions" for "phases" (ibid.). If the Viennese had only been attempting to affirm Freudian views derived through adult analysis, Klein's explorations were leading her to reconfigure the analysis of adults and analytic theory altogether. However, what both brands shared was a set of foundational concepts: conflict, the inveterate push from an earlier time, interpretation, the transference, and the presence of a past dominated by unconscious instinctual wishes that might be accessed with reductionist logic. They differed only in the location of the antecedent pathogenic fixation points, the nature of the instinctual determinants, and the quality of the defenses that might be mobilized against them.

The Psychoanalytic Study of the Child had been partly created as a vehicle to support Anna Freud's research. The editors may have very well enthusiastically welcomed a case study that was informed by the Viennese founders and delivered by way of a most prestigious Institute to boot. "Frankie" was born.

Ten years earlier, Bornstein had reported on an analysis of a two-and-a-half-year-old girl, concerned with genital damage (1935), a contribution that affirmed certain Freudian assertions about the development of little girls within the framework of recognized foundational concepts. It was a relatively brief report.

Bornstein's 1949 description of Frankie was far more ambitious, closely detailed, selectively directed toward defenses, with less emphasis upon affirming nuclear complexes.[1] Frankie was a boy who was emotionally challenged almost from the beginning of his life; his mother strained in her attempts to assist him. Commenting on "developmental" matters, Bornstein regarded him on track—at least as reflected in his ease at toilet training. She set about attending to his phobic symptoms as indicative of conflict. While Little Hans had been understood as a child defending himself against Oedipal longings and castration, Frankie was increasingly viewed as principally protecting himself against affects. Bornstein's dominant concern was not inter-systemic conflict—the heretofore preferred center for Freudians and Kleinians alike—rather, it was *intra-systemic*, one aspect of the ego in struggle with another. This

---

1. In the interim, Anna Freud's pre-developmental opus "The Ego and the Mechanisms of Defence" had been published (1936).

was certainly an innovative proposal. Bornstein illustrated the value of extending into defense analysis, while holding child analysis to its customary foundational concepts. Anna Freud's many studies of developmental lines, studies that would all but eclipse her earlier contributions, were still not available for prime time.

Reading Bornstein's case material, one cannot help but be taken with her patience and determination as she tries to steer Frankie toward controlling his surfeit of affects and omnipotent excesses. Her forbearance extends over many years. Toward the treatment's end, however, Frankie declares that he is King Boo-Boo and can do whatever he wishes; he is seriously out of control. This behavior sounds alarm bells and some of Bornstein's patience flags a bit. She eventually confronts Frankie: she opines that such talk can lead to crazy houses (Bornstein, 1949, 214–216 [134]). That threat—a threat that for Frankie is particularly disquieting—brings him back in control, and the treatment soon ends. If this analysis had been intended to demonstrate a sequential treatment process that tracks a path conceptually akin to the adult model, Bornstein's authoritatively punitive intervention deflects it from the customary unwinding of the terminal phase.

Four analysts, recognized for their work with children, took on the task of presenting their own stories of this old tale in the form of commentaries. They not only provide a variety of thoughtful reflections on a documented text, they also uncover a concealed state of flux in the here-and-now psychoanalytic climate.

Alvarez (2015) recognizes that among analysts there are disputes over "whys." Her credentials include a rich information base about Freudian and Kleinian differences. She urges analysts to free themselves from informing theoretical maxims—from explanatory "whys"—and to shift to observational "whats." The implication is that too much of what we see is informed by what we believe. Alvarez acknowledges that this is her first reading of Frankie. She praises its textual virtues and urges more attention to empirical data.

Child analysts, Freudian, Kleinian and other "-ians" have customarily embedded their theories in a linear framework, in accord with the maxim "the child is father to the man." Alvarez silently affirms this view, while Hoffman (2015) provides an impressive reinforcement of Bornstein's commitment to linearity. In his admirable and comprehensive summary he reasserts the centrality of intra-psychic conflict and further endorses the value of applying a model of continuity in a therapeutic setting.[2] Hoff-

---

2. Harrison (2015) also will find herself at least partly allied to this position.

man underwrites Bornstein's extending intra-psychic conflict to include conflict within systems—defenses against affects. He suggests contemporary psychiatrists would benefit were they more aware of this process. There may be no more enthusiastic proponent of Bornstein's view than Hoffman. His is an exposition conveyed through and buttressed by a heritage of respected in-house teachers; this is obviously not his first reading.

Galatzer-Levy is not prepared to go there. He finds foundational concepts in a different place, the realm of nonlinear dynamics and complex systems. Equally inspiring and as clearly expressed as Hoffman's, his approach is more influenced by the move forward arising from nonlinear features rather than the push from behind by instincts. If linear thinkers contend that the child is father to the man, nonlinear thinkers argue that the whole is more than the sum of its parts. Galatzer-Levy contextualizes case studies and understands the transformative impact of feedback loops in the framework of his theories about networks. Reductionism and conventional views of transference are not very useful for monitoring a treatment tracked within a nonlinear framework. Hence, a different way of thinking is proposed, a way that requires attending to transformative activities and "the personal remaking of the network of meanings." Galatzer-Levy also expresses concern that a child psychoanalysis constructed upon a linear framework may give rise to authoritative interventions and lead to an educational experience rather than an analytic one—although that outcome is possible in any therapeutic setting conducted by a zealous overseer. While Galatzer-Levy's contribution demands much of a student, the rewards of an attentive read are certain to follow.

Harrison (2015) offers an intriguing mix. She wants to bring together developmental science and customary analytic models—that is, nonlinear (discontinuous) and linear (continuous) ones. She views the psychoanalytic text in the context of interactive relationships that embrace both features. Hers is a complex proposal attempting to be integrative. It is centered around the view that caregivers are co-creators of the development of children. A disharmonious interchange very early in life can impact on all that occurs thereafter, and she suggests that Frankie might very well fit that bill. This dominating "linear" view, however, is tempered by comments about nonlinear processes. In fact, in her metaphor the linear is "sandwiched" between nonlinear activities. For her, what transpires in an analytic setting is a co-created story, transitionally stabilizing, then disrupting, then needing repair. It is with the repairing that the treatment moves forward. Whatever the range of her theorizing, however, relationships—and the propensity of their effect to be continuous—does not stray far from her center. It is the meat in the sandwich.

To summarize: This exercise of looking back at Frankie usefully evokes varying narratives, narratives that try to put together the way things were, how they got that way, and whether this "classic" provides a suitable model for contemporary pedagogues. But while assessing these variants in historical excursions, it becomes possible to uncover the presence of a more pressing matter concealed within the shadows of the here and now. Frankie arose at a time when certain foundational concepts went unchallenged; they were the rules of the only game in town. These four in-depth fresh views of this "classic" suggest that the time to challenge that listing may finally be at hand. As we convene to consider suitable candidates for admission into our contemporary foundational scheme, nonlinearity clamors for a seat at the table.

REFERENCES

ABRAMS, S. (2007). Updating Little Hans: An Introduction to the Section. *Psychoanalytic Study of the Child* 62:21–27.

ALVAREZ, A. (2015) Discussion of Berta Bornstein's "The Analysis of a Phobic Child" (1949). *Psychoanalytic Study of the Child* 68 (this volume).

BALSAM, R. H. (2003). Women of the Wednesday Society: The Presentations of Drs. Hilferding, Spielrein, and Hug-Hellmuth. *American Imago* 60:303–342.

BORNSTEIN, B. (1935). Phobia in a Two-and-a-Half-Year-Old Child. *Psychoanalytic Quarterly* 4:93–119.

———. (1949). The Analysis of a Phobic Child: Some Problems of Theory and Technique in Child Analysis. *Psychoanalytic Study of the Child* 3:181–226 (also in this volume).

FRANK, C. (2009). *Melanie Klein in Berlin: Her First Psychoanalyses of Children.* London and New York: Routledge.

FREUD, A. (1936). *The Ego and the Mechanisms of Defense.* In *The Writings of Anna Freud,* vol. 2. New York: International Universities Press, 1966.

FREUD, S. (1919). *A Young Girl's Diary.* Ebook #752, Project Gutenberg, 2006.

GALATZER-LEVY, R. M. (2015). A Nonlinear Lens on Berta Bornstein's "Frankie." *Psychoanalytic Study of the Child* 68 (this volume).

GLENN, J. (1992). Hermine Hug-Hellmuth, Her Life and Work. *International Review of Psycho-Analysis* 19:389–390.

GUIRAO, D. M. (2012). Hermine Hug-Hellmuth Biography, http://psicotera peutas.eu/hermine-hug-hellmuth-biography/.

HARRISON, A. (2015). Co-Creativity and Interactive Repair: Commentary on Berta Bornstein's "The Analysis of a Phobic Child." *Psychoanalytic Study of the Child* 68 (this volume).

HOFFMAN, L. (2015). Berta Bornstein's "Frankie": The Contemporary Relevance of a Classic to the Treatment of Children with Disruptive Symptoms. *Psychoanalytic Study of the Child* 68 (this volume).

HUG-HELLMUTH, H. (1922). Vienna Psycho-Analytical Society. *Bulletin of the International Psychoanalytic Association* 3:512–513.

The Analysis of a Phobic Child[1]

Some Problems of Theory and Technique in Child Analysis

BERTA BORNSTEIN

This paper attempts to clarify some theoretical and technical aspects of child analysis by correlating the course of treatment, the structure of the neurosis, and the technique employed in the case of a phobic boy who was in analysis over a period of three years. The case was chosen for presentation:

(1) because of the discrepancy between the clinical simplicity of the symptom and the complicated ego structure behind it;

(2) because of the unusual clearness with which the patient brought to the fore the variegated patterns of his libidinal demands;

(3) because of the patient's attempts at transitory solutions, oscillations between perversions and symptoms, and processes of new symptom formation;

(4) because the vicissitudes and stabilization of character traits could be clearly traced;

(5) and finally, because of the rare opportunity to witness during treatment the change from grappling with reality by means of pathological mechanisms, to dealing with reality in a relatively conflict-free fashion.

I

FRANKIE, A 5½-YEAR-OLD BOY OF SUPERIOR INTELLIGENCE WHO WAS eager to learn, was brought into analysis because of a severe school phobia. He

---

The Psychoanalytics Study of the Child 68, ed. Claudia Lamemt, Robert A. King, Samuel Abrams, Paul M. Brinich, and Rona Knight (Yale University Press, copyright © 2015 by Claudia Lament, Robert A. King, Samuel Abrams, Paul M. Brinich, and Rona Knight).

1. From a series of lectures given at the Menninger Foundation, Topeka, Kansas, September 1947. Minor typographical adjustments have been made to the reproduction of Bornstein's original (1949) publication.

liked to play with other children and was friendly and amenable with them, but shy and withdrawn in the presence of any stranger. He became panic-stricken if his mother or nurse were out of sight. Even when left with his father in his own home, he was occasionally overwhelmed by attacks of anxiety. His phobic symptom had existed for more than two years.

Frankie was the older of two children of intelligent middle-class parents. His father was a kind man with slightly compulsive character traits. His relationship to the child was predominantly protective and had the character of friendly interest. However, he resented the tension which the child's neurotic behavior caused in the family. His reproaches were not openly directed against the boy, but against his wife, whom he did not consider affectionate enough to the child. Moreover, he accused her of having surrendered Frankie's care to a nurse.

The mother reported that Frankie was a planned child, that her pregnancy had been uneventful, and that she had felt happy and contented in anticipating her first baby's arrival. The delivery was normal, the child healthy, yet the very first moment she held the baby in her arms, she had felt estranged from him. The little boy's crying had given her an uncanny and uneasy feeling. She felt quite different toward her second child, a girl.

She herself was an only daughter, between an older and a younger brother. Her own mother had not displayed any warmth toward her, but was preoccupied with the older boy. This brother was "selfish, undisciplined, queer, and insisted on obtaining whatever he craved"; she used the same words in describing her son Frankie. Just as she had lived in terror of her brother, she now lived in terror of her son. Yet, in spite of her determination not to repeat her mother's behavior, her own feeling of aloofness toward Frankie was an exact repetition of her mother's attitude toward her. She was completely unaware of the fact that her primary rejection of Frankie was her unconscious revenge on her brother; later, after Frankie's neurosis made her suffer, her identification with her mother made her devote herself exclusively to Frankie.[2] In the end, however, the child's phobic symptoms, which made her and the nurse his prisoners, discouraged her profoundly, and made her realize her defeat as a mother. Thus she became not only eager to seek therapeutic help for the child but was also ready to identify herself with the analyst. Actually, her relationship to her son changed radically during the course of the treatment.

Frankie's first disturbance, his constant screaming and crying as an infant, were incomprehensible to the mother. She was convinced that the child's reactions were caused by unsatisfactory feeding in the hospital. And it is a fact that as soon as the intervals between feeding periods were decreased, the screaming attacks became less violent and less frequent. He was a bottle-fed baby and was described as a greedy eater. Night feeding was continued for an unusually long time and when, at the age of 5½ months, the 2 A.M. feeding was stopped, the child again evidenced his discontent. For several months he continued to

2. She gained insight into the motivation of her attitude only during the course of the child's analysis. She then understood that her longing to find a protective substitute mother had resulted in her dependence on her son's nurse.

scream at this hour. It could not be ascertained whether the baby's crying and screaming spells were unusually violent or whether they seemed so because the parents were oversensitive. As a matter of fact, the parents did not dare to fall asleep because of their anticipation of the baby's screaming.

When Frankie was 2, it became especially difficult to put him to bed at night. Regularly, he screamed for an hour before he fell asleep, and also whenever he awoke during the night. A third screaming period occurred at the age of 4½ years and was stopped only after the nurse threatened to punish him. As we shall learn later, it was during this period that the child developed his unusually severe insomnia which subsided only in the last period of the analysis.

We were told that toilet training did not lead to any neurotic reaction. Bowel control was easily established at the age of 1. Bladder control at night was established at the age of 3. However, Frankie refused to use any bathroom outside of the home, but instead retained urine for hours.

His sister Mary was born when Frankie was 3 years and 3 months old. Upon the mother's return from the hospital he displayed marked anxiety. He grew more ill-tempered toward his mother, and his coolness toward her increased to such an extent that she became disturbed and made conscious efforts to win the child's affection. Despite her strong urge to devote herself to her little daughter, she left the baby in the care of a second nurse while she and Frankie's nurse were at the boy's disposal. Thus she hoped to prevent any further cause for the boy's jealousy. Yet her concerned attention did not improve Frankie's relationship to her. He refused to let his mother touch him and reserved all the intimacies of his care for his nurse. His distrust of his mother, especially during illness, became so intense that he accepted neither medicine nor food from her. Nevertheless he insisted tyrannically on her presence at all times and had outbursts of wild aggression if she did not adhere meticulously to his demands. When she occasionally wanted to leave him, he became violent, panic-stricken, and clung to her desperately. But immediately after, when left alone with the nurse, his outburst subsided, and the tyrannical child became curiously submissive.

The mother had suffered considerably from Frankie's rejections. In his clinging attitude she began to see a sign of the child's love, and she was so deeply impressed by his fear and his need of her protection that she succumbed to his phobic arrangements.

The child's anxiety reached its first peak when he was brought to nursery school at the age of 3 years and 9 months. At that time, his sister's nurse had just left the home, and he had to share his own nurse with the baby. He went to school for only two days. Each time, he had to be taken home because of his wild attacks of fear and screaming, and nothing could make him return to school. A second attempt to send him to a different school was made when he was 4½. Although the mother not only accompanied him to school, but actually stayed in the classroom with him, his anxiety did not subside. After two weeks, this attempt also was given up.

At the time of the third attempt, the teacher noticed that Frankie observed the activities of other children with the greatest interest, that he wanted to join their play, but could not move from his mother's side. Only when he could believe his teacher's promise that his mother would not leave the room without his knowledge, was Frankie able to play with the other children. However, even then he periodically interrupted his play to check on his mother's presence. Because of the intensity and duration of the child's anxiety, analysis was advised by the school.

The analyst suggested that treatment be postponed until after a period of preparation for analysis in which the school was to co-operate with the analyst.[3] This pre-analytic phase was designed to create a conflict in the child between his symptom and reality (8). To be sure, Frankie was already suffering from an internal conflict as shown by his phobia. However, as long as his phobic demands were met, he was insulated against anxiety or its equivalent, and in this state there was no reason for him to want to overcome his phobia. By our pre-analytic scheme we hoped to produce in him insight into his need for help, without which no psychoanalytic treatment can make any progress.[4] Thus, as soon as the child showed signs of a firm positive attachment to the school, his teacher was to inform him that his mother could no longer be permitted to be present. When the child protested that he could not remain alone, he was to be told that there was a person, the analyst, who might be able to help him stay at school, and to withstand the pain of his mother's absence. This pre-analytic scheme worked just as we had planned. Frankie, conscious of his conflict and his desire for help, was brought to the analyst, who now could act as a mediator between him and the school. The analyst "persuaded" the school to extend the trial period, and to agree that his mother be permitted in the classroom. We also had to promise that his mother would be present during the analytic sessions. By this arrangement the analyst quickly became an important person for the child and the ground was prepared for a positive transference patterned after the child's relationship to his nurse—a relationship which at that time the analyst did not know in all its complexity.

The first period of Frankie's analysis was characterized by his desire for help. As long as he was in a state of anxiety, his understanding of analysis and his willingness to co-operate were remarkable.

3. The psychological insight of the school's authorities and teachers was of great help. Such co-operation with the analyst is not frequent and should be commended.
4. For a further discussion of the need for an introductory phase in child analysis, see Anna Freud (16).

His dramatic play during his first session led straight into his conflicts, just as in adult analysis the first dream often leads into the core of the patient's neurosis. His play revealed at once the experiences that had led to his phobia and thus betrayed the meaning of his symptom.

Frankie started his first session by building a hospital which was separated into a "lady department," a "baby department," and a "men's department." In the lobby, a lonely boy of 4 was seated all by himself, on a chair placed in an elevated position. The child's father was upstairs visiting "a lady" who, he informed us, when questioned, "is sick or maybe she's got a baby, maybe—I don't know, never mind." He made the point that newborn babies and mothers were separated in this hospital. Casting himself in the roles of a doctor and a nurse, he attended to the babies in a loving way, fed and cleaned them. However, toward the end of the play, a fire broke out. All the babies were burnt to death and the boy in the lobby was also in danger. He wanted to run home, but remembered that nobody would be there. Subsequently he joined the fire department, but it was not quite clear as to whether the firemen had started the fire or put it out. Frankie announced: "Ladies, the babies are dead; maybe we can save you!" Actually only those lady patients who had no babies were rescued by him. The one whom he several times—by a slip of the tongue—had addressed as "Mommy," however, was killed in the fire. No particular attention was given to the men's department. Most of the men had died anyway.

This game, which was repeated in the analysis for many weeks, betrayed the intensity of the boy's fury against his mother and sister. He could not forgive his mother for her unfaithfulness. He took her going to the hospital as a desertion of him and a sign of her lack of love. She must suffer the same tortures which he had suffered when she left him. He said, as it were: "I don't love you either; I hate you, I don't need you, you may die in the hospital. If you hadn't had a baby I would love you."

The dramatization of this biographical episode of his relationship with his mother was expressed repeatedly in a later period of his analysis, when in his play he reversed the roles: it was he who did the abandoning. A little boy escaped with his nurse into foreign countries and the mother was unable to find him. She looked for him but was usually killed by an army of enemies while he watched the execution from a hidden place. Sometimes he and his nurse joined the enemy army, sometimes he returned with his nurse to live with his father, who minded the mother's loss as little as did the boy.[5]

5. For more about this interesting detail in Frankie's play, which reveals his relationship with his father, see p. 193 [110].

Frankie, who so thoroughly punished his mother by the withdrawal of his love, naturally lived in continual fear of retaliation. He could not stay at home or go out without his mother because he needed the presence of just that person against whom his aggressive impulses were directed. The presence of the ambivalently loved person prevents the phobic from being overwhelmed by his forbidden impulses and assures him that his aggressive intentions have not come true. But while the unconscious hatred directed at the protecting person is usually difficult to uncover in the analysis of adults, it was still very close to the surface in this 5½-year-old boy (10).

The following methods of technical approach might have been applied in the subsequent analytic period:

> 1. We might be tempted to interpret to the boy the various motivations for his aggression against his mother and the newborn baby as: (a) his revenge for her abandonment of him—an aggression which was close to his consciousness; (b) the desire to take his mother's place, which was repressed and indicated only by the loving way in which he took care of the babies when playing doctor and nurse, and by his peacefully living with his father after his mother had been killed; (c) his desire to kill his mother, which we might interpret, as Melanie Klein probably would, in terms of the child's original sadistic intentions to destroy the mother by disembowelment (30). (In the last period of his analysis these fantasies were openly expressed by the child.)
>
> This approach, in which the ego is brusquely forced to face unconscious impulses, would result either in a quick suppression of the phobic symptom or in the strengthening of the phobia and of the resistance. The suppression of the symptom would make the patient temporarily independent of further analysis, but his ego, still in jeopardy from this suppression, would not have won the freedom which is essential for sound development. The strengthening of the phobia might lead to a stage in which the analyst himself would become an object of the phobia, preventing the continuation of the analysis.
>
> 2. By our participation in the play, we might refrain from any interpretation and thus, or actively, encourage the child to express his hostility in further play actions. This catharsis might soon lead to a diminishing of his phobia. The cathartic approach would mean, in terms of the id, a temporary discharge of tensions, but would leave the conflict between ego and id untouched. This would correspond to the pre-analytic procedure which Freud described in 1895 before he introduced the theory of psychodynamics. A return to such therapeutic procedures is encountered not infrequently at present.
>
> 3. We might devaluate the conflict by reassuring the child that such conflicts are frequent, natural, and understandable. This would mean

a consolation and encouragement for the ego but would tend to scotomize the conflict instead of analyzing it (25).

4. The therapist might take a criticizing attitude, by appealing to the
child's desire to grow up and not to indulge in such infantile phobic
mechanisms (4). This approach, also directed to the child's ego, would
be an appeal to give in to superego and reality demands, and would
amount to an overpowering of his ego.

Any of these four ways might be applied, depending on the therapist's
aims and personality. They all might lead to a quick disappearance of
the symptom.

In order to bring about an *ego change* we chose for interpretation from
the different themes revealed in the child's play that element in which
the patient represented his ego. It was evident to us that he himself
was the lonely 4-year-old boy in the hospital game, although feelings
of sadness and loneliness had not been mentioned by him in his play.
On the contrary, in his game he demonstrated only the *defense* against
loneliness and sadness.

By placing the little boy's chair in an elevated position he had reversed
the reality situation, presenting himself as omnipotent and successful.
Thus he became a person who actually knew what went on in the hospital, who directed the events, and who had no reason whatever to feel
excluded and unhappy. The omnipotence, as well as the destruction of
mother and infant, were used as defenses by which he denied the affect
of sadness. But before the defense proper could be dealt with, it was
necessary to have the child recognize and experience such affects.

We must remember that at the time of the analysis Frankie himself did
not know anything of his sadness. This sadness had been the original
response of the child's ego to an external occurrence of traumatic effect. It had existed only temporarily and was not particularly noticed by
those about him. The patient had successfully concealed from himself
the affect of sadness which evidently had been too painful for him to
bear. He had replaced it by his aggressive and tyrannical demands, to
which he later reacted with his phobic symptoms. Both aggression and
anxiety were the end product of an initial sadness, and without recap-
turing that initial affect so that the patient was aware of it, no real ego
change could be brought about.

The warded-off affect is a barrier to a successful interpretation of the
conflict and therefore must be made conscious before any further step
can be taken, lest the ego be pushed into a course beyond its integrative
power (15). Bringing an affect into consciousness furnishes an opportunity for the unraveling of both genetic and dynamic elements. The

re-experiencing of the original affects provides the emotional ground for the subsequent interpretation of unconscious material and makes it possible for the child to deal with a conflict consciously (17). Our aim, of course, was to make him conscious of the fact that behind the sadness, aggression, and anxiety, there was an intense, unrewarded, and repressed longing for the mother.[6]

In order to introduce this emotion into the child's consciousness without arousing undue resistance, the loneliness of the little boy in his game became the subject of our analytic work for several weeks. The analyst expressed sympathy for the lonely child who is barred from his mother's sickroom and who is too little to understand why his father is admitted. Frankie responded to the analyst's sympathy with growing sadness, which could be discerned only from his facial expression. The analyst's sympathy made it possible for him to tolerate this affect.

Once he had been able to face his sadness, Frankie showed relatively little resistance when his specific situation was examined. We asked whether by any chance he was a child who had been left alone while his mother was in the hospital. Or had someone taken care of him during that difficult period? He turned to his mother with the question: "Was I alone, Mommy?" and before she could answer, he told about his father and his nurse's presence, adding that his nurse would "never, never leave him alone."

By taking advantage of the variations of the hospital game slowly introduced by the child, we were able to go into the details of his life immediately before his sister's birth and again after the mother's return from the hospital. We learned from him how strong his affection for his nurse had been even before his sister's birth; that she had appeared a far more reliable person than his mother, who frequently went out and left him alone with the nurse. Gradually he remembered periods of separation from his parents before the sister's birth. Once when his parents left for vacation he stayed at his grandparents' home with his nurse.[7] One of his memories referred to his watching the departure of

---

6. It may appear that bringing an emotion to consciousness is a scanty result of many weeks of analytic work. However, it is noteworthy that the uncovering of recent emotions is often extremely painful for the child, more painful than the direct interpretation of deep unconscious content, which is frequently easily accepted by children and taken as a permission to obtain instinctual gratification.

7. I shall not follow up this episode because analysis did not reveal that any definite trauma occurred during this visit. However, incidental remarks and Frankie's behavior toward his grandfather led me to assume that the patient experienced a castration threat from his grandfather at that time. It would seem that this trauma did not have any immediate pathological effect on the child. The analytic material suggests that subsequent events led retroactively to a revival of that experience—a delayed effect comparable to that which similar occurrences had on "Little Hans."

his parents in a plane,[8] and his subsequent illness. He assured us that the nurse never left his side while the parents were absent.

This ample material referring to abandonment corroborated the appropriateness of selecting his sadness as the first content of our interpretation. To him, being sent to school was an aggravating repetition of former separations: it happened just after his sister's nurse had left and his own nurse and mother had to share in the care of the baby. Thus, he lost not only his mother but also his nurse "who would never, never leave me alone." *This repetition of the traumatic experience of being abandoned* brought about the climax of his anxiety.

In his play, and later, in direct memories, he revealed the specific contents of his fear. He was afraid that he might not be able to stop the school bus which brought the children home, that he might not recognize his own home, that he might never find his way home, and, worst of all, even if these obstacles were overcome, the door of the school bus might not open and he would be trapped.

His school phobia and the mother's stay in the hospital were thus linked. His fear of not finding his way home corresponded to his unconscious, revengeful wish that his mother who had abandoned him would never return, an interpretation which was confirmed by many play actions and verbalizations.

The same aggression against the mother underlay his fear that he would not recognize his house. When the mother returned from the hospital, he, of course, recognized her, but behaved as if he could not acknowledge her to be his mother. The fear of being trapped, which later became an important overt factor in his neurosis, referred to his original death wish against the newborn baby. The one who was to be trapped was his little sister. In a later phase of his analysis he said: "If Mommy had not opened her belly, my sister would never have come out" (30).[9]

The feeling of jealousy toward the sister whose birth had caused him such suffering found almost no overt expression. Frankie had learned to spare himself jealousy by denying the baby's existence almost completely during her first two years of life. He ingeniously escaped the pain of jealousy by creating exactly the same feeling of frustration in his mother as that which was gnawing at him. He refused to accept any affection from her, while he encouraged the nurse to cuddle him in his mother's presence.

---

8. An interesting relationship seemed to connect this incident of the plane with the later development of the child's neurosis, particularly as manifested in his elevator phobia.

9. See also p. 207 [124].

The contradiction in his attitude toward his mother was the next step in our own interpretation. He was shown the discrepancy between his inability to be without her and the rejecting way in which he treated her. Our interpretation suggested that he had exaggerated his affection to his nurse because he wanted to take revenge for the disappointments he had suffered at the hands of his mother. Throughout the months following this interpretation he told us that his nurse had forced him to obedience by threats. We understood that some of his criticisms against his mother were based on the nurse's deprecating remarks. Moreover, he intimated that there were some secrets between him and the nurse which he was determined not to reveal, and about which we learned only after the nurse had left the home. "Only God knows about my secret," he used to say, "and even God may not know it."

By continually connecting his recent experiences and emotions to their genetic counterparts, his sadness and jealousy, the pathological tie to his nurse was loosened. The analysis of the triangular relation between the mother, the nurse, and himself enabled him to desist from arousing his mother's jealousy. Only now his own jealousy appeared in its proper place, openly directed against his little sister.

Once the hostility toward his mother was diminished, his relationship to her seemed greatly improved, and his repressed love came to the fore. With this resolution the manifest school phobia subsided. He was able both to stay in school and to attend his analytic sessions without his mother's presence. This situation continued even after the nurse left. He took her leaving without an unduly exaggerated reaction, dared to express his sadness, and remained free of fear. In spite of all these encouraging signs, his neurosis was by no means dissolved.

In describing the first phase of Frankie's treatment it appears that we dealt with what might be called the preoedipal constituent of his disorder. Although his hostility as well as the clinical symptom revolved exclusively around female persons, such as his mother and nurse, two circumstances make one hesitate to speak of this phase of Frankie's disorders as preoedipal. There were indications that he had entered the oedipal phase prior to the onset of his phobia, but that this oedipal phase was interrupted by the outbreak of his neurosis. Furthermore, as we shall see later, the nurse was partly a representative of the father.[10] This may be one reason why, in the clinical manifestation of his illness, so little material regarding his father came to the fore at this period.

10. See also pp. 210 [128] ff.

Although Frankie's conquest of his aggressiveness toward his mother now made it possible for him to re-experience and to express his normal positive oedipal conflicts, he did so only in the analytic session. At home, the child's reaction to the father seemed to be emotionally neutral. He was, for instance, apparently unaffected by his father's frequent arrivals at and departures from home during wartime and even the analyst's reference to this failed to provoke any direct response. Only in his dramatic play and fantasy material did he reveal his hostility toward men. Innumerable play episodes also betrayed Frankie's interest in procreation and his urge to know "what was going on" between his parents.

In the most frequent of his play dramatizations, a father was absent and a mother was alone. Then an apparently friendly man, a butcher, a policeman, or a vegetable man (each impersonated by Frankie), came to dinner. The "friendly" visit always ended with an attack on the mother who was killed. The ending was always the same: the visitors were taken by the police and sentenced to death by the judge, both of whom were again personified by Frankie.

It was our next task to connect these fantasies with his actual experiences. This was achieved by confronting him with a paradox: his lack of emotion about his own father's coming and going, and the excitement the child showed in his play when visitors arrived. The mother had reported that prior to the outbreak of his neurosis, Frankie had shown signs of irritability toward visitors, especially toward his grandfather. This irritability was markedly increased when his phobic symptom disappeared. Neurotic anxiety was supplanted by the aggression against which the phobia had been mobilized in an earlier period.

It became evident that the image of the father had been split into two groups of substitutes: male relatives of his mother, of whom the most important was his grandfather, and various tradesmen and craftsmen who Frankie asserted were the nurse's intimates.[11]

In the course of discussing his irritation toward visitors, Frankie admitted that there was actually no reason for him to assume that visitors would attack his mother. Nevertheless, he felt that he had to guard her against threatening dangers, especially if she were out of his sight. "She might run away," he said. "She might be run over, or her car might break, or men might kill her in the subway." We finally understood that he was afraid that all of these dangers would lead to a second hospitalization, just as when his mother had had her baby.

11. See footnote 7.

The circle was closed. The danger which threatened the mother from relations with men would result in what was the gravest danger to him: the arrival of a new baby. He had to guard against a repetition of this traumatic experience.

It was this concern that was responsible for the insomnia which became acute at this point of his analysis. There had been previous occurrences of insomnia when he was 2½ and again when he was 4½. Now again it took him hours to fall asleep. He listened silently and anxiously to the noises at night. Whenever his parents spent an evening at home, he ran back and forth between the living room and his bedroom. He wanted to know, as he expressed it, what plans they were making. They might eat something special and he wanted to share it. Or someone might come and hurt his Mommy. Ideas about the problem of procreation filled the hours of his severe insomnia.

Our attempts to discover what Frankie thought about birth and procreation met only with resistance. Even with our help, he could not verbalize his sexual theories, but expressed them in further dramatizations. His games presented scenes of attack duplicating those which he undoubtedly assumed were taking place in his parents' bedroom. The role of the attacker soon aroused anxiety, and he shifted in his play to the role of an observer of the attacks.

When he began to present this new content, and for some time thereafter, he became quite excited. It is not easy to describe his complex emotional state at such moments. It was a mixture of rage and triumphant conquest, of irritability and anxiety. These emotions changed rapidly and erratically without any obvious reference to the content of the dramatic play characterized by overactivity. Gradually the character of his dramatizations changed: the wild emotions became pacified, the kinesthetic storm was subdued to meaningful gestures. One element which was already present in his wild performances became the predominant and all-important feature: a strong inclination to gain pleasure by use of his eyes. This voyeuristic element led him to a new impersonation, that of an omniscient God.

In his new role he made the analyst a frightened, sleeping child into whose ears God whispered dreams of wild colliding horses, of violent scenes in which "Daddy throws Mommy out of the window so that she has to go to the hospital for eighteen days." The "sleeping games" revealed his suspicions of something frightful happening between his father and mother during the night—something he would have liked to observe. As God, he had the right to see and watch everything. His new role of God provided him with greater power than he had previously enjoyed as attacker, judge, or policeman—roles in which he had experienced the triumph of the conqueror, but also suffered the pain of the conquered.

The dynamics of these games may be reconstructed as follows: when Frankie made the analyst act the part of a child whose dreams were supplied by God's whispers, he was revealing his reaction to the noises emanating from his parents' room. The child obviously completed visually what had been suggested audibly. He was unable to endure his own conception of what was taking place and tried to overcome this terror by putting himself in control of the events—by becoming God who can create dreams by his whisper.[12]

Later, however, when he realized that God was not only his own creation but a concept shared by others and that he could not rule "his" God to the extent necessary to be protected from anxiety, he replaced his fantasy of an omniscient God by an imaginary television apparatus which belonged exclusively to his fantasy and thus was completely at the disposal of his wishes and plans. ("God sees everything, but the television apparatus sees only if *I* turn it on.") The television apparatus brought the child closer to reality. When he was God, he made the analyst dream about those frightful scenes between his parents, while with the introduction of his imaginary television apparatus, he himself attempted to face those scenes. The analyst was made a co-observer of eating scenes in restaurants, for which Frankie provided the music (another auditory manifestation) while explaining the observed events to the analyst. He reassured the analyst many times that the observations were "make believe" and actually he never again reached the previously described state of excitement and anxiety. By means of his invention of the television apparatus, he removed himself not only from the scenes he imagined, but also from the feelings of desire and concomitant guilt which those scenes aroused.

It was noteworthy that with his exchange of the machine for God, the content of his problems was no longer expressed on the phallic level, but in oral terms. The aggressive element persisted, but apparently the content of his fantasies became more acceptable to his dawning conscience when expressed in the relative innocence of oral gratifications.

The following is one of the scenes observed through the apparatus: Father was in the restaurant and ordered the most delicious food for Mother from the restaurant owner. Then he had a secret talk with the owner. As soon as Mother had eaten, she collapsed and died; the food was poisoned. (In his thoughts, eating was linked with being impregnated, for which Frankie had not yet forgiven his mother, and for which he still punished her by death.) Father and the owner of the restaurant were unconcerned by her death; they continued

---

12. His role of God might be construed as an identification with the sexual father, but this was only partly true. The identification with the father was, in this instance, a defense against a greater danger, the yielding to passivity. The basic identification was with the mother, whose sexual role Frankie really craved.

their pleasant talk and play, shoving Mother under the table.[13] Some drawings of this time show God and God's wife feasting at a dinner table, disturbed by "little gnomes" who alternately attack God and his wife.

These games helped the investigation and understanding of a past period of his life: We had reason to assume that when he was 4½, his screaming attacks had reappeared as his reaction to audible primal scene experiences. His father once wrote us that in former times, "in his prankish days," he used to pinch his wife and throw her into the air, "all in fun and for exercise . . . , I can imagine what it must have seemed like to someone who heard it but did not see what actually happened." Frankie's running back and forth between his bedroom and the living room occurred in reaction to auditory stimuli and continued until his nurse quenched his active interest and nightly curiosity by a threatening and punishing attitude.

With the process of internalization of his conflicts the actually threatening nurse was replaced by imaginary objects, mainly wolves, who stood guard under his bed and kept him from getting up and investigating what might be happening in the parental bedroom.

These imaginary wolves under his bed were able, like the God he had played, to see what he did and to surmise his intentions. As soon as he put out hand or foot to go into his parents' bedroom,[14] the wolves would snap at him; "but they would let me go to the bathroom." For a protection from their attacks the boy armed himself with many weapons, preferably with a long stick, in order to beat the wolves down when they raised their heads. He maintained that they observed all his movements, and he in turn countered with an equally watchful attitude. His configuration of the wolves contained as elements the punitive and protective parent figures as well as his own impulses. The wolves punish his intentions and prevent their fulfillment. Their symbolic role as superego was

13. This scene is rich in its overdetermined factors; it permits the reconstruction of Frankie's oedipus complex. The element, "Mother is shoved under the table," refers to the child's resentment against his mother, who did not pay any attention to him when he, sitting under the table, tried to disturb his parents' meal. The next element, "Father and restaurant owner confer about the food for Mother (from which she dies)" is an indication of Frankie's wish to participate in his father's sexual activities. Frankie's position as restaurant owner was evident in many daydreams: he possessed "all the restaurants in New York." This detail makes us anticipate that Frankie's hostility toward his mother contained also some envy of her role as father's wife. Owner and father-Frankie and father do together what otherwise mother and father do. We shall see later how strong the child's desire was to take the passive role with the father.

14. The element of uncovering the hands and feet is overdetermined and it is obviously a presentation of its opposite, i.e., a reverse of the original warning against touching his genital under the bedcover.

strikingly confirmed in a drawing which Frankie called the WOLVES' STATUE. It showed an oversized wolf (in human form) with outstretched arms, floating above Frankie in his bed, under which a number of smaller sized wolves (also in human form) were engaged in mysterious activities, obviously of a sexual nature. In his comments on this picture, Frankie said: "It shows what the wolves hope for, what they will look like some day."

The dread of wolves which had haunted the child for weeks finally led to the analysis of his castration fear. In his stories and in his play, the mother's attackers who previously had been punished by death, now were punished by almost undisguised castration. In his pictures he endowed God with monstrously elongated arms and legs, only to cut off these limbs with scissors. Immediately after such operation he tried to undo this symbolic act of castration by drawing innumerable new arms and legs. Frankie derived reassurance from the idea that destruction is not necessarily irrevocable and consequently dared to express the thoughts of castration without any symbolic disguise. Mother's attackers were imprisoned and he, as a doctor, subjected the prisoners to operations which usually threw him into a state of exaltation. Playing the doctor, he exclaimed: "Those criminals, they have to be operated on. Off with their wee-wees. It has to come off!" In his play he guarded himself against any awareness of his fear by identifying himself with the person performing the act of castration. His fear of the anticipated retaliation found expression in his behavior toward his pediatrician. Frankie had always been a difficult patient, but during this period he absolutely refused to be examined, and assaulted the doctor by throwing blocks or potatoes which he carefully had stored under his bed for this purpose.

The emphasis in our interpretation was on Frankie's preoccupation with the mechanisms of undoing, and his identification with the aggressor. After this, we were able to approach the theme of his castration fear by confronting him with a comparison of his impersonation of a cruel doctor and the kind attitude of his own doctor; with the fearlessness of his prisoners in contrast to his own frightened aggressiveness toward his doctor.

In view of the anxiety which was kept in abeyance by his identification with a castrative figure, particular caution was necessary in the interpretation and dissolution of this identification. Abrupt release of such large quantities of anxiety would have produced a traumatic effect. Therefore it seemed indicated to decrease this defense only gradually. In a preparatory period of several weeks, we "amused" ourselves by imagining how frightened the brave prisoners of his fantasy would feel if *they* were suddenly exposed to the reality of a doctor's office. By our bantering his fantasy-prisoners, Frankie was enabled to take a more tolerant view of these frightening thoughts which he had formerly warded off by identification with the aggressor. Through this playful approach we prepared him for the fact that it was he himself who feared for his genitals, or at least that in the past he had once done so, even if the past were only ten minutes ago. Introducing *humor* (23) as a benign defense, we saved Frankie the full impact of the suffering which accompanies castration fear. He learned to understand that the wolves represented not only the prohibiting nurse and the father, but also himself with his strong voyeuristic and castrative impulses.

Although his masturbation was not yet approachable, the decrease of his castration fear enabled him to bring his sexual curiosity into the open and to ask the questions to which he had tried to find the answers by his compulsive running back and forth to his parents' room.

The material obtained from his play actions, in which men violently attack women, was interpreted to him in terms of his fantasies about intercourse. The treatment made it possible for him to re-enter the oedipal phase, and the father then acquired that emotional importance in the child's reality which was due him in terms of the oedipal relationship. Yet despite this progress, we did not expect his behavior in this new phase to be free of neurotic disturbances.

II

When, at the age of 6½, Frankie's wolf phobia had yielded to analysis, a breakthrough of uninhibited active phallic behavior occurred. He no longer contented himself with symbolic expressions, fantasies, and play actions as at the beginning of his analysis. Now he tried to carry out in reality all those actions against which he had previously protected himself by his phobia. Even God, and the television apparatus, by means of which he had satisfied his voyeuristic impulses, no longer sufficed for his needs. He began to gratify his sexual curiosity by directly questioning his parents and the analyst about intercourse.

He could not bring himself to accept the differences between the sexes. Although Frankie had many opportunities to convince himself in real life of their existence, in analysis he denied them with unusual firmness; even during the period when he made active investigations of his sister's body, he was not able to accept what he had seen. Finally, when he could no longer maintain this denial, he resorted to the theory that it was *only* his sister, and not other females, whose genital was mutilated. Hers had been, as he said, "pinched off" or "screwed off"—as a punishment. (Reasons for this punishment were not obtainable at this time.)

The obvious danger of castration emanating from his sister made her disgusting to him and made him shift his voyeurism toward adult women. Under the assumption that their genitalia might provide the

reassuring sight of a penis, he lifted the maid's skirt, then tried stealth-
ily to do the same with his mother and the analyst. When all his investigations could not confirm his fantasy that all human beings had
a penis, he felt disquieted, repelled, and stopped his investigations
altogether. And as always when his fear reached a climax, he stopped
verbal communication in analysis, and replaced it by dramatic play.
The traumatic experiences which had so intensified his castration fear
were now elaborated in harmless play activities by means of which he
achieved some mastery over these experiences and some lessening of
his fears.

One of his favorite dramatizations during this period contained an allusion
to his masturbation in connection with his castration anxiety. He repeated the
following play endlessly: The parents are away. The children ruin pipes and
electric appliances and accuse the dogs of having caused the damage. The
plumber and the electrician are called in, but they cannot repair the damage.
In rude words they warn the children against playing with material "which is
not meant for playing," and threaten to kill the children if they disobey. Upon
the mother's pleading, the plumber and electrician finally undertake the repair,
but ask an exorbitant fee.

This game shows us with particular clarity the means of defense which
predominated after Frankie's phobic mechanism—avoidance—had
subsided. They are the mechanisms of denial, projection, and undoing.
He denies the trauma of irreparability, and thereby defies the analyst's
statement that all women are born without a penis and must remain so.
He projects onto the dogs his feeling of guilt for the forbidden masturbation. He represents as the *restorers* of masculinity those grown-ups
(plumber, electrician, doctor, and nurse) whom he fears as castrators.
They undo the damage committed by the children as he himself undoes
castration when he adds innumerable elongated arms and legs to his
drawings of the God whose limbs he has just cut off.

And finally the defense by undoing and restoring was also evident in
the role in which he cast his mother. She, whom Frankie had previously
made responsible for all evil, now became the instrument for providing help. (This referred to Frankie's knowledge of his mother's role in
reality.) He knew that it was she who had insisted on the nurse and the
analysis for him; with the allusion to the plumber's exorbitant fee he
indicated the hope that by means of bribery, the analyst, like the nurse,
would help against the danger of castration.

Frankie demanded that the analyst be the threatening, merciless adult in his
game. The analyst observed that the child reacted to her rendition of the role
of the punitive adult with an increasing excitement which at least resembled

the mounting tension of sexuality. Therefore the analyst only intermittently sustained the designed role of the merciless adult in the play, occasionally adding to the character of the cruel plumber and electrician the reassuring element that reality was not quite as punishing as Frankie obviously wanted it to be. As the analyst went through the motions of the plumber, she would mumble under her breath: "Wouldn't I be happy if I could fix not only broken pipes but everything that is broken in the world. Children would be less scared if that were true." Or, on another occasion, breaking through her role of the merciless electrician, the analyst would say, "All right, if that child insists on my telling him that the switches are beyond repair and he has to die for having broken them, I'll tell him so. But that's all nonsense. No person should say such a thing to a child. That's not the way to learn. After all, things can be touched without being spoiled."

Frankie reacted to our reassuring interpretation with an annoyance that revealed intense resistance. We came to understand that this resistance was aroused by our having thwarted an important dynamic function of his game, i.e., the discharge of tensions emanating from traumatic experiences which were related to his castration anxiety and its masochistic exploitation. The attempt to confront him with the unreality of his play confronted us instead with the fact that our step was premature.

The child's insistence on the repetitious game and on the analyst's role in it placed her in a serious predicament: Continuation of the game might have shown us what particular experience he was driven to repeat in his play; there was, however, the danger that the child would take our participation in his play as permission for further indulgence in masochistic pleasures, which might have facilitated a masochistic fixation. On the other hand, had we refused to continue this game altogether, the child might have taken our refusal for a moralistic condemnation which would have undermined his positive relationship to the analyst at this crucial moment; moreover, it would have induced him to conceal the material from the analyst and himself.

The alternative to a direct interpretation of the masochistic pleasure involved in the game also seemed contraindicated chiefly because experience in child analysis has shown that, by such direct interpretative reference to the child's play, it might easily lose its natural function of pleasure, communication, learning, and sublimation (6, 35). It might become a stereotyped or sexualized activity which would interfere with or block further sublimation. Pathological attitudes should not be analyzed in reference to constructive, relatively conflict-free (28) activities, but, if possible, in manifestations such as dreams, slips, neurotic symptoms, and the like.

In Frankie's case, while noting the unconscious content of his play for further use, we first approached his ego reactions, namely his feelings of guilt. We did so not during the game but later, in a direct conversation, when the child was occupied with something emotionally neutral. We asked: "Who in your life has given you so many do's and don'ts? To some of them you don't stick at all, while you do stick to others and nothing can make you change your mind." Or else: "Who told you that it is such a crime to touch certain things, and who told you that punishment would follow the touching of things? Once you told me that you were sure that your little sister has lost her penis. What did she do to deserve it and who do you think was mean enough to punish her that way?"

If such questions are timed correctly, by which we mean, in moments of diminished tension, the patient will respond favorably. The favorable response will not necessarily consist of recollections or of an answer to the analyst's questions. If a child is only ready to tolerate what the analyst says without covering his ears, he shows that he is making the first step in acknowledging the existence of a problem. If a week later the same problem is approached, the child may be prepared to assimilate the question put to him. Unfortunately, such a slow pace is unavoidable in child analysis. Children are in much greater danger of being flooded by instinctual demands, and their fear of real external danger is much greater than that of adults. Therefore resistances are, if anything, stronger in children than in adults.

It took a long time before we succeeded in making Frankie aware of the connection between his masturbation and his feelings of guilt. The violence of his resistance made it clear that he was not yet capable of allowing the subject of masturbation to be discussed, or even of acknowledging it as a problem in his life. He stated that he had never masturbated. (His parents and nurse had actually never observed masturbatory activities.) He told us, however, about other children's negligible misdeeds in tones of great disapproval. While we would soon expose such a mechanism of projection to an adult, in child analysis we gladly encourage this indirect method. By discussing the problems of other children we are able to prepare our young patient for the acceptance of his own. It seemed to us significant progress—a step closer to reality—when Frankie projected his own misdeeds on other children, rather than on such fantasy figures as the dogs in the incident of the "spoiled pipes."

Children often omit from their analytic sessions all references to the external world. When this happens we must rely on the parents' reports. For this reason, and other well known ones (16) a continuous relationship with the parents is necessary. At the time we were skirting Frankie's problem of masturbation, the parents reported that he was sporadically showing unmanageable and quarrelsome behavior at home. After a long period of trial and error in the analysis it was understood that the periodic flare-ups were due to some notion he had about menstruation.[15]

Once again, Frankie was unable to verbalize this affect-laden material of his observations. Indeed, his fear at this time was so great that he could not even dramatize his experience in his play. He could express himself only in his paintings and drawings. They served him as *preparation for verbalizing* contents which he was not yet ready to communicate directly. As long as fear was overwhelming, his paintings were shapeless, as if under the dominance of the primary process. Any spot could mean anything, just as in the pictures of very young children. When the content had lost its terror it was represented in his drawings in a manner appropriate to his age.

Many sheets of paper were flooded with red paint or red ink. Finally, the analyst broke the sequence of silent sessions with an interpretative question: "Frankie, your pictures are red as blood, and Mommy tells me that you are unbearable at home. You quarrel with her and all the other women. Even with your sister Mary. What has made you so angry at women lately?"

To such questions Frankie responded either with violence or with complete silence. He increased the speed with which he flooded the paper and the carpet with red paint. The analyst continued: "I wonder, Frankie, whether you haven't seen some blood at home, and you didn't know where the blood came from, and you did not know what had happened. Is it that what makes you so angry?"

In response to our interpretations, his bloody pictures gradually assumed definite form. One of his pictures showed a toilet with blood in it, another a naked man urinating into a toilet, the red paint still dominant. He explained: "Here you see a man's wee-wee and blood is flowing all over the place." This picture showed that all previous explanations regarding sex differences had been of no avail, but were actually repudiated by him.

Another picture, called "Bleeding Bones," he explained with the following story:

"Once there was a lady who had 100,000 bones. And the lady was a very poor lady, and her bones fell off; they came off and she died very soon. And this lady when she died, had 106 cuts which she had all her life. But she only pretended to be dead. She was really wicked and very horrible. She wanted to be wicked to everybody."

15. The child analyst who repeatedly observes such periodic flare-ups of aggression and sexual excitement is in a good position to confirm Daly's important findings about the "menstruation complex" (9).

The analyst's interpretation now focused on the child's increased aggression against women as a reaction to his observations. We realized that since bleeding women aroused his fears and distrust, he retaliated by attacking all the women in his house.

Learning from Frankie that he had actually seen blood not only in the toilet, but also on his mother's bedsheet, we reminded him of his old anxieties about the injuries he thought had threatened his mother from men. And although all this had frightened him, we both already knew that he himself would also have liked to do that which he thought his father did, namely to hurt his mother; and the sight of blood on his mother's sheet and in the toilet might have stirred up both his fears and desires.

His aggression toward women was intensified by the rough and threatening way in which women had reacted to his explorations and attacks. Even his mother had reacted to one episode of his sadistic love play by saying: "I'll break your neck!" The following song was a direct reaction to such an episode: he accompanied the song in his own way, by smashing a wastepaper basket, reflecting both his own phallic sadistic impulses and the destructive impulses aroused by women's actual counterattacks:

"Break the lady's head,
break, break the lady's head,
break it with a knife, a sword,
throw her up and then fight high,
cut the foot halfway off
and then we take it up with God.
God will throw the bottle where a leg is.
He will throw it on you,
And the lady's head will be broken off."

Since both reality and the analyst's statements refuted his firm conviction that women had a penis, he shifted his curiosity and his attacks to their breasts, their buttocks, and their possessions. His father, aroused by the child's attacks, attempted to restrain him forcibly. Although the child rebelled and forbade his father's interference with, "Don't butt in when I fight with Mommy. I can do whatever I want. You are not the boss. I am not afraid of my wolves anymore," his phallic activity finally gave way because of the repeated rejection and punishment he suffered from both parents.

Whereas in his phallic phase women had been of importance to him and he had felt charmed by their beauty, in his anal-sadistic phase his attacks were directed indiscriminately toward both women and men. The goal of his attacks shifted from assaults on women for the purpose of penetration to that of eliciting an aggressive response from the person he attacked. With a provoking smile he tossed around his own toys and other people's belongings, threatened to smash plates, his mother's vases and furniture, and wanted to destroy his father's and the analyst's papers.

His sexual excitement was unmistakable when after such an attack, he laughingly shouted: "Don't grab me!" He continued such assaults until he had provoked a counterattack. Then, with glee in his eyes, and with arms outstretched, he shouted, "I surrender, I surrender." Once, when asked which he preferred, to attack or to *be* attacked, he answered seriously, "One wouldn't be fun without the other."

To our repeated interpretation that this behavior was caused by his misconception of adult love life, he finally confessed that the anticipated counterattack was his immediate goal. The provocative violence in his behavior served the purpose of gratifying his passive drives which could not yet be called masochistic; he did not desire punishment. Once when he received a slap, he exclaimed with surprise and indignation, "But that hurts! I don't want to be hurt!" During a discussion of punishment, he insisted that he did not want a painful spanking, but something he called "a love spank," or "a love pat."

The compulsiveness of his provocative behavior led us to suggest that he was probably acting out some past experience. After many long and difficult periods of resistance Frankie finally revealed the carefully guarded secret, the "something he would never tell the analyst" —a bedtime ritual in which the nurse had participated. When he was a good, obedient little boy, he was tucked in by her, turned around on his belly, and patted on his buttocks as a reward.

It was a repetition of this gratification of his passive desire which he now sought from everyone.

III

So far, we have given the material in almost chronological sequence, in order to round out the clinical picture and to illustrate the actual course of the treatment. Such further chronological presentation of complex analytic material would leave the reader with a feeling of confusion. Therefore we shall now discuss two of Frankie's symptoms, without regard to the order of their appearance in the analysis: his retention of urine and his elevator phobia.

The retention of urine could be traced back to the age of 3, shortly after bladder control had been established. One of the stories in the first period of Frankie's analysis indicated that the act of urination was connected with threats of castration:

"Two giants once ate up a river, so each river said: 'Get bigger so that the giants won't be able to eat you up.'" A big river equals a big penis "which holds lots of water."

Frankie had confessed with shame that he refused to use strange bathrooms because he thought that they were inhabited by giants who might *bite* off one's penis. However, when the retention of urine became the subject of his analysis, he denied ever having had such a fear, and claimed that the analyst had invented it.

Previously we had learned about a number of his oral impregnation theories, among which the most prominent had been that a woman conceived by swallowing a man's penis or, as revealed in his restaurant games, by taking in poisoned food. Frankie's present impregnation fantasies still contained the element of poison, but now poisoning was linked with urination: the drinking of wine led to impregnation. In analysis he squirted the analyst with his water pistol, aiming at her mouth, and shouting: "I'll poison you, I'll poison you. My arrows are poisoned with germs." Many times he slipped, and said "sperms" instead of "germs."

Here the analyst should have become aware that the sense of urgency which he betrayed in his actions indicated an attempt to demonstrate more than a mere theory, namely a past experience which he could not verbalize. Such emotional urgency appears to us as a clinical indication that we are dealing not with a fantasy but with a reality experience—and furthermore, an experience the impact of which probably came before verbalization was possible.

Frankie's play with the water pistol showed his masculine intention toward women. When we pointed out the contradiction in his behavior, namely his excessive retention of urine (at this time from eight to nine hours) and his pleasure in squirting water, he recalled that in the past he had gaily and wilfully urinated on the floor. His nurse had threatened and shamed him into obedience. He did not recognize that his prolonged retention of urine was his defiant revenge upon the nurse.

The retention of urine exemplified his conflict between active tendencies and passive desires and it was patterned after the conflict between him and the nurse when she was intolerant of his urethral eroticism. At first, Frankie's wilful urination had been the expression of his exhibitionistic masculine tendencies. The nurse grabbed him whenever she saw him prepare to urinate and carried him into the bathroom against his will. He recalled that soon after this the struggle with her became more pleasant than the intended urination. Therefore he often *pretended* to urinate into the corner of the living room in order to be picked up by her and carried to the toilet.

At the time of his analysis, there was no open manifestation of any desire to be carried. On the contrary, we knew from his parents' complaints that, even as a very young child, he had a marked objection to being touched, lifted, or carried about. In view of the fact that the child's later struggle was directed at preventing passive locomotion, we concluded that he had once experienced great pleasure from equilibrium sensations, and that this pleasure must subsequently have had undesirable consequences for him.

We assumed in our reconstruction that he had urinated while being carried by the nurse and that the loss of urine had added to the pleasure of passive locomotion. We further assumed that the nurse must have threatened or punished him for this, and that his retention of urine also was aimed at preventing a repetition of that experience. Her threats or punishment must have contributed to his later anxiety over the loss of urine.

We may then recapitulate the history of his urinary symptom as follows:

At first, acting as if he wanted to urinate in the living room was a means of forcing the nurse to carry him to the toilet and provided him with gratification through passive locomotion. Later, however, the retention of urine became an adequate defense both against losing control during passive locomotion, and against being touched. His panicky fear of being touched pointed to an originally pleasurable tactile experience. He recalled that he often refused to urinate in order to force the nurse to take out his penis.

We assume that the craving to be touched was not satisfied in the way he expected. He must have expected a gentle handling whereas the nurse, annoyed by his provocative behavior, was rough and may even have accompanied her actions with direct castration threats, an assumption supported by the previous story of the giants in the bathroom.

In another of his stories he further confirmed this reconstruction: "A king killed his mother when he was three years old. He wanted her to cut trees in his garden, a hundred thousand trees. And she should do it with her *hands*. But she was fresh, she dared to ask for an axe—therefore she must die."

He told this castration story after an episode at school when he refused to submit to a medical examination by the school physician, a woman. The only fear which he would admit was a dread of the smallness of the consultation room. He denied any fear that the doctor might harm him although he had reported only the day before that his school friends claimed this doctor "is used to cutting off wee-wees." "Anyhow," he continued, "I will not permit a ladydoctor to look at my penis."

We might add here what the child could not express: The smallness of the consultation room revived recollections of the bathroom in which the scenes with the nurse had taken place. It was as if he were saying by his refusal: "I am afraid that women in 'small rooms,' even if only looking at my penis, might arouse my desires. Women are as fickle as my beloved nurse. When I wanted to have my penis touched she hurt it." Her hands, instead of giving pleasure, might perform castration with an axe as the mother did in the king's story. (The experience in the bathroom with his nurse had contributed to his claustrophobic ideas of being trapped in small rooms.)

His panicky fear of being touched was a defense against the desire to obtain this passive satisfaction. While at the beginning wilfully retaining urine was a means of obtaining the gratification of being touched, subsequently the retention of urine—which by now had become an established symptom—was a means for defense against this danger. Furthermore, his urinary inhibition guarded him against his masturbatory wishes. By not urinating he avoided both the temptation to touch and the act of touching. He had even learned to direct the stream of his urine without touching his penis.

Frankie had already indicated his fear of losing control in his first phobic attack at school when he was afraid that he would not be able to stop the bus and the car would pass his house. He projected onto the school bus his own fear of being overwhelmed by a tidal wave of anxiety, and of being helpless in its grip.

On his second and last schoolday in the first school he was brought home crying and inconsolable. In analysis he described his plight in the following words: "I was crying and crying, because I had no handkerchief. Again his complaint is against being overwhelmed—this time by crying which he could not stop. He rejected our suggestion that he might at that time have feared the loss of bladder control, but then volunteered the statement that he could not bear the smell of the toilet at school, that the cot on which he should have rested smelled of urine, and he insisted that the teacher had threatened to lock up bad children in the bathroom.

Such a stream of recollections is unusual in child analysis. Whenever it occurred in Frankie's case it was a precursor of therapeutic gain. Soon after this, the retention of urine was given up.

While the child's memories were concerned with tears, a more basic fear was concerned with the loss of urine, a striking example of the oft-claimed connection between urination and tears. We should like to note here that the fear of uncontrollable flowing of tears and of urine both correspond to the uncontrollable flow of neurotic anxiety (26).[16] The main complaint of phobic patients is the danger of being overwhelmed by an uncontrollable flow of anxiety.

We shall now present, in some detail, Frankie's elevator phobia, which was one of his most impressive symptoms since it was a compound of all the etiological factors involved in his neurosis. It contained his ag-

16. K. R. Eissler has suggested that the biological root of full-fledged phobic attacks is the sensation of the uncontrollable flow of urine.

gression against and identification with his father on the oedipal level; his aggression against and identification with his mother; his death wish against his sister and his desire to take her place, and finally it included his masturbation conflicts: the fear of erections, the fear of losing control over his own emotions, and the fear of being lifted, all of which were components of the danger of castration.

The child summarized the dangers which the ride in the elevator involved as follows: "The elevator might crash down, or the door might not open, and I would be trapped."

We recall that when Frankie was 4½ he spent hours at night trying to get out of bed to observe his parents and his nurse. His nurse curbed this restlessness by threats. She said she would call the elevator man to teach him not to disturb people. The threat was effective, and the boy stayed in bed. Whenever he heard the sound of the elevator, he was terrified, expecting the man to come in and take him away. He wished that the elevator would crash with the operator. Then what he wanted to have happen to the dreaded elevator man, by his familiar mechanism, recoiled against himself, and he feared that the elevator might crash down while he was in it. Here the factors of aggression and retaliation stemming from his oedipus complex are encountered again; the elevator man represented his father, a fact which Frankie himself recognized.

A fear concerning his mother was also involved in his elevator phobia. Here his memories led into a period of life before his sister was born. He was deeply moved when he recalled that his father used to greet his mother by lifting her "high, high up in the air . . . I always thought, he'll suddenly throw her out of the window.[17] Daddy whirled Mommy around. I hate this if someone does it to me. It makes you feel crazy." Beneath the verbalized displeasure was longing and envy of the mother because of the pleasure he suspected she derived from being lifted up by the father. The idea that his father would throw his mother out of the window found its analogy in the fearful expectation that "the crazy elevator man" would lose control over the elevator, so that suddenly Frankie would find himself "deep down in the cellar under the building." He would encounter the same fate that he wished for his mother.

The following dream mirrors his desire for participation in the sexual excitement which he believed his mother experienced when his father playfully lifted her up.

"Some boy came to my house and we wanted to make a fire escape so that cars could go down one side and people could go down the other. The boy that I invited to my house—he fell down, way downstairs. Then the room starts to go down, the whole room, and Mommy tried to hold on and Mommy tried to keep up. And my sister fell into the business—into the room. *She* started to go down. Mommy did not fall down (Daddy helped to keep up things). I was falling

17. The same element is present in the sleeping game. See p. 192 [109].

down with the rest. Finally we all landed in the cellar." (Actually, the emphasis on "going down" was a representation of its opposite, being lifted up.[18])

This dream would seem to be a scarcely distorted representation of some experience of the primal scene, an experience which had been condensed with the frequently observed lifting scenes between his father and mother, and both experiences must have impressed him with the idea that a unity existed between father and mother from which he felt excluded. In his dream, he tried to participate in this unity: "I was falling down with the rest. Finally we *all* landed in the cellar."

The elevator phobia revealed another element, one which was contained within the phobia. This was a claustrophobia which was the result of Frankie's desire for being carried in his mother's womb and his defense against it.

Being carried symbolized to the child a means of unification with the mother's body (28). The perfect way to insure himself against his mother's desertion would be to be inside her body. He reflected this fantasy by stressing the great advantages the fetus has in being so closely united with the mother, or, as he expressed it, "in being tied to her." His desire for the womb was accompanied by a great fear of it. It was seen as a castrating organ, and was visualized as a "lion's mouth," and a "trap which can bite or pinch off an arm or a leg." He projected his own aggression upon the womb, especially when he realized with frustration that his little sister had enjoyed the unity with mother at a time he was already separated from her. In one analytic session, he told us that he had actually wished that his sister should be trapped in the mother's womb; in his own words, "If Mommy had not opened her belly, my sister would have never come out."

The wish for his sister's entrapment aroused a fear of retaliation, but this time from all small spaces, such as buses, bathrooms and elevators. Being trapped in the elevator was the punishment for the identical wish

18. It might be of value to summarize what we learned through Frankie's preoccupation with equilibrium sensations and the feeling of being lifted. This preoccupation and the conflicts it aroused were the result of: (1) His pleasure as a young child, when his nurse lifted him, and the fear that her castration threats made him attach to the act of being lifted. This was tied up with his dread of an uncontrollable flow of urine—and of anxiety. (2) His fear and loneliness at the airport when his mother had been "lifted away" from him in the plane. Somehow, the child connected this flight with the later birth of his sister. It is actually a fact that the mother became pregnant during this trip with her husband. In other words, Frankie felt, "If one is lifted, one becomes pregnant. I would like to be lifted. I would like to have a child, as my mother did. But being lifted, and being mother, means losing my penis. I want to be lifted, but I dare not pay the price for it." Naturally, Frankie did not reason out all of these factors in this manner. Our presentation is a reconstruction of the way he *felt*—his emotional, rather than intellectual, reasoning.

against the sister. We find in his claustrophobia a condensation of his identification with his sister, the aggression against her, and the ensuing danger to himself.

When he was confronted with the contradiction between his desire to be a fetus and his fear of being trapped in small places, he explained that the embryo did not mind the restriction in space since it participated passively in the mother's locomotion. These thoughts had found expression in the following questions in which the connection between passive locomotion and the flow of urine was again emphasized. "Does the child feel every little step of the mother or does only the mother feel the child kicking around?" And another time, "What does the mother say if the child wee-wees into her?"

In view of these questions his claustrophobia appears as a fabric in which activity and passivity are interwoven. This appears to us as a possible reflection of an early ego state in which activity and passivity had not yet found separate representation.

The movement of the elevator became for Frankie an important factor through its affinity to kinesthetic sensations. The ride in the elevator was dangerous because it aroused his sexual sensations. He projected his own sexual excitement onto the elevator man and assumed that the operator, aroused by passive locomotion, would lose control over the elevator. He would therefore be unable to stop the elevator which would either continue to move indefinitely up and down, or would crash down in a sudden fall. This explains why Frankie called every elevator man "crazy," and why he drew dozens of pictures of "crazy elevators" which rolled up and down and could not stop, so that "the passengers would become dizzy and crazy like being whirled around."

For Frankie the up-and-down movement of the elevator had gained another symbolic meaning. It was equal to an erection, an analogy which the child directly communicated, and which at long last made it possible for us to approach his problem of masturbation.

Several times during the course of his analysis he had made allusions to this problem, for instance when he feared the wolves would snap at his fingers and later, when he dramatized the game of "bad children" who spoil pipes and electric appliances, and even more openly, when we discussed his retention of urine. But our previous attempts to interpret to him the connection of this material with his masturbation had been of no avail. The child assured us that masturbation had never occurred in his life. However, he finally admitted that he derived some pleasure from another activity. It consisted in the contraction of the pelvic muscles and Frankie told us that he indulged in it for hours. We consider these manipulations as a masturbatory equivalent.

Frankie could not recall ever having been reprimanded for masturbation or threatened with castration for it. He did remember, however, that the nurse had interfered with his sister's masturbation and that she had warned him that retaining urine might cause a poisoning of the blood. To our questions as to the character of the disease of blood poisoning, he responded without any hesitation: "Blood poisoning? You might lose a finger or a leg!" and the following associations showed that to him, blood poisoning meant bleeding like a woman, being castrated like his sister, losing control over one's own emotions—in short, "going crazy." Frankie's behavior was occasionally called "crazy" when he indulged in his outbreaks of uncontrollable wildness. Since he had occasionally experienced erections during such outbursts, he felt that there was a link between phallic sexuality and craziness. He told us that erections were once a desired experience, especially if they could be brought about indirectly. He admitted that he had sometimes consciously used retention of urine as a means of producing erections. Later he discovered accidentally that by contraction of the pelvic muscles he could likewise produce erections. However, at the height of his elevator phobia he complained he could not produce any erections despite conscious efforts to do so.

The hour-long contractions of the pelvic muscles had either led to or were accompanied by painful spasms in the umbilical region. He called these sensations "wee-wee ache," and had always feared that these symptoms were proof that he had the dreaded disease of blood poisoning, especially since he had actually experienced pains when retaining urine for hours. These pains represented the hysterical nucleus which is regularly to be found at the root of an obsessional neurosis (21). When analyzing this symptom, the pains around the navel shifted to the penis where the sensations probably had their origin. By the displacement of the sensation from the penis to the navel, he utilized an existing identity between his sister and himself. The furrow of the navel appeared to him similar to the female genital, and while his castration fear still did not permit him to accept the female genital itself as the point of similarity, he proudly pointed out that he had a navel like his sister's, that in this respect he was like her. By accepting the fantasy of being similar to his sister—by being a girl—he achieved the escape from the dreaded castration by an external force. We remind the reader that Frankie had been convinced that his sister had been deprived of a penis because she, like the "bad children" in the plumber game, had spoiled her genital by touching it.

Frankie's pelvic contractions, his first obsessional symptom, were a defense against the temptation of manual masturbation. In contrast to adult compulsive patients in whom the secondary struggle against anal-sadistic impulses is in the foreground,[19] Frankie's first compulsive symptoms still showed their connection with masturbation in an undistorted way. His prohibition against touching referred directly and consciously to the genital. The curbed impulses for masturbatory satisfaction had produced a state of tension which contributed to his insomnia. He called this state, in which he lay awake for hours, "boredom in bed," and vainly attempted to distract and amuse himself with games. He crowded his bed with a variety of toys in order always to be sure of finding something to play with. Unfatigued, he manipulated his toy vehicles, cards, and toy money for hours. As soon as the analyst explained that his need for

19. The conspicuous absence of anal material in this patient can be explained by the fact that a temporary compulsive neurosis *in statu nascendi* subsided quickly under analysis.

toys in bed was a means of assurance against the temptation to masturbate, he strengthened his defense by extending his taboo to the touching of his toys at night.[20] He now substituted thought operations for the handling of the toys, which originally had diverted him from manual masturbation. He learned to play all his card games in his "head only," and was proud of being able to count his money "even without money." The fantasies which accompanied his masturbatory equivalent emphasized likewise the taboo of touching. They were centered around the automatic working of imaginary machines. "I need not even press a button to make trains or my elevator move upward," he explained. He imagined a truck or train or a passenger car going over a bridge, or "up, up, up the hill" and "slowly, slowly, down." To our question as to how his penis behaved during these fantasies, he answered that he tried to direct the descent of vehicles carefully so that the erection would not subside too quickly. "It goes up and down again, just as I want, and I try not to let it drop."

The blocking of sexual satisfaction had resulted in an uncontrollable outbreak of sadism and aggression. While he refrained from using his hands for masturbation he could not refrain from grabbing, in an almost obsessional manner, whatever he could get hold of. He destroyed possessions of his own as well as those of adults. It may well be that the breaking of objects symbolized the destruction of his own genital were he to touch it (11). His obsessional symptoms were transitory, but his preoccupation with certain thought operations made us aware of a nascent compulsive character. A tendency to brood about problems of life and death and morals emerged while he still indulged in sadistic outbursts. All these uncontrollable sadistic acts were designed to provoke repercussions, which in their turn served to gratify his passive desires.

Eventually he started to masturbate and his confession of manual masturbation was made through his drawings. Silently he spent many hours drawing hands. At first his hands could not be recognized as such. Later he used the analyst's hands and his own to trace around, but often left out a finger, once more indicating the danger of "blood poisoning," "losing a finger or a leg." Eventually, when interpretation had diminished his anxiety so that he could verbalize his problem, he could draw whole figures with complete limbs without resorting to tracing. This sequence of drawings from shapeless to accurate representations shows how the lifting of anxiety promotes simultaneously both greater sexual freedom and sublimation.

IV

Until now our presentation of Frankie's case may have given the impression that we centered our analysis primarily around the unconscious content of the child's symptoms and ignored his actual life experiences.

---

20. The other side of his taboo of touching was expressed in his worry lest other people touch his eating utensils. He developed a preoccupation with contagious diseases which might be contracted through touch.

However, we omitted to stress those parts of his treatment which referred to his current life only because we wished not to distract the
reader's attention from the formative process of Frankie's neurosis. In
presenting these processes we have been forced to schematize and sim-
plify some of them, but we hope that the reader will recognize that the
forces which are now to be described as a sequence were often at work
simultaneously.

In analyzing two of Frankie's symptoms—the retention of urine and
the elevator phobia—we learned about certain behavior patterns. In
the past, they had been mainly related to his nurse, but now they were
centered in his father and reflected his fight against his passive desires. His passivity determined much of the nature and structure of his
problem.

His symptoms were the carriers of the past and represented his experiences with his nurse. The dawning character formation could be observed in changes of his behavior, which were related to his continuing
impressions and experiences pertaining to his father. The progressive
analysis of his symptoms freed energy for the development of his character. But the passive drives which he turned toward his father stimulated
the ancient memories of past passive gratifications connected with his
nurse.

We mentioned that she was partly a representative of the father. It
would be more correct to say that for the child, the father was a representative of the nurse. In many respects the status of the nurse in
the family, and her behavior, were confusing to the child, because they
involved functions usually associated with the father's role. To Frankie
it was she who laid down the rules and regulations and the mother
seemed to be almost as dependent on her guidance as he himself was.
This was actually true in periods of the father's absence, and facilitated
the fusion of the father's image with that of the nurse.

When the nurse left the house, Frankie tried to re-enact the bed ritual with
his mother, who complied with his wishes for a while. After a few weeks, probably disturbed by the importance the patting ritual had acquired for him, his
mother gradually dropped it. It was this satisfaction the frustrated child sought
to obtain by his aggressive acts against women.

The women's reaction to his sadistic outbursts again made him retreat from
them and turn to his father. For a short time his role toward his father was like
the one he had had toward his nurse after she had frustrated his masculine
impulses, and this made him resort to his infantile dependence, which the nurse
had been willing to gratify. Frankie had gone through at least three phases of
obedience. All of these three phases followed periods during which his active
strivings had been frustrated. His obedience was always dictated by his desire to

obtain passive gratification and all three phases were abruptly ended when his expectations were disappointed. First he behaved like an obedient child with his nurse, who gladly accepted that pattern since it eased her responsibility for the child's care; she was motherly and kind when he was ready to play the role of the dependent little boy, but was intolerant of his active self-assertions. Next he acted as his mother wanted him to. He expressed love for her and suppressed all the signs of anxiety for which she had previously reprimanded him. In the third phase, in his relationship to his father, he indulged in long discussions on philosophical subjects, ranging from the existence of God, to the justification of laws, political and racial problems and, above all, questions about life and death—again behaving in a way satisfying to his father.

This intellectual relationship provided some gratification to his passive desires. His intellectual growth during this period was marked but this desirable sublimation was soon disturbed. The profuse passive gratification which he saw his little sister enjoying became a direct and potent stimulus to his own cravings. The longing for passive physical contact made him keen and alert in his observations and he meticulously noted any passive gratifications his mother and sister received from his father. When he saw his father stroke his sister's hair, he became depressed and longed for similar gratifications.[21] In order to experience the pleasures of a baby, he regressed to a behavior even more infantile than his sister's. He insisted on being washed and dressed like an infant, demanding this "love service" from his father. Once when his family was in a hurry to go out with him, he suddenly undressed completely and insisted that they dress him.

During this passive period he wanted to take the role of the woman, which meant, in his terms, to possess everything a woman has, while ignoring the difference in the sex organs. He said that he wanted breasts like his mother's, and silky hair like his sister's. He asked his father to rest in bed beside him and he spoke openly about his wish to give birth to children.

His conscious desire for feminine satisfaction and the idea of change of sex was expressed in his attitude toward injections. While formerly even the thought of an injection resulted in unmanageable resistance, he now suddenly craved injections. In one of his uncontrollable outbursts during his analytic sessions he shouted ecstatically while looking at a picture of a boy he had been painting, "Give him an injection, make him a girl, make him a girl!"

His persistent courtship of his father was partly successful. He managed to achieve some anal-passive gratification in various ways, such as having his father throw a ball against his buttocks and rubbing his buttocks against the father's knee. The anal gratification aroused genital sensations (erections had been observed on such occasions) and he then craved to have the genital region

21. In his analytic sessions at this period, he cut off the hair of all dolls before he could express this longing. We assume that the child displayed here a delayed reaction of jealousy which would have been appropriate when mother and nurse took care of his sister as an infant. The jealousy was focused on the father, since the father was to him at this time the phallic representative of mother and nurse.

treated by his father in the same way that he had wanted the nurse to treat it. He induced his father to button his fly, and the coyness he displayed on such occasions made the father recognize the child's attempt at seduction, and caused him to become reserved. Here the patient must have felt a disappointment similar to the one he had experienced at an earlier age when his nurse, and, later, his mother withdrew gratifications. Like the father, they probably did so because his insistence and the intensity of his desires alarmed them.

After Frankie failed to obtain gratification from his father, he concluded that his mother was granted those gratifications which his father denied him, because she had no penis. Therefore, since the fulfillment of his passive desires was not obtainable without the loss of his penis, Frankie's fears forced him away from his father.

Frankie's castration fears compelled him to make an attempt to achieve an independence commensurate with his age. On the one hand, he joined the older boys in their play, and roamed the street far beyond his permitted limits. On the other hand, in his fantasies his desire for the passive role still prevailed. His passive cravings had, however, undergone marked changes and now were no longer pleasurable, but aroused anxiety. The passivity, which up to then had been openly and fearlessly expressed, was worked into a fearful fantasy of being kidnapped by strangers. He was preoccupied with this fantasy for months. The image of men lifting him up and carrying him away contained derivatives of earlier observations when he had seen his father lifting his mother. His ambivalent desire to be lifted and carried was condensed into the kidnapper fantasy, similar to that described in the elevator phobia.

The essential feature of these new kidnapping fantasies was that they contained no open reference to genital or anal gratifications and that the *factor of passive locomotion was dominant*. As long as these fantasies were of moderate intensity, carrying two toy revolvers sufficed as a magic gesture to ward off anxiety. But whenever his repressed passive desires increased in intensity, the fantasy of being kidnapped lost its playful features, and he went into attacks of violent panic in which he was unable to distinguish between the world of fantasy and reality.

Such an attack of panic was once observed within the analytic hour. It followed his return from a vacation trip. On the train, he happened to hear that two criminals had broken out of jail, and were hiding somewhere in the country. His first response to the news was to refuse to see the analyst anymore. The next day, against his will he was taken to her office by his father. As soon as he saw the analyst, he lost all control, burst into tears, and assaulted her. He made attempts to choke her, and threatened to burn down her country house. (He had frequently referred to this house as a "hideaway," or "witch place," and had jokingly called the analyst a kidnapper, who kept kidnapped children hidden under the house.) His panic subsided when the analyst interpreted that he suspected her of hiding escaped criminals in her "hideaway," in order to give him up to them.[22]

We must assume that the train ride had touched off his conflict about passive locomotion and increased his susceptibility to anxiety.[23] The news of the jailbreak, therefore, stimulated his fantasies about being kidnapped, and he repeated in analysis the reactive panic he had experienced when his nurse had threatened to give him up to the police or the elevator man.

It would seem therefore that behind his peremptory refusal to see the analyst there was an unconscious challenge to be kidnapped. Indeed he provoked his father to take him forcibly to the analyst, thus succeeding in making the father his kidnapper.

To avoid such states of panic which the intensity of his passive desires repeatedly brought about, Frankie was forced to evolve an entirely new attitude. He began to ignore reality. Signs of passivity were eradicated and were replaced by feelings of omnipotence. He gave his parents nonsensical orders and was greatly annoyed if they were not carried out; he struck his sister and parents for not obeying unspoken orders. His world was divided into two camps: rulers and slaves—and he belonged to the world of rulers and supermen, who were characterized by incredible cruelty. He demanded that his father read him books in the middle of the night, and insisted on being served steak at two o'clock in the morning. In his analytic hour, he threatened that those who did not obey his orders would be sent to jail. When asked whether this could ever happen to him, he assured the analyst that if committed to such an institution, he would always find means of escape. He said: "They couldn't get me in, even if they carried me"—indicating again his wish for passive locomotion and the resulting fear.

The analyst suggested that he was identifying himself with his tough radio heroes and criminals in order to ward off his passive desires. This interpretation had a negative therapeutic result. He reacted to it by strengthening this particular defense. His demands became even more fantastic, and from time to time his behavior resembled that of a megalomaniacal patient. He claimed that he was actually a king: "Even if you don't know it and if you don't believe

22. The following elements were involved in the transference: The child reacted to the interruption of the work as if the analyst had abandoned him although it was the child and not the analyst who went on vacation. This separation from the analyst had revived the trauma when his mother had left him and then returned with a baby. The analyst is also accused of having children who live under her house. The child is saying—as it were—the analyst, like the mother, is unfaithful. She had taken advantage of his absence to give birth to another child and will give him up to kidnappers.

23. Trains always seemed dangerous vehicles to him, for the travelers were at the mercy of the conductor, who could create deadly accidents at will. In his games Frankie dramatized the following scene: Children are separated from their mothers during a train ride. German soldiers masked as friends enter the train, shoot the mothers, and take the children prisoners. Frequently the father and conductor are killed either by the German army or by burglars, and the children are left to the robbers, who are cannibals and murderers.

it." The fantasies of omnipotence were extensive; he called the exalted role he played in the universe, King Boo-Boo.

King Boo-Boo is master over life and death. Anyone who disobeys his orders will die. King Boo-Boo's thoughts are sufficient to cause another person's death. Sometimes some of his victims die, although they do not know of their own death and pretend to be alive.

King Boo-Boo also has power in political matters. "The USA only thinks she is a democracy, whereas in reality he governs her as a king. His army is stronger than that of the USA and Russia together. He is more cruel than Hitler, but people are so afraid of him that they don't dare to hate him. His soldiers and slaves love him so much that they finally *want to do* whatever he wishes" (an obvious projection of Frankie's passivity). Once in an outburst of exaltation he screamed:

"All the people, they like me better than anyone else in the world. I am better and I can kill everyone I want. I can even kill President Truman, I'm tired of him. I'm rid of him. I am going to make a new war against America. I am the manager of the world. I see that it goes around quick enough. I'm the executive committee. 'Execute her! execute her!' I said." (This referred to his little sister whose picture he had just drawn and which, at this point, he began to cut up.)

A few minutes after this outburst, he tried to be Frankie again, but could not endure this role. While he was casting our parts in play, he shouted: "I am the policeman, I am the delivery man, I am the truck man, I am all the men together in the whole world!" Frankie's earlier fantasies about God were the predecessors of his later King Boo-Boo imagery and had contained similar elements of cruelty. His role of the all powerful served two purposes: it was a defense against the fulfillment of the wish for passive gratification, and, at the same time, it was a means of obtaining that very gratification.

His dictatorial behavior at home and his fantastic ignoring of reality took on such proportions that it became questionable whether he could remain in his usual environment. This acute situation threatened the continuation of his treatment and necessitated special measures. As a last resort we had to bring to the child's attention the serious consequences his behavior would entail.

It was necessary that he be told that his behavior had actually one aim: to be sent away. This would be the realization of the one thing he had dreaded most: to be separated from his parents. We should like to amplify on the session which followed, and which brought about the decisive change in Frankie's attitude.

The analyst found him in the waiting room, the paper basket on his head, hilariously throwing books and blocks at his mother. After much maneuvering the analyst got him into the office. When alone with him, she asked him what he *really* thought the effect of his actions would be. She conceded that he acted as if he were a great king and as if he expected complete submission from his environment. But she expressed her doubts that he himself really believed in the truth of these ideas. She called to his attention the fact that his behavior would not have the desired effect and that no matter what he did, nobody would accept him as a superman or as King Boo-Boo. Frankie replied quickly: "Oh, they will find out some day, and they will do what I want!" The analyst then suggested that Frankie might not even know exactly what it was he really wanted and that he would probably achieve just the opposite of what seemed desirable to him.

Referring to several incidents during the analytic sessions in which he had acted out his King Boo-Boo ideas, she told him that even her positive relationship to him was influenced by his "actions." "Even before you enter my office, I can't help thinking: 'For goodness sake, what will Frankie try to do today; what is he going to break and to destroy today?'" He interrupted quickly: "Oh, you shouldn't care. You get paid for that, even more than it costs."

He was then asked whether he knew what had brought about this change in his behavior; after all, there had been a time when he had cared quite a bit for people, and when he had wanted to be with his mother all the time. Frankie replied triumphantly: "So that's fine; now I am cured of my fears, and I don't want to be with Mommy."

The analyst did not agree with him as to his being cured. She thought that he was still very much afraid, just as scared as he was at the time when he did not want to come to his session because he believed the analyst was a kidnapper. Only now he tried to hide his fear even from himself. He had never let her tell him what she actually thought about his kidnapper fantasies and about King Boo-Boo. But now she was seriously worried about his behavior. Therefore, she must show him that his King Boo-Boo behavior would end in something of which she had always thought he was terribly afraid. She had understood only recently that he really wanted to be carried off by someone, to be lifted and taken away. Didn't he himself see that he was behaving now just as he had when he used to attack people and then scream with fear, "Don't grab me! I surrender, I surrender!" Perhaps he was again looking for the old excitement, always waiting to see whether people would not eventually do the very thing which he dreaded.

The analyst told him she was compelled to assume that he wanted to create a situation where his being sent away was the only possible outcome. She was reminded of his nurse's threats to have elevator men and policemen come up and take him away. Perhaps these thoughts had always been somewhat pleasurable to him, although he had been aware of *only his fears.*

The child listened calmly, although this was quite unusual in this period of unmanageable wildness. Eventually he asked seriously: "Where can you send me? My parents promised they would never send me to a camp or to a boarding school if I didn't want to go there. And you yourself told me that children cannot go to jail. And a reform school wouldn't even take me because I'm very good at school."

Thereupon the analyst told him about hospitals which specialized in treating children whose sickness led them to behave in unacceptable ways.[24] He interrupted: "But I'm not sick; I have no temperature." The analyst stated that people who seriously believed that the world was divided into two camps "of an almighty king and the rest slaves" are seriously ill, even without a temperature and belong in special hospitals. He replied: "But Hitler could do whatever he wanted. Only, if I had been Hitler, *I would not have killed myself. I would have waited until they come and do something to me.*" Suddenly realizing that the analyst referred to mental illness, he became quite frightened and asked, "Do you think I'm crazy? Do you think I belong in a crazy house?"

Without waiting for an answer, he wanted to know in detail how those hospitals were run, how children were kept there, whether they were visited by their parents, what kind of toys they had, whether they were permitted to have knives and blocks and whether they were analyzed there. Our answers obviously disappointed him; they did not fit into his picture of exciting fights between attendants and patients and between kidnappers and the kidnapped.

The psychodynamics of this analytic session brought about a decisive therapeutic gain which may be explained as follows:

1. The beginning of the analytic session permitted Frankie to re-experience and to act out the full grandeur of his world of fantasy. He had an opportunity to demonstrate his narcissistic omnipotence, his disdain for reality, and his belief in the inferiority and weakness of the analyst.
2. The next analytic step was a thrust into his unconscious, and a demonstration that his unconscious aim was to enforce a separation from home. This was a contradiction of his omnipotence which even the almighty King Boo-Boo could not overlook.
3. He readily picked up the suggestion about enforcing a separation and revealed his unconscious desire by the great interest he showed in the place to which he would be sent. By asking one question after another, he began to consider the reality of what would happen if his unconscious desires were really fulfilled. This process then effected a valuation of what might have appeared in brilliant colors if left in terms of the unconscious. The ego discovered that fulfillment of these unconscious desires was drab and monotonous if carried out in reality. Thus, step by step, he gratified his wishes in his imagination and simultaneously learned that the price he would have to pay was not in proportion to the pleasures to be obtained.[25] The analyst succeeded in proving that this

24. The particular technique used in this session was an emergency measure in a very crucial situation, and should not be viewed as a typical or terminal procedure.
25. Two other factors may have contributed to the child's willingness to accept the interpretations of this decisive hour: The analyst had discussed with his parents the possible necessity of removing him from the family. The parents were depressed by the prospect, and the patient had probably sensed their depression and the seriousness of the situation. The analyst, through her active interference, had again contributed to his identification

defense was not perfect but would lead finally to the victory of his passive desires by commitment to an institution. Only then did Frankie start to doubt the wisdom of carrying his King Boo-Boo fantasies into reality. It is of interest to note why our earlier interpretations of his feelings of omnipotence as a defense against passivity did not have the desired effect. As long as the analyst merely discussed his megalomaniacal behavior as a defense without interpreting in detail his unconscious desire, she was doing nothing to impede the use of this mechanism. If anything, her remarks only helped him to consolidate this defense.

The threat which the child felt in our discussion of "craziness" had contributed to the deflation of his kidnapper fantasy. The final devaluation of the kidnapper fantasy and of the defense of being King Boo-Boo came about after we succeeded in showing him how the warded-off desire for passive gratification was contained even in this very defense. In addition, it was designed to result in satisfaction which he might have missed as an infant. After all, we said, acting as an almighty king was indeed a repetition of infantile behavior. We referred in particular to those scenes in which he demanded food in the middle of the night and we compared his behavior to that of a hungry infant whose screaming usually brings the desired food.

Nothing in our interpretation caused Frankie more despair than the analogy between his temper tantrums when his wishes were not fulfilled and the attacks of screaming and fury which an infant shows when its hunger is not immediately satisfied. Here we touched on what we probably might consider his "primal trauma" in a period in which he, hungry for milk and affection, screamed for hours. This, as the reader will recall, had happened when night feeding was stopped at the age of 5 months.

In brief, in the following months we were able to discuss with Frankie's active participation his feeling of omnipotence and his belief in the omnipotence of his thoughts. In so doing we followed Ferenczi's conception, presented in his paper, *Stages in the Development of the Sense of Reality* (13).

After our frequent interpretations of his feelings of omnipotence as derivatives of infantile behavior Frankie announced that he had something to tell us. He had a "remembering machine," a "projecting machine"—which he could turn backward as far as he liked. In it he saw that the analyst's mother had killed the analyst at the command of King Boo-Boo, because she, the analyst—when a baby—had screamed so violently that she had disturbed the whole world. When

---

of her with his image of the nurse who, like the analyst, had threatened him, but on the other hand, had also acted as his protector.

our discussion led to the motives for his projecting his feelings of frustration and fear onto the analyst, he gave way to a fit of rage and ran away from his analytic session. Pale and disturbed, he hid in the family car, and requested his mother to "throw the analyst out," or else he would smash the car. It took several hours to calm him. We had to discuss with him the fact that though he might not remember his infancy, he must have heard many comparisons of his own baby behavior with that of his sister, and he must have received the impression that his parents had never forgiven him his screaming at night. His sister had always been praised as a good, quiet baby which must have made him even more angry at her. Perhaps it was not only the analyst who should have been killed as a baby by her mother—maybe he had often wished the same would happen to his sister, so that his family could not rave about her. Finally we had to enlist his mother's help in reassuring him that in spite of her despair about his early screaming attacks, she now felt no resentment whatsoever toward him. Since her relationship to him had become genuinely warm, this reassurance was of therapeutic help.

The following months during which the child was able to work through the conflict about his passivity were a period of consolidation during which he was preparing himself for the termination of his analysis.

The prospect of ending the analysis revived for him the pain of separation from his mother at the time his sister was born. This prompted us to use these last months for further working through his relationship to his mother. During the weeks of our analytic interpretation of his early oral frustrations, his anger against her was reactivated and he demonstrated an unusually strong oral envy and aggression. Whenever he suspected that his mother preferred his sister to him, whenever she did anything for the little girl, he either gave vent to his fury against his mother and sister, as in earlier periods, or became depressed. The investigation of these moods produced a flood of material referring to early orality. We could witness the changes which his oral impulses underwent and how the freed energy was diverted for reaction formation and sublimation.[26]

26. When Frankie came into analysis he was a greedy child who devoured huge bags of "animal crackers" during his analytic hour and frequently asked for more food from the analyst. His orality was characterized by possessiveness and cruelty. God was drawn as a creature with a huge mouth, and he frequently described God's teeth in detail. Devouring was a frequent element in his dramatizations, and impregnation was linked with oral incorporation. Punishment was seen in oral terms. During his analytic hour, he often had fantasies of cutting his sister into pieces, cooking her, and preparing "totem" meals. In the period of working through his oral aggressive fantasies an expression of oral sharing appeared. He bought candies with his own allowance and offered them generously to the analyst, her secretary, and the patient whose session followed his. He made plans to give a present to his sister before his analysis was ended and in an especially generous mood wanted to invite her to share an analytic session with him.

His desire to devour huge quantities of food was sublimated into his interest in the origin and preparation of food. Food, the object of incorporation, became the subject of

Even when he was on the verge of giving up most of his megalomaniacal fantasies, he still used King Boo-Boo's "remembering machine" to deny his own past experiences of frustration, aggression and fear of retaliation. He first claimed that this machine did not remember what had happened in his own life but knew exactly the analyst's misdeeds and *her* mother's rage. Under the cover of the remembering machine, and through the voice of King Boo-Boo he expressed his aggressive fantasies regarding his intrauterine existence.

For example, King Boo-Boo—in contrast to all other people—could remember when he, the king, was still an embryo "and ate up his mother from the inside and also any other children she wanted to have." Only gradually could King Boo-Boo's "remembering and projecting machine" be focused on Frankie's own childhood and on more than the intrauterine period. Presently we could ask him to focus it on the transference situation and on events which had recently occurred in his analysis.

He wanted to know exactly who would take his particular hour after he had finished his analysis, and it seemed to us an important step when Frankie could say laughingly, "I hope that you won't take a child younger than me." And only in those last months of analysis was it possible for Frankie to realize the twofold nature of his transference to the analyst. On the one hand, he repeated the dependence which originally he had developed toward his nurse, and, on the other, the aggression with which he reacted to any frustration caused by his mother.

Only now could he be shown, for instance, that his rage and his fear at the thought that the analyst would give him up to kidnappers was also based on his fear of abandonment. He feared that the analyst would turn away from him as he had withdrawn from his mother when she came home from the hospital.

An important and new therapeutic gain was achieved when Frankie realized that his megalomaniacal behavior and fantasies were a defense not only against his passive strivings (kidnapper fantasy) but also a protection against suffering and death. Though he had rejected God and life-after-death at an early age, he had felt in need of some substitute consolation. He had tried to gain this consolation by making himself believe that at least a creation of fantasy, King Boo-Boo, was endowed with immortality. And when he was faced with the demand that he give

---

investigation and learning. At school he wrote a long paper about the food of Indian tribes in which there was no reference to taste or to the act of eating as such; his report was exclusively devoted to the technique of food preparation and the use of eating utensils. His oral possessiveness was not only sublimated into the sharing of food and theoretical food interests, but he discovered the institution of keepsakes. Keepsakes, not only for the child, but also for the adult, mean, "I do not devour you as a whole, but I take a little piece of you and let you live." Frankie's tendency to start a collection of keepsakes, such as the little toys and vases which he asked the analyst to give him, impressed her as a definite sign that his oral greediness had developed into a socially acceptable though still narcissistically colored attachment.

up even this buttressing fantasy he once more had resorted to phobic mechanisms, albeit this time only in his thoughts.

The following incident which occurred at a time when he was eager to attend a day camp during the summer will illustrate this: Having injured his leg, Frankie was worried that this injury might prevent him from starting on time. So he mentally rehearsed his phobic mechanisms, all the ways of avoiding a repetition of such accidents. He told his sister that he would not leave the house so as not to hurt himself before going to camp. To her response that she had once hurt herself in their own house, he replied: "That's right, but I could just sit in my room and I would not move at all." She, however, showed him that there still could be dangers, since he might fall off his chair and hurt himself that way. To this he retorted: "Well, I could stay in bed. I wouldn't even dress, and then certainly nothing could happen to me." He was somewhat ashamed when reporting this plan to the analyst, adding: "That's very stupid, I know. For instance, it would be dumb not to use the subway because you might catch a cold from germs. I know that germs are all over the world and I might get a cold anywhere." Then he said triumphantly: "But it would not be stupid to stay away from school, or from camp if the Mayor tells you to, because there is an epidemic of infantile paralysis." Here for the first time Frankie took a reasonable stand toward real dangers, which mirrored a significant and far-reaching change in his superego formation. It may be worthwhile to review the long road which had led to this achievement.

When Frankie entered his analysis, he was completely enslaved by his symptoms. His preoccupation with his mother and with the need for assurance that he could obtain gratification without endangering his existence, resulted in a constriction of his ego. He had not accepted any external ideals and there were hardly any indications of internal prohibitions. These are the signs of a severe lag in the formation of a superego.

During his oedipal phase, his fears were displaced from real objects such as his mother, his nurse, and his father, to imaginary objects and situations. The fears referring to his mother were shifted to "uncanny places" in which there was danger of being trapped, such as bathrooms, elevators, and small consultation rooms. His fears referring to his father were projected to imaginary objects like wolves from which he expected retaliation for his aggressive impulses. As the reader will remember, the resolving of those fears temporarily resulted in an eruption of instinctual impulses as, for instance, when he rejected his father's authority with the words, "I'm no longer afraid of my wolves, I can do whatever I want."

Considering what had caused the lag in superego formation, we must refer to two factors. One is that his environment did not provide him with a clear-cut frame of reference as to objects of identification. For example, his mother acted like a child in relation to the nurse, and it was the nurse who exercised authority. Yet he sensed that the nurse took a secondary position whenever his father made his sporadic and brief appearances during wartime and that she was paid to take care of him. The second and more important factor was that this nurse combined her prohibitions with libidinal gratifications. Normally, as the oedipal phase ends, the prohibitions of the environment are internalized and accepted. The sexual demands are renounced and these prohibitions and the growing demands of reality are consolidated to form the core of the superego. In Frankie's case, however, his nurse's prohibitions were sexualized as soon as they were expressed, and therefore instead of forming the basis of a superego, these sexualized prohibitions laid the foundation for a masochistic perversion.[27]

It was only after the nurse's departure that we could observe the first brief and unsuccessful attempts at building a superego. We refer to Frankie's interest in laws and regulations. At about that time he suggested to his family the founding of a "Club for Democracy and Being

27. Throughout Frankie's analysis we pursued the vicissitudes of his passive drives, hoping that our observations would permit us some general assertions with regard to the origin of passive homosexuality in boys, as well as of masochism. We must admit that his analysis did not offer sufficient material to draw final conclusions about either. Whether the activation of Frankie's brief perversion was accelerated by some prohibition by the patient's nurse or even caused by it, is not the point of our discussion in this context. Whatever the biological roots of Frankie's passivity, his turning toward his father as a love object was preceded by the traumatic rejection of his phallic activity by nurse and mother, the two most important feminine figures in his life. We have reason to believe that the rejection itself had been preceded by manipulation of the child's genitalia by the nurse. Whatever his biological readiness for this passive satisfaction, it is still important that he had been habitually passively gratified by his nurse. By tradition, by training, and because of convenience, it is certainly a temptation to settle the question of genesis by recourse to the biological explanation. However, the ascription to constitutional factors as an explanation serves to block rather than to help our understanding. It is permissible only after we have exhausted all other possibilities. We should rather focus on those environmental elements which seem to be unique in each case, elements which although apparently accidental, may contain the common factors in the development of passive homosexuality and masochism.

The present disagreement among analysts on this topic will yield to constructive discussion after more analytic material on children will have been collected and scrutinized. Although child analysis will not solve the problem of the biological components of passivity and masochism, it may help to clarify it by bringing to light in greater detail the environmental influences. Especially if the parents' personalities are well-known to the analyst, he may be able to make a fair appraisal of the extent to which the environment may have been conducive to favoring or blocking the behavior which the child shows. It will probably be easier to observe fine gradations and to weigh the relative influence of external and biological forces in the analysis of children than in that of adults.

Good." He invented rules and punishments, but they were so exaggerated that no one could abide by them. The slightest infringement was punished by complete annihilation, such as being "stamped to death by an elephant" or "being tied to a lion's mouth."

Once he drew a diagram for his father, explaining to him the battles which it represented. It showed a head and in it two "control towers" of good and bad Frankies. The "control towers" were responsible for the outcome of those battles. He himself could not control these battles, since "there is no bone connecting my mouth with my head or the control tower." He added, however, that there might be a chance that his good part and the good control tower would win the battle if his father were ready to do exactly what Frankie wanted him to do. Here he showed again the pattern of libidinizing the fulfillment of a duty. But this fantasy also shows the dawning of internal demands, expressed in his wish that the forces of good should win, although this internal prohibiting agent is still feeble and impotent.

We must draw the reader's attention to one more factor of this child's superego pathology. It is most significant in the development of his psychic structure that his earlier internalized superego configuration— King Boo-Boo—was not felt as something separate from his ego. Most children who have created such a primary and tyrannical superego, let it modify their behavior. Their ego accepts the superego as a prohibitory influence. When Frankie first invented King Boo-Boo, his ego, on the contrary, sided with this figure, and derived from it, in so doing, the strength and permission to act out an unrestrained omnipotence. This omnipotence served as an aggrandizement of his ego which had been tortured, humiliated, and frightened throughout the years of his neurosis.

Once he could give up acting out his King Boo-Boo fantasies, he could transfer his omnipotence to others who represented his ego-ideals. He could accept his father as a strong and enviable figure without becoming passively dependent on him. He had given up his wish for physical gratifications and therefore his anxiety had vanished. He could now compete in healthy and constructive ways with people of his environment, such as his athletics teacher, whom he admired for his strength and his justice, and the camp director, whom he praised for his ability and experience. In short, he had accepted the fact that there were people from whom he, a little boy, could learn.

The material produced in the next to the last hour of his analysis illustrates his new-found capacities.

The first topic related to the termination of his analysis. He had difficulty in bringing up his impending separation from the analyst, although he was now able to speak about his past separation from his mother. Frankie's acknowledgment that he did not really want to part from his analyst for good came indirectly. He suggested that the present which was to be given to him at the end of his analysis should be postponed until Christmas, rationalizing that "by that time, those particular trains will be of a better make." The analyst admitted that she herself did not consider the analysis completely finished, but that she trusted his ability to get along without her and to come back whenever he might need help. Thereupon Frankie showed his readiness to depend on people in the outside world for protection by announcing with a solemn expression his decision to let King Boo-Boo die. "Do you know that King Boo-Boo will not live always? I've made up my mind. Tomorrow is the day he is going to be 100 years old, and before that, he is going to commit suicide. First, all other people will die; his soldiers have killed all the other people; and then all his soldiers will commit suicide because they know King Boo-Boo will die and they do not want to live without him."

We hinted that though his King Boo-Boo was to die, Frankie was still not willing to admit that death was something he could not control; otherwise, he would have allowed King Boo-Boo to die a natural death. Frankie understood. He laughed wholeheartedly.

During this conversation he was toasting a biscuit over a gas flame. The biscuit suddenly caught fire and flared up. Frankie let it drop to the floor. For a second his clothes were in danger of catching fire. He showed no panic, but did what he was told. Only his sudden pallor betrayed his justifiable fright. Suddenly he went to the window and asked the analyst: "Would you let me jump out of the window? I mean just jump to the next roof [a distance of about twelve yards]?" He tried to convince her that he could hold on to the telephone wire, and when told that the analyst would not let him jump, he asked: "Why not? Would you jump?" "No," was the reply, "I would be afraid of being killed." Frankie asked: "What would you like better—to die jumping down, or to be trapped here?" When the analyst answered that she would neither like to jump nor to be trapped, but that if there were a fire, she would obey the instructions of the fire department, and even jump if told to, he replied: "I think I would too, if I were told; but I would not do it gladly."

What Frankie needed in order to let King Boo-Boo die was the reassurance that not only he, a little boy, but every person is exposed to injuries, sickness, and death, and that mastering reality is a difficult task for all of us.

In this significant hour we see recapitulated all the elements which we encountered in his first analytic session when he dramatized the lonely boy and the fire in the hospital. We could observe that the derivatives of his initial fears were firmly embedded in an adequate relationship to reality without eliciting fear, although the contents of his past conflicts were present to his mind.

A prognosis in child analysis is not easy. We are by no means sure that we have forestalled a later recurrence of Frankie's neurosis. But when he stood at the window, gauging the distance to the next roof, when at last fear, fantasy of omnipotence, and reality had become synthesized in one constructive act, when he was able to ask how we guard ourselves from danger—when he could face danger without resorting to pathological anxiety or belief in magic and omnipotence—then we knew that the secondary process had won a victory over the primary process. And this we thought, was the utmost a boy of 8½ can achieve—even with the help of child analysis.

BIBLIOGRAPHY

1. ABRAHAM, K. "A Constitutional Basis of Locomotor Anxiety," *Selected Papers*, Hogarth, 1942.
2. ABRAHAM, K. "Zur Psychogenese der Strassenangst im Kindesalter," *Klein. Beiträge z. Psa.* Internet. Psa. Verlag, 1921.
3. ALEXANDER, F., AND FRENCH, T. M. *Psychoanalytic Therapy*, Ronald Press, 1946.
4. ALLEN, F. *Psychotherapy with Children*, Norton, 1942.
5. BONAPARTE, M. "Passivity, Masochism, and Frigidity," *Intern. J. Psa.*, XVI, 1935.
6. BORNSTEIN, B. "Clinical Notes on Child Analysis," this annual, I, 1945.
7. BRUNSWICK, R. M. "The Preoedipal Phase of Libido Development," *Psa. Quar.*, IX, 1940.
8. BURLINGHAM, D. T. "Probleme des psychoanalytischen Erziehers," *Zeit. f. Psa. Paed.*, XI, 1937.
9. DALY, C. D. "The Role of Menstruation in Human Phylogenesis and Ontogenesis," *Internat. J. Psa.*, XXIV, 1944.
10. DEUTSCH, H. "The Genesis of Agoraphobia," *Internat. J. Psa.*, X, 1929.
11. FEDERN, P. "Beiträge zur Analyse des Sadismus und Masochismus," *Internat. Zeit. f. Psa.*, I, 1913, and II, 1914.
12. FENICHEL, O. "Remarks on the Common Phobias," *Psa. Quar.*, XIII, 1944.
13. FERENCZI, S. "Stages in the Development of the Sense of Reality," *Contrib. to Psa.*, Badger, 1916.
14. FRENCH, T. M. "Some Psychoanalytic Applications of the Psychological Field Concept," *Psa. Quar.*, XI, 1942.
15. FRENCH, T. M. "Integration of Social Behavior," *ibid.*, XIV, 1945.
16. FREUD, A. *The Psychoanalytical Treatment of Children*, Imago, 1946.
17. FREUD, A. *The Ego and the Mechanisms of Defence*, Internat. Univ. Press, 1946.
18. FREUD, S. "The Economic Problem in Masochism," *Coll. Papers*, II.
19. FREUD, S. "Analysis of a Phobia in a Five-Year-Old Boy," *Coll. Papers*, II.
20. FREUD, S. "Notes Upon a Case of Obsessional Neurosis," *ibid.*, III.

21. FREUD, S. "From the History of an Infantile Neurosis," *ibid.*, III.

22. FREUD, S. *The Problem of Anxiety*, Norton, 1936.

23. FREUD, S. "Der Humor," *Ges. Schriften*, XLI.

24. FROMM, E. *Escape from Freedom*, Farrar & Rinehart, 1941.

25. GERARD, M. W. "Alleviation of Rigid Standards," in Alexander, F., and French, T. M. *Psychoanalytic Therapy*, Ronald Press, 1946.

26. GREENACRE, P. "The Predisposition to Anxiety," *Psa. Quar.*, X. 1941.

27. GREENACRE, P. "Pathological Weeping," *ibid.*, XIV, 1945.

28. HARTMANN, H. "Ich-Psychologie und Anpassungsproblem," *Internat. Ztschr. f. Psa.*, XXIV, 1939.

29. HERMANN, I. "Sich Anklammern-Auf Suche gehen," *ibid.*, XXII, 1936.

30. KLEIN, MELANIE. *Psychoanalysis of Children*, Hogarth, 1948.

31. LAMPL-DE GROOT, J. "The Pre-oedipal Phase in the Development of the Male Child," this annual, II, 1946.

32. LEWIN, B. D. "Claustrophobia," *Psa. Quar.*, IV, 1935.

33. LOEWENSTEIN, R. "Phallic Passivity in Man," *Internat. J. Psa.*, XVI, 1935.

34. MENNINGER, K. A. *Man Against Himself*, Harcourt, 1938.

35. RADO, SANDOR. Review of Anna Freud's *Einführung in die Technik der Kinderanalyse*, in *Zschr. f. Psa.*, XIV, 4, 1928.

36. SCHILDER, P. "The Relations between Clinging and Equilibrium," *Internat. J. Psa.*, XX, 1939.

Discussion of Berta Bornstein's
"The Analysis of a Phobic Child"

ANNE ALVAREZ, Ph.D.

Bornstein's paper is a true psychoanalytic study of a child, if ever there was one. The fine tracing and discussion of the technical detail, together with the clarity and exposition of the theoretical underpinning make it a truly deep and thorough study and a model for those of us doing this work and trying to understand what indeed we do and why. I should say that although I have read the writings of the (then) Hampstead Clinic's borderline workshop (Kut Rosenfeld and Sprince, 1965), I had not read this outstanding paper by Berta Bornstein, and I wish I had done so long ago.

I shall begin with some comments about psychoanalytic theory and then go on to discuss Bornstein's abundant and fascinating analyses of technique. I shall conclude with some observations on the child's psychopathology.

THEORETICAL QUESTIONS

ALTHOUGH THERE IS MUCH ATTENTION IN THE LARGE MIDDLE sections of the paper to the oedipal problems that beset this very disturbed and demanding young child, it was interesting to see the degree of space also given to the pre-oedipal issues. We are told early on in the paper that the mother of "Frankie" said that his infant crying had given her an uncanny and uneasy feeling, and that he himself found

Dr. Alvarez, Ph.D. and M.A.C.P, is a Consultant Child and Adolescent Psychotherapist (and retired Co-Convener of the Autism Service, Child and Family Department, Tavistock Clinic, London). She was Visiting Professor at the San Francisco Psychoanalytic Society in November 2005, and her latest book, *The Thinking Heart: Three Levels of Psychoanalytic Therapy with Disturbed Children* was published in April 2012 by Routledge.

The Psychoanalytic Study of the Child 68, ed. Claudia Lament, Robert A. King, Samuel Abrams, Paul M. Brinich, and Rona Knight (Yale University Press, copyright © 2015 by Claudia Lament, Robert A. King, Samuel Abrams, Paul M. Brinich, and Rona Knight).

it very hard to wait between feeds, until their frequency was increased. Then, at five months of age he again began to scream with what seems to have been desperation and outrage when the 2:00 A.M. feed was cut. He became a very demanding and difficult little child, turning to his nurse away from his mother. Bornstein points out (p. 188 [104–105]) that Frankie had been defending himself against great sadness, and that behind this lay a great longing for his mother's love. So the oedipal problems that are described later are definitely seen to be accompanied by an earlier problem in Frankie's relationship with his mother, referred to as his "primal trauma" (p. 217 [135]).

Both levels of Frankie's difficulty are described in fine and telling detail. However, what struck me, and might also strike other modern readers not necessarily of a post-Kleinian persuasion like my own, is the lack of integration of the two levels in—and into—the clinical observations. That is, I would expect that nowadays we might be more likely to view the oedipal issues, even the more perverse elements, as being colored and infused by earlier pre-oedipal problems, not in addition to them but *within* them. For example, we are told that Frankie turned to his nurse, partly to punish his mother for having another baby, but also possibly to punish her for not loving him enough from the beginning of his life. Yet this is not referred to as a possible element in his rage in the clinical material. (I wondered, indeed, whether his mother might have been frightened of him—"uncanny" is a strong word to use about a little baby—and whether such possible fear may have contributed to her weakness with him and avoidance of him, which we hear more about later but which may have been there from the start.) In any case, the question could arise concerning the nature of the child's early internal objects. Was there something missing in his internal maternal holding object (Winnicott, 1960)? (See the issue of a deficit in internal objects in Alvarez, 2012.)

To continue with the discussion of integration of the oedipal and pre-oedipal levels: there is much discussion of Frankie's passivity and the masochistic sexuality which accompanied it (it certainly had the flavor of something that could have gone on to some sort of perversion, or at least homosexuality, as Bornstein suggests), but I wondered if a further element in the passivity may have been his genuine infantile need to be carried more. Babies have normal developmental needs to be passive some of the time, that is to be held and rocked and soothed, and we can wonder whether his mother's uncanny feelings interfered with a tender and more confident holding of him. One patient of mine who had been raised in an Eastern European orphanage loved the idea of breakfast in bed—which is of course what every feeding young infant with an actual mother caring for him or her gets. In such orphanages bottles tend to get propped up against cushions and holding and rocking is at a minimum. I also wondered whether the dream of the wild elevator man might have carried some elements, not only of the oedipal situation of father's bouncing of mother into the air, as Bornstein suggests, but perhaps of his play with his own baby son too, which might have been a bit more exciting than an oversensitive baby could take. (See Winnicott on holding and the fear of falling, 1960, and Tustin, 1986).

A tiny, picky complaint, which is easy to make after the years of work with autistic and psychotic patients (see Tustin and Winnicott, as above), but I think nowadays we would not assume "down" really stood for "up," or tears for urine. Terror and despair are emotions taken more seriously in their own right now that those human needs that go beyond the sexual have received so much attention in the literature.

A final theoretical point, concerning the psychoanalytic theory of defense. We owe to Anna Freud the emphasis on the respect for defenses, to Kohut and the intersubjectivists the concept of pre-stages of defense, and to Bornstein herself for mentioning the protective element in Frankie's defenses (Freud, 1936; Kohut 1977; Stolorow and Lachmann, 1980). I would like to amplify this point by suggesting that an element in a defense may be not only denial, or wishful longing that things be otherwise, but an expression of a desire that things could be or might be different, or it may be an expression of a rightful need (not a wish) that this is how things should be or should have been (Alvarez 1992, 2012). I will come on, in the section on technique, to Bornstein's extremely sensitive respect for Frankie's need for defenses, but just one caveat. On p. 214 [131] she interprets Frankie's strength as a defense against his passive desires, and I found myself objecting that the defense could be seen as not only defensive, but as containing a rightful *need* for strength and safety. Yet a few pages later, on p. 219 [137], she says Frankie realized that his megalomaniacal behavior was not just a defense against passive strivings but also a protection against suffering and death. So my objection is mostly answered, with the proviso that we need to interpret not only what the defense is a protection against but what it manages, however imperfectly, to achieve. This is a question of technical balance, whether we stress the strength aspect or the fear and weakness it protects against, and the balance may need to shift from moment to moment. This can save the child's dignity and spare him humiliation. Then we can help him to find, with the help of his objects, different and better ways of feeling safe and strong.

TECHNICAL ISSUES

I was a bit in doubt over the way the pre-analytic scheme was described. Probably few child psychotherapists would agree now with the assertion (p. 184 [101]) that "no treatment can proceed without insight into the need for help." The patient population that we are seeing nowadays in the National Health Service in the United Kingdom especially is full of conduct-disordered children who think the world needs to change, not them; neglected children who can barely conceive of a thing called help; and borderline children with weak egos and concrete thinking who hardly know what an insight would be. Yet they come, first only perhaps by being brought reluctantly, then begin to use the treatment and often develop real and deep attachments to their therapists and to the clinic. The point when they develop the insight that they need may occur only near the end of treatment. I also thought the way in which Bornstein facilitated the positive transference by "persuading" the school to let mother stay on longer was unfortunate, in that she might have done the same thing in a less seductive and more honest way, that is, because she genuinely thought the child wasn't ready to separate yet.

Another point: In the past, I would probably have taken the classical Kleinian view like Max in Sendak's story *Where the Wild Things Are* (Sendak, 2000), who says, "Let the wild rumpus start!"—that is, "Let the patient and therapist face the negative transferences from the start" (Klein, 1945). Now, however, with the damaged children we are seeing, I think Kleinian-trained child psychotherapists are more delicate and tactful and less confrontational at the beginning, too. So it is a process of easing in, but perhaps we do not acknowledge it or conceptualize as have our Anna Freudian colleagues (Hurry, 1998).

Bornstein provides a masterly outline of a choice of technical approaches that could have been taken in relation to Frankie's aggression toward his mother and baby sister as revealed in his play in the first session (p. 186 [102–103]). In the first option, Bornstein says "we might be tempted to interpret to the boy the various motivations for his aggression against his mother and the newborn baby—that is, his vengeful feelings, his desire to take his mother's place, and his original sadistic intentions to kill her, as suggested by Klein" (1945). Bornstein suggests that such a brusque forcing of the child to face unconscious impulses would result either in a quick suppression of the phobic symptom (fear of separation from his mother) or in the strengthening of the phobia and of the resistance. I would have preferred the word "could" to "would," as it is not easy to calibrate our assessment of the level of ego capacity in our patients at any given moment. However, I agree that the risk would be great—the risk, that is, of overwhelming a child with a discovery of actual impulses toward his real mother. A modern object-relations-trained therapist might prefer to work either in the transitional area (Winnicott, 1953), by talking about the figure of the boy in the play only and of the figure's power and aggression, or she might try to find a deft, tactful, and not too heavy way of mentioning the negative transference, in terms of his irritation about having to come to this lady. Either of these routes would take the pressure off the idea of actual murderousness toward his actual mother.

By contrast, Bornstein suggests that we might refrain from interpretation and just participate in the play, thus fostering catharsis of the child's hostility. But, she points out, this could leave the conflict between ego and id untouched. I would like to suggest that there is a middle way between explanatory interpretations and "just play" (Joseph, 1998), a way that I have termed the use of descriptive or amplifying comments (Alvarez, 2010, 2012). These comments refer to the "whatness" of experience, rather than the whyness, and can help to add meaning to behavior or experience, one slow step at a time. As the meanings begin to expand around the single thoughts or experiences, the ripples, as it were, can begin to spread to other thoughts, and connections can begin to be made. This can gradually build up the child's thinking capacity toward the more two-part "why-because" interpretations outlined in Bornstein's first choice. These latter can be given to a child with a stronger ego and a good symbolic capacity. This is not far from the choice finally taken by Bornstein on page 187 [104], although she spoke to the sadness, not the aggression of the little boy figure in the play. I felt, however, that we might also explore his insistence on being the boss and how much he liked that feeling. As another alternative, Bornstein discusses appealing to the child's ego and rationality but dismisses this as leading to scotomization. I am sure she is right. She also suggests that the analyst might criticize the child trying to strengthen his superego, and this would (could?) overpower his ego.

In her fifth and final choice, Bornstein chooses to discuss the little figure's sadness with some sympathy, and this has an important effect on Frankie. She suggests that Frankie was aware of neither the sadness nor of his unrewarded and repressed longing for his mother, thus making him aware of this too directly might have caused his ego to be "pushed into a course beyond its integrative power." It is interesting that what she said involved a sort of uncovering interpretation, yet, via the figure of the doll, Frankie was able to accept it. I would only add, as I said earlier, that working via the doll might have offered, in addition, a way of approaching the aggression together with the nature of the mother-figures toward whom it was directed. It might be interesting to see if he could have described what it was about these figures that made them deserve death. In other words, we might also be better able to approach the more paranoid-schizoid elements in relation to a bad internal object. People often find it easier to talk about their aggression via a two-person psychology in which the object takes the blame! However, Frankie was able to respond to her sensitive reference to sadness, and this is a tribute to both of them.

On p. 192 [113], it was fascinating to see the value of Bornstein's use of humor when approaching Frankie's fear of castration by the wolves. In addition, her observations (p. 197 [114]) are brilliant and a lesson to us all on the prematurity of her attempts to introduce a good object into the cruel electrician material. She felt that his annoyance at her attempt suggested he still needed to process his trauma and also his masochistic excitement. On p. 198 [115] she raises the interesting and complex issue of whether our continuing to play the game and not challenge would involve a collusion with sadomasochism. This is an endlessly difficult issue, and we walk a tightrope with such cases. She is concerned that too direct an interpretation of the masochistic pleasure can kill the play altogether. Indeed, Betty Joseph makes a similar point in discussing masochism (Joseph, 1982), where she says in her conclusion how difficult it is for the patient to give up his high excitements for the ordinary sober pleasures of everyday life. I agree, but I think we need to introduce to our patients the idea of a third option between excitement and sobriety—that is, the idea of a different kind of excitement. Not all excitements are perverse or over the top. The child's play could be more constructive but still exciting. We have to monitor the range but also the type of excitement the child is feeling during his play, and we sometimes need a slightly firmer technique to help him or her calm down, as mothers do with toddlers hurtling too close to a glass coffee table, for instance, when they say "now calm down; there'll be tears before bedtime if you don't"; or when a perverse child gets into a frenzy, we must not be too strict and rejecting, but still firm enough to de-escalate things somewhat.

DIAGNOSTIC ISSUES AND CONCLUSION

On many occasions, Bornstein refers to her patient as a neurotic or phobic boy. Yet she also describes a very impatient, demanding, and indulged boy. I suppose nowadays we might outline some elements of budding character disorder, or to use a more modern term, "personality disorder," which accompanied the neurotic fears. On p. 220 [138], Bornstein says that when he entered therapy, he was completely enslaved by his symptoms, had a constricted ego, lacked external ideals and internal prohibitions. In those days, of course, both in psychoanalytic circles and in child psychiatry, it would be seen to be wrong to give a child a diagnosis of personality disorder because it would seem to be damning a child. Now, however, we therapists have had to learn to be mindful of the difference between a purely defensive process and one that has solidified into something addictive or even perverse. Child psychiatrists are now interested in differentiating different types of conduct disorders and in following their trajectories to adulthood (Viding, 2004). We need different techniques when we realize, for example, that a child has moved on to a stage of *liking* to hurt people, not just needing to hurt in order to project his own victimhood. And as Bornstein points out throughout this paper, where the ego would be overwhelmed, we need to go much more slowly in revealing indigestible truths.

What about those children with weak superegos? Frankie was helped to give up his grandiose fantasies, his contempt for authority figures, and to develop real respect and admiration for figures who were both good and strong. This involved a huge development in his personality, a development encouraged with much tact, wisdom, and firmness on the part of an apparently outstanding clinician and psychoanalytic thinker.

REFERENCES

Alvarez, A. (1992). *Live Company: Psychoanalytic Psychotherapy with Autistic, Borderline, Deprived and Abused Children*. London and New York: Routledge.

———. (2010). Levels of analytic work and levels of pathology: The work of calibration. *International Journal of Psychoanalysis* 91, no. 4: 859–878.

———. (2012). *The Thinking Heart: Three Levels of Psychoanalytic Therapy with Disturbed Children*. Hove, East Sussex, UK: Routledge.

Bornstein, B. (1949). The Analysis of a Phobic Child: Some Problems of Theory and Technique in Child Analysis. *Psychoanalytic Study of the Child* 3:181–226 (also in this volume).

Freud, A. (1936). *The Ego and the Mechanisms of Defence*. London: Hogarth (1986).

Hurry, A., ed. (1998). *Psychoanalysis and Developmental Therapy*. London: Karnac.

Joseph, B. (1982). "Addiction to near death." In E. B. Spillius and M. Feldman, eds. (1989), *Psychic Equilibrium and Psychic Change: Selected Papers of Betty Joseph*. London: Routledge.

_____. (1998). Thinking about a playroom. *Journal of Child Psychotherapy* 24, no. 3: 359–366.

KLEIN, M. (1932). "The psycho-analysis of children." In *The Writings of Melanie Klein*. Vol. 2. London: Hogarth (1975).

_____. (1945). "The Oedipus Complex in the light of early anxieties." In *The Writings of Melanie Klein*. Vol. 1: *Love, Guilt and Reparation and Other Works*. London: Hogarth (1975).

KOHUT, H. (1977). *The Restoration of the Self*. New York: International Universities Press.

KUT ROSENFELD, S., AND SPRINCE, M. (1965). Some thoughts on the technical handling of borderline children. *Psychoanalytic Study of the Child* 20: 495–517.

SENDAK, M. (2000). *Where the Wild Things Are*. London: Red Fox / Random House.

STOLOROW, R. D., AND LACHMANN, F. M. (1980). *The Psychoanalysis of Developmental Arrests*, Madison, CT: International Universities Press.

TUSTIN, F. (1986). "Falling." Chapter 11 (pp. 183–196) in *Autistic Barriers in Neurotic Patients*. London: Karnac.

VIDING, E. (2004). Annotation: understanding the development of psychopathy. *Journal of Child Psychology and Psychiatry* 45, no. 8: 1329–1337.

WINNICOTT, D. W. (1953). Transitional objects and transitional phenomena: A study of the first not-me possession. *International Journal of Psychoanalysis* 34:89–97.

_____. (1960). "The theory of the parent-infant relationship." In *The Maturational Processes and the Facilitating Environment*. London: Hogarth.

_____. (1962). "Ego integration in child development." In *The Maturational Processes and the Facilitating Environment*. London: Hogarth.

Berta Bornstein's "Frankie"

The Contemporary Relevance of a Classic to the Treatment of Children with Disruptive Symptoms

LEON HOFFMAN, M.D.

In this paper the lasting effect of the work of Berta Bornstein is described, particularly the technique of interpreting defenses against unpleasant emotions when beginning an analysis with a young child. This technique is illustrated in the analysis of the patient she called "Frankie" (1949). Although her work is rarely cited (perhaps because she did not publish widely as a result of the dominance of the oral tradition at the New York Psychoanalytic Society and Institute), her work remains central for child psychoanalysis and psychodynamic psychotherapy, with the evolution of the experience-near technique of interpreting defenses against unpleasant emotions. The applicability of Bornstein's ideas to contemporary ideas about affect regulation and the treatment of disruptive children is discussed.

Leon Hoffman is Director, Pacella Parent Child Center; Co-Director, Research Center; and Training and Supervising Analyst (Child, Adolescent, Adult Analysis) at the New York Psychoanalytic Society and Institute.

Some ideas in this paper were (1) presented by Leon Hoffman and Ruth Karush at the Classic Paper Series: On "Clinical Notes on Child Analysis" by Berta Bornstein (1945), at the New York Psychoanalytic Society and Institute, November 20, 2010; and (2) will be expanded in Hoffman, L. and Rice, T. with Prout, T. (In Press). *Regulation-Focused Psychotherapy for Children with Externalizing Behaviors* (RFP-C) (Routledge).

The Psychoanalytic Study of the Child 68, ed. Claudia Lament, Robert A. King, Samuel Abrams, Paul M. Brinich, and Rona Knight (Yale University Press, copyright © 2015 by Claudia Lament, Robert A. King, Samuel Abrams, Paul M. Brinich, and Rona Knight).

INTRODUCTION

PETER FONAGY, MARY TARGET, AND THEIR COLLEAGUES (SEE, FOR example, Bateman and Fonagy, 2011), D. W. Winnicott (1953, for example), as well as Robert Emde (1999, 2000), Stanley Greenspan (Greenspan and Shanker, 2004) and their colleagues, among others, are well known to the mental health professional field because they utilize the findings of developmental and cognitive psychology to further the development of psychodynamic theory and psychodynamic technique. This paper addresses the lack of attention given to the work of so-called classical child and adolescent psychoanalysts,[1] dating back to Berta Bornstein (1945, 1949, 1951) and Anny Katan (1961). These two psychoanalysts, though their names are no longer on the tongues of most contemporary mental health clinicians, provide us with seminal still-relevant contributions demonstrating the centrality of verbalization of emotions and the understanding that all patients, particularly children, automatically avoid (that is, unconsciously defend against) the conscious experience of painful emotions.

In a pithy communication, Katan (1961) describes how a child verbalizes his/her perceptions of the outer world before he/she can verbalize feelings. Katan stresses that verbalization of feelings by the child leads to greater control and mastery and that verbalization helps the child distinguish between what is fantasy and what is real. These functions promote a greater sense of integration in the child. Katan makes a crucial point: "Children whose acting upon their feelings predominates over verbalizing their feelings can in this way establish a pattern which predisposes them to become 'actors out' in later life" (p. 186n). In other words, in modern parlance, we would say that children, who have difficulties consciously experiencing their painful emotions and putting those emotions into words, have emotional regulation difficulties and may develop a tendency to develop behavioral symptoms, Oppositional Defiant Disorder, or other Disruptive Disorders.

Half a century later, affective neuroscience has begun to demonstrate the prescience of Katan's observation. In a functional magnetic resonance imaging (fMRI) paradigm, the labeling of negatively valenced emotive faces with affect-congruent words has been demon-

---

1. To look at one data point: Bornstein (1945) is cited 36 times in the PEP database, and her 1949 paper, 69 times; Anny Katan (1961), 124 times; Winnicott (1953), 595 times (the most popular author on PEP). More recent discussions of children include Fonagy and Target (1996b), which is cited 216 times (retrieved August 8, 2013).

strated to reduce neurophysiological correlates of emotional distress, including amygdalar and limbic region activation (Lieberman, et al., 2007). As the affective neurosciences become increasingly interested in exploring implicit mechanisms of emotion regulation processes (Etkin, 2011), the contemporary importance of elaborating the historical roots of such processes in child and adolescent psychoanalysis is clear.

Historical Development of the Technique of Interpretation of Defenses against Unwelcome Affects

In the 1920s, Anna Freud (1926a) observed that children generally did not develop a transference neurosis. Melanie Klein (1927) maintained that this failure to demonstrate a transference neurosis was a result of the preparatory phase (where the analyst acted in an exaggeratedly benign and giving way). Anna Freud (1945) argued that "even if one part of the child's neurosis is transformed into a transference neurosis as it happens in adult analysis, another part of the child's neurotic behavior remains grouped around the parents who are the original objects of his pathogenic past" (p. 130). In contrast to Anna Freud's attention to the parent's role in the child's life, Klein (1927) espoused the idea that in analytic work with children, the analyst should not be concerned with the child's relationship to the outside world, and that reality issues and work with the parents were unnecessary and corrupting factors in a child's analysis because they interfered with the development of a transference neurosis.[2]

Anna Freud (1926b) continued to stress that, as superego and auxiliary ego figures for the child, parents were crucial to the child's life and therefore were needed to maintain the treatment. She recommended that the analyst needed to form an alliance with the child so the child could trust the analyst, as well as with the parents, in order to help them support the analysis both emotionally and realistically.

One resolution to the conflicting approaches between the Kleinian view and the Anna Freudian view was accomplished with the development of defense analysis with children. This technique may be an unacknowledged forerunner of Paul Gray's (2005) conceptualizations about the lag in the utilization of defense analysis with adults (Hoffman, 2000).

---

2. Tyson, P. (1978) illustrates the difficulties involved in sorting out transference manifestations in very young children.

Anna Freud (1966) explained, "So far as we were concerned, we explored above all the alterations in the classical technique as they seemed to us necessitated by the child's inability to use free association, by the immaturity of his ego, the dependency of his superego, and by his resultant incapacity to deal unaided with pressures from the id. We were impressed by the strength of the child's defenses and resistances and by the difficulty of interpreting transference, the impurity of which we ascribed to the use of a nonanalytic introductory period. This latter difficulty was removed later by Berta Bornstein's ingenious use of defense interpretation for creating a treatment alliance with the child patient."[3]

BERTA BORNSTEIN

In her classic 1945 paper, Berta Bornstein clearly and succinctly introduced the technical approach to helping children, particularly children who do not or cannot directly express their painful emotions. Bornstein described in great detail the technique of interpreting defenses against painful feelings in children. By clinical example, she demonstrated how this can be done without inflicting painful narcissistic injury on patients.[4] By addressing the child's defenses against painful emotions instead of directly confronting the child's unwelcome thoughts and fantasies, the therapist can connect with the child in a much more sensitive and, thus, effective way. Bornstein's ideas form the basis of the contemporary approach to addressing a patient's defenses.

Berta Bornstein stands out as a major contributor to the evolution of technique in child analysis and psychodynamic psychotherapy. Her work spanned two major phases in the early years of child analysis. The first phase occurred in the 1920s when Anna Freud (1926b) enumerated the major elements of child analysis: the development of the child's insight into his illness, the uses of play, the limitations of the transference, and the work with the parents. The focus of analytic thinking gradually changed to the structural point of view (addressing the balances among the Id, Ego, and Superego) (S. Freud, 1923; Miller,

---

3. A detailed historical account of the development of Bornstein's work can be found in Keable (2011).

4. Interestingly, the first child analyst to stress the importance of avoiding narcissistic injuries in children was Hermine Hug-Hellmuth. Her existence was practically effaced by the Vienna psychoanalytic community, likely as a result of the shame involved when she was murdered by her nephew, Rolf. She began her work with children well before Anna Freud and Melanie Klein (Hoffman, 1995).

1996) and to understanding that many functions of the ego, such as defenses, are out of the person's awareness. Anna Freud (1936) described and discussed a variety of defense mechanisms in the classic *Ego and the Mechanisms of Defense*. She later expanded and elucidated these ideas in her discussions with Joseph Sandler and others (Sandler and Freud, 1985).

The structural theory should actually be called the dynamic theory. Addressing the child's psychodynamics changed the focus of analytic technique. Rather than focusing on trying to quickly unearth the patient's unconscious fantasies (which often required a great deal of speculation on the part of the analyst), the analyst's major focus, at least in the early part of treatment, was not on trying to decipher the patient's unconscious wishes, but rather trying to understand how the patient utilized, unconsciously, a variety of defense mechanisms to protect him or herself against painful and conflicted feelings and wishes.

Unfortunately, too many nonanalytic clinicians and nonclinicians and even analysts, when they think of "Freudian" psychoanalysis or classical psychoanalysis, imagine a practitioner whose aim is to penetrate the patient's unconscious and immediately interpret in a symbolic way, "what the person was thinking."[5] In fact, such a technique can be called "wild analysis." This erroneous fantasy about an analyst's practice, rightly, stimulates a great deal of fear and anxiety about analysts, who are perceived as either mind readers or charlatans, leading to an avoidance of analysts.

It is striking how so many psychoanalysts and psychotherapists are unaware of the concept and technique of a defense-focused psychotherapy with children, and the basic analytic technique of analysis of defense against painful affects. Arietta Slade (1994), for example, provides an example of the counter-therapeutic value of a direct "id or content interpretation" (p. 102). She discusses how play with the child should be allowed to unfold without needing to prematurely decode the "meaning" of the play. Slade addresses the importance of integrating the child's affect in the play (p. 92). Yet she does not address the value of addressing the child's defenses against affects. This equation of classical technique with automatic "decoding" by the psychoanalyst is a common misunderstanding that may have contributed to the idea that "classical" analysts utilize an experience-distant technique in contrast to other contemporary analysts.

5. For example, Mitchell (1998) states that "traditional classical interpretations were regarded purely in semiotic terms, as a decoding, a translation of the manifest meanings of the patient's associations into latent unconscious meanings" (p. 839).

Studying Bornstein's work can help elucidate the careful, experience-near technique of "defense analysis" and the analyst's respectful approach to a patient.

BERTA BORNSTEIN'S ANALYTIC DEVELOPMENT

Berta Bornstein began her training in 1925 in Berlin. She would discuss technical problems with Anna Freud when the latter would come with her father to stay at Simmel's Tegel Castle sanitarium in Berlin. And in 1929, Bornstein went to Vienna. Anna Freud recognized her gifts as an analyst long before Berta Bornstein emigrated from Vienna to New York in 1938. Her publications that appeared between 1930 and 1936 showed insight into the key to the treatment of a child, which is the child's need to be understood according to the level of his ego development.

After World War II, child analysis flourished in London, where Anna Freud developed the Hampstead Clinic, later renamed the Anna Freud Centre. Child psychoanalysis blossomed in New York under the leadership of Berta Bornstein. It was at the Anna Freud Centre that Fonagy and Target (1994 and 1996a) conducted their retrospective study of 763 cases from the Anna Freud Centre, finding that the usual weekly psychotherapy sessions for disruptive children was ineffective or even damaging. That study can be credited with the beginning of our contemporary focus of the systematic evaluation of psychodynamic treatments of children and adolescents.

Berta Bornstein's first major discussion of how to address a child's defenses appeared in 1945 and is modestly titled "Clinical Notes on Child Analysis." As is seen in that paper, Bornstein had a talent for transmuting potential painful statements into those that stirred a child to reflect rather than to defensively retreat. In 1949 she published a long description of the treatment of "Frankie," in which she explicated her approach to defense analysis and why interpretation of affect should be the initial approach to the child. (Below I will discuss the beginning of the analysis with Frankie in detail, addressing its relevance to contemporary treatment dilemmas.)

Bornstein's lectures, her supervisory work, her papers, and her personal communications illustrate her uncommon facility to see the world through the senses of the child. Her work stands alone, with the exception of Anna Freud, in the exposition of technical methods of child analysis. Yet despite her emphasis on work with children, much of Berta Bornstein's teaching also is applicable to adults because the analysis of a neurotic adult addresses the arrested elements in his or her personality. Child analysis for Berta Bornstein always included analysis of defense and conflict, of resistance, and of transference reactions. "She became a Special Member of the New York Psychoanalytic Society, a Faculty Member of the New York Psychoanalytic Institute, a training and supervising analyst, an Honorary Member of the American Psychoanalytic Association, and a Member-at-Large of the International Psycho-Analytical Association"[6] (Blos, 1974, p. 37). She was the leader of child psychoanalysis at the New York Psychoanalytic Institute and remains influential to this day (Keable, 2011).

Becker (1974), Feigelson (1974), and Kabcenell (1974) (all of whom had direct experience with Bornstein at NYPSI) describe Bornstein's exquisite sensitivity to children and their developmental needs. As Feigelson (1974) states, this sensitivity was communicated in her teachings about the importance of play in child analysis. He notes: "Her rules for the understanding of play were:

> 1. Every element in the play has a meaning which is over-determined.
> 2. Every *repetitive* play contains an unconscious conflict related to the child's symptom.
> 3. Repetitive play frequently contains a symbolic expression either of masturbatory activity or of the fantasy connected with it.
> 4. The content of repetitive play often reflects a particular traumatic experience.
> 5. Repetitive play which contains more impulsive characteristics seems to indicate that a past reality experience (not just a fantasy) prior to the development of verbalization is being expressed." (p. 22)

Berta Bornstein died just before her seventy-second birthday in 1971 while vacationing at her beloved summer home on the island of Vinalhaven in Maine. She was still actively engaged in her work (Blos, 1974). Anna Freud referred to Berta Bornstein as one of the decisive contributors to child analytic technique and acknowledged that "The introductory phase was dropped when Berta Bornstein developed the analysis of the defenses."

It is interesting to note Ted Becker's (1974) comment about Bornstein, that, "Although in some of her case reports Berta Bornstein clearly described how she analyzed latency children in the initial phase of their treatment, she herself never drew attention to the fact that she had introduced a modification of the technique of child analysis; namely, the analysis of defense against affects before analysis of defense against

---

6. The designation of Berta Bornstein as a Member-at-Large by the IPA is notable in that it provided official honorific recognition of the global importance of her work (Tyson, R. L., personal communication, August 23, 2013).

drives. It remained for others to underscore this important modification" (p. 5).

Bornstein's central contribution allowed analysts and psychodynamic psychotherapists to develop and continue to refine an *experience-near technique,* in which the analyst does not have to impose her or his guesses of the child's unconscious wishes. This effective technique, then, became easily transportable to all psychodynamic psychotherapists.

Berta Bornstein (1945, 1949) spelled out the technique of defense analysis in children in papers that are still clinically and theoretically applicable yet rarely referenced. The development of the technique of defense interpretation with children (whether the child participates in analysis or psychodynamic psychotherapy) allows the analyst or therapist to observe, understand, and appreciate the power of affects and the value of the defenses to the child and to point out (interpret) the defenses against unwelcome affects[7] (Becker, 1974). In her treatment of Frankie, Bornstein (1949) describes how she helped Frankie cope with his unwelcome, unpleasant emotions.

"FRANKIE"

Bornstein's careful clinical description of Frankie's initial presentation provides us with a textbook-like description of:

1. how to begin any dynamic treatment with a young child;
2. how to proceed sequentially in the beginning of an analytic treatment.

Section I covers the first year of analysis, and section II covers the next phase. Section III discusses the analysis of Frankie's retention of urine and his elevator phobia, without regard to the sequence of the occurrence of the material, and in section IV, Bornstein discusses his behavior pattern, including his severe out-of-control behavior. In fact, many of Frankie's behavioral disturbances would be categorized today as one or other version of Disruptive Disorders.

In this discussion I focus on the beginning of the analysis, which eventually led to the resolution of Frankie's school phobia and allowed further analytic work. I will discuss the opening phase in detail and discuss two interventions toward the end of the first year.

---

7. Bertram Ruttenberg from Philadelphia reported that during supervision with Bornstein, when a supervisee would say what he thought during a session, she would say, *"No, but what did you feel?"* (personal communication, October 14, 2005). See discussion in footnote 10 in this paper.

OPENING PHASE

The opening phase is the locus of Bornstein's original contribution, without which the subsequent analytic work could not have been accomplished. I will describe one paradox that is evident from a close reading of the text of the case. On the one hand, as already noted, many authors, including Anna Freud, credit Bornstein with the introduction of the technique of interpreting defenses against affects (see Hoffman, 2007). On the other hand, it is difficult to extract from Bornstein's written material the actual technique she utilized when interpreting the defenses against affects. The culture at NYPSI has always been clinical, with students learning from their analysts, supervisors, and teachers rather than from published papers. Thus, in the latter part of the twentieth century, there were very few publications by many of the significant teachers at NYPSI, especially child analysts. Instead, the oral tradition flourished so that Bornstein's teaching was transmitted to Ted Becker, who had been her analysand and then her student and colleague; Becker transmitted the knowledge to subsequent generations of analysts at NYPSI (Cohen, 2002; Keable, 2011). Clearly, the oral tradition was more important than written documents for those who were directly or indirectly influenced by Bornstein. Unfortunately, relying on the oral tradition to transmit knowledge from one generation of analysts to another has obvious limitations because of the inherent difficulties in its applicability to the education of a broader audience.[8]

BERTA BORNSTEIN'S INTRODUCTION TO THE TREATMENT: LESSONS FOR CONTEMPORARY MENTAL HEALTH CLINICIANS

Frankie was 5½ years old, experiencing a school phobia when he entered treatment. "He became panic-stricken if his mother or nurse were out of sight. Even when left with his father in his own home, he was occasionally overwhelmed by attacks of anxiety. His phobic symptom had existed for more than 2 years" (Bornstein, 1949, p. 181 [99]). Frankie's

---

8. In the tripartite educational model, one's own personal treatment and supervision of psychotherapy and psychoanalysis by one's senior colleagues are the most important aspects of a psychotherapist's and psychoanalyst's education. Teaching the nuances of treatment techniques, which are communicated in those intimate settings (consciously and unconsciously, verbally and nonverbally) cannot be matched by the written word of even master clinicians (see discussions about learning from Paul Gray in person in contrast to his writings) (Phillips, 2006, and Sonnenberg, 2013). It is beyond the scope of this paper to discuss the ramifications of this aspect of education for the development of the field. See footnote 9 in this paper as one example of the oral tradition.

sister was born when he was 3 years and 3 months, and the first peak of his anxiety occurred "when he was brought to nursery school at the age of 3 years and 9 months" (p. 183 [100]). As a result of severe anxiety and fear manifested by wild, out-of-control behavior, he could remain in school for only two days. A second unsuccessful attempt to go to school (lasting only two weeks in the class) occurred when he was 4½, and during a third attempt at school attendance, the school recommended psychoanalysis.

This presenting clinical picture is not unusual to those who work with young preschool children, though the intensity of the symptoms may be greater than ordinarily seen. It is important to note, however, that Frankie exhibited symptoms prior to his sister's birth. For example, Bornstein notes: "The delivery was normal, the child healthy, yet the very first moment she held the baby in her arms, she [mother] had felt estranged from him. The little boy's crying had given her an uncanny and uneasy feeling. She felt quite different toward her second child, a girl" (p. 182 [99]).

Bornstein conjectures that the mother's rejection of Frankie was a result of her unconscious revenge on her older brother, who had been preferred by her own mother. In today's vocabulary one can posit that there was an early attachment difficulty in the child activated by the mother (and in fact, she did abrogate a great deal of the child care to a baby nurse but did improve as a result of the child's analysis). However, one also needs to consider the possibility that Frankie was born with some neurophysiological sensitivity that interfered with his attachment behavior to mother and increased his sensitivity to adverse stimuli. Not every child with a rejecting mother develops severe symptoms. Bornstein notes that "Frankie's first disturbance, his constant screaming and crying as an infant, were incomprehensible to the mother" (p. 182 [99]). It is plausible to imagine that a child with a more adaptable temperament, for example, would have needed less soothing than Frankie obviously required and that his mother could not provide without professional intervention.

I stress this possibility because in our contemporary culture, children will usually come to psychoanalysis or intensive psychodynamic psychotherapy if shorter-term treatments have failed to work. And, as we have learned from Fonagy and Target's (1996a) retrospective review, the more severe a child's behavioral disturbance, the greater treatment-intensity is required. It is reasonable to conjecture that many of these more-disturbed children have some kind of temperament or neurophysiologic sensitivity and have parental figures that cannot provide the increased soothing they require as infants and may not be cognizant of the value of an early intervention.

Clearly, at 5½, Frankie is one of those children for whom psychoanalysis is indicated. Appreciating that the child's maladaptive behavior is a result of a dyadic problem (or perhaps even a family issue) is not only scientifically more accurate but allows the analyst to approach the parent in such a way as to not increase the guilt of the parents, who already likely feel solely responsible for their children's problems.

In the beginning of the analysis, Bornstein describes Frankie's play. In the play . . .

> a lonely boy of 4 was seated all by himself, on a chair placed in an elevated position. The child's father was upstairs visiting "a lady" who, he informed us, when questioned, "is sick or maybe she's got a baby, maybe—I don't know, never mind." He made the point that newborn babies and mothers were separated in this hospital. Casting himself in the roles of a doctor and a nurse, he attended to the babies in a loving way, fed and cleaned them. However, toward the end of the play, a fire broke out. All the babies were burnt to death and the boy in the lobby was also in danger. He wanted to run home, but remembered that nobody would be there. Subsequently he joined the fire department, but it was not quite clear as to whether the firemen had started the fire or put it out. Frankie announced: "Ladies, the babies are dead; maybe we can save you!" Actually only those lady patients who had no babies were rescued by him. The one whom he several times—by a slip of the tongue—had addressed as "Mommy," however, was killed in the fire." (Bornstein, 1949, pp. 184–185 [102])

Bornstein describes how this game was repeated for many weeks, and it was clear that Frankie lived in continual fear of retaliation because of his death wishes to his mother for her betrayal by having a newborn; he developed a phobia, having to stay near his mother all the time, to make sure that no harm would come to her, in other words to protect her and himself from his anger toward her.

As a good teacher addressing her students and as a good scientist weighing the value of various potential interventions, Bornstein describes four alternative ways of addressing the play: (a) interpreting possible motivation for his aggression; (b) allowing the child to play, enabling him to experience a catharsis, without the analyst commenting; (c) reassuring the child by generalizing the fears; or (d) appealing to the child's wish to be big. Her description of these various alternatives is so instructive that they bear repeating verbatim.[9]

9. In this section, one can imagine Bornstein's voice and appreciate the esteem of her work as a teacher and as an analyst by those who had direct contact with her.

1. We might be tempted to interpret to the boy the various motivations for his aggression against his mother and the newborn baby as: a. his revenge for her abandonment of him—an aggression which was close to his consciousness; b. the desire to take his mother's place, which was repressed and indicated only by the loving way in which he took care of the babies when playing doctor and nurse, and by his peacefully living with his father after his mother had been killed; c. his desire to kill his mother, which we might interpret, as Melanie Klein probably would, in terms of the child's original sadistic intentions to destroy the mother by disembowelment. (In the last period of his analysis these fantasies were openly expressed by the child.)

Bornstein notes that "This approach, in which the ego is brusquely forced to face unconscious impulses, would result either in a quick suppression of the phobic symptom or in the strengthening of the phobia and of the resistance. The suppression of the symptom would make the patient temporarily independent of further analysis, but his ego, still in jeopardy from this suppression, would not have won the freedom which is essential for sound development. The strengthening of the phobia might lead to a stage in which the analyst himself would become an object of the phobia, preventing the continuation of the analysis."

2. By our participation in the play, we might refrain from any interpretation and thus, or actively, encourage the child to express his hostility in further play actions. This catharsis might soon lead to a diminishing of his phobia. The cathartic approach would mean, in terms of the id, a temporary discharge of tensions, but would leave the conflict between ego and id untouched. This would correspond to the pre-analytic procedure which Freud described in 1895 before he introduced the theory of psychodynamics. A return to such therapeutic procedures is encountered not infrequently at present.
3. We might devaluate the conflict by reassuring the child that such conflicts are frequent, natural, and understandable. This would mean a consolation and encouragement for the ego but would tend to scotomize the conflict instead of analyzing it.
4. The therapist might take a criticizing attitude, by appealing to the child's desire to grow up and not to indulge in such infantile phobic mechanisms. This approach, also directed to the child's ego, would be an appeal to give in to superego and reality demands, and would amount to an overpowering of his ego. (p. 186)

"Any of these four ways might be applied, depending on the therapist's aims and personality. They all might lead to a quick disappearance of the symptom" (pp. 186–187 [104]).

In our contemporary climate how do we communicate to mental health professionals as well as to parents that a more intensive and lengthier technique is more valuable for a child with this constellation of symptoms, given the paucity of systematic follow-up data for child analysis and dynamic therapy? Certainly three of the interventions described by Bornstein would be instituted by parents or professionals with most children who exhibit the symptoms with which Frankie suffered: cathartic expression, reassurance and universalizing his problem, or condemning him for his "babyish" behavior. It is more difficult to imagine nonanalytic situations in which one would very quickly interpret the child's unconscious wishes to hurt his mother, thus, forcing him to face unbearable impulses of retaliating against the mother for bringing a rival into this world.

Bornstein is correct when she states that utilization of one or other of these various techniques may very well result in symptomatic relief, which after all is what parents want when their child is suffering, the way Frankie was. In fact, the contemporary popular cognitive and behavioral techniques utilize versions of catharsis, universalizing, and cognitively finding alternative, more adaptive ways to cope with anxiety-provoking states. Only when these techniques fail will the typical parent agree to a more intensive psychotherapeutic treatment.

BORNSTEIN CENTRAL CONTRIBUTION: DEFENSE AGAINST PAINFUL AFFECTS

Bornstein contrasted her technique with other techniques; and, in fact, her introduction to the technique of analytic exploration is a clinical gem. She says:

> In order to bring about an *ego change* we chose for interpretation from the different themes revealed in the child's play that element in which the patient represented his ego. It was evident to us that he himself was the lonely 4-year-old boy in the hospital game, although feelings of sadness and loneliness had not been mentioned by him in his play. On the contrary, in his game he demonstrated only the *defense against* loneliness and sadness [my stress].
>
> By placing the little boy's chair in an elevated position he had reversed the reality situation, presenting himself as omnipotent and successful. Thus he became a person who actually knew what went on in the hospital, who directed the events, and who had no reason whatever to feel excluded and unhappy. *The omnipotence, as well as the destruction of mother and infant, were used as defenses by which he denied the affect of sadness* [my stress]. (p. 187 [104])

How do we understand the concept of "ego change," and how is the analytic technique of addressing the child's defended-against painful affects more helpful in the long run than the techniques that attempt to quickly ameliorate the maladaptive symptoms? In other words, how is this analytic technique mutative?

A recent communication by Lotterman (2012)[10] provides us with the most cogent explication of what Bornstein, as well as other analysts, mean by the term "ego change." This description of how "ego change" occurs is a potential theoretical basis for the mutative mechanism of action when one recognizes and addresses defenses against painful affects.

Bornstein's first aim was to help the child become consciously aware of his sadness before addressing his conflicts and anxiety over his aggression. She notes that *"it is noteworthy that the uncovering of recent emotions is often extremely painful for the child, more painful than the direct interpretation of deep unconscious content, which is frequently easily accepted by children and taken as a permission to obtain instinctual gratification"* [my stress] (p. 188n. [105]).

Lotterman describes the importance of affect as a singularly important marker for effective psychoanalytic work. "How affect comes to light in the clinical setting is discussed, as well as how it and defenses against it can be worked with to deepen the psychoanalytic process" (p. 305). It is noteworthy that Lotterman does discuss the relative absence in the adult analytic literature of discussions about the utility of trying to understand the patient's affects and defenses against them (compare Hoffman's 2000 discussion of the pervasive exclusion of child analytic ideas from general analytic discourse).

Lotterman considers the *"ego* to refer to the operative aspects of the *I*—for example, its functions and defenses (including perception, reality testing, and so on). Its main task is to regulate the relationship between the drives and external reality. The ego in this respect is the central processing unit of the mind as a mental apparatus, and its functions are impersonal" (p. 311n.). From this perspective the term "ego change" refers to an increase in a person's abilities to regulate his or her responses to the ongoing pressures from within and without. These ideas are very similar to the neuropsychological construct of emotion regulation[11] (Gross, 2002, as one example). Lotterman succinctly states: "Emotions expedite adaptation" (p. 311).

10. Lotterman's (2012) work is an example of the disconnection between the work of adult psychoanalysts and that of child and adolescent analysts. In fact, Lotterman was not aware of Berta Bornstein's work (personal communication, September 6, 2012).

11. I am indebted to Timothy Rice, M.D., for his noting that defense mechanisms are, in essence, unconscious emotion-regulating mechanisms. In a recent paper, Gross (2013)

A child, like Frankie, who could not regulate his emotional responses, could hardly be expected to adapt to the various stressors of his inner life or to his environment. As Ritvo (1996) states: "the regulation and control of aggressive impulses is central to Frankie's difficulties" when he was a child (p. 375).[12]

Bornstein's genius lay in her ability to intuitively understand the importance of helping the child regulate his emotions, especially those painful emotions that he could not tolerate to experience consciously. One can only assume that as a result of her clinical experience and her clinical intuition, she understood, as Anny Katan (1961) came to describe later, that helping a child consciously experience painful emotions would lead to ego growth (or in the language of contemporary psychology, growth and development in the affective, cognitive, and social spheres).

Lotterman states that "the repression of affect is often less effective in protecting the ego than is the repression of ideas and fantasies" (p. 305) and, thus:

> The exercise of bearing painful affects also strengthens the ego's functioning and coherence. The ego is called upon to mobilize its strengths in order to tolerate the pain and anxiety of disturbing emotions, and as a result, the ego's mastery and confidence in its own power increase. The ego's ability to become conscious of pathogenic fantasies increases in parallel with an increase in the ability to tolerate shame, guilt, and anxiety. Parts of the self that have been disavowed because they are connected with unacceptable affects can now return to awareness and can resume functioning, restoring the lost vitality of self-experience. Earlier repression of these aspects of the self, deprived it of a sense of aliveness and spontaneity.
>
> And when an affect becomes bearable, emotions and fantasies are reconnected to the entire personality, reinforcing the experience of wholeness. In this process, painful, disavowed affects are mitigated by an awareness that these feelings do not define the entire personality. (p. 329)

From this contemporary perspective, Bornstein's choice of technique is remarkable. She did not interpret unconscious wishes—that is, aggression against mother (and baby); did not simply allow for catharsis; did not simply reassure the child; and did not promote superego injunc-

---

has noted for the first time in his published work the connection between defense mechanisms and affect-regulating mechanisms. These ideas have been expanded in Rice, T. R. and Hoffman, L. (2014). Defense Mechanisms and Implicit Emotion Regulation: A Comparison of a Psychodynamic Construct with One from Contemporary Neuroscience. *Journal of the American Psychoanalytic Association* 62(4):693–708.

12. Ritvo (1996, 2003) treated Frankie analytically post-college.

tions against his symptoms—that is, she did not attempt to make him feel ashamed, guilty, or humiliated. Rather, she focused on the child's defenses against his unbearable affects (sadness and loneliness).

In order to grow and develop and feel greater mastery and confidence in himself, the child needs to develop greater tolerance of unbearable affects. The introduction of the need to understand the child's current emotional state and then interpreting the child's defenses against such painful affects proved to be a nodal point in the evolution of child psychoanalytic technique and child psychodynamic technique. Bornstein notes:

> The warded-off affect is a barrier to a successful interpretation of the conflict and therefore must be made conscious before any further step can be taken, lest the ego be pushed into a course beyond its integrative power. Bringing an affect into consciousness furnishes an opportunity for the unraveling of both genetic and dynamic elements. The re-experiencing of the original affects provides the emotional ground for the subsequent interpretation of unconscious material and makes it possible for the child to deal with a conflict consciously. Our aim, of course, was to make him conscious of the fact that behind the sadness, aggression, and anxiety, there was an intense, unrewarded, and repressed longing for the mother. (pp. 187–188 [104–105])

Bornstein goes on to describe how she first addressed the theme of loneliness by talking about the sadness and loneliness of the child in Frankie's play.

> The analyst expressed sympathy for the lonely child who is barred from his mother's sickroom and who is too little to understand why his father is admitted. Frankie responded to the analyst's sympathy with growing sadness, which could be discerned only from his facial expression. The analyst's sympathy made it possible for him to tolerate this affect.
>
> Once he had been able to face his sadness, Frankie showed relatively little resistance when his specific situation was examined. We asked whether by any chance he was a child who had been left alone while his mother was in the hospital. Or had someone taken care of him during that difficult period? He turned to his mother with the question: "Was I alone, Mommy?" and before she could answer, he told about his father and his nurse's presence, adding that his nurse would "never, never leave him alone."
>
> By taking advantage of the variations of the hospital game slowly introduced by the child, we were able to go into the details of his life immediately before his sister's birth and again after the mother's return from the hospital. We learned from him how strong his affection for his nurse had been even before his sister's birth; that she had appeared a far more reliable person than his mother, who frequently went out and left

him alone with the nurse. Gradually he remembered periods of separation from his parents before the sister's birth. Once when his parents left for vacation he stayed at his grandparents' home with his nurse. One of his memories referred to his watching the departure of his parents in a plane, and his subsequent illness. He assured us that the nurse never left his side while the parents were absent.

This ample material referring to abandonment corroborated the appropriateness of selecting his sadness as the first content of our interpretation. To him, being sent to school was an aggravating repetition of former separations: it happened just after his sister's nurse had left and his own nurse and mother had to share in the care of the baby. Thus, he lost not only his mother but also his nurse "who would never, never leave me alone." *This repetition of the traumatic experience of being abandoned* brought about the climax of his anxiety (pp. 188–189 [105–106]).

A CONUNDRUM

Studying this material proves to be confusing. Unquestionably Bornstein's clinical gift is evident in her ability to decipher the centrality of the child's sadness and the defenses of omnipotence and grandiosity that he utilized to mask the sadness at being abandoned and fearing further abandonment. On reading this material one wonders how or whether the defenses of grandiosity and omnipotence were actually addressed and interpreted. Reading the material makes one wonder whether the actual technique utilized was *recognizing* the presence of those omnipotent defenses, *ignoring* them, and recognizing that the important affect *to address* was the loneliness.[13] Bornstein first discussed that affect in the play, sympathizing with the child in the play. With her undoubtedly keen eye she noticed sadness in Frankie's face, indicating that he could now tolerate the sad affect. Without making a direct connection to the play, Bornstein asked Frankie about his real life, allowing for elaboration of his traumatic situation.

Cohen (2002) states that Bornstein

> focused on the child's defenses and their analysis. She saw that the defenses operated against affects, and that those used by the child to ward off unpleasant feelings were the same as those used against the drives. It was by first addressing the defenses that one could expect to uncover unconscious conflict. Miss Freud adopted Mrs. Bornstein's technique of defense analysis and gave up the preparatory phase.

13. On rereading the case, Ritvo (1996) similarly questioned how defenses were actually addressed by Bornstein. He states that "Although the analysis was presented with emphasis on the defenses, one gains the impression from the case that in resorting to 'unconscious thrusts,' defenses were bypassed" (p. 375).

How is one to do this? What sounds to be a straightforward, if not simple task turns out to require considerable skill, especially with the highly conflicted and defended latency child. Sensitivity to the child is required, the ability to identify with him, to enter his world, and to recognize and sense accurately his defenses and the affects that lie behind them. Ted Becker had this gift (as did Mrs. Bornstein): an uncanny intuition with children. He truly understood children and what they felt. (p. 508)

Two vignettes illustrate directly Bornstein's interpretation of Frankie's defenses. At one point toward the end of the first year, Bornstein describes Frankie's play.

Playing the doctor, he exclaimed: "Those criminals, they have to be operated on. Off with their wee-wees. It has to come off!" In his play he guarded himself against any awareness of his fear by identifying himself with the person performing the act of castration. His fear of the anticipated retaliation found expression in his behavior toward his pediatrician. Frankie had always been a difficult patient, but during this period he absolutely refused to be examined, and assaulted the doctor by throwing blocks or potatoes which he carefully had stored under his bed for this purpose.

The emphasis in our interpretation was on Frankie's preoccupation with the mechanisms of undoing, and his identification with the aggressor[14] [my stress]. After this, we were able to approach the theme of his castration fear by confronting him with a comparison of his impersonation of a cruel doctor and the kind attitude of his own doctor; with the fearlessness of his prisoners in contrast to his own frightened aggressiveness toward his doctor. (pp 194–95 [112])

A little later, Bornstein says

In view of the anxiety which was kept in abeyance by his identification with a castrative figure, *particular caution was necessary in the interpretation and dissolution of this identification* [my stress]. Abrupt release of such large quantities of anxiety would have produced a traumatic effect. Therefore it seemed indicated to decrease this defense only gradually. In a preparatory period of several weeks, we "amused" ourselves by imagining how frightened the brave prisoners of his fantasy would feel if *they* were suddenly exposed to the reality of a doctor's office. By our bantering his fantasy-prisoners, Frankie was enabled to take a more tolerant view of these frightening thoughts which he had formerly warded off by identification with the aggressor. Through this playful approach we prepared him for the fact that it was he himself who feared for his genitals, or at

---

14. The challenge, of course, is how to help the novice address these defenses in a way that does not attack the child's narcissistic vulnerability.

least that in the past he had once done so, even if the past were only ten minutes ago. Introducing *humor* as a benign defense, we saved Frankie the full impact of the suffering which accompanies castration fear.[15] He learned to understand that the wolves represented not only the prohibiting nurse and the father, but also himself with his strong voyeuristic and castrative impulses (p. 195 [112–113]).

CAN THIS TECHNIQUE BE TAUGHT?

How to help novices implement effective technique is difficult to describe. In fact, every therapist and analyst has to develop his/her own empathically connected technical approach with children, with the aid of his/her own treatment and supervision. Reading examples of the work of master clinicians like Bornstein provides scaffoldings to which one provides one's own personal accoutrements. Mirroring or trying to exactly duplicate the technique one hears or reads about may be counterproductive because it would lack the personal stamp of the clinician and his/her patient.

SELECTED CONTEMPORARY PRACTICES BASED ON BERTA BORNSTEIN'S TECHNIQUES

The major lesson to be learned from this review is that from the earliest sessions, the analyst observes the child's affects and defensive reactions to about-to-be-felt feelings. Thus, from the earliest points in a psychodynamic treatment, the analyst or therapist can address how the child copes with unpleasant feeling states, regardless of his or her age or wish to communicate in words. By understanding how the child copes with his or her unpleasant affects, the analyst understands how the child manages his or her conflicted wishes. Thus, over time, as the analyst interprets defenses against warded-off affects, the child is able to master those unpleasant affects more effectively and is able to reveal a greater amount of conflicted material with an unfolding of the increasingly manifold layers of meaning.

Since children often ignore or reject interpretations, it may be difficult to assess whether changes in the psychotherapeutic material are a

15. Ritvo (2003) comments on the recrudescence of these conflicts post-college: "At the time he returned to analysis, faced with taking a major step to adult status, Frankie was mired in a regressive oedipal conflict in which his aggressive, competitive strivings against authoritative, paternal figures evoked anxiety and symptom formation. The fantasized defeat and collapse that would follow represented the prohibiting superego defense against ambitious strivings, turning the aggression against the self" (p. 41).

response to fresh understanding or the result of a new defensive strategy without new understanding (compare Kennedy, 1979, and Hoffman, 1989). There are instances when it would be reasonable to infer that children do have insight into their conflicts, such as by understanding or creating a new metaphor, by asking many questions about a particular stressful situation, such as a vacation, and so on. Child analytic authors have also stressed that mutative interpretations occur within the context of the transference, as the child interacts with the therapist/analyst in a manner similar to interactions with his/her parents (P. Tyson, 1978).

A key sign of improvement and development would be the increasing tolerance and expression of painful affects, such as anxiety, anger, jealousy, and longings to be cared for. Although interpretation of defenses is ubiquitous in the analytic and psychotherapeutic work with children (as well as with adults), it seems *that systematically addressing a child's defenses, as an organizing method of technique has not been fully appreciated.*[16]

In a series of papers, Judy Yanof (1996a, 1996b, 2000) discusses the lack of appreciation of analysis of defense in children. She discusses the decreased weight that has been given to interpretative techniques (interpretation of defense and transference interpretation) in contrast to, for example, more recent emphasis on the child's play itself as a helpful promotion for the child's development. Unquestionably, in doing psychotherapeutic or psychoanalytic work with children, noninterpretive techniques are ubiquitous. Interestingly, Alan Sugarman (2003) discusses how developmental interventions, such as physically having to set limits, may in fact be examples of "transference of defense interpretations at a concrete level" (p. 189). In other words, the therapist communicates via his or her actions (not just with words). Sugarman (2006) notes that a goal of treatment is to free up the patient's mental processes in order to promote his or her symbolic capacities (p. 982).

Judith Chused (1996) has also stressed the paramount importance with children of the analyst's developmentally appropriate nonverbal communication to the child, whether the child is "neurotic" or "developmentally delayed." Since children often have difficulties in hearing the therapist, alternative ways have been devised in communicating interpretations to children, such as talking about other children rather than about the patient him- or herself.

In addressing the difficulties therapists encounter when they attempt to directly and verbally address feelings with children, Yanof (1996b)

---

16. To my knowledge, only Winston, et al. (1994) have systematically studied therapists addressing defenses (in adults).

adds that "Verbal interpretations to children may fail not merely because they are verbal, but because we may tend to interpret drive derivatives too directly. Drive derivatives are less disguised in child material.
Despite this, the child has as much, if not more, trouble than the adult
in owning his own feelings and taking responsibility for them. *The child
analyst may be tempted to call attention to the unconscious wish or unacceptable affect and by so doing bypass the child's defense.* This may increase the
child's resistance and risk cutting off further elaboration of material.
In addition, bypassing the defense restricts opportunities for the child
to work on the maladaptive defense" [my stress] (p. 108).

Robert Tyson (1994) describes analytic instances with children and
adults both, in which the patient's negativism is a defensive expression.
Tyson cites Bornstein's (1951) idea that latency-age children employ
negativism defensively to protect themselves from narcissistic injury
(p. 295).

Ruth Karush (2006) describes such an example in the analytic work
with an aggressive little boy. She states that the boy's "intrapsychic defense mechanisms were no match for the dangers that could be heard,
seen and felt. The external forces that threatened Teddy gave an unarguable reality to the internal ones and called for real defenses in the
form of violent behaviors" (p. 17).

I myself (Hoffman 1989, 2000, 2007) describe the utilization of a
defense-focused technique with children, discussing the therapeutic
value of this seemingly narrow intervention strategy, within a more global
approach with the children, which includes the utilization of play and
verbal interaction, addressing the child's transference, providing supportive interventions, promoting a relationship between the clinician and the
child, and, most importantly, promoting a relationship with the parents
in order to explain to them the technique utilized, gather information
about the child's life in order to understand the play and interactions
with the child more effectively, and provide some parent guidance without assuming a "good" parent role, always stressing that they are the
parents who need to decide the best course of action with their child.[17]

CONCLUSION: VALUE OF ADDRESSING AND INTERPRETING
DEFENSES WITH DISRUPTIVE CHILDREN

There is an important distinction between psychotherapeutic and psychoanalytic work with adults and with children. Adults who enter treat-

17. See case example at: http://www.commonlanguagepsychotherapy.org/fileadmin/
user_upload/Accepted_procedures/interpretingdefenses.pdf (accessed July 3, 2014).

ment need to have sufficient motivation to enter the process. Children usually do not have the same motivation, nor do they have the same impetus to decide whether or not to enter treatment. With children, especially *with disruptive children, it is the parents or teachers who suffer from the child's symptoms, not so much the children themselves.* Furthermore, children look at their problems much more from the point of view that something in their environment is causing the problem. They do not have the same capacity as adults for reflection and introspection. Children first and foremost want the environment to change—to adapt to their symptoms, whether the symptoms are behavioral problems or phobic anxious symptoms (that is, whether the symptoms fit under the rubric of "externalizing" or "internalizing" disorders). A child, for example, might say, "If the teacher stopped picking on me, I would stop fighting." Another child might say, "If you got rid of the monster, I would then go to sleep." Adolescents to some extent fall midway between preadolescent children and adults. Parents can insist that young children enter treatment. A certain amount of self-motivation is required from adolescents. Older adolescents are, of course, much more like adults than younger children, in that parents usually cannot insist that they enter treatment.

Disruptive children do not openly express a sense of responsibility for their misbehavior, nor do they have insight into internal reasons for their problems. Systematically addressing the disruptive symptoms as defenses can be an effective way of engaging the child as well as ameliorating his or her symptoms.

The ability to work psychotherapeutically with disruptive children is Berta Bornstein's greatest legacy.

BIBLIOGRAPHY

BATEMAN, A., AND FONAGY, P. (2011). *Handbook of Mentalizing in Mental Health Practice.* Arlington, VA: American Psychiatric Publishing.

BECKER, T. E. (1974). On latency. *The Psychoanalytic Study of the Child* 29:3–11.

BLOS, P. (1974). Berta Bornstein—1899–1971. *Psychoanalytic Study of the Child* 29:35–37.

BORNSTEIN, B. (1945). Clinical notes on child analysis. *Psychoanalytic Study of the Child* 1:151–166.

———. (1949). The analysis of a phobic child: Some problems of theory and technique in child analysis. *Psychoanalytic Study of the Child* 3:181–226 (also in this volume).

———. (1951). On latency. *Psychoanalytic Study of the Child* 6:279–285.

CHUSED, J. F. (1996). The therapeutic action of psychoanalysis: Abstinence and informative experiences. *Journal of the American Psychoanalytic Association* 44 (4): 1047–1071.

COHEN, D. (2002). Introductory remarks to Ted E. Becker Memorial Meeting. *Journal of Clinical Psychoanalysis* 11:507–509.

EMDE, R. N. (1999). Moving ahead: Integrating influences of affective processes for development and for psychoanalysis. *International Journal of Psycho-analysis* 80 (pt. 2): 317–339.

———. (2000). Affect dialogue (vol. 1, no. 1, 1999): Commentary by Robert N. Emde. *Neuropsychoanalysis* 1 (1): 69–74.

ETKIN, A. (2011). Emerging insights on implicit emotion regulation. *Neuropsychoanalysis* 13 (1): 42–44.

FEIGELSON, C. I. (1974). Play in child analysis. *Psychoanalytic Study of the Child* 29:21–26.

FONAGY, P., AND TARGET, M. (1994). Who is helped by child psychoanalysis? A sample study of disruptive children, from the Anna Freud Centre retrospective investigation. *Bulletin of the Anna Freud Center* 17:291–315.

———. (1996a). Predictors of outcome in child psychoanalysis: A retrospective study of 763 cases at the Anna Freud Centre. *Journal of the American Psychoanalytic Association* 44:27–77.

———. (1996b). Playing with reality: I. Theory of mind and the normal development of psychic reality. *International Journal of Psycho-analysis* 77:217–233.

FREUD, A. (1926a). An hysterical symptom in a child of two years and three months old. *International Journal of Psychoanalysis* 7: 227–229.

———. (1926b). Introduction to the Technique of the Analysis of Children. In *Writings*, vol. 1, pp. 3–69. New York: International Universities Press.

———. (1936). *The Ego and the Mechanisms of Defense.* New York: International Universities Press, 1966.

———. (1945). Indications for child analysis. *Psychoanalytic Study of the Child* 1:127–149.

———. (1966). A short history of child analysis. *Psychoanalytic Study of the Child* 21:7–14.

———. (1974). A Psychoanalytic View of Developmental Psychopathology. In *Writings*, vol. 8, pp. 57–74. New York: International Universities Press.

FREUD, S. (1923). The Ego and the Id. In *The Standard Edition of the Complete Psychological Works of Sigmund Freud*, vol. 19 (1923–1925): *The Ego and the Id and Other Works*, pp. 1–66. London: Hogarth Press and Institute of Psychoanalysis.

GRAY, P. (2005). *The Ego and the Analysis of Defense.* 2nd ed. Northvale, NJ: Jason Aronson.

GREENSPAN, S. I., AND SHANKER, S. G. (2004). *The First Idea: How Symbols, Language, and Intelligence Evolved from Our Primate Ancestors to Modern Humans.* Cambridge, MA: Da Capo Press.

GROSS, J. J. (2002). Emotion regulation: Affective, cognitive, and social consequences. *Psychophysiology* 39:281–291.

———. (2013). Emotion regulation: Taking stock and moving forward. *Emotion* 13 (3): 359–365.

HOFFMAN, L. (1989). The psychoanalytic process and the development of insight in child analysis: A case study. *Psychoanalytic Quarterly* 58 (1): 63–80.

———. (1995). Review of George MacLean and Ulrich Rappen's (1991) *Hermine Hug-Hellmuth: Her Life and Work*. *Psychoanalytic Quarterly* 64:600–603.

———. (2000). Letters. *Journal of the American Psychoanalytic Association* 48:1617–1618.

———. (2007). Do children get better when we interpret their defenses against painful feelings? *Psychoanalytic Study of the Child* 62:291–313.

KABCENELL, R. J. (1974). On countertransference. *Psychoanalytic Study of the Child* 29:27–33.

KARUSH, R. K. (2006). The vicissitudes of aggression in a toddler: A clinical contribution. *Psychoanalytic Study of the Child* 61:3–19.

KATAN, A. (1961). Some thoughts about the role of verbalization in early childhood. *Psychoanalytic Study of the Child* 16:184–188.

KEABLE, H. (2011). The Freudian tradition at one hundred years through the lens of Berta Bornstein. *Psychoanalytic Review* 98:723–742.

KENNEDY, H. (1979). The role of insight in child analysis: A developmental viewpoint. *Journal of the American Psychoanalytic Association* 27:9–28.

KLEIN, M. (1927). Symposium on child-analysis. *International Journal of Psychoanalysis* 8:339–370.

LIEBERMAN, M. D., EISENBERGER, N. I., CROCKETT, M. J., TOM, S. M., PFEIFER, J. H., AND WAY, B. M. (2007). Putting feelings into words: Affect labeling disrupts amygdala activity in response to affective stimuli. *Psychological Science* 18:421–428.

LOTTERMAN, A. C. (2012). Affect as a marker of the psychic surface. *Psychoanalytic Quarterly* 81:305–333.

MILLER, J. M. (1996). Anna Freud. A historical look at her theory and technique of child psychoanalysis. *Psychoanalytic Study of the Child* 51:142–171.

MITCHELL, S. A. (1998). From ghosts to ancestors: The psychoanalytic vision of Hans Loewald. *Psychoanalytic Dialogues* 8:825–855.

PHILLIPS, S. H. (2006). Paul Gray's narrowing scope: A "developmental lag" in his theory and technique. *Journal of the American Psychoanalytic Association* 54:137–170.

RITVO, S. (1996). Observations on the long-term effects of child analysis. *Psychoanalytic Study of the Child* 51:365–385.

———. (2003). Conflicts of aggression in coming of age: Developmental and analytic considerations; observations on reanalysis. *Journal of Clinical Psychoanalysis* 12:31–54.

SANDLER, J., AND FREUD, A. (1985). *The Analysis of Defense: The Ego & the Mechanisms of Defense Revisited*. New York: International Universities Press.

SLADE, A. (1994). Making Meaning and Making Believe. In A. Slade and D. Wolf, eds., *Children at Play: Clinical and Developmental Approaches to Meaning and Representation*, pp. 81–107. New York: Oxford University Press.

Sonnenberg, S. (2013). On Sidney Phillips: Paul Gray's narrowing scope. *Journal of the American Psychoanalytic Association* 61: NP13–NP21,doi:10.1177/0003065108320864. The online version of this article can be found at http://apa.sagepub.com/content/61/4/NP13.

Sugarman, A. (2003). Dimensions of the child analyst's role as a developmental object. Affect regulation and limit setting. *Psychoanalytic Study of the Child* 58:189–213.

———. (2006). Mentalization, insightfulness, and therapeutic action: The importance of mental organization. *International Journal of Psycho-Analysis*, 87 (pt. 4): 965–987.

Tyson, P. (1978). Transference and developmental issues in the analysis of a prelatency child. *Psychoanalytic Study of the Child* 33:213–236.

Tyson, R. L. (1994). Neurotic negativism and negation in the psychoanalytic situation. *Psychoanalytic Study of the Child* 49:293–312.

Winnicott, D. W. (1953). Transitional objects and transitional phenomena: A study of the first not-me possession. *International Journal of Psycho-Analysis* 34:89–97.

Winston, B., Samstag, L. W., Winston, A., and Muran, J. C. (1994). Patient defense/therapist interventions. *Psychotherapy: Theory, Research, Practice, Training* 31 (3): 478–491.

Yanof, J. (1996a). Language, communication, and transference in child analysis. I. Selective mutism: The medium is the message. *Journal of the American Psychoanalytic Association* 44 (1): 79–100.

———. (1996b). Language, communication, and transference in child analysis. II. Is child analysis really analysis? *Journal of the American Psychoanalytic Association* 44 (1): 100–116.

———. (2000). Barbie and the tree of life: The multiple functions of gender in development. *Journal of the American Psychoanalytic Association* 48 (4): 1439–1465.

A Nonlinear Lens on Berta Bornstein's "Frankie"

ROBERT M. GALATZER-LEVY, M.D.

This reading of Berta Bornstein's case of "Frankie" half a century after its publication focuses on the knowing attitude that pervades her description of child analysis and child development, and this attitude is used to explain interventions that appear harsh and anti-analytic to today's reader. Using concepts from nonlinear dynamic systems theory and, particularly, network theory help to both understand what is troubling in the case description and how these problematic features came to be part of the case description. The mistaken view that development is linear leads to attempts to get development "on track" and a view that the goal of analysis is well-defined psychological maturity, as opposed to the ongoing freedom to explore the psychological world in new and creative ways. Bornstein's authoritative style was not only coercive of her young patient but also of the reader who is invited to uncritically agree with her formulations. It is suggested that the appeal of this way of writing is best understood in the broad historical context within which the work with Frankie was undertaken.

A CASE STUDY IS NEVER ABOUT THE PATIENT. NOR IS IT ABOUT THE analyst, nor the analyst-patient dyad. It is not even about the triad of patient-analyst (author)-reader. Any case study lives within ever-widening contexts of meanings whose appearance is contingent on what fragment of the network of meaning we choose to focus on and how we chose to focus on that fragment of the network. The child who was "Frankie" lived within a family and school that were in turn embedded within a particular historical moment and culture. Representation of the larger

Dr. Galatzer-Levy is Clinical Professor of Psychiatry and Behavioral Neurosciences, University of Chicago, and on the faculty of Chicago Institute for Psychoanalysis.

The Psychoanalytic Study of the Child 68, ed. Claudia Lament, Robert A. King, Samuel Abrams, Paul M. Brinich, and Rona Knight (Yale University Press, copyright © 2015 by Claudia Lament, Robert A. King, Samuel Abrams, Paul M. Brinich, and Rona Knight).

culture and history came to him primarily through his family and school, but also through the sights and sounds of the street and over the radio. In similar fashion, his analyst lived within a network of meanings and life situations that, coming at the close of the Second World War, cried out the urgency of order and sanity. How can we, six and a half decades later, who are heirs to the disavowal of larger contexts that made questions of psychoanalytic technique in postwar New York to be of overwhelming importance when so much else that matters more should have seemed more urgent, recognize our own continued isolation of these questions from the large networks of meaning in which they exist, and so come to read Frankie's story in a richer fashion?

My use of the term "network" in this paper is meant to be both intuitive and precise in the sense that it refers to a very broad conceptual framework for thinking about complex systems based on the observation that important properties of a wide variety of systems are captured by thinking of them as nodes, which are active agents, and the interconnections of those nodes. Amazingly, important features of systems ranging from biological organisms to the Internet to interpersonal relations, economic markets, and linguistic structures are clarified by applying ideas from this broad conceptual network framework (see, for example, Easley and Kleinberg, 2010). This discussion originates in viewpoints informed by and borrowed from network theory, though it does not use the formal results of that theory.

Berta Bornstein's case of Frankie is a landmark in multiple psychoanalytic domains—ego psychology as theory and technique, the technique of child analysis, conceptualization of latency-age developmental processes, and description of the implicit picture of the place of analysis and child analysis as it dominated American thinking about children's mental health following the Second World War. Follow-up of the case by Ritvo (1996) added to its importance as part of pioneering efforts to study the long-term effects and efficacy of child psychoanalysis as well as to map the changing nature of analytic work with children. Reexamining the paper sixty-five years after its publication inspires a group of thoughts about the problems faced by Frankie and his analyst, the solutions Bornstein advocates, and the challenges of decoding its significance for succeeding generations of analysts and others who would help distressed children.

The analyst who is accustomed to thinking in terms of nonlinear dynamics system theory and the theory of complex systems is immediately struck by some seemingly superficial features of the paper. At the end of the paper, as it appears in the 1949 original, there is a very clear diagrammatic timeline, labeled "Case Material, Frankie." It lays

out major events in Frankie's life (including the analysis), his symptoms, the phases of the analysis, and the contents of analysis in orderly
parallel sequences. The diagram is like the narrative of the analysis
that constitutes the body of the paper, highly ordered into a coherent
sequence. This orderly sequencing of material derives from at least
two sources—Bornstein's attempt to write a persuasive narrative and
the analyst's vigorous attempts to bring order to the analytic process.
As Spence (1983, 1989) demonstrated, the suasive narrative commonly
achieves its end at the expense of accurate descriptions of the events of
an analysis. Linear descriptions provide orderly stories that are convinc-
ing to those of us who implicitly believe in a linear world. The linear
description suggests a traditional scientific process of observation and
the credibility such scientific process suggests. Such linear descriptions
systematically prune the branching interconnections of elements of the
narrative, leaving the appearance of clear causal connections. In traditional scientific experiments an effort is made to identify all possible
cofounding variables and to manipulate a single experimental variable
with the result that the researcher can say with confidence that, at least
under the specific experimental conditions, the change in the experimental variable causes observed changes in outcome. Frankie's analysis
is described in a manner suggesting an orderly laboratory experiment
in which specific changes in the boy's psychological function followed
on well-defined, causative interventions. But in Frankie's analysis, unlike an ideal laboratory experiment, confounding variables cannot be
held steady while the consequences of single interventions are observed.
By removing the links between elements of narrative and links to the
multiple worlds outside the analysis from the narrative, Bornstein gives
her narrative an authority that would not be possible had these links
been included in it, a suggestion of an orderly laboratory experiment,
which, in fact could not have taken place. Had the links to other events
not been pruned from the story they would not only have shown it to be
more complex than Bornstein suggests, they would also have shown the
existence of feedback between elements of Frankie's situation. A main
finding of the theory of complex systems is that the existence of such
feedback loops alters the nature of causality in the system, producing
qualitatively different kinds of causality and insuring that the kind of
linear description that Bornstein provides cannot accurately describe
what occurred.

The most obvious missing link in the narrative is to the person of
the analyst. Frankie's analyst is never identified in the paper, and until
the last paragraph of the paper she is consistently referred to in the
third person. Only in this last paragraph is the voice of the omniscient

narrator replaced, and then only for two sentences, by a first-person-plural pronoun: "then *we* knew that the secondary process had won a victory over the primary process. And this *we* thought, . . ." (italics added, p. 223 [142]). Even here it remains unclear whether "we" refers to the author and the reader (as is suggested by the preceding paragraph, "we see recapitulated . . ." [ibid.]), the royal "we," Frankie and the analyst (which seems unlikely given the ideation), or possibly the analyst and her supervisor. Whichever of these possibilities apply, the analyst and author place themselves as objective and independent observers of the analysis, which makes the narrator's voice the voice of authority, not only by the pronominal rhetorical ploy, but, more important, by removing the network of connections between the analyst and the rest of the world from the description of the analysis.

THE VOICE OF AUTHORITY

The paper itself can be read in many ways. It has had enormous influence in the psychoanalytic literature. It is cited in seventy-five publications, as of July 18, 2014, in the PEP database. Most of these publications treat the Frankie paper as containing definitive and correct information. Bornstein's statements about development and technique are accepted truths by virtue of her having stated them, despite the paper's containing many radical views and despite a follow-up publication that is clearly critical of the clinical work described in it. More rarely, some writers state that Bornstein's ideas are simply incorrect or reflect discarded views of child analysis and child development. These negative assessments tend, like the approving statements, to be bald statements of opinion. In either case, Bornstein's text is rarely treated as the subject of critical inquiry, that is, its arguments and the evidence for them are not systematically explored and subject to argumentation about their validity.

It might be said that a similar approach to clinical reports is common in psychoanalysis, where citation is often used to pay tribute to earlier contributors rather than to address the merits of the ideas in their publications. But even in this context the extent to which Bornstein is cited as a definitive source, as a canonical text, is unusual.

Looking at the text in more detail, the reason for the readers' response becomes evident. Bornstein tells us, concerning a manipulation of Frankie orchestrated with the parents and school, and citing Anna Freud, "By our pre-analytic scheme we hoped to produce in him insight into his need for help, *without which no psychoanalytic treatment can make any progress*" (p. 184 [101], italics added). Further along, Bornstein describes how the child was confronted with the logical inconsistency of his emotional stances: "The contradiction in his attitude toward his mother was the next step in our own interpretation. He was shown the discrepancy between his inability to be without her and the rejecting way in which he treated her" (p. 189 [107]). In the next sentence Bornstein states that a further elaboration of this interpretation was "suggested" to Frankie but there is no hint of suggestion, tentativeness, or doubt in the first sentence. Bornstein knows and informs both the reader and Frankie that logically inconsistent feelings are unacceptable. Bornstein goes on to describe Frankie's association over the coming months. These associations are not treated as evidence of the correctness or limitation of the interpretation. The focus, instead, is on this material as detail that has been uncovered as a result of the interpretation. As stated in the opening sentence of the paper, Bornstein's attempt is to "clarify" certain matters—not to explore, not to study, not to examine, but to "clarify," that is, to apprise the reader of truths known to her.

Bornstein's approach to Frankie parallels her approach to the reader, except that, having more power in her relationship to Frankie, her method of persuasion need not be as subtle as it is with her reader. She is free to manipulate him using his terror as a means to force his cooperation. If empathy fails to suggest the ethical problems in her approach, recall the overt torture of prisoners as described, for example, in *Nineteen Eighty-four* (Orwell, 1949) or "enhanced interrogation" as practiced at Guantanamo (Alexander and Bruning, 2008; United States. Congress. House. Committee on the Judiciary. Subcommittee on the Constitution Civil Rights and Civil Liberties. 2008; United States. Congress. Senate. Committee on Armed Services. 2009), which involved the identification of specific anxieties in the detainees and threats or actualities of exposing them to those terrifying situations. This is exactly what Frankie's analyst threatened or arranged for others to threaten would happen to Frankie in order to win his compliance with her therapeutic interventions.

At the same time, Bornstein is among the first clinical psychoanalysts to recognize that mechanisms of defense, manifest as resistance, to the analytic process deserve and require respect since they protect analysands from unacceptable levels of anxiety, distress, and potential trauma. She would no more thoughtlessly intrude on these defenses to get to the supposedly deeper layers than a surgeon would rip away flesh to expose a diseased organ. Insofar as aggressive, unskilled efforts to attack defenses succeed, say by bald confrontation, Bornstein implicitly argues, they leave the patient in a state in which analysis would be impossible, and insofar as they fail, the analysand is left in a state of redoubled resistance. These ideas are a logical extension, as Bornstein points out, of Anna Freud's recognition that mechanisms of defense are integral to normal psychological functioning (A. Freud, 1936). They reflect the clinical implications of ego psychology as it emerged in the United States in the 1940s and 1950s. Hartmann's seminal writings on ego function particularly emphasized their protective and adaptive function (Hartmann, 1939a; Hartmann, Kris, and Loewenstein, 1946). The obvious clinical significance of this point of view is that resistance, as a manifestation of these functions, needs to be respected. Yet, applied to the analytic situation, Bornstein did not extend this respect to the search for a comprehensive understanding of defenses. There was little clinical effort to uncover and elucidate the origins, dynamics, or adaptive function of defenses manifest as resistance. The respect accorded them is that owed a powerful enemy, and the analyst's job is seen as overcoming these interferences in the primary analytic work of elucidating unconscious conflicts. It would be many decades before clinicians recognized that the analysis of resistance is not primarily intended to interrupt this important psychological function but rather to increase its flexibility and adaptive function by recognizing that, in addition to having a "trailing edge" that impeded development, it also has a "leading edge" that moves development forward (Tolpin, 2002).

The postwar ego psychologists came to see the defensive functions of the ego in clinical psychoanalysis through a lens of suspicion. Mechanisms of defense manifest as resistance not only placed roadblocks in the path of understanding unconscious conflicts but the attempts to bypass them by means other than confrontation by a direct interpretative approach risked introducing analysis-destroying "parameters" into the clinical work (Eissler, 1953). At best, the resulting parameters could be dealt with only by rigorous work that eliminated the effects of having introduced them. But, more likely, analysts who introduced parameters would ultimately fail to analyze because resisted material would be lost to further analytic work. Eissler made these assertions only a few years after publishing analytic work with adolescents, in which he approvingly described what he would a short time later refer to as "parameters" (Eissler, 1949, 1950, 1958). In any case, a corollary of Bornstein's notion that child analysis requires manipulation of the patient, and Eissler's idea that analysis is spoiled by such manipulations, is that child and adolescent analysis can never be analyses in the sense the term is used for work with adults. It is, at best, psychoanalytically informed education carried out within a psychoanalytic setup that includes elements of true analytic work around id impulses and the conflicts surrounding them.

It was not only in the area of resistance to analysis that Bornstein addressed ego function. She was also concerned about the child's adaptation to school and home and attended to these with an eye to issues of character development. She saw Frankie's misbehavior during analytic sessions as an opportunity to educate his ego toward socially acceptable conduct.

In sum, Bornstein's approach to ego function was educative in the sense of using whatever methods might be most effective to alter problematic ego functions. In Frankie's analysis no effort is made to help him understand or rethink the defense operations in which he engaged, nor is the possibility considered that they reflected what seemed to Frankie to be optimal solutions to the problems he faced. In fact, insofar as manipulations interfere with the capacity to observe and think, many of the interventions described are inconsistent with thinking and understanding on the part of the analysand. In this sense, I believe, they are profoundly anti-analytic.

Let us compare the way of working described in Frankie's case to Freud's psychoanalytic method. Freud operated on the working assumption that where meaning for a psychological action appeared to be absent, as in a symptom that made little sense, disguised underlying fantasies were at work that formed the basis for that action. Psychoanalytic cure rested, for Freud, on the discovery of those fantasies and the reworking of them, which became possible as consciousness permitted them to interact with a wider range of ideas and knowledge, thus permitting for a more satisfactory re-solution of the conflict that had led to the action. This central thesis was supported by three kinds of data. First, there was the clinical observation, that as analysands developed ever more clear ideas about a pathogenic fantasy, symptoms disappeared. Second was the observation that the addition of elements into an associative thread promoted the emergence of yet more connecting elements to that thread. Specifically, accurate-enough interpretations, linking previously disparate elements of the thread, resulted in the emergence of further associations that enriched the connections within the thread. Third, Freud discovered that a wide range of nonpathological behaviors, including dreams, paraprexes, jokes, and artistic creations, could be usefully elucidated on the assumption that they grew from the same unconscious fantasies that shaped neurosis and that the interconnection leading to them were fundamentally of the same nature as those leading to neurotic symptoms.

All aspects of these processes, from describing fantasies as specifically connected nodes of concrete images, to the interconnection between fantasies and their representations in words, to the transformations of networks of fantasies through the introduction or removal of links can be modeled using network theory. In fact, Freud, following ideas first put forward in *On Aphasia* (Freud, 1891) and further developed—though in so condensed and dense a fashion in chapter 7 of *The Interpretation of Dreams* (Freud, 1900) that they have been little pursued in later analytic writing—outlines such a network theory, referring to the nodes as neurons and the connections between them simply as connections.

While the range of underlying fantasies that analysts use to explain symptoms has enlarged beyond those that Freud originally thought to be foundational, the fundamental analytic strategy of discovering and bringing to light those fantasies remains central to much analytic practice. At the same time, most analysts have come to believe that something beyond interpretation occurs in successful analyses, although there is not a consensus either about what elements of technique and activity fall within this category, nor is there a consensus about what interactions between analyst and patient interfere with fundamental analytic processes. In a sense, this is no surprise since we do not currently have a clear formulation of what constitutes fundamental analytic processes. At this point it is clear that observational foundations of the Freudian approach do not fully support his central hypothesis about the therapeutic action of analysis as interpretation, and that in any well-conducted analysis much else goes on besides the uncovering of unconscious fantasy. But what else this is and how it relates to analytic cure remains unclear.

While analytic experience supports the idea that oedipal fantasies are important elements in the psychology of many analysands, it also supports the idea that the spectrum of unconscious fantasy is far broader than Freud imagined. Furthermore, there are many more ways in which these fantasies relate to psychological actions than Freud was able to enumerate. For example, and particularly relevant to Frankie's analysis, as Klein (1935, 1945) and Bion (1962, 1963, 1967) observe, fantasies about the ways in which fantasies are dealt with shape the workings of unconscious mentation. It is not an unreasonable hypothesis that one or several of these noninterpretive elements of the analytic situation accounts for analytic cure. While the claim that there are universal unconscious fantasies may not stand up well to critical evaluation, there do seem to be invariant structural features of the fantasies that can be accounted for on the basis of the structure of human cognition (see, for example, Levi-Strauss, 1963). Good arguments have been made that it is the creation of meaningful stories that encompass the symptoms as well as other aspects of the analysand's life, rather than the uncovering of preexisting fantasies, that explains the significance of the emergence of such stories in well-conducted analyses for the relief of psychological distress.

A possible model of analytic process, which builds on Freud's neural network model in chapter 7 of *The Interpretation of Dreams*, conceptualizes mental life as involving networks of interconnecting nodes of psychological function. The connections between these nodes (and hence also groups of nodes) may vary and change over time in response to many factors, with the result that some groups of nodes may become effectively detached from other groups of nodes, or new connections may be established or detached and links reestablished. The overall operation of the system reflects the properties of the nodes and their interconnection. For example, a repressed fantasy may be thought of as a group of nodes that are not attached to conscious mental processes in a manner in which the conscious processes can influence them. Interpretative work that brings the fantasy to consciousness establishes a link between conscious mental functioning and the formerly repressed fantasy, such that the fantasy can be effected by conscious mental processes and thereby be transformed. The work of analysis is to establish useful connections between elements of psychological functioning. Where disconnection was, connection shall be!

A particularly important aspect of analytic work concerns the governing fantasies concerning stability of the links themselves. Elsewhere, I have argued that the goal of analytic work is to bring the analysand (or rather the system analyst–analysand) to the "edge of chaos," where transformation on linking occurs sufficiently rapidly that new possibilities for function can be engaged without losing structure to such an extent that the system becomes disorganized, and that the reward of such work is that analysand's continuing capacity to explore and transform the links in the network of meaning, that is, the capacity for ongoing analytic process in the absence of the person of the analyst (Galatzer-Levy, in press).

An aspect of this model that should be emphasized is that the links need not be limited to connections within the individual psyche. The links may be to aspects of other persons' psychological functioning and to other aspects of the larger community.

If we tentatively accept that this idea of analytic process involves an ongoing dynamic reorganization of links, we can think of any process that interferes with linking and its ongoing reorganization as anti-analytic. Manipulations designed to suppress and otherwise drive from awareness any aspect of psychological functioning, whatever the intentions of the manipulations are, in this conceptualization are anti-analytic, as is any attitude that limits the patient's freedom to think based on the analyst's

authority. From this point of view many of the interventions with Frankie
were profoundly anti-analytic. It might be argued that Bornstein's claim
that certain interventions were necessary for an analysis to take place
find support in the idea that by interrupting the boy's actions, Frankie
is forced to transform the expression of the fantasies into much more
flexible modes of words and play. These are much more promising representations for the kinds of psychological work described by Bornstein
as analysis. Indeed, once in analysis, Frankie expressed and worked with
a range of very important fantasies, some of which were closely related
to the action the analyst interfered with. At the same time, having effectively removed action from the arena of analysis, the central questions
of why Frankie felt that his fantasies necessitated action could never
come into the analysis, and they never did.

It is clear from his subsequent analysis that Frankie's childhood analysis did not fully clear the path for his satisfactory development. This
can be considered from various points of view. As Freud (1939) pointed
out, no psychoanalysis is complete nor can it engage matters that do not
come into the analysis. Transferences that fail to emerge for whatever
reason, whether they are defended against or do not at the time of the
analysis have adequate urgency, can, of course, not be analyzed. Yet
this is hardly the only reason for the limitation of psychoanalytic work.
In fact, what from certain perspectives appears to be accomplishment
may also be seen as its limitation. Thus, for example, Ritvo (1996),
commenting on Frankie's return to analysis as a young adult, endorses
it as an accomplishment of the childhood analysis that Frankie would
see a return to the psychoanalytic situation as a solution to his distress.
This seemingly positive result could be seen from a different angle as a
serious limitation of psychoanalytic work, in which Frankie was left impaired with regard to finding other means of working through difficulties that confronted him. It has long been agreed that one of the hopes
for outcomes of psychoanalysis is a capacity for something referred to
as "self-analysis," but what this capacity is is less than clear.[1] Sometimes
"self-analysis" is thought of as an ability to think about and come to understand one's self, using the methods learned in analysis, such as free
association. In this vision the process of self-analysis is conscious. The
same individual plays roles of both analyst and analysand. A contrasting
vision of self-analysis involves the idea that the core result of a successful
analysis lies in the freeing of the analysand to engage in an ongoing,
largely unconscious, playful engagement with the problems and opportunities of living. This may be regarded as the freeing up of mental life

1. The clinical basis for these observations are due to Samuel Wiess, M.D.

to involve an activity that is referred to in artificial intelligence as "simu-lated annealing." As a substance like molten glass cools and solidifies, it takes on a structure that is ever more resistant to change. Frequently this structure is less than optimal in that it leaves points of strain in the solidified material. These in turn make the material brittle and subject to fracture. Slowing the process of cooling or repeatedly warm-ing the material and then lowering the temperature allows the glass to find a more optimal structure in the sense of reducing irregularities and hence points of strain. In working with actual physical substances like glass and metal, it was found that an optimal annealing process often involved allowing the substance to solidify in significant measure, thereby taking on some structure and then heating it again to a point at which some of the structure is maintained and some of it is lost, so that, on recooling, new and more-close-to-optimal solutions may be found. An analogous means of optimizing solutions to problems occurs when, after a fairly good solution has been found, partial disorganization is reintroduced and the problem is resolved, often leading to a superior solution (see Galatzer-Levy, 1988). This process of partially disorganiz-ing and disrupting solutions can either at some point be terminated or may be continued indefinitely. One way of looking at self-analysis is as the ongoing application of simulated annealing to emotional mental functioning, and that the purpose of analysis, which itself is a process of simulated annealing, is to allow the individual to continue this activ-ity across the course of life. The outcome of Frankie's analysis suggests that he had not developed this capacity during his analysis and, in fact, had come to be neurotic in a manner that strongly suggests great in-flexibility. Reading about Frankie's analysis from a nonlinear viewpoint we must wonder whether the multiple manipulative interventions to which he was exposed succeeded in limiting rather than expanding his capacities for playful engagement in an ongoing reorganization of the networks of meaning by which he lived.

This discussion began by describing the multiple contexts in which Frankie's analysis could be placed and thereby suggesting, in network language, that limiting the networks of meaning in which it belonged limited our understanding. The larger context in which the analysis occurred can only be inferred from the text, which does not include a statement of when and where the analysis occurred. Yet, Bornstein and many of her contemporaries' positions as European refugees, whose world had been demolished by Nazism, is clear. Arendt (1951) convinc-ingly argues that the central aspect of totalitarianism is the destruc-tion of the capacity for thought and its replacement by unthinking action. Elsewhere (Arendt, 1970), she argues that violence, the attempt to destroy the humanity of another, is the core of the response to injustice. One may at least wonder whether Bornstein's approval of an essentially violent response to Frankie's action, oriented irrationally, takes its origin in the larger context of her life, namely the experience of how attitudes like Frankie's, in the hands of persons with physical power, can devastate the world. This view would explain both the urgency Bornstein felt to civilize Frankie, and her willingness to support a cruel process that aimed at limiting his fantasies to those that could be encompassed within her conceptualization of analytic materials. While it would take considerably more evidence than can be presented in this paper to demonstrate the idea, one cannot help but wonder if the particularly rigid attitude toward action that dominated American East Coast psychoanalysis in the 1940s and 1950s had important origins as a reaction to the European chaos from which its authors had physically escaped.

Memorializing Berta Bornstein, Peter Blos (1974) described how she often fell asleep during case presentations only to wake up near the end and make salient comments. Most experienced analysts have known admired colleagues who exhibit similar behaviors. These analysts can, on the basis of minimal input, say something that seems deep and interesting about a case in a manner that invites awe rather than skepticism. Depending on the frame of mind of the audience, these abilities may be attributed to the remarkable capacity to mine a fragment of data for information, astounding levels of empathy (an immediate knowing of another's mental state in depth), a capacity for pattern matching that rapidly recognizes similarities of the case under discussion with other cases, a rapid application of a general theory, or simply a willingness to throw out a poorly substantiated idea in a form that invites belief. One has the feeling in reading the case of Frankie that, like Frankie and his family, the reader is invited to a state of passive acceptance of Bornstein's authoritative statements but left perplexed as to whether accepting them involves an irrational bowing to authority or, rejecting them, of foolish disregard of true wisdom. What is clear is that this attitude of authority invites the abandonment of the creative exploration of alternative possibilities, the personal remaking of the network of meanings that is at the core of the analytic process.

BIBLIOGRAPHY

ALEXANDER, M., AND BRUNING, J. R. (2008). *How to Break a Terrorist: The U.S. Interrogators Who Used Brains, Not Brutality, to Take Down the Deadliest Man in Iraq.* New York: Free Press.

ARENDT, H. (1951). *The Origins of Totalitarianism.* New York: Harcourt, Brace (1951).

———. (1970). *On Violence.* New York: Harcourt, Brace & World.

BION, W. R. (1962). *Learning from Experience.* In *Seven Servants.* New York: Aronson, 1977.

———. (1963). *Elements of Psycho-Analysis.* In *Seven Servants.* New York: Aronson, 1977.

———. (1967). *Second Thoughts: Selected Papers on Psycho-Analysis.* London: Heinemann.

BLOS, P. (1974). "Berta Bornstein 1899–1971." *Psychoanalytic Study of the Child* 29:35–37.

BORNSTEIN, B. (1949). "The Analysis of a Phobic Child: Some Problems of Theory and Technique in Child Analysis." *Psychoanalytic Study of the Child* 3:181–226 (also in this volume).

EASLEY, D., AND KLEINBERG, J. (2010). *Networks, Crowds, and Markets: Reasoning about a Highly Connected World.* New York: Cambridge University Press.

EISSLER, K. (1949). *Searchlights on Delinquency: New Psychoanalytic Studies.* Dedicated to Professor August Aichhorn on the Occasion of His Seventieth Birthday, July 27, 1948. New York: International Universities Press.

———. (1950). "Ego-Psychological Implications of the Psychoanalytic Treatment of Delinquents." *Psychoanalytic Study of the Child* 5:97–121.

———. (1953). "Effect of the Structure of the Ego on Psychoanalytic Technique." *Journal of the American Psychoanalytic Association* 1:104–143.

EISSLER, K. R. (1958). "Notes on Problems of Technique in the Psychoanalytic Treatment of Adolescents—With Some Remarks on Perversions." *Psychoanalytic Study of the Child* 13:223–254.

FREUD, A. (1936). *The Ego and the Mechanisms of Defense.* New York: International Universities Press.

FREUD, S. (1891). *On Aphasia: A Critical Study.* Trans. E. Stengel. New York: International Universities Press (1953).

———. (1900). *The Interpretation of Dreams.* In *The Standard Edition of the Complete Psychological Works of Sigmund Freud,* ed. J. Strachey, vols. 4–5. London: Hogarth Press.

———. (1939). *Analysis Terminable and Interminable.* In *The Standard Edition of the Complete Psychological Works of Sigmund Freud,* vol. 23. London: Hogarth Press.

GALATZER-LEVY, R. (1988). "On Working Through: A Model from Artificial Intelligence." *Journal of the American Psychoanalytic Association* 36:125–151.

———. (in press). "The Edge of Chaos: A New Nonlinear View of Psychoanalytic Technique." *International Journal of Psychoanalysis.*

HARTMANN, H. (1939a). *Ego Psychology and the Problem of Adaptation.* New York: International Universities Press.

———. (1939b). "Psychoanalysis and the Concept of Health." In *Essays in Ego Psychology,* 3–18. New York: International Universities Press.

HARTMANN, H., KRIS, E. AND LOEWENSTEIN, R. (1946). "Comments on the Formation of Psychic Structure." In *Papers on Psychoanalytic Psychology,* 27–55. New York: International Universities Press.

KLEIN, M. (1935). *A Contribution to the Psychogenesis of Manic-Depressive States: Love, Guilt and Reparation.* New York: Delacorte Press.

———. (1945). "The Oedipus Complex in the Light of Early Anxieties." In *Love, Guilt and Reparation & Other Works 1927–1945,* 370–419. New York: Delacorte Press / Seymour Lawrence.

LEVI-STRAUSS, C. (1963). *Structural Anthropology.* Garden City, NY: Anchor Books.

ORWELL, G. (1949). *Nineteen Eighty-four: A Novel.* New York: Harcourt, Brace.

RITVO, S. (1996). "Observations on the Long-term Effects of Child Analysis." *Psychoanalytic Study of the Child* 51:365–385.

SPENCE, D. (1983). "Narrative Persuasion." *Psychoanalysis and Contemporary Thought* 6:457–481.

———. (1989). "Narrative Appeal vs. Historical Validity." In *Scientific Symposium: Clinical Controversies and the Interpersonal Tradition.* New York, 1986. *Contemporary Psychoanalysis* 25:517–523.

TOLPIN, M. (2002). "Doing Psychoanalysis of Normal Development: Forward Edge Transferences." In *Postmodern Self Psychology: Progress in Self Psychology,* ed. A. Goldberg, vol. 18, pp. 167–190. New York: Analytic Press.

UNITED STATES. CONGRESS. HOUSE. COMMITTEE ON THE JUDICIARY. SUB-COMMITTEE ON THE CONSTITUTION CIVIL RIGHTS AND CIVIL LIBERTIES. (2008). *Torture and the Cruel, Inhuman and Degrading Treatment of Detainees: The Effectiveness and Consequences of 'Enhanced' Interrogation: Hearing before the Subcommittee on the Constitution, Civil Rights, and Civil Liberties of the Committee on the Judiciary,* House of Representatives, 110th Cong., 1st sess., November 8, 2007. Washington, U.S.: G.P.O.

———. CONGRESS. SENATE. COMMITTEE ON ARMED SERVICES. (2009). The Treatment of Detainees in U.S. Custody: Hearings Before the Committee on Armed Services, United States Senate, 110th Congress, 2d sess., June 17 and September 25, 2008. Washington, U.S.: G.P.O.

Co-Creativity and Interactive Repair

Commentary on Berta Bornstein's "The Analysis of a Phobic Child"

ALEXANDRA HARRISON, M.D.

My comments focus on a consideration of three issues central to child psychoanalysis stimulated by rereading the classic paper by Berta Bornstein, "The Analysis of a Phobic Child: Some Problems of Theory and Technique in Child Analysis": (1) the importance of "co-creativity" and its use in analysis to repair disruptions in the mother-child relationship; (2) working analytically with the "inner world of the child"; and (3) the fundamental importance of multiple simultaneous meaning-making processes. I begin with a discussion of current thinking about the importance of interactive processes in developmental and therapeutic change and then lead to the concepts of "co-creativity" and interactive repair, elements that are missing in the "Frankie" paper. The co-creative process that I outline includes multiple contributions that Frankie and his caregivers brought to their relationships—his mother, his father, his nurse, and even his analyst. I then address the question of how child analysts can maintain a central focus on the inner world of the child while still taking into account the complex nature of co-creativity in the change process. Finally, I discuss insights into the multiple simultaneous meaning-making processes in the analytic relationship to effect therapeutic change,

Dr. Harrison is a Training and Supervising Analyst in Adult, Child, and Adolescent Analysis at the Boston Psychoanalytic Institute, and an Assistant Clinical Professor in Psychiatry at Harvard Medical School at the Cambridge Health Alliance.

The Psychoanalytic Study of the Child 68, ed. Claudia Lament, Robert A. King, Samuel Abrams, Paul M. Brinich, and Rona Knight (Yale University Press, copyright © 2015 by Claudia Lament, Robert A. King, Samuel Abrams, Paul M. Brinich, and Rona Knight).

including what I call the "sandwich model," an attempt to organize this complexity so that is more accessible to the practicing clinician.

In terms of the specific case of Frankie, my reading of the case suggests that failure to repair disruptions in the mother-child relationship from infancy through the time of the analytic treatment was central to Frankie's problems. My hypothesis is that, rather than the content of his analyst's interpretations, what was helpful to Frankie in the analysis was the series of attempts at interactive repair in the analytic process. Unfortunately, the case report does not offer data to test this hypothesis. Indeed, one concluding observation from my reading of this classic case is how useful it would be for the contemporary analyst to pay attention to the multifaceted co-creative process in order to explain and foster the therapeutic change that can occur in analysis.

INTRODUCTION

I WELCOMED THE CHANCE TO REREAD THIS CLASSIC PAPER. NOT ONLY is it enjoyable reading, but it also provides us important data to use in considerations of analytic process. Bornstein offers us many observations of a young child and his play, as well as a style of reporting these observations that makes them feel fresh and real. In addition, her descriptions of the problematic relationship patterns in the family— between "Frankie" and his parents, his parents with each other, and Frankie and his nurse—seem familiar to those of us who work with young children and their families (Bornstein, 1949, p. 181–182 [99]). It is good to be reminded that as early as 1949 child analysts acknowledged the importance of the role of the parent and even teachers in the child analyst's work, for example in allowing the mother to be present in the analytic session and in engaging the teachers as collaborative partners in the preparatory phase of the analysis (p. 184 [101]).

Bornstein provides an ongoing account of her psychoanalytic formulations of Frankie's behaviors both in and outside the analysis during the course of the treatment. She also describes her thinking about analytic technique. For example, in "the hospital game," she presents a series of alternative choices for technical intervention, and her choice to focus on Frankie's defense against sadness and longing for his mother is one that I imagine many contemporary child analysts would also make (p. 185 [101–102]). The Frankie paper is an example of a case report, the typical way psychoanalysts have communicated about their work, beginning with Freud.

Yet, there are limitations to this kind of writing. As Bornstein herself admits, there is a "discrepancy between the clinical simplicity of the symptom and the complicated ego structure behind it" (p. 181 [98]). Even if read as a long and fascinating narrative, the reader may become confused at times as Bornstein's focus shifts among libidinal phases and from one dynamic conflict to another. The reader may feel as if he or she is riding the waves with Bornstein, struggling with how to tame "King Boo-Boo." This is unquestionably a valuable experience. The problem is, however, that there is a hidden fact of some importance in the account of Frankie's analysis. The hidden fact is that Bornstein is as much a creator of the narrative as is her little patient.

Let me explain what I mean. The case report offers primarily one kind of data—a progressive account of the sense the analyst makes of Frankie's behavior and verbal communications to her in the analytic sessions, understood with the help of her analytic theory. There is a little history at the beginning of the paper and now and then some descriptions of what is going on in Frankie's "real life," but most of this lengthy paper is the content of Frankie's analytic sessions and what Bornstein makes of them. There is justification for this approach to psychoanalytic writing. However, if we attempt to bring child analysis into the present and hopefully even into the future, it might be beneficial to use insights from contemporary theory about how human beings grow and change, and that is hard to do with such a case report. In this commentary, I will make an argument for why it would be useful to make such an attempt.

Contemporary developmental theory, derived significantly from the direct observation of infants in their caregiving relationships, claims that the capacities of the growing child emerge from *interactions between infant and caregiver* that occur moment to moment in repetitive fashion during daily life (daily caregiving routines) (Sander, 2008). I am referring to such essential competencies as the ability to regulate state of arousal and emotions, motor coordination and sensory processing and integration, and shared subjectivity and theory of mind. Children, of course, differ in the degree and quality of these competencies, and they even seem to be born with differences in their potential for developing them. For example, each child has his or her own particular temperament, profile of sensory sensitivities, preparedness for social engagement, and emerging cognitive style. Also, each caregiver brings his or her own set of capacities, influenced by mood, past history of early caregiving experience, and internal representation of the child. When you include all these additional factors, you have a different perspective on complexity than the one Bornstein noted.

I submit that taking into consideration some of this kind of complexity would be helpful to the practicing child analyst, and it also more generally offers insight into child psychoanalytic theory and practice. But how to do it? The first step is for child analysts to become more familiar with contemporary developmental science. The second step would be to supplement analytic case reports with additional types of data. Finally, it would be useful to find a way to put these insights together with the analyst's unique ability to make sense of the child's subjective world as it is communicated to her through words and symbolic play.

First, I will give a brief *theoretical background* to provide a context for this discussion. I will conclude the theoretical section with a discussion of my major emphasis, the concept of "co-creativity" and the repair of mismatches in the caregiving relationship. Then I briefly discuss the difficulties involved in putting together these different kinds of data—the psychoanalytic and the developmental—and ask whether it is possible to preserve the inner world of the child as a focus if these other theoretical considerations and the data associated with them are included in psychoanalytic formulations. Finally, I will offer an initial attempt at a solution to this challenge of integration, what I call the "sandwich model." The sandwich model is an attempt to integrate current developmental science with psychoanalytic theory and practice in a way that can be useful to the practicing child analyst (Harrison, 2013). The organizing principle of the sandwich model is *multiple simultaneous meaning-making processes.*

THEORETICAL BACKGROUND

EARLY CHILD ANALYSTS AND THE EARLY CAREGIVING RELATIONSHIP

As I have noted, it is impressive to see the emphasis Bornstein gave to the mother's difficulty bonding with Frankie as an infant. The importance of the mother-child relationship was demonstrated early on by Anna Freud and Dorothy Burlingham in their work in the war nurseries (Kennedy, 2009). These observations were amplified by Spitz's powerful observational data from foundling homes (Spitz, 1965) and by Winnicott's writing about the mother-child relationship derived in part from his observations as a pediatrician (Winnicott, 1982). Henry Herman's ideas about the flow of energy between infant and mother inspired another pioneer from Anna Freud's circle, Margaret Mahler, whose classic writings about separation-individuation and "refueling" derive from extensive observation of her mother-infant groups (Mahler, 1974). The intergenerational transmission of problematic patterns in the mother-infant relationship was described by Anna Freud's followers, for example, Selma Fraiberg in her famous paper, "Ghosts in the Nursery" (Fraiberg and Adelson, 1975). Lieberman further elaborated this work as the theoretical basis for her "parent child psychotherapy" (Lieberman, Silverman, and Pawl, 2000).

DEPRESSED MOTHERS

As noted, both Anna Freud and Selma Fraiberg described the effect on the child of the mother's traumatic reactions and depression. In Bornstein's paper, she describes Frankie's mother as planning her pregnancy and feeling "happy and contented" anticipating the birth of her first child, "yet the very first moment she held the baby in her arms, she had felt estranged from him" (p. 182 [99]). It is not hard to imagine that Frankie's mother was suffering from postpartum depression. We have learned much more about maternal depression and its effect on the child's development since Bornstein wrote about Frankie.

Most research on the effect of maternal depression on the developing child has focused on depression in the postpartum period (Murray et al., 1992; Murray and Cooper, 1997; Murray et al., 2010; Murray et al. 2011; Campbell, Cohn, and Meyers, 1995). This research has shown that children of mothers with postpartum depression are affected at every developmental stage, from infancy through early adulthood. Maternal depression has been linked with depression, behavior problems, and other psychopathology in their offspring (Tronick and Weinberg, 1997). In a 2009 review of postpartum depression, maternal depression was found to negatively affect early maternal bonding processes, mother-infant interaction, and cognitive and motor development (Tronick and Reck, 2009, p. 148). These unfortunate effects on the infants of depressed mothers appeared to be related to the mother's impaired parenting skills. The results of microanalysis of mother-infant interactions as well as in-home observations demonstrate distortions in the emotional communication between mother and infant caused by the mother's depression (Weinberg et al., 2006).

Researchers found that depressed mothers tend to fall into two groups—mothers who are intrusive and mothers who are disengaged and withdrawn (Tronick and Weinberg, 1997). Interestingly, it appears that the experience of having a withdrawn, disengaged mother in infancy seemed to produce a particularly adverse effect. The withdrawn mother does not offer the baby a predictable set of behaviors with which to organize his behavior, and the baby is left to regulate himself without a mutually regulating partner. These babies may grow up to be depressed and irritable children (Tronick and Reck, 2009). This picture of an irritable child is consistent with Bornstein's description of Frankie. Again, however, without observational and more historical data, we can only hypothesize about this idea.

It is also important to note that I am not saying Bornstein's formulations of Frankie's mother identifying Frankie with her resented brother, or of Frankie's jealousy of his sister, do not hold value. As we continue to note, most current developmental models include a multitude of variables, as I will explain in the final section on "Multiple Simultaneous Meaning-Making," and the parental representation of the child is another important variable.

ATTACHMENT THEORY

In the 1950s and 1960s, John Bowlby developed his ideas about a motivational system that was different from Freud's instinctual drives. Instead of being motivated by the desire for nurturance or love, Bowlby proposed that the infant was primarily motivated by the need for comfort and security, including physical proximity to his primary caregiver. The security of this attachment would then allow the infant to explore the world (Bowlby, 1958, 1969). Through the mother's sensitive and attuned caregiving, the infant would come to expect reliable comfort when in distress and develop an internal representation of the caregiving relationship, or an "internal working model." Bowlby described a repertoire of innate infant behaviors designed to maintain proximity with the caregiver—the infant's reaching for and clinging to the mother, and the infant's smile and vocalizing. He referred to the mother as the baby's psychic organizer and the baby's ego and superego. In contemporary attachment studies, as predicted by Bowlby, the secure caregiving relationship has been shown to provide the means for the development of *emotional self-regulation* (Cummings and Cicchetti, 1990; Schore, 2001; Beebe and Lachmann, 2014, pp. 24–40).

Attachment theory has generated fifty years of productive research utilizing the strange situation paradigm (SSP), designed by Bowlby's student Mary Ainsworth, and the Adult Attachment Inventory (AAI), developed by Ainsworth's student Mary Main (Hesse and Main, 2000). The SSP, which includes a series of separation and reunion experiences between infant and mother in the laboratory, categorizes infants into "secure" or "insecure" or "disorganized" in their attachment according to their behavior during the reunions (Main and Solomon, 1990). "Disorganized attachment" identified in the SSP is said to predict psychopathology in older children, and the AAI is said to predict the attachment status of the mother's unborn child on the basis of her relationship with her own mother (Hesse and Main, 2000). Criticism of attachment theory generally focuses on the failure of the theory to take account of the powerful factor of *culture* and the claims of the predictive value of the SSP and AAI, particularly the *confusion of "correlation" with "prediction,"* given the multitude of variables affecting the caregiving relationship and the complex interactions among them.

On the other hand, it is hard to imagine formulating Frankie's problems without taking into account what we now know about attachment. The description of Frankie's mother's "uncanny and uneasy feeling" when she heard the infant Frankie cry strikes at the heart of the mother's inability to comfort her baby and the lack of an initial "secure base" in Frankie's life. Frankie's "marked anxiety" and rejecting response to his mother at their reunion after the birth of his sister, seems to indicate an insecure attachment pattern when he was three years old. In fact, Frankie's "tyrannical" control of his mother, his "outbursts of wild aggression" if she did not comply with his demands, and his "violent, panic-stricken," desperate clinging to her if she had to leave, suggests a "disorganized attachment," the pattern associated with psychopathology in the older child. Of course, all of this is inference, because in the absence of adequate data we can only guess at Frankie's attachment style.

Bornstein does identify Frankie's initial trauma as occurring in the early mother-infant relationship and as related to his mother's inability to connect with and comfort Frankie. However, she suggests that Frankie's wild aggression derived primarily from his rage at his mother and his wish for revenge. In contrast, an attachment theorist might see Frankie's behavior less as an organized intention to exact revenge and more as the disorganized, dysregulated aggression commonly seen when a young child with no method for repairing the rupture caused by the separation from his mother is reunited with her. *However, as we shall see in our discussion of multiple simultaneous processes, the latter formulation does not exclude the possibility of a retaliatory symbolic meaning in Frankie's inner world.*

TEMPERAMENT AND SENSORY REACTIVITY

Temperament can be defined as "what a child brings to the interaction with the environment to create personality," pointing out that nowadays we tend to talk about "individual differences" instead of temperament, but that individual differences tend to be a "blend of temperament and environment" (Snidman, 2011). Temperamental differences in children are reflected in different thresholds of reactivity in the amygdala. If the amygdala output effects are studied—output to the larynx (crying), and output to the skeletal motor system—studies identify a group of "timid" children who have inherited a low threshold of reactivity of the amygdala. There is a lot of overlap between the sensory-integration scale and the temperament scale, and some people think they are not so different. If part of your definition of sensory-integration disorder is that there is an overwhelming response to sensory information that the child is born with, you could call it temperament.

It is well known that high reactive temperament and insufficient developmental regulatory competencies may complicate a child's attempts to cope with adverse life circumstances and even everyday transitions (Kagan et al., 2007; Kagan, 1989). Child clinicians—pediatricians, occupational therapists, pediatric neurologists, early intervention therapists—typically consider these characteristics of a child in their assessments. Yet it is uncommon for psychoanalytic formulations to include mention of a child's temperament and especially his or her sensory reactivity. In fact, when making an argument for castration anxiety generated by his nurse's patting him on the bottom as a source of his masochistic passivity, Bornstein appears to reject a "biological" contribution to his conflicts as if such an idea challenged her psychoanalytic formulation (Bornstein, 1949, p. 201 [118]). Yet, in this commentary we are accumulating evidence for the inclusion of multiple factors in our psychoanalytic formulations, and we need the data to do that. We know that Frankie's infancy was characterized by violent screaming. The history states that he was calmed by more-frequent feeding, suggesting that he was hungry and could not accommodate the feeding schedule initiated by the nurse.

While not contending that motives and beliefs are irrelevant, proponents of the contribution of temperament to personality suggest that children are born with biases that predispose them to acquire different kinds of motives, beliefs, and actions (Kagan, 1989). The temperamental bias that has been most studied is related to the concept of approach versus withdrawal when faced with novel and challenging events (ibid.). A group of high-reactive children, born with a lower threshold of limbic-hypothalamic activation to unfamiliarity and challenge, react more strongly to even small increases in uncertainty than does the average child (ibid.). In the case of children with these innate sensitivities, the child may be expected to have more difficulties with transitions—the transition to bed and sleep, the transition from sleep to wake and then to school—than the typical child. I would wonder—though, again, one can only wonder without more data—whether Frankie's continued bouts of screaming and his difficulties settling to sleep at night, as well as his trouble making the transition to school are suggestive of a high-reactive, or "inhibited," temperament (ibid.).

Many studies underscore the crucial importance of sensitive caregiving to the highly reactive child (Cummings and Cicchetti, 1990; Kochanska, 1995; Murray et al., 2011; Suomi, 1997; Tronick and Weinberg, 1997). A helpful way to conceptualize this process is to imagine that in *the co-creative process the high-reactive infant contributes a propensity for creating mismatches*. He is more often unavailable—sometimes actively dysregulated and other times withdrawn in a dysregulated state—when his mother seeks to connect with him, and comforting him is a greater challenge.

CO-CREATIVITY: THE REPAIR OF MISMATCHES

Perhaps the preeminent method of studying co-creativity in infant development is the face-to-face still-face (FFSF) paradigm (Tronick, 2007). The experiment involves an interruption of engagement between mother and infant as the mother is instructed to suddenly become unresponsive to her infant while maintaining her face-to-face position with him or her. The dramatic effect this interruption in social engagement with the mother has on the infant is demonstrated by behavioral responses—gaze aversion, crying, self-regulatory gestures, arching back, loss of postural tone—and also by physiological changes such as changes in heart rate, skin conductance, and salivary cortisol level (Gunnar and Donzella, 2002; Murray et al., 2010).

Challenging the earlier developmental paradigm of a harmonious caregiving relationship established and maintained by the sensitive attunement of the mother, FFSF experiments in the late 1980s demonstrated that the baby makes a substantial contribution to the type and quality of the early relationship. That is not to say that the relationship is symmetrical; the infant is helpless in maintaining its regulation—physiological (temperature, nurturance)—and requires "good enough" caregiving to manage affective regulation. However, microanalysis of mother-infant playful interactions showed that the well-functioning mother-infant pairs spent approximately 70 percent of the time in affective mismatch (Tronick, 1989). In addition, the infants were the initiators of at least half of the interactions (ibid.). In his Mutual Regulation Model, Tronick explained that both mother and infant were engaged in a reciprocal interactive process of regulating affect and intention, and "good" mother-infant pairs were characterized less by harmony than by their ability to *repair* small mismatches in their efforts to connect with (and regulate) each other (ibid.). This conceptual model allows for the true complexity of the infant (the factors that make the infant a unique being from the start) to enter into the equation, such as, the infant's temperament, sensory profile, or developmental immaturity, as well as what had been previously emphasized—features of the mother's caregiving style. Bornstein does not dismiss Frankie's contribution to the failure of repair of mismatches in the caregiving relationship in infancy, but she does not give evidence of co-creative process in her formulations of the etiology of Frankie's dysregulated states.

It is remarkable to consider the fact that most of the time they are interacting, mothers and babies are working to achieve a match, but as soon as they reach an emotionally matching situation, one or the other will shift, and they will return to a mismatch and again begin trying to find each other. It follows that patterns of interaction in the infant-caregiver relationship are all co-created—including patterns of attachment—and also that the key to healthy development in the infant resides not so much in the matches or mismatches between them but rather in the capacity of the partnership to repair. It is this that I imagine was impaired in Frankie's relationship with his mother.

We see in Bornstein's account of Frankie's analysis that the infant's contribution (temperament, oversensitivity, effective communication of needs by crying) is left out of the picture. Even more important is the consistent observation that from the beginning and at the subsequent major life transitions documented in the paper—the birth of Frankie's sister, his beginning school—*Frankie's and his mother's ability to repair the strain placed on their caregiving relationship was inadequate to allow him to move forward comfortably in his development.*

Night feeding was said to be "continued for an unusually long time"— until five and a half months, and when the 2:00 A.M. feedings were discontinued, he screamed at this hour for several months. I would imagine that most contemporary parents in the United States and also infant specialists would think that night feedings beyond five and a half months were not unusual, and the fact that Frankie continued to protest when no one responded to his cries with nurturance would also not seem strange. Bornstein states, "It could not be ascertained whether the baby's crying and screaming spells were unusually violent or whether they seemed so because the parents were over-sensitive. As a matter of fact, the parents did not dare to fall asleep because of their anticipation of the baby's screaming" (Bornstein, 1949, p. 182 [100]). This appears to be the beginning of the unhappy cycle of mutual overcontrol between Frankie and his caregivers. Already as an infant, Frankie was coming to anticipate frustration in his efforts to repair the mismatches in his caregiving relationship. This frustration had sensori-affective-motoric meaning for Frankie before he gained the capacity to symbolize, but it is likely that features of this unmetabolizable distress in a caregiving relationship remained in the attachment domain of Frankie's repertoire of meanings and influenced the emergence of "King Boo-Boo."

It is easy to imagine that the problematic trajectory of mutual overcontrol—Frankie's domineering behavior and mother's acquiescence—in a maladaptive attempt to repair mismatches, began in the newborn period, in response to a combination of factors such as maternal depression (perhaps aggravated by paternal unavailability and an undermining competition with the nurse) and a highly reactive infant. In addition, the capacity to repair mismatches takes different forms at different stages of development. The ability to play games—you may lose—is such a form, as is the capacity to take turns with siblings at home or peers on the playground, the ability to comply with teachers' directions, and even the willingness to give up the defense of omnipotence enough to learn—all require competency in healing mismatches. Unfortunately, we do not have the data to support statements about the quality of Frankie's relationships with peers, nor—although we know of course that Frankie resented his sister and had hostile, aggressive fantasies about her—even much about the actual quality of his sibling relationship.

It is my opinion that the repair of mismatch becomes the driver of healthy development in the young child (and perhaps in older children and even adults). We can now see that the capacity to repair mismatches comes to belong to the child, though it is forged in the caregiving relationship. But how is the failure to repair mismatches experienced in the subjective world of the infant and in the inner world of the older child who can symbolize?

THE INNER WORLD OF THE CHILD

Bornstein states, "It took a long time before we succeeded in making Frankie aware of the connection between his masturbation and his feelings of guilt. The violence of his resistance made it clear that he was not yet capable of allowing the subject of masturbation to be discussed, or even of acknowledging it as a problem in his life" (p. 199 [116]). How do we know that the "long time" it took before Bornstein succeeded in making Frankie aware of his masturbation guilt was due to his "resistance"?

In fact, how do we "know" the child's inner world? The analyst develops hypotheses about the child's inner world from the child's words or symbolic play, but the adult's hypotheses are heavily influenced by her theory. In this case, Bornstein is looking for Frankie's intrapsychic conflict about masturbation. I am not suggesting that she was incorrect in her formulation; I am only suggesting that there are many alternative narratives that an analyst might have constructed from Frankie's communications. It is also true that because of their immature cognitive capacities and the objects and experiences that are salient to children of a particular developmental age, they make a different sense of their daily experience than adults do. The young child's developmentally appropriate meanings are very different from our own (Harrison and Tronick, 2007). Although psychoanalysis has come to accept the idea, introduced by the Relational School of psychoanalysis and by analysts influenced by developmental science, that patient and analyst are co-contributors to the analytic process, child analysts do not often acknowledge the degree to which the meanings generating formulations and interpretations are co-created (Stern et al., 1998). This may be in part because the practicing clinician needs a narrative to guide him- or herself in the analytic work, and an awareness of multiple possibilities at every moment would interfere with the coherence, and thus the usefulness, of the narrative. In Bornstein's case there is a continuous narrative that shifts and turns, with Frankie's play and stories.

This narrative moves from Frankie's anger at his mother for his sister's birth, which fueled his fear of her retaliatory abandonment (p. 185 [102]), to his desire to take his mother's place in caring for a baby, and his wish to kill his mother (p. 186 [103]), to Frankie's deep sadness at the primary abandonment by his mother (p. 187 [104]), and a repressed longing for his mother (p. 188 [105]), and then to his "urge to know 'what was going on' between his parents" (p. 190 [108]), his primal scene fantasies of his mother being injured, attacked by a man (p. 191 [108]), and then a voyeuristic impulse associated with a fantasy that he was an omnipotent god (p. 192 [109]).

My view of the analytic exchange is that patient and analyst share bits and pieces of meaning with each other in a constantly evolving flow of partial meanings, periodically pausing to settle on a relatively coherent meaning they explicitly or implicitly choose as having special importance, this meaning being necessarily different from what either had at the beginning, and then they move on. If we could see inside the head of patient and analyst we would see that the momentary meanings that acquire salience for both of them (and this is true to some degree in adult analysis as well) are not actually exactly the same for each person.

Bornstein mentions Melanie Klein and criticizes what she imagines Klein would do with Frankie (p. 186 [103]). The comparison of rival schools of psychoanalysis from the point of efficacy presents us with a fascinating problem. How can two analysts working under the assumption that their theory—which they have a compelling conviction to be the best or even the only correct theory, and which they are convinced informs their technique such that their technique is better than the other school's technique—*both make their patients better?* If one theory were much better than the other, would not all other theories have died out? Perhaps it is not the content of the interpretations, not the theory that holds the key to therapeutic outcome. Perhaps we can find an answer to this dilemma in the concept of multiple simultaneous meaning-making.

Multiple Simultaneous Meaning-Making and the "Sandwich Model"

My reading of the case suggests that a major difficulty for Frankie was the failure to repair ruptures in his caregiving relationships. The positive result of the analysis indicates that he was able to gain capacity to repair strains and ruptures in relationships, but because of the data we are offered in the case report, we do not know how this was accomplished. That is because what we are given is mainly a narrative consistent with the analyst's theory. Current developmental theory prepares us to make sense of much more data than this kind of narrative.

What we would like to be able to examine is more data about Frankie's early caregiving relationship, including moment-to-moment observations about what Frankie and his caregivers—particularly his mother—contributed to the interactive patterns. We would like to have data about interactive patterns in the analytic relationship—especially data that demonstrates attempts at repair of the inevitable strain or ruptures in the relationship—and most useful would be this kind of data in the micro-process, not large enactments. This kind of data demonstrating the moment-to-moment co-creative process would require a record of the nonverbal communication of the kind that is captured on video.

I imagine that one of the ways Frankie grew in the analysis was to create new meanings—mostly more-adaptive ones—with his analyst, even though they were not the only meanings they could make together. The co-creative process of making meaning requires the child to communicate an element of meaning from his inner world, during which process the meaning already begins to change as the child struggles to represent it, and then requires the analyst to try to make sense of it and offer that new sense back to the child. The child then responds, further adding to the evolving meaning. As we have learned from developmental research, this process takes place in multiple domains of experience and function—for example, in nonverbal coordination of rhythms of body and voice, in bodily sensations—as well as in verbal and symbolic communication, and in different time scales—seconds and split seconds as well as in narrative time (Beebe, Jaffe, and Lachmann, 1992; Beebe and Lachmann, 2014; Harrison, 2014). What I am describing is a reparative process. It repairs the rupture in the old meaning that has come apart, by creating a new one to take its place. It also *represents* the repair of the rupture in the relationship with the caregiver; again and again it gives the child an experience of creating something of value with another person. This process generates confidence in mastery, faith in the power of relationships, and hope for the future.

But if we emphasize aspects of Frankie's development that involve small interactive patterns in his caregiving relationships and the domain of nonverbal communication in his analysis, then do we have to give up our analytic theory that helps us make sense of what is going on in the child's symbolic "inner world"? To address this dilemma, I have developed a conceptualization that I call the "sandwich model" (Harrison, 2014). This concept is grounded in the elaborated dyadic expansion of consciousness model of Edward Tronick (Tronick, 2007).

The premise of the sandwich model is that a "layered" approach is necessary to understand the process of exchanges that result in therapeutic change. In the three layers of a sandwich, the top layer, or top slice of bread of the sandwich, represents a broad view of the change process; it is nonlinear and includes the feature of uncertainty, a general principle of dynamic systems theory. The middle layer, or meat of the sandwich, is explained by *theories that are immediately and clinically useful to a therapist,* such as in this case, Anna Freud's psychoanalytic theory. This is a primarily linear theory and uses language and play symbols to "tell a story of what happened." This layer is necessary because the clinician needs a way of making sense of her patient's communications in each session and over the course of weeks and months, and the most effective way of doing this is through constructing a narrative. The bottom layer, or bottom slice of bread of the sandwich, is the micro-process; this layer includes the moment-to-moment patterns of coordinated rhythms that both communicate meaning and provide the essential scaffold for all higher-level change processes. The micro-process also requires a nonlinear theory to make sense of its variability and emergent properties. Taking a bite out of the sandwich will include a "polysomic bundle" of communicative behaviors (Harrison and Tronick, 2011).

The way Bornstein worked with Frankie involved engaging his inner world of symbolic meaning with emotional accuracy. She needed a linear theory in order to explain his behavior on the basis of his inner thoughts and feelings, for example, his fantasies. Adding a nonlinear perspective of the way people grow and change through interactive processes enriches this domain of understanding. The nonlinear theoretical perspective takes into account variability and uncertainty and explains interactive patterns of exchange through which new organization—or meaning—emerge. The nonlinear perspective on interactive processes can encompass the idea of intrapsychic conflict, as such conflict involves interactive processes within the individual.

CONCLUSION

Child analysis includes multiple domains of therapeutic action occurring simultaneously with the intention of making sense of the child's inner world as he or she communicates it in a partial and constantly evolving form. Formulations that analyst and child make together that have special value to them may not derive their value from the accuracy of their content. They may instead derive their value from something about the way that they came to it together, such as linking an idea and a particularly important behavior or two ideas in the context of an affectively important moment. In this paper, I explore the possibility that it is repairs of ruptures that form the leading edge of therapeutic action. How is this different from the relational idea of analyzing enactments? It may not be, if "enactments" are seen as occurring in multiple domains of activity and time scales and if they are accepted as constantly taking place, just as the mother and infant are constantly trying to find a match and as soon as they find one, losing it and starting on the road to find another.

In this case, the data are not presented to assess the hypothesis that repair of ruptures was an important element of the therapeutic result, nor to deal with many of the complexities of co-creativity; this is not surprising, since the analysis was done more than sixty years ago. But the case suggests to me the importance to contemporary analysts of collecting more and different kinds of data (such as videos or transcripts) that would allow us to examine various hypotheses and complexities in the analytic process. This broad perspective seems particularly important for child analysis to remain vibrant and important in the twenty-first century.

BIBLIOGRAPHY

BEEBE, B., JAFFE, J., AND LACHMANN, F. (1992). A dyadic systems view of communication. In N. J. Skolnick and S. C. Warshaw, eds., *Relational Perspectives in Psychoanalysis*, pp. 61–81. Hillsdale, NJ: Analytic Press.

BEEBE, B., AND LACHMANN, F. (2014). *The Origins of Attachment: Infant Research and Adult Treatment*. London and New York: Taylor & Francis.

BORNSTEIN, B. (1949). The analysis of a phobic child. *Psychoanalytic Study of the Child* 3:181–226.

BOWLBY, J. (1958). The nature of the child's tie to his mother. *International Journal of Psycho-Analysis* 39:350–373.

———. (1969). *Attachment and Loss*. New York: Basic Books.

CAMPBELL, S. B., COHN, J. F., AND MEYERS, T. (1995). Depression in first-time mothers: Mother-infant interaction and depression chronicity. *Developmental Psychology* 31:349–357.

CUMMINGS, E. M., AND CICCHETTI, D. (1990). Towards a transactional model of relations between attachment and depression. In M. T. Greenberg, D. Cicchetti, and E. M. Cummings, eds., *Attachment in the Preschool Years: Theory, Research, and Intervention*, pp. 339–372. Chicago: University of Chicago Press.

FRAIBERG, S., ADELSON, E., AND SHAPIRO, V. (1975). Ghosts in the nursery: A psychoanalytic approach to the problems of impaired infant-mother relationships. *Journal of the American Academy of Child Psychiatry* 14(3): 387–421.

GUNNAR, M., AND DONZELLA, B. (2002). Social regulation of the cortisol levels in early human development. *Psychoneuroendocrinology* 27 (1–2): 199–220.

HARRISON, A. M. (2013). The music and dance of therapeutic action: The sandwich model. *International Journal of Psychoanalysis* 95(2): 313–340.

———. (2014). Imagining Chloe in infancy. In B. Beebe and F. Lachmann, eds., *Origins of Attachment: Infant Research and Adult Treatment*, pp. 178–185. New York: Taylor & Francis.

HARRISON, A., AND TRONICK, E. (2007). Now we have a playground: Emerging new ideas of therapeutic action. *Journal of the American Psychoanalytic Association* 55 (3): 853–874.

HARRISON, A. M., AND TRONICK, E. Z. (2011). "The noise monitor": A developmental perspective of verbal and nonverbal meaning-making in psychoanalysis. *Journal of the American Psychoanalytic Association* 59(5): 961–983.

HESSE, H., AND MAIN, M. (2000). The organized categories of infant, child, and adult attachment: Flexible vs. inflexible attention under attachment related stress. *Journal of the American Psychoanalytic Association* 48 (4): 1055–1097.

KAGAN, J. (1989). The concept of behavioral inhibition to the unfamiliar. In J. Reznick, ed., *Perspectives on Behavioral Inhibition*, pp. 1–25. Chicago: University of Chicago Press.

KAGAN, J., SNIDMAN, N., KAHN, V., AND TOWSLEY, S. (2007). The preservation of two infant temperaments into adolescence. *Monographs for the Society of the Research in Child Development* 72 (2).

KENNEDY, H. (2009). Children in conflict: Anna Freud and the war nurseries. *Psychoanalytic Study of the Child* 64:306–319.

KOCHANSKA, G. (1995). Children's temperament, mother's discipline, and security of attachment: Multiple pathways to emerging internalization. *Child Development* 66 (3): 597–615.

LIEBERMAN, A. F., SILVERMAN, R., AND PAWL, J. H. (2000). Infant-parent psychotherapy: Core concepts and current approaches. In C. H. Zeanah, Jr., ed., *Handbook of Infant Mental Health*, 2nd ed., pp. 472–484). New York: Guilford Press.

MAIN, M., AND SOLOMON, J. (1990). Procedures for identifying infants as disorganized/disoriented during the Ainsworth Strange Situation. In M. Greenberg, D. Cicchetti, and E. Cummings, eds., *Attachment in the Preschool Years*, pp. 121–160. Chicago: University of Chicago Press.

MAHLER, M. (1974). Symbiosis and individuation—The psychological birth of the infant. *Psychoanalytic Study of the Child* 29:89–106.

MURRAY, L. (1992). The impact of postnatal depression on infant development. *Journal of Child Psychology and Psychiatry* 33:543–561.

MURRAY, L., ARTECHE, A., FEARON, P., AND COOPER, P. (2011). Maternal postnatal depression and the development of depression in offspring up to 16 years of age. *Journal of the American Academy of Child & Adolescent Psychiatry* 50 (5): 460–470.

MURRAY, L., AND COOPER, P., EDS. (1997). *Postpartum Depression and Child Development*. New York: Guilford Press.

MURRAY, L., HALLIGAN, S., GOODYER, I., AND HERBERT, J. (2010). Disturbance in early parenting of depressed mothers and cortisol secretion in offspring: A preliminary study. *Journal of Affective Disorders* 122:218–223.

RECK, C., HUNT, A., AND WEISS, R. (2004). Interactive regulation of affect in postpartum depressed mothers and their infants: An overview. *Psychopathology* 37:272–280.

SANDER, L. (2008). *Living Systems, the Evolving Consciousness, and the Emerging Person*. New York: Analytic Press.

SCHORE, A. N. (2001). Effects of a secure attachment relationship on right brain development, affect regulation, and infant mental health. *Infant Mental Health Journal* 22:7–66.

SNIDMAN, N. (2011). Lecture on Temperament. University of Massachusetts Boston Infant-Parent Mental Health Fellowship/Postgraduate Certificate Program.

SPITZ, R. (1965). *The First Year of Life: A Psychoanalytic Study of Normal and Deviant Development of Object Relations*. New York: International Universities Press.

STERN, D., SANDER, L., NAHUM, J., HARRISON, A., LYONS-RUTH, K., MORGAN, A., BRUSCHWEILER-STERN, N., AND MORGAN, A. (1998). Noninterpretive mechanisms in psychoanalytic therapy: The something more than interpretation. *International Journal of Psychoanalysis* 79:903–921.

SUOMI, S. (1997). Early determinants of behaviour: Evidence from primate studies. *British Medical Bulletin* 53:170–184.

TRONICK, E. (1989). Emotions and emotional communication in infants. *American Psychologist* 44:112–119.

———. (2007). *The Neurobehavioral and Social Emotional Development of Infants and Young Children*. New York: Norton.

TRONICK, E., AND RECK, C. (2009). Infants of depressed mothers. *Harvard Review of Psychiatry* 17 (2): 147–156.
TRONICK, E., AND WEINBERG, M. K. (1997). Depressed mothers and infants: Failure to form dyadic states of consciousness. In L. Murray and P. Cooper, eds., *Postpartum Depression and Child Development*, pp. 54–81. New York: Guilford Press.
WEINBERG, M., OLSON, K., BEEGHLY, M., AND TRONICK, E. (2006). Making up is hard to do, especially for mothers with high levels of depressive symptoms and their infant sons. *Journal of Child Psychology and Psychiatry* 47 (7): 670–683.
WINNICOTT, D. W. (1982). *The Maturational Processes and the Facilitating Environment*. New York: International Universities Press.

CLINICAL CONTRIBUTIONS

What Child Analysis Can Teach Us about Psychoanalytic Technique

STEVEN LURIA ABLON, M.D.

Child analysis has much to teach us about analytic technique. Children have an innate, developmentally driven sense of analytic process. Children in analysis underscore the importance of an understanding and belief in the therapeutic action of play, the provisional aspects of play, and that not all play will be understood. Each analysis requires learning a new play signature that is constantly reorganized. Child analysis emphasizes the emergence and integration of dissociated states, the negotiation of self-other relationships, the importance of co-creation, and the child's awareness of the analyst's sensibility. Child analysis highlights the robust nature of transference and how working through and repairing is related to the initiation of coordinated patterns of high predictability in the context of deep attachments. I will illustrate these and other ideas in the description of the analysis of a nine-year-old boy.

MY CHILD ANALYTIC PATIENTS HAVE INSISTED I LISTEN TO THEIR ideas about how they need to communicate the pain that brings them to treatment. They do this by letting me know how we are going to interact, how our play and talk needs to evolve. If I fail to recognize what they have in mind, they are surprisingly forgiving and return to their unconscious plan. They have said things like "Stop talking and play; watch and you will learn." One child asked "How many children do

Dr. Ablon is a Training and Supervising Adult and Child Analyst at the Boston Psychoanalytic Society and Institute. He is an Associate Clinical Professor, Harvard University Medical School at Massachusetts General Hospital. Dr. Ablon is a published poet whose most recent book is *Night Call*.

The Psychoanalytic Study of the Child 68, ed. Claudia Lament, Robert A. King, Samuel Abrams, Paul M. Brinich, and Rona Knight (Yale University Press, copyright © 2015 by Claudia Lament, Robert A. King, Samuel Abrams, Paul M. Brinich, and Rona Knight).

you have?" When I asked what he thought, he said, "Dr. A., don't you know how many children you have?" Perhaps their youth, their developmental energy, and their being less bound by conventions of social interaction and expectations of therapeutic process make them freer. They point out when conventional approaches are not useful. Children seem to have an innate developmentally driven sense of analytic process (Klein, 1932, 1961). A five-year-old boy at the beginning of analysis cut out a drawing of a good boy and bad boy. He wanted to throw out the bad boy, but I wondered if we could keep it in his folder. Three years later when finishing up, he found the bad boy and the good boy and stapled them together. But I think our adults may know as much about the process as he did. Perhaps if I were more skillful with my adult patients, I would not need my child patients to clarify technical issues.

I am going to tell you about the treatment of a boy who first came to see me at age nine and how he made me think about technique. Of course, there is no technique separate from the uniqueness of each therapeutic experience.

Sam was referred because he was deeply unhappy and had severe temper tantrums. He picked up large pieces of furniture and hurled them around. He was frightened to be alone, was indecisive, and perfectionistic. If the family went for ice cream, when asked what flavor he would like he would stand for hours trying to decide. He always wore sweatpants and a sweatshirt with the hood pulled up over his head so you could hardly see him. In school he would erase his work over and over until there were holes in the paper. He had frequent nightmares that kept him and the family up at night. He was quite bright and did well in school but was anxious and without confidence. At school kids picked on him and sometimes locked him screaming in his locker. He was particularly interested in science, and his favorite activity was to go to the science museum. Sam has one sibling, a brother four years older who had demanding educational needs that took a great deal of time and energy in the family. His brother was unhappy and angry and would boss Sam around and hit him. The parents' impression was that Sam resented all the attention his older brother required, but Sam didn't say so directly.

Sam's parents were both in their early forties. His father was a mathematics professor who specialized in complex problems of probability. He acknowledged that he was on the obsessional side and was good at weighing all the possibilities. He was nurturing and attentive with Sam and his brother. Sam's mother was an art historian who took the boys hiking, camping, and fishing. She struggled with periods of anxiety, depression, and angry outbursts. During Sam's treatment it became clear that these outbursts were overwhelming for him.

The summer before Sam came to see me he had a bicycle accident, fell, and broke his jaw. He had to have his jaw wired in the operating room. Sam's development had been normal, and he had no other hospitalizations or major injuries. Because of his brother's learning problems, Sam had extensive testing and no difficulties were found. He and his parents were eager to undertake a more intensive treatment involving four-times-a-week sessions. They described how his problems were extremely disruptive for the family. They weren't sleeping. They couldn't go anywhere because he would have tantrums or become paralyzed with indecision. They talked about how hard they tried to help Sam, tried to be caring and sympathetic, but were infuriated with him most of the time. During Sam's treatment I met with both parents every several months, and they were supportive and cooperative. My meetings with the parents focused on helping them have a more empathic attitude toward Sam's struggles and solidifying my alliance with them so that they could have confidence in the treatment and me and support our work. I met with Sam four times a week from age nine until shortly before his graduation from high school.

When I first met Sam he was a pale thin boy with curly blond hair hidden under the hood of his gray sweatshirt. Although he turned his head somewhat away from me, I could see he had a sparkle in his eyes and that he listened intently. I explained to Sam that in our time together we could get to know each other and learn about feelings and worries as we talked and played with the things in the office.

As we began meeting, Sam set about playing the game Life. In this game you spin the wheel, numbers come up, you get a car, go around the board, and various events happen depending on where you land. You go to college, get a job, get money, get married, buy a house, have children, pay taxes, and may get blown backward by a tornado. The idea is to become a millionaire or multimillionaire. Sam chose this game among many possibilities. One playing board comes with the game. Over the time from age nine to age fourteen, with my help Sam invented nine additional boards that were played in sequence one to ten and then resumed again. He told me what to write in the spaces of the new boards, and we discussed new rules.

The themes of our play included acquiring enormous supplies and then repeating the boards so the game would never end. The game became a trying-on of life possibilities. There was the issue of following the rules, such as paying taxes, and dealing with adversity, such as a tornado, and a space called "Revenge" where he could extract money from me or send me backward in my life.

After several months of treatment Sam said, "You know I have been thinking about our game. We have been scrooges, just getting money to have it, to keep it, more and more of it, not doing anything with it for our families or ourselves. Our wives and children have no place to sleep even though we are so rich. Why don't we buy things with our money, like businesses, Rolls Royces, jet planes, yachts, and mansions?" These aspects of the play helped Sam acknowledge, bear, and put in perspective overwhelming painful feelings of deprivation. When I accumulated the most money, Sam told me, "Since you are doing so well, getting so much, I am going to be mean. I am going to get revenge. You'll be very sorry." In this way Sam began to elaborate his feelings of envy and destructiveness.

Sam often told me dreams. He said, "I'm tired. I had a bad dream and was awake for three hours. My mother told me to ask you what I can do at night, like exercises I could do so I wouldn't be so scared."

I answered, "Perhaps you could tell me about the dream and the dream would help us understand what scares you." Sam said, "I dreamed I was at a friend's house on top of a hill and there were aliens who looked just like people. They were sleeping in a hammock. Our piano was on the lawn of his house, and his mother said to practice. That made the aliens angry, disturbed them and woke them. They pulled off their masks and chased me so I would stop playing the piano. They weren't going to hurt me. They just wanted me to stop." I said, "What comes to mind about the dream?"

Sam said, "After dinner my mother reminds me to play the piano. Except when I am tired, I don't mind. Last night my father was away, so I came and woke my mother. She takes five minutes to fall asleep again, so I usually wake my father, who falls right back to sleep." I said, "The aliens were angry, so perhaps the dream has to do with angry feelings."

Sam continued, "My parents don't get angry when I wake them up."

I think Sam was telling me how his mother got angry like an alien and how he felt like an alien, overwhelmed by his anger and alienated from the real world where people live in a harmonious way. I think he feels like what the poet A. E. Houseman wrote, "I, a stranger and afraid In a world I never made" (2005).

Several months later Sam told me, "I was at a book fair at our school. I am getting a lot of science books. My father used to read chapters of science books to me at night since I was six years old. One book said there was no water on Mars. Later the book said there was ice on Mars. I remembered and wrote to the company. They sent me a free book and said they would correct it in the next edition. I am going to look in the book today and see if they fixed it." I said, "You know, it sounds like you are good at remembering things, like very special times with your father." Sam agreed and began playing Life. I thought he was telling me about his wish for closeness with his father and me in the transference. I also thought the water on Mars was about his growing confidence knowing and trusting his feelings and experience.

At this point in the game of Life Sam was involved in making rules for picking cards. He wondered if it was really good to pick as many cards as you want, and I asked, "What might not be good about taking as much as you want?" He replied, "If everybody picked and picked and never stopped, that wouldn't be good." Sam used a new tactic, freezing me, so he could go on picking. Then he wrote a rule about how after a long time there was a limit on picking. Sam wondered, was this rule okay with me? We could make rules if they were okay with both of us. That was fair wasn't it? I said I thought so. In this way Sam seemed to be trying to master his voracious and competitive feelings, his longings for power, nourishment, and love. He explored: Are there limits to our desires? Is collaboration possible? How can rules and a superego be manageable? Sam said when he picked a card, before he turned it over he could feel if it was good or bad. He said happily, "We will be able to play this game a very long time." I thought Sam was exploring his wishes never to have to leave and be separate, and his fantasy of a magical way to know and control his life.

Sam and his father read chapters every night, and Sam and I played Life. We found common worlds together. I was a therapeutic companion and adventurer into a world that is a scary place. Our game was an introduction for Sam to another way of looking at himself. Sam built his self-esteem and his confidence in his memory and observations. We would have a long time to be in this place together. We would share navigational and educational efforts.

Two years later Sam said, "I'm tired. I ran to the front of the school, but I was too late, and I missed my car pool. I tried to call my mother, but some kids closed the door and locked me out of the school. I have been teased for twelve years. I don't let myself have feelings about it anymore. I'm used to it. The popular kids who get terrible grades and do no work and talk on the phone all night and have their parents furious at them call me a nerd and too smart. I don't know why they pick on me. I am not mean in return. Maybe it is because I don't let them copy my papers. They say I am too honest. My parents were both teased."

"My parents say my grades aren't important to them as long as I try hard. I want to go to MIT and be an engineer. I don't want to have a lot of money but enough to be comfortable and have things for my children. If I do earn a lot of money, I'll give it to the homeless. I think the most important thing is liking what you do. I have a few good friends at school. They are nice and smart like me." Sam worked on the pain of how he was treated by other kids and, earlier, by his brother, who beat him up, and his mother in her angry outbursts. He explored his evolving sense of self and self-esteem.

Talking and playing the game of Life, we remained intimately connected in our experience together. When Sam was about fourteen he told me, "You know, when you win a lot, it hurts." I asked what it was like? "Pain, a terrible pain in my stomach, an angry feeling." (He left and went to the bathroom.) "When I don't get money I was hoping for, I also feel a lot of pain, but it is also sadness in my stomach. You are doing well now, and there will be no more luck left in the dice for me." I added, "I'll use it up, like your brother, Jack, and his school troubles." Sam replies, "Jack didn't want a baby brother. I fight with him all the time." Sam's ability to experience and bear his feelings, including in his body, had continued to increase.

Sam had become much less symptomatic and was no longer teased in school. He had developed an interest in computer networks and had a few friends who shared this interest. While in school, he became the head of a large computer network that traded information and programs. Much like the game of Life, he established the rules about participating in this network and becoming a new member. He discussed having to restrict or fire people from the network. He also became adept at computers. For Sam, the game of Life led to a game of Internet life. As the head of the network, Sam had two aliases, Sinbad the Sailor and Icarus. These were different aspects of him—the adventurous part of him and the megalomaniac, grandiose part that flies too high and crashes. In the game of Life the grandiose aspect of his aspirations were explored, and he learned not to overdo it and to build a safe structure.

Many classmates asked him for help with their computers, and I learned a considerable amount myself. At times I worried whether this was a problem in the countertransference. Was I getting too much pleasure from my cyber-world education? Occasionally I wanted to ask him for help with problems I was having with my computer, but I resisted. We continued to play Life while we discussed the computer issues and continued to learn about power, aggression, connection to other people, grandiosity, and superego concerns.

In junior high school Sam said, "I am feeling better. I was sick. I had two dreams. In one I went from one room to the next passing a refrigerator, and something tried to attack me. I ran outside and was with friends. A gorilla came up to me. It was jumping. It was a friend in a gorilla costume. I saw a TV program about a woman who studied gorillas in Africa and found out that they fight and are vicious and kill like humans. I also dreamed a friend of mine was searching for his brother and found him in a swimming pool. There were lobsters in the shallow end and a small shark in the deep end. The shark bit one boy, but he got out of the pool." Sam paused, and I said, "The dreams have attacking, biting, and killing feelings in them, feelings that everyone has but are scary." Sam replied, "I am angry that my parents and my brother are going rafting, and I can't go because I am not old enough. It's not fair. There hasn't been much rain, so there will be a lot of rocks."

By the time Sam was in high school he was able to express his awareness of the therapeutic process, transference, interpretation, and the role of the past. "I had this dream last night. I was walking, going to this place. I didn't even know what it was. This guy says, 'We are going to go into the past.' There is an audience, and somebody I know in the audience. I wander in the dark, go home to tell my parents. I need to say a chant so I won't get stuck in the past. I somehow tell my parents that they have to come with me. They come, and the guy says the chanting. It is light and the guy isn't a kid. Everyone in the audience was going to be stuck in the past.

"It is a weird dream. The father, mother, and boy remind me of Mike, a classmate, and his parents. When Mike beat me up and threatened me if I told, his parents were called to see the principal and Mike was suspended. I remember Mike's big hand on me. Maybe I want them to be trapped in the past, punished, to be mean to them." I think that Sam is now aware that as he masters and puts in perspective his intense feelings of anger, sadness, and fear, he will not be stuck in the past. The guy saying the chanting is himself and me. Perhaps the chant is also about Sam's conflict about growing up and unconsciously wanting to stay in the past.

As we continued to meet through high school Sam played the game of Life less. He talked about his work and his friends, which was still a small, circumscribed group. He went to a local university and saw me once a week. At college he was surprised to find that people considered him an interesting and socially engaging person. He had many friends including girls. He was well liked, admired, and sought after. He had a number of girlfriends, and by the end of college he settled into a committed relationship. After college we no longer met, but I heard that he took a job with a technology company and has gradually assumed greater and greater responsibility. A couple years after college, he and his girlfriend married and subsequently had children.

DISCUSSION

It is heuristically valuable to define play as a free-ranging voluntary activity that occurs within certain limits of time and place, according to accepted rules. In adults and children both play is reversible and provisional. Play carries with it the awareness that it is different from ordinary life. It is accompanied by feelings of tension and joy. For adults, play evolves to a considerable extent from thing-play to thought and word play. Nevertheless in adults nonverbal expression is an important element of play. Talk can be also action and play (Greenberg, 1995). Some aspects of play in adults are puns, humor, metaphor, synonym, irony, sarcasm, and expletive. Play can take place on the substrate of word symbols, such as dreams, legends, mythic figures, and icons of popular culture (Ablon, 2001).

Sam's analysis clarified the importance of an abiding understanding and belief in the therapeutic action of play (Cohen and Solnit, 1993; Huizinga, 1938; Loewald, 1987; Neubauer, 1987; Sanville, 1991; Solnit, Cohen, and Neubauer, 1993; Waelder, 1933; Winnicott, 1971a). Play in the therapeutic setting augments what in fact is an innate capacity for synthesis and organization of affect (Bettleheim, 1976; Borch-Jacobsen, 1992; Hadamard, 1945; Tomkins, 1962, 1963). Play supports developmentally progressive and adaptive forces in children and adults (Brown, 1994; Hurry, 1998; Piaget and Inhelder, 1969; Peller, 1954; Sander, 1983). As Marguerite Duras said, "When the past is recaptured by the imagination, breath is put back into life." Play makes possible a greater capacity to bear and master the most painful feelings, such as murderousness, rage, destructiveness, love, passion, the erotic, sadness, longing, fear, anxiety, and helplessness.

When therapy goes well, a unique play is possible in which the therapist tries to appreciate the symbolic, affective communication and attempts to communicate this appreciation with tact and sensitivity in symbolic terms and, when accessible, in verbal terms. In this process Winnicott helpfully warns about the uses of interpretation: "Interpretation outside the ripeness of the material is indoctrination and produces compliance. . . . A corollary is that resistance arises out of interpretation given outside the area of the overlap of the patient's and the analyst's playing" (1971b, p. 41). As Ferenczi (1921, 1933) emphasizes, the countertransference is the main obstacle to a successful treatment. During Sam's treatment I often worried whether playing these games of Life, elaborating these boards as I was instructed would be viewed by my teachers and colleagues as collaborating with an endless defensiveness. They sat on my shoulder, and I heard them saying *What about analysis of defense, interpretation, medication for depression, for OCD, and behavioral interventions for being teased?* Not that any of these ideas would not have been good additional considerations, but I worried that they should replace what Sam and I were doing. Did I just enjoy playing this game? Did I like learning about computers too much? Did I enjoy having the grand wizard of this prominent network as my patient?

All analyses like Sam's require that we stretch ourselves beyond what is familiar to us in the analytic dialogue and in our psychology. Each analysis requires learning with each patient a new play signature that is constantly reorganized as the analysis evolves. Patients bring to us what is most excruciating and what they have not been able to share with others and with themselves. In Sam's case he brought his deprivation, hunger, murderousness, and fear of abandonment. For the therapeutic experience to be authentic and reach the heart of things, I had to increase my capacity for confusion, helplessness, retaliatory longings, intense competition, and hunger. Every analysis requires an extension and reorganization of our psychic patterns and equilibrium. This can be very demanding, painful, and rewarding in terms of expanding our psychological capacities and unresolved conflicts. It is necessary if we are to accompany our patients in the places that they need to go.

Early in my training Dr. Semrad (1968) would ask, "Will you try and help this patient bear his/her pain?" I knew better than to say no or of course, because how did I know if I could? At these times I turn to my ego ideal, Yoda, and remember, "There is no try, just do." My patients remind me of this every day. When Sam wanted to add more boards and I thought six was enough, I just did it. With adults it is more subtle, like when an adult patient needs to tell me how inadequate and unhelpful I am, I am tempted to try to change this blistering attack with an interpretation.

Sam's play facilitated the emergence and integration of dissociated states. There was the traumatized boy with the broken jaw hidden under his hood. There were Sinbad and Icarus. There are many small splits into different personae and psychic states, like the enormously hungry boy, the strict punitive boy, the vengeful boy. In the elaboration of these self-states and personae they become integrated (Frankel, 1998). Self-states include interaction patterns, state-dependent memories,

cognitions, moods, and affects. As Winnicott (1968) wrote: "The patient can be giving the analyst a sample of the truth; that is to say of
something that is absolutely true for the patient, and when the analyst
gives this back, the interpretation is received by the patient who has
already emerged to some extent from this limited area or dissociated
condition" (p. 209). These dissociated states and especially the small
splits are not as easily recognized in adults.

   With parts of us split off we cannot feel fully alive. A forty-year-old
woman who was very successful in her artistic career came to see me
because of severe anxiety and low self-esteem. After two years in analysis
it emerged that three little people lived in her—an angry child, a sad
child, and a hurt child. After four more years in which parts of many
hours found her in a dissociated state, the feelings accompanying experiences of emotional and sexual abuse emerged. By her sixth year in
analysis, as she was finishing up, the three little people were part of her.
She said being one person, being whole, allowed her to be alive, and it
was a wonderful and precious feeling. In child analysis the integration
and acceptance of disavowed or dissociated aspects of experience is
central, and this is equally true in adult analysis. In adult analysis it is
more disguised because adults rarely play a hungry crocodile, a scared
rabbit, an angry bear.

   In the action and interaction in our game of Life and our time together, Sam and I created symbols and renegotiated self-other relationships through action, mutual influence, and regulation and recognition. These essential processes of therapy are crucial with adults but are
seen less clearly. This is because of the level of action and interaction
in child analysis. The provisional aspect of Sam's and my experience
together is highly mutative. As Montaigne (2003) said, "Nothing is so
firmly believed as what is least known." Different views of our voyage
and us together are all at play, and none have hierarchical status. This
is just as crucial in adult analysis, where a patient tells me that I am
irritable and hostile, and I say "That may be true."

   With Sam there is an acceptance that not all play will be understood
and, as in life, many things will remain uncertain and unknowable.
As Voltaire said, "Doubt is not a pleasant condition but certainty is
absurd." This is just as present in adult analysis and allows the process
to elaborate and surprise (Reik, 1936). Sam's and my experience is a
co-creation and involves mutual recognition. In this way I am known
to Sam and am not anonymous. My child patients tell me all about
their observations of my moods, my mannerisms, my temperament, and
much more. One teenage boy in analysis was telling me about his ideas

about all varieties of sex. He then turned to me and said, "Dr. Steve, don't you think sex rules?" I thought I might say sex is important but so are many other things. I thought if I agreed he might tell his mother that I think sex rules. I decided he probably knew I think sex rules, and I needed to not be afraid to accompany him. So I said, "Yes, I think sex rules." This deeper knowledge our patients have of each of us is a crucial therapeutic factor that supersedes our theoretical orientation and accounts for the success of different therapeutic approaches for children and adults.

Child analysis also emphasizes the robust nature of transference (Freud, 1912). I was his older brother, whom Sam destroyed as he acquired all the supplies for himself. I was the mother with frightening rage attacks, against whom Sam felt empowered to take revenge. I was the father who was patient, loyal, loving, and admirable as well as sometimes infuriatingly obsessional. The transference was even more striking in the analysis of a five-year-old boy whose father was alcoholic and frightening. One day in the middle of a three-year analysis he said to me, "Dr. A., your voice is deeper and you haven't shaved. You can't walk, and you swear all the time. You have been drinking ninety-nine bottles of beer." I wanted to feel my chin and see if I had forgotten to shave.

Sam's and my use of the game of Life also involved principles described in the work of Harrison and Tronick, employing the microanalysis of video-recorded therapy and Tronick's model of the Dyadic Expansion of Consciousness. Their work elucidates how repair is related to the initiation of coordinated patterns of high predictability. The rhythm of the hours and of turn-taking during the game "functions as a carrier wave that maintains the momentum of the meaning-making process, and in doing so it also conveys meaning, such as 'We are working together to find a "Directionality" to our meaning-making.' Once established, directionality self-amplifies and leads toward a greater coherence and complexity of shared meaning. In the moment-to-moment process of a psychoanalytic session, repetitive patterns are common. In the expansion model they are given a central role in the change process" (Harrison and Tronick, 2007, p. 859). Is this not a powerful factor for an adult on the couch four times a week?

The growing attachment between Sam and me was crucial for our work. In order to make this attachment it was crucial to enter into Sam's unique world. The use of play to elaborate the expression of Sam's experience, no matter how unclear to me, powerfully catalyzed the necessary attachment. This was important even though the play space seemed repetitive and highly idiosyncratic (Rayner, 1992). Some children play in a repetitive, stereotypic way that seems unchanging and not therapeutic. My experience is that such play has small nuances in the play and manner of relating that are progressive and therapeutic. Sometimes this is very difficult to discern, but I believe the child has some awareness of this movement. Such play is also the child's attempt at mastery and to protect against extremely difficult feelings. A related issue is that in our work each of us has preferences regarding the play signatures we find interesting or tedious.

I think this is just as powerful in adult analysis. For example, a woman came to see me weekly for almost a year while she looked for a therapist (Ablon, 2008). I did not want to do this. She did not want to think about what this might mean. She did not inquire about my reaction to what she said about my colleagues whom she interviewed. Even though we got along well, she did not consider my being her therapist. She found a therapist and several years later moved to another city where she was in analysis. She wrote to thank me and say she came to discover that her time with me was like her largely forgotten time with a foster family when she was little and her mother was sick in the hospital. This patient created a pattern of relating to me that put us in a long-forgotten but yet not-forgotten time of her life, a time she could not integrate as a child or when she consulted with me but which she eventually mastered in her later analysis.

The child and adult have to make their own discoveries, like Freud said, and surprise us (Freud, 1908). How much is healing and integration facilitated by the nonverbal, the play, the relational, the experiences in the intensity of transference and countertransference? These intertwined forces are blended in their own unique way in each child and adult treatment.

BIBLIOGRAPHY

ABLON, S. L. (2001). Continuities of tongues: A developmental perspective on the role of play in child and adult psychoanalytic process. *Journal of Clinical Psychoanalysis* 10: (3, 4): 345–365.
_____. (2008). Doubt. *American Journal of Psychiatry* 165 (5): 563–564.
BETTLEHEIM, B. (1976). *The Uses of Enchantment: The Meaning and Importance of Fairy Tales.* New York: Alfred A. Knopf.
BORCH-JACOBSEN, M. (1992). *The Emotional Tie: Psychoanalysis, Mimesis, and Affect.* Stanford, CA: Stanford University Press.
BROWN, S. L. (1994). Animals at play. *National Geographic* 186 (6): 2–35.
COHEN, P. M., AND SOLNIT, A. J. (1993). Play and therapeutic action. *Psychoanalytic Study of the Child* 48:49–63.

FERENCZI, S. (1921). The Further Development of an Active Therapy in Psycho-Analysis. In *Further Contributions to the Theory and Technique of Psycho-Analysis,* pp. 198–217. New York: Brunner/Mazel, 1980.

———. (1933). The Confusion of Tongues Between Adults and the Child. In *Final Contributions to the Problems and Methods of Psycho-Analysis,* pp. 156–167. New York: Bruner/Mazel, 1955.

FREUD, S. (1908). Creative Writers and Day-Dreaming. In *Standard Edition* 9:141–153.

———. (1912). The Dynamics of Transference. In *Standard Edition* 12:97–108.

FRANKEL, J. B. (1998). The play's the thing: How essential processes of therapy are seen most clearly in child therapy. *Psychoanalytic Dialogues* 8:149–182.

GREENBERG, J. (1995). Words and acts: The round robin. Newsletter of Division 39, American Psychological Association, April.

HADAMARD, J. (1945). *The Psychology of Invention in the Mathematical Field.* Princeton, NJ: Princeton University Press, Appendix II.

HARRISON, A. M., AND TRONICK, E. Z. (2007). Now we have a playground: Emerging new ideas of therapeutic action. *Journal of the American Psychoanalytic Association* 55 (3): 853–874.

———. (2011). "The noise monitor": A developmental perspective of verbal and nonverbal meaning-making in psychoanalysis. *Journal of the American Psychoanalytic Association* 59 (5): 961–983.

HOUSEMAN, A. E. (2005). *The Collected Poems.* Ware, UK: Wordsworth Editions.

HUIZINGA, J. (1938). *Homo Ludens: A Study of the Play Element in Culture.* Boston: Beacon Press, 1955.

HURRY, A., ED. (1998). *Psychoanalysis and Developmental Therapy.* London: Karnac Books.

KLEIN, M. (1932). *The Psycho-Analysis of Children.* London: Hogarth Press.

———. (1961). *Narrative of a Child Analysis.* London: Hogarth Press.

LOEWALD, E. L. (1987). Therapeutic play in space and time. *Psychoanalytic Study of the Child* 42:173–192.

MONTAIGNE, M. E. (2003). Essays. In *The Complete Works,* trans. Donald M. Frame. Everyman's Library. New York: Alfred A. Knopf.

NEUBAUER, P. B. (1987). The many meanings of play: Introduction. *Psychoanalytic Study of the Child* 42:3–9.

PELLER, L. (1954). Libidinal phases, ego development, and play. *Psychoanalytic Study of the Child* 9:178–198.

PIAGET, J., AND INHELDER, B. (1969). *The Psychology of the Child.* New York: Basic Books.

RAYNER, E. (1992). Matching, attunement and the psychoanalytic dialogue. *International Journal of Psycho-Analysis* 73:39–54.

REIK, T. (1936). *Surprise and the Psycho-Analyst.* New York: E. P. Dutton.

SANDER, L. W. (1983). Polarity, Paradox, and the Organizing Process in Development. In *Frontiers of Infant Psychiatry,* ed. J. D. Call, E. Galenson, and R. L. Tyson, vol. 1, pp. 333–346. New York: Basic Books.

SANVILLE, J. (1991). *The Playground of Psychoanalytic Therapy.* Hillsdale, NJ: Analytic Press.

SEMRAD, E. (1968). Personal communication, Massachusetts Mental Health Center, 1968.

SOLNIT, A. J., COHEN, D. J., AND NEUBAUER, P. B. (1993). *The Many Meanings of Play.* New Haven, CT: Yale University Press.

TOMKINS, S. (1962, 1963). *Affect, Imagery, Consciousness.* Vols. 1 and 2. New York: Springer.

VOLTAIRE, F.-M. A. (1977). *The Portable Voltaire.* New York: Penguin Books.

WAELDER, R. (1933). The psychoanalytic theory of play. *Psychoanalytic Quarterly* 2:208–224.

WINNICOTT, D. W. (1968). Interpretation in Psycho-Analysis. In *Psycho-Analytic Explorations,* ed. C. Winnicott, R. Shepherd, and M. Davis, pp. 207–212. London: Karnac, 1989.

——. (1971a). *Playing and Reality.* New York: Basic Books.

——. (1971b). *Playing: A Theoretical Statement in Playing and Reality.* New York: Basic Books.

Toward a Psychoanalytic Way-of-Being in the Game of Life

Discussion of a Paper by Steven Ablon

ALFRED MARGULIES, M.D.

There are no clinical techniques not always already embedded within a psychoanalyst's way-of-being-in-the-world. This claim, grounded in the author's reading of Steven Ablon's "What Child Analysis Can Teach Us about Psychoanalytic Technique" (in this volume), takes us to Ablon's exemplary psychoanalytic comportment, with a particular focus on poetics, playfulness, practicality, and pluralism. These complex, intertwined features of child psychoanalysis have had a broad and deep impact on contemporary adult psychoanalysis, influencing praxis, conceptions of therapeutic action, ethics, and workaday worldview.

A BIT LIKE WINNICOTT'S (1960) AWARENESS THAT THERE IS NO BABY without a mother, despite our literature implying otherwise, there is no analytic technique without a clinician. More specifically, there are no techniques not always already embedded within a psychoanalyst's way-of-being-in-the-world. Similarly, of course, there is no paper on technique without an author who is also embedded in a complex way of being (and so too for a discussant). Think of noble grapes and terroir, the total environment—soil, weather, sun, vintner—in which a grape expresses itself and creates a typical wine, recognizable and yet highly distinctive to that region, neighborhood, and even to the specific vineyard.

Dr. Margulies is Training and Supervising Analyst, Boston Psychoanalytic Society and Institute; Associate Professor of Psychiatry, Harvard Medical School, at the Cambridge Health Alliance.

The Psychoanalytic Study of the Child 68, ed. Claudia Lament, Robert A. King, Samuel Abrams, Paul M. Brinich, and Rona Knight (Yale University Press, copyright © 2015 by Claudia Lament, Robert A. King, Samuel Abrams, Paul M. Brinich, and Rona Knight).

And so when Steven Ablon presents a paper on the contributions of child analysis to adult psychoanalytic technique, I am drawn to the kind of analytic worldview he inhabits. What analytic ways-of-being are distinctive to this author, clinician, and person who is living this particular technique? Of course, I do not want to miss the precise abstractions of technique that are being offered for our consideration, but rather to consider that these highly nuanced abstract specifics also have a complex articulation within a worldview and a way-of-being that is always already interlaced within a world of ways of approaching another who comes for a psychoanalysis.

Though we of course need to pay attention to mistakes and failures, we would be wise to pay special attention to the most exemplary clinical cases, those with satisfying outcomes and with the most straightforward, thick descriptive feel of the complex experience of actually doing psychoanalysis. These cases offer the promise to be highly instructive because they have the texture of experience and of personal presence of both analyst and patient. As with Ablon's paper, a clinical world is recreated, one we can feel into, one that we are being invited to enter, to try on, in our effort to expand our own analytic way-of-being and worldviews. I have the good fortune of knowing Steve Ablon personally, and so the reader should know that I am biased in his paper's favor. But my bias is not mere bias; it is because I know, a bit, the man and his way of comporting himself. Like his paper, he is poetic, playful, and practical. This discussion is predicated on the value of that way of comportment and my trying to tease out its outlines and implications.

So let's review our situation, and I'll begin with a question: Ablon's paper seems essential, and yet still we must ask: Just why is it necessary? After all, one would naturally think that the two worlds of psychoanalysis—adult and child—would be seamlessly connected. But one would be wrong because, oddly, the two seem to live on different planets.

This, however, is no accident; rather it is in part a consequence of historical attitudes and, yes, politics and the sociology of ideas. For one, that's how some of our field's luminaries in the classical era treated the different worlds. The attitude went something like this: Child analysis was of some interest, but it is not real analysis and has little to offer adult psychoanalytic technique. That is, if the fundamental technical method and goal is resistance analysis, then other methods, goals, and ideas (like developmental theory) become distractions and, worse, resistances themselves. Stick to the task of the analysis of resistances to the transference. Moreover, if you would use child analytic techniques for adults, be aware that you have introduced parameters, mixing alloys into the gold of pure analysis. Now, there is much truth here, particularly if you want to graduate.

But do we still believe this to be the case? Can we join the two domains of adult and child analysis? A city slicker once asked a Down East Mainer for travel directions and, after a thoughtful moment, got this reply: "Well, you can't get thay-ah from hee-ah." Are we bewitched by our binaries? Ablon offers us a path from here to there, and, I submit, it is not so much in the technical particulars, but rather in the manner he inhabits his analytic way of being, one suffused with the care of and for his patients. His paper reflects, and, yes, inspires an attitude, an exemplary way of being, for the practitioner. And so I will use my descriptors of Steve Ablon and his paper, and most importantly his way of being as an analyst—playful, poetic, practical—to organize the rest of my remarks and lessons for the adult practitioner. And I'll add one more to cap my poetic alliteration: pluralistic (or the polyphony of theory).

But first, tying it all together before I take it apart, let me begin with the central image I would use for the opening scene of my movie about this paper: Pan to a game board, to two figures—a boy and a man—deeply absorbed in a game and in each other. Now focus on the title emblazoned in bold letters across their field of vision: "THE GAME OF LIFE." How wonderful is that! A perfect image, a poetic symbol, a Lacanian upholstery button, tacking down the infinite threads of this paper and the child analytic process. As Ablon and Sam play, the child invents new and better rules for their game. Now don't we all wish we could come up with better rules for the game of life in this imperfect, maddening, heartbreaking, and soul-crushing world? And if we are so lucky, we could all use a good friend and companion. So let's now look at the poetics, play, practicality, and plurality in this game of life.

POETICS

Poetry, a Homer scholar once put it, lies somewhere between music and the word. But I submit we might also think of poetry at the intersection of the unthematized, of the not-yet-thought, the overflow of symbol, image, body, memory, fantasy, and the larger semiotic world beyond language per se.

Child analysis has developed as a matter of necessity the practice of the ready-to-hand use of displaced signifiers: think of it—a therapeutic toy box filled with a world of symbols just within reach. And symbolization always outstrips what we can say about it. Lacan (1993) refers to a strong, resonant signifier as an "upholstery button"—the point of infinite intersection of the associative threads of mind embedded in the infinite chains of signifiers of language—"rings of a necklace that is a ring in another necklace made of rings" (Lacan 1977, p. 153)—an infinite, inexhaustible play of signifiers! And I like this term "play of signifiers" because this opens on to a kind of adult play so dear to Freud, that is, "word play"—puns, word puzzles, and jokes!

Poetics as a quality of thinking approximates elusive meanings and gives pleasure to insight. Poetics is then an aesthetic but also a praxis, a practice, a way of engaging the world, honed in child analysis within the sublime poetics of play. So let's move to the mystery of play—and here it amuses me to think of the child analytic frame as a kind of regularly scheduled play date! Can Dr. Ablon come out and play? What a great idea!

PLAY

Don't you love to watch young animals—puppies or cats or lion cubs—in play, anticipating the game of their lives? They wrestle and nip at each other, they fight, then roll over and pee, establish dominance, reestablish; they jump up, they get into trouble, they romp, they play. If you'd like a good laugh, just look up videos of puppies mobbing the family cat. Or the extraordinary border collie with a vocabulary of hundreds of words running to his toy chest to pick out any complex object—for example, the brown furry cube—that his owner might describe. Sheer joy, libido. No doubt about it, play is adaptive, evolutionarily selected, like a growth hormone, to prepare the animal for its niche in its world.

A very recent popular press review in *The New York Times* (Dobbs, 2013) on the research on play cogently summarized: "Studies suggest that free, self-directed play in safe environments enhances resilience, creativity, flexibility, social understanding, emotional and cognitive control, and resistance to stress, depression and anxiety. [Author: Now what psychopharm agent dares make claim to all of that!] And we continue to explore as adults, even if not so freely."

That is, we have come to realize: there is therapeutic action in play itself! Here I recommend a new "CPT" code (that is, Current Procedural Terminology) for insurance companies: complex play, with or without medications. . . . And, let me be clear, I would use this code for adults too. Now Klein in her genius realized for the child that the analog to free association is play. But following the summary I just mentioned— "And we continue to explore as adults, even if not so freely"—shouldn't we reverse the vector of this analog? Isn't free association the adult's way of playing with the richness of his own mind, a richness that he has forgotten? How is it that almost every child forgets how to draw with the same exuberance, creativity, and skill she had before age ten? One of my daughters began a short story for her elementary school with the following first line: "The day began like a hangnail. . . ." Her teacher marked up the paper in red, telling her that that was not a proper first line. Children get domesticated out of their own creativity and joy. Can the adult find her way back? Picasso is reputed to have said: "It took me four years to paint like Raphael, but a lifetime to paint like a child." Indeed, isn't this in the spirit of free association, the goal of a freed-up mind freely exploring itself so that a person less encumbered might choose more freely how to live, how to fashion her own particular approach to the game of life? Play then is libidinal, erotic, joyous, life-affirming, creative—and, particularly if you have a friend, a companion, a chum along with you, libido is not overrun by aggression, but, like playing poker for small stakes, has just enough aggression to give it an edge and make it more interesting. But just what kind of person, we wonder, is this analytic companion within a child's world?

It is easier to accept in child work that the analyst is a new object, in a sense, not fully captured by the term "transference." As with all analytic relationships, there is something altogether new and a bit surreal in the relationship, like orchids raised in greenhouses. This relationship mobilizes desire, even love, often when desire has been previously trampled or remains undeveloped. Sometimes the child is alone and not yet aware that he is alone. For example, though it was not Sam's situation, the autistic child needs to grow from aloneness into loneliness. That is, the analyst needs to help catalyze aloneness into the possibility of loneliness. The child needs to appreciate his condition of aloneness as such, that is, to find his way into the desire of another as an other. In short, he needs to need a friend, a Sullivanian chum. And from there, he needs to learn how to make and keep friends and relationships. This need, then, is a marker, a metric, if you will, of growth for all children, and one that Ablon beautifully describes.

The person of the analyst is, then, the upholstery button of the object world, the signifier of many relationships all at once, from diverse, simultaneous transferential configurations to the many new possibilities of relationship, including friend, chum, and object of love, hatred, competition, and desire. Perhaps a better metaphor than upholstery button is that of polyphony, as in Bach or the joining of voices in Mozart—all present, intertwined, and coming together in the person of the child analyst. With Sam, Ablon becomes that complex nexus of object voices; Ablon and Sam create the polyphony together—something new and profound, a goal for all analyses!

PRACTICALITY

Practicality is the quintessential American trait, oft criticized—and rightly—but at its best, practicality keeps us grounded, empirical, and with our eye on the ball. Child analytic technique, after all, was born of a certain practicality in that stroke of genius by Melanie Klein to create an analog to free association. Here are some other child analytic practical adaptations:

Transference: Transference is not foregrounded in interpretation! Child analysts are almost apologetic here, but they needn't be. Indeed, such a perspective might serve as a corrective to the sometimes fetishistic contemporary focus on the transference, particularly on self-disclosure, enactment, and the funneling of all statements through a transference-countertransference lens, as if that is all there is. An analysis needs room to breathe. And so, consider this: overly emphasized, transference (and countertransference) analysis might also be a powerful resistance to other aspects of exploration! (Here I would refer to papers by Christopher Bollas [2007] and, from a Lacanian perspective, Bruce Fink [2007].)

Resistance: The term "resistance" has connotations of battlefield, confrontation, or, at the very least, work. As with transference-countertransference analysis, an overfocus on resistance may itself be a resistance, for example, a resistance to engagement, as on the first page of Ablon's paper, when the child says: "Dr. A., don't you know how many children you have?" The child has a point, something like: "Talk to me as if you are a person!" Why should he play with a blank screen, a cipher? He wants a person, present, now.

Further, resistance is not always best addressed head on; sometimes we get further through indirection, displacement, titration, and not getting stuck in the Chinese finger locks of struggle. I sometimes think of aikido and the art of flow in martial arts, of going with a force rather than against it, destabilizing its natural contrariness and thereby opening up, freeing up, toward the goal of free association. Child analysts, as Ablon demonstrates, become quite adept at this art form of loosening up resistance.

"Therapeutic action": Our metaphors of therapeutic action are revealing of how we conceptualize the human situation. No wonder there is a backlash to "psychiatry's bible," the *DSM* (*Diagnostic and Statistical*

Manual). Among all of those myriad diagnoses, where is the person? How is it that we can fold the universal grieving process into something pathological? Where is the notion of health? Consider the pediatricians' term "failure to thrive" and their use of growth charts of weight and height over time. Isn't this growth model more to the point—and for our adult patients too? Are they thriving or not, and where and in what areas of their lives?

If you are implicitly oriented to growth and thriving, then you will take careful account of strengths and potential, just as you would in gardening. Growth, as in pruning a tree to strengthen its core, takes note of advantages, limitations, and natural inclinations, needs for light, air, water, and nutrients. We try to optimize a tree's natural biological imperatives (let us call this "libido" or life force). We hope, keep close tabs, all the while looking to the future and its possibilities.

Though keenly aware of Sam's paralyzing symptoms and problems, Ablon particularly appreciates Sam's intellectual strengths and many gifts, including Sam's kindness and his sweetness. We pause in appreciation of this remarkable boy struggling to make sense of his world. Now, if you reflexively think of growth and thriving, implicitly you will also think of context, the setting, the terroir of growth, which will lead you to the specifics of this child in his world, or "Winnicott's baby."

Winnicott's baby, or no child without a mother, is the child embedded in family and social and cultural matrix. That is, just as there is no child without a mother, there is no mother without her milieu. And this gives me pause, because, unlike the adult analyst, the child analyst as a matter of course has regular interaction with the child's caretakers! And so this engagement changes abstraction to something close to the child's reality. Though not explicitly addressed in Ablon's paper, there is then countertransference to the child's parents, sibs, caregivers: Welcome to my world. Now if you think of child in context, you implicitly know that the world can be a hard place to survive, to endure, much less to thrive in, which leads you to advocacy—and this is where the practical meets the ethical and the existential.

With a different imperative than usually confronts the adult analyst, there is a necessity to assess real-time trauma versus fantasy. That is, trauma is not only something that might have happened in the past with its entire overdetermined tangle of memory and fantasy, but there is the ongoing reality of trauma, including adults in collusion. Trauma entwines itself in the child's unfolding future, distorting growth and limiting possibilities, threatening to dominate his worldview. Exquisitely existential, trauma is then an alive process—and these lessons are important for adult analysts to keep in mind, too.

CONCLUSION: PLURALISM, THE POLYPHONY
OF THEORY, AND THE GAME OF LIFE

Despite our sharply etched public panels on different schools of psycho-analysis, I suspect most practicing analysts inhabit a more integrative, poetic, and practical position that draws from many traditions. Further, I submit that the American version of child psychoanalysis is for many of us a strong template for this pluralism. We worry less about getting technique right and more about using the portal of awareness of our analytic worldview to help others apprehend and appreciate theirs. For example, interviewing on inpatient wards, I move quickly, freely, draw-ing on many principles I have learned from child analysis and other traditions. I seldom am concerned per se with interpreting the transfer-ence; I readily use images, music, and cultural symbols. I am present face-to-face; together we look out on the world, this game of life and its heartbreaking absurdity. With more time we might explore parallels to other clinical situations and other schools and avenues of healing.

"Co-creation"—that vaunted relational term—has long been an ac-cepted child analytic practice and breakthrough. Winnicott's (1958) magnificent "Squiggle Game," that is, first you make a mark on the pa-per and then I will make a mark on your mark, and what will we come up with together? We will play off of each other's creativity and—just like Picasso and Braque and Matisse—we will become richer for it. How will our creativities, our unconscious souls, merge, and how will this reflect what each of us literally brings to the table? The child gets it, and without needing words: Come let us play together!

In this sense child analysis is relational, classical, oedipal, preoedipal, symbolic, loaded with Lacanian signifiers, Kleinian, needing Bionian containers to detoxify and metabolize, filled with self and narcissism, and yet self and other in the Lévinasian (1987) sense: we surprise each other with the infinity of one another, of not really being able to totally know the other before us. It is all there, in this play, this "Game of Life," just like the Talmud or Achilles' magical shield, with cities in peace, cit-ies at war—the whole world right there in the game, the game of life.

The last we know, Sam is no longer playing The Game of Life; he is, rather, living his life, and well. Ablon has been a companion, a guide, a friend, a chum, and, of course, a projective screen that deepens the resonance and richness. That is, Steve Ablon inhabits an exemplary psychoanalytic way-of-being—and that, to me, is what is most compel-ling about this paper. He is a natural analyst, a natural healer, someone who's been there, and someone who knows the way. And then he says good-bye, and the child goes off into the world.

Lastly, I looked up "The Game of Life" online, and here is what I found on its box cover, beneath its title, the phrase "Twists & Turns." Now this really pleased me, because, over two thousand years ago the poet Homer began *The Odyssey* with another famous first line: "Sing to me of the man, Muse, the man of twists and turns, driven time and again off course . . ." (Homer, 1996, p. 77). Now how great is that! Prior to the dawn of written language, when there was only song and poetry, homesick Odysseus, inventor of the Trojan horse, knew how to twist and turn with life. Homer sang the poetics of practicality and engagement, of learning how to survive in a difficult world. No wonder all of the Greeks, young and old, sang and delighted in the tale of the man of twists and turns.

But, the game box of "The Game of Life" has one more message that polishes its perfection with a Zenlike, Delphic, and existential question that embeds the journey of every adult analysis:

"A thousand ways to live your life! How will you live yours?"

REFERENCES

BOLLAS, C. (2007). On Transference Interpretation as a Resistance to Free Association. In *The Freudian Moment*. London: Karnac.

DOBBS, D. (2013). Playing for All Kinds of Possibilities. *New York Times*. April 22, sec. D, p. 7.

FINK, B. (2007). *Fundamentals of Psychoanalytic Technique. A Lacanian Approach for Practitioners*. New York: Norton.

HOMER (1996 trans.). *The Odyssey*. Trans. Robert Fagles. New York: Penguin.

LACAN, J. (1977). The Agency of the Letter in the Unconscious, or Reason Since Freud. In *Écrits: A Selection*, pp. 146–178, trans. Alan Sheridan. London: Tavistock.

_____. (1993). *The Seminar of Jacques Lacan: Book III, The Psychoses 1955–1956*. Trans. Russell Grigg. London: Routledge.

LÉVINAS, E. (1987). *Collected Philosophical Papers*. Trans. A. Lingis. Phaenomenologica, vol. 100. Dordrecht, The Netherlands: Nijhoff.

WINNICOTT, D. W. (1958). Symptom Tolerance in Paediatrics (1953). In *Collected Papers: Through Paediatrics to Psychoanalysis*. London: Tavistock.

_____. (1960). The Theory of the Parent-Infant Relationship. *International Journal of Psycho-Analysis* 41:585–595.

Postscripts

Reflections on the Post-Termination Phase

RUTH K. KARUSH, M.D.

This paper delineates a deeper and more flexible approach to the termination of an analysis. When a patient returns following the ending of a treatment, the analyst has the opportunity to observe the effects of the termination on her former analysand. If the ending of an analytic treatment is not handled sensitively, much of what has been accomplished may be undone. Also, the quality of the post-termination contact itself may affect the long-term outcome of the analysis. The analyst's availability after termination is important if the termination has set off feelings of abandonment. Clinical vignettes are used to demonstrate how patients may need to touch base with the analyst or actually return for a period of continued treatment. The process of terminating is crucial in setting the stage for continued self-analysis or for the return to analytic treatment.

Dr. Karush is Dean of Education, the New York Psychoanalytic Society and Institute, and Training and Supervising Analyst in Adult, Child, and Adolescent Analysis, the New York Psychoanalytic Society and Institute. She is also Past President of The Association for Child Psychoanalysis.

A version of this paper was presented as the Marianne Kris Memorial Lecture at the 2013 Annual Meeting of the Association for Child Psychoanalysis. As I mentioned during that lecture, many years ago I consulted Marianne Kris when I wanted to begin psychoanalysis. She gave me two pieces of advice: first, that I should let my husband play tennis, and, second, that I should resign from my residency and stay home with my children. Her first piece of advice was easy for me to follow, but the second was not. Rather than resign, I chose to follow her example and pursue a career in child analysis. I am grateful to Dr. Kris for having referred me to my analyst and also for (perhaps inadvertently) helping me keep my priorities straight.

The Psychoanalytic Study of the Child 68, ed. Claudia Lament, Robert A. King, Samuel Abrams, Paul M. Brinich, and Rona Knight (Yale University Press, copyright © 2015 by Claudia Lament, Robert A. King, Samuel Abrams, Paul M. Brinich, and Rona Knight).

234

IN CERTAIN SITUATIONS, CHILD AND ADOLESCENT ANALYSANDS MAY return to the analyst following termination, either to touch base or to seek further treatment.[1] A patient's return may enable the analyst to critique not only the long-term outcome of her analytic work but also the effects of the termination on the patient. These two aspects of the analysis are, of course, inseparable: if the ending of an analytic relationship is not handled with sensitivity, much of what has been accomplished may be undone. Furthermore, the quality of post-termination contact itself may affect the long-term outcome of the analysis. This paper examines the post-termination phase both as a source of insight into the effects of termination and as an opportunity to continue helping the patient negotiate new challenges.

MOURNING IN THE POST-TERMINATION PHASE OF A CHILD'S ANALYSIS

Although it is common to speak of mourning after the termination of an adult analysis, we may not adequately consider the mourning that the child or adolescent patient experiences when he ends treatment. We understand mourning as the process by which psychic equilibrium is restored following the loss of a meaningful love object. Mourning is a normal response to termination and, in adults, may last up to a year. The process of mourning involves the gradual relinquishment of the cherished relationship and its concurrent internalization. For the child, losing the analyst may be extremely painful. The child must relinquish the transference object who holds his infantile wishes and has the skill to interpret and contain the transference. The child also loses the analytic situation, in which he receives the undivided attention of a person who understands him deeply and has been a partner in a unique therapeutic relationship. No matter how well we prepare our young patients for termination, they must complete certain tasks alone: the child has to face the loss of the analyst alone, and he must hold on to a good-enough internal image of the analyst and the self while experiencing an enormous loss. We hope that our child and adolescent patients can

---

1. We psychoanalysts, I believe, are always interested in the course of our patients' lives. Sometimes we are lucky enough to hear from a family member or even, as Freud did, to meet up with our patient again. When Little Hans was nineteen years old, he introduced himself to Freud as the boy whose infantile neurosis was the subject of Freud's 1909 paper. Freud was impressed by the youth and amazed that Hans remembered almost nothing about the events from his childhood that had led his father to seek help for his phobic four-year-old son.

take on some of the functions of the analyst, but this, of course, is also dependent on the level of development that the child has reached.

The Decision to Terminate

How do we decide when a child is ready to terminate? Criteria for the ending of a child's analysis, according to Sandler, Kennedy and Tyson (1980), include restoring the child to the path of normal development, the resolution of the transference, and the child's developmentally appropriate adaptation in his life outside the treatment setting. Similarly, in his criteria for termination, Abrams (1978) raised four questions: (1) Are the dynamic issues engaged? (2) Have specific drive derivatives become manifest? (3) What is the direction of restructuring? (4) Has the resolution of past conflicts found a more fortunate pathway? Even when these criteria have been satisfied, the child analyst has more to assess. She must pay attention to "the natural thrust toward growth and development." Abrams added that it is inadvisable to end a treatment without a conviction that a "progressive [developmental] push is present and continuingly imposing its influence." One way that a child analyst can test the forward movement of development is to continue a treatment into the next phase of development before deciding to terminate. An example is the case of four-year-old Sam, who came into analysis because he wanted to be a girl. In his analytic treatment, through imaginary play, we learned that Sam's stated desire to be a girl was, in fact, a defense against intense castration anxiety. This boy did well in his analysis and, in about three years, had worked through many of his conflicts. When the analytic sessions changed from dramatic play versions of Cinderella and Snow White to challenging games of chess and volleyball, I felt we were into a new phase. He and his parents thought he was ready to terminate, and, since I could see that he was solidly entrenched in latency, I felt comfortable with his ending his treatment.

Although much has been written on the subject of termination—including numerous papers, a casebook edited by Anita Schmukler, and a book on the termination process entitled *Good Goodbyes* by Kerry and Jack Novick—the decision to terminate a particular child's analysis remains fraught with complexity. Not only are other people such as parents, pediatricians, teachers, and coaches involved, but also there are activities, such as sports and time for playing with other children, that must be considered when contemplating the termination of a child's analysis. And analytic endings are emotionally challenging for the analyst as well as for the patient.

The Difficulty of Saying Good-bye

Recently, I received a startling e-mail comprised of two simple sentences: "I love you. I miss you." A four-year-old boy whose treatment had been terminated because of family circumstances had dictated the message for me to his mother. I was touched by the message and realized that I also missed him. The psychoanalytic relationship is unique among intimate relationships, in that its ultimate goal includes separation. As Martin Bergmann noted in 1997, "In real life, only death and hostility bring a libidinal relationship to an end. The kind of termination that psychoanalysis demands is without precedent."

After termination the analysand mourns the loss of the analyst and, at the time that he feels vulnerable and bereft, must face demanding emotional tasks alone. It is disturbing that, given the analysand's vulnerability, many of our common termination practices may undermine the patient's leave-taking and harm the positive internal image of the analyst and the analytic relationship that was created in the analysis. This is especially true for the terminations of child and adolescent analytic treatments chiefly because the child or adolescent often does not have the same important role in the decision to terminate that our adult patients do.

In the post-termination period of a good-enough analysis, there may be eruptions of latent transferences, the repetition of earlier trauma, the alteration of the positive image of the analyst, and regressive symptomatic relapse. The internal image of the analyst may remain one that is predominately positive, or it may change to one that is primarily disappointing or even persecutory.

Sometimes, the patient's parent(s) may mourn the loss of the analyst even more than the child does.[2] In fact, there are parents who refuse to terminate their relationship with the analyst even though their child has separated and moved on. For example, I still see the mother of my second child-analytic case—now discussing her teenage grandchildren. We are getting old together, and I find myself wondering how termination will occur: Which of us will be the first to die or to be unable to continue our meetings?[3]

2. Several years ago, I was at a movie theater when a man called out "Dr. Karush." He turned out to be the father of a former child analytic patient, and he appeared delighted to give me an unsolicited report on his now grown-up son.

3. In this case, I had asked the patient about how she might feel if her mother wanted to continue to talk to me even if she did not. She expressed both positive and negative feelings about her mother seeing me. She expressed the feeling that her mother had always been in competition for my attention and that, in a way, her mother was stealing me or breaking the rules of the game. On balance, though, she, as a teenager, believed it would be beneficial for both of them if her mother continued to meet with me.

Child analysts themselves may find it particularly difficult to say good-bye to a child whom they have watched mature over years and with whom they have been so intimately involved. Although an analyst may recognize the need for the child to separate and end his or her treatment, the analyst may be encumbered by countertransference feelings that may affect termination in ways that are counterproductive or even detrimental.

HARRY: THE ANALYST'S ANGER AND HOPELESSNESS

Kerry and Jack Novick wrote in 2000 that the analyst's role after termination is to maintain her stance as an analyst, available for future consultation if needed, while acknowledging her continuing "respect, admiration and objective love" for the patient after analysis. That is a tall order for child analysts, but really for all analysts. Terminations often occur under less-than-optimal circumstances. In child analyses, there are often many people involved in the decision to end a treatment, and the analyst has to cope with a myriad of countertransferences.

I had begun to see Harry when he was three and a half. He was about to be thrown out of nursery school for his aggressive behavior toward the other children. His parents had divorced before his birth, and neither parent, because of their own psychiatric problems, was available to parent him. Luckily, he had a loving, practical, and stable nanny. A plan for intensive treatment was supported by the maternal grandfather, and the nanny went into the nursery school to shadow Harry. He lived with his mother, who came to meetings with me on an infrequent basis. The court had mandated that Harry's visits with his father be supervised.

Harry made significant progress both emotionally and socially over his four years of treatment. When his nanny had a baby of her own, Harry got very angry and his behavior regressed. He was particularly angry with me and told his mother that he was not going to see that "old woman" anymore. At his annual physical, his pediatrician recommended that Harry see a behavior specialist for "anger management." It was Harry who informed me that he was seeing a new therapist—a man. I investigated, and indeed his family had arranged for him to have behavior therapy. They believed he could continue to see me once a week. I explained that I would be terminating Harry's treatment because it would be confusing for any child to see two therapists at the same time, and also that I could not really help Harry on a once-a-week basis. I arranged a rather short termination period for Harry. By the time we were supposed to end, he understood that he was angry with me for not making sure that there were no babies to take attention away from him. In our very final session Harry said that he really preferred to stay in treatment with me. He said, "Is that no longer an option?"

I was brought up short by Harry's very mature question. Immediately I realized my countertransference feelings of anger had led me to respond in a way that was not in Harry's best interests. I had felt discounted and dismissed by the family and by Harry, although I believed that his treatment had been crucial in getting his development almost on a normal track. Luckily, my nearly eight-year-old patient realized that something was going very wrong. Together we began to discuss what options the two of us had, and we proceeded to make a more appropriate plan.

I don't think it is uncommon for an analyst to feel angry and hopeless when parents or others insist on a termination or a reduction in the frequency of a child's treatment. It is important to try to remain flexible and try to negotiate an ending that, at the very least, will not be harmful to the patient and undermine the work that has already been done.

JUDY: THE ANALYST'S FLEXIBILITY

Judy was a very bright nine-year-old who was plagued with counting rituals. It was clear from the early evaluative sessions that Judy would benefit from an analytic treatment. She was enraged with her mother, whom she felt was critical of her weight and of her closeness to her father. Judy's mother felt that her daughter should be seen in family counseling, but she agreed to have Judy come to see me. The father brought Judy to my office four times a week although the family's home and Judy's school were rather far away. I had been unable to locate an analyst closer to Judy's home. Judy did very well in her treatment and understood that her rituals protected her mother from her rage. She was a youngster who spent her sessions talking, and she was obviously very happy to have someone who would listen. When the first summer approached, her mother planned that Judy would go to camp before spending a month traveling with her. When September came around, I did not hear from the family. I left a phone message and an e-mail. Finally, I said that it would be good for Judy and I to at least have the opportunity to say good-bye. It was difficult because I had personally very much enjoyed the work with this insightful, lively, and articulate girl.

We set up a few meetings, and Judy explained that things were a lot better. Her mother had arranged for her to go horseback riding after school. Her rituals were practically gone, and she was not fighting with her mother. For the first time she said that my office was just too far away. I told Judy that she could always call me and, if she wanted, she could come back to see me. I realized that Judy was stuck in an unfortunate place. She knew that her mother did not want her to see me and, although furious with her mother, she did very much love her. When Valentine's Day arrived, Judy told her father that she had to see me. We arranged two meetings. Judy was very upset. All of her counting rituals were back. "I cannot stand it! It's worse than ever!" she said. We both knew that Judy needed to resume her analysis, and we both also knew that her mother might be able to support the treatment if she didn't have to commute a long distance to the analyst. A child analyst, whose office was within walking distance from Judy's school, luckily had time available. This doctor agreed to see Judy and, as far as I know, that treatment went well. With his final payment, Judy's father wrote thanking me "for everything." It was bittersweet.

TANYA: THE ANALYST GETS A SECOND CHANCE

Tanya is a seven-year-old second grader with a two-year-old younger brother. At the age of five she entered analysis for several reasons. One was that she demanded to use a pull-up diaper and wrap herself in the shower curtain when she would have a bowel movement. This symptom had various ramifications, including the fact that she occupied the family's only bathroom for a considerable length of time. With intensive work, Tanya's symptom was mostly understood and remitted. Her parents could not see the need for continued intensive work, and we had a brief termination period. Tanya, however, developed another bathroom symptom. Now she could not go to sleep without getting up multiple times to urinate. Tanya believed this problem was her parents' fault because they stopped coming in to check on her numerous times before she fell asleep. She also had to be the last one to use the bathroom before the family left the apartment. She had another curious ritual of rubbing her finger around her belly button to "get the last drops out." Her treatment was reestablished.

In one session during the second year of analysis, Tanya came over to the couch and sat very close to where I was sitting. This was unusual for her. Most of her time was spent at the art table making elaborate projects. She said she wanted to tell me a dream she had had the night before: *"I was getting out of the car and a person stole me. My parents knew where I was. They were not going to care of/about me. They were not going to look for me."* I said that the dream seemed very sad and it reminded me of something. Tanya said it reminded her of how her parents had stopped coming in to her room at bedtime. She continued, "They didn't do it slowly, preparing me—you know slowly come in to the room less times. They didn't care about me." I said, "Do you mean, you didn't think they understood how you were feeling—that you needed time to get used to going to sleep on your own?" "They just decided and that's it," she declared. I said, "You seemed to have felt very unprepared and not cared for." "Yes, but sometimes my body thinks it's all my fault." "That is confusing," I said. I went on to say that we had learned that her pooping problem had something to do with her anger about her brother. Tanya said, "Maybe they should have prepared me better for how it is to have a brother." I said that the dream made me wonder about her feelings about me. She seemed startled. "What do you mean?" she asked. I said, "Well, remember when your parents decided that you didn't need to see me any longer?" Perhaps, I said, she had felt that I hadn't cared enough about her. Maybe she felt I should have made more of a fuss. Instead, we ended, and she may have felt that I hadn't even looked for her. She had to get another problem to come back to see me. To my surprise, Tanya said, "Yeah—you really are like my mother—you just don't care about me." The dream led to a rich exploration of the transference. Not only were her feelings of rage explored, but also we could see how much she longed to be close to me/mother.

The work with Tanya is instructive. Although she had felt disappointed by my acquiescing to her premature termination, which made her question my commitment to her, she had held on to the belief that deep down I did really care about her and wanted to be helpful. She thought that I should not have let her go and she felt I had abandoned her before she was ready. These feelings had their roots in her feelings of abandonment when her mother gave birth to her brother. The child patient is not always able to orchestrate the return to her analyst as Tanya was. But it is important that the analyst be open to the return of her patient. I think that Tanya had felt rejected and abandoned by me, and she thought if I had really cared about her, I would have demanded that her parents keep her in treatment. Had Tanya not been as determined as she was, I think that the good work we had done together would have been in jeopardy.

DANIEL: UNRESOLVED TRANSFERENCE AND SECURE ATTACHMENT

I considered the almost three-year analytic treatment of a latency-age boy to have been very successful. Daniel, who had entered analysis because of nightmares, brought up terminating after we had been working together for two and a half years, and we began to discuss the possibility. He, however, experienced a return of his frightening nightmares. This recurrence, I interpreted to him, was a way he could show me, and also his parents, that he was not quite ready to leave. He expressed his worry about how he would get along without me. His parents did not seem to know what he would like for his birthday as, he believed, I did. We postponed the date for terminating and continued our work which now included his worries about leaving. In his last session Daniel reported a dream: *"I'm taking a trip all by myself. There are dangers on each side of the road. But I go straight ahead. I think there is a rainbow at the end—in gray."* Daniel thought this was a wonderful dream. He felt he could make it on his own, and he shook my hand good-bye. I had thought that the rainbow "in gray" had only to do with the work we had done on Daniel's color-blindness and that it was a kind of "inside joke." Thinking about it today, I regret not pointing out and discussing more fully his profound sadness on leaving his analysis.

But even Daniel managed to find his way back to my office almost twenty years after he had left. At the age of nine, he had been extremely inhibited and restricted. Twenty years later, he was open, lively, and communicative. He was in the same area of work as his father and was quite successful in his own right. What was troubling Daniel when he returned was his inability to "commit to a relationship." It was not that he hadn't been in relationships, but after several months or a year, he became even less involved or even "bored." The relationship in which he was currently involved had now reached that point. To be honest, I felt a little chagrined to have Daniel back in my office with what seemed to be a rather significant problem. I think, at that time, I had subscribed to the misconceived and unfortunate ideal that after a successful analysis one would not hear from her analysand again. I maintained this ideal despite knowing that our child patients still have to negotiate many developmental stages and, even more importantly, that psychoanalysis is not a vaccination against the impact of life's trials and traumas.

Twenty years earlier, I was very pleased with the outcome of Daniel's, now Mr. T.'s, childhood analysis. At the time of the termination of that treatment, his development seemed back on track. He was doing well in school, with peers, and with his family. It was clear to me then and even clearer now that Mr. T. had dealt mainly with his fears of his aggression and that he had not analyzed his longings for love and attention from his mother or myself. When Daniel ended his analysis, he was solidly in latency and he was not interested in talking about his loving feelings for me. He also was not yet involved in dating girls.

In his adult analysis, Mr. T. developed an erotic transference to me, which was then analyzed. This work, I believe, allowed him to move ahead, get married, and have a family. Mr. T. had maintained a good, internal image of me. He said, "As a kid, I had always believed you would be there for me and would always consider my feelings." When Mr. T. returned to see me, his strong attachment to me and his unresolved oedipal feelings were apparent. One might consider that more work should have been done on the positive transference in his childhood treatment. Or one could say that the positive transference had been beneficial to the treatment alliance, the analytic progress, and perhaps future self-analysis. If a patient of any age returns after the termination of an analysis, the analyst should not, I think, immediately feel that the treatment was a failure.

Attachment research (Lyons-Ruth, 1991) provides the model of the securely attached child as one who can express affection unambivalently, use a parent as a source of help or guidance and vigorously pursue the goal of comforting contact with the parent when under stress, as well as assert initiative and opposition without fear of rejection. Thinking from the perspective of attachment theory, a securely attached patient would be comfortable going off on his own and struggling independently with new problems as they arose. The securely attached patient would also not hesitate to contact the analyst if he or she felt the need. In a similar way, the analyst would feel comfortable making herself available if she held the attachment model in mind.

MR. D.: IDEALIZATION AND DISAPPOINTMENT

Another man, Mr. D., returned to see me after a fifteen-year hiatus. When he returned, I was more prepared to see how I might help him and I did not consider his first analysis to have been a failure. Mr. D. had begun an analysis as a seven-year-old second grader. His father, an older man, was charismatic, successful, and powerful. He was, however, quite ill with cancer at the time. This first analysis was complicated by the father's death early in the treatment and by the patient's speech problems and dyslexia. Mr. D. was depressed and longed for his father, who had been particularly fond of him. Mr. D.'s mother's grief over the loss of her husband made her unavailable to her grieving son. He was mainly taken care of by a warm and devoted nanny. Both Mr. D.'s mother and his older brother irrationally blamed him for the father's death because the father had delayed treating his cancer in order to impregnate his wife with their second son, my patient.

As a child, Mr. D. aspired to be like his father. He worked in his analysis to deal with his sense of smallness, defectiveness, and inadequacy. He was a daredevil in sports and in his general behavior. His use of counterphobic defenses was interpreted and he began to understand his impulse-driven behavior. With analytic work, Mr. D. agreed to leave a high-powered boys' private school for a special school for children with learning disabilities. There, he was able to excel academically and ultimately returned to a mainstream private school.

In preadolescence, Mr. D. felt unable to continue his treatment with me. He thought that he needed to speak to a man because he didn't feel comfortable talking to me about sex. He saw his mother's behavior as both seductive and demeaning, and he felt that I, in the transference, was also like that. He believed strongly that he had to separate from his mother and from me the analyst/mother. I referred Mr. D. to a male analyst and then I didn't hear from him until several years after he had graduated from college. Mr. D. returned to see me despite the fact that both the male analyst he consulted during college and his mother were opposed to his returning to treatment with me.

Mr. D. returned as a young entrepreneur with joint custody of his three-year-old daughter. He had never married the child's mother but was very involved with his daughter's care. Mr. D. believed that he needed to see me because he had unresolved issues with his mother and because he felt I would be the one, since I had known his mother, who could understand his difficulties. I pointed out Mr. D.'s idealization of me and even wondered whether he was seeing me just to aggravate his mother. Mr. D. then confided that his mother did not like me because when she had seen me, she had felt that I was critical of her parenting. She felt I was harsh. After lengthy discussion, Mr. D. felt he needed to "finish up" with me, and I agreed to begin a second analysis.

In the second treatment, the main themes revolved around his guilt over his oedipal victory. He believed that he had helped his mother succeed in the family business. He continued to feel that his mother was inappropriately seductive and had ensnared him into working for her. By working on the transference, Mr. D. was able to leave the family business in favor of his own venture. He also began to develop a more reasonable and mature relationship with a seemingly appropriate woman.

Also present in the second treatment was Mr. D.'s disappointment in the first analysis. He reviewed his last memories of his father lying on a hospital gurney. He recalled how the two of us had played out hospital scenarios with Playmobil figures. The intense feelings of pain and anguish were still present, and Mr. D. felt angry that all of his treatment had never eradicated those affects. He had hoped that his many years of treatment would have erased those feelings and he was disappointed that they still existed and would reemerge in his thoughts from time to time.

THE ANALYST AS A SUSTAINING NEW INTERNAL OBJECT

Last summer, I happened to pick up my office phone one July evening. I did not recognize the woman's voice but I did recognize her name. She was a former patient of mine who had come into analysis as an early adolescent because of many problems, including an eating disorder. I must admit she had given me a run for my money. But over the four years we worked together she had improved and had become insightful about her conflicts. We terminated when she went to college in another city, and I gave her a referral to an analyst in that city. When she went to graduate school abroad, I gave her another referral. I knew from that analyst that my former patient had gone to see her, but I hadn't heard from my former patient in about ten years. The woman on the phone asked me for a referral for a friend of hers. She said, "You are good with referrals" and proceeded to tell me a little about her friend. I asked my former patient how she was and what she was doing. She told me, "Today is my due date and I am going to have a little boy. I don't expect he will arrive today. First babies can often be late. . . ." We spoke for a short while and I wished her good luck.

After our conversation, I sat in my office thinking about why my former patient had called me on that day. Of course, I was glad that she seemed happy and to be doing well. I thought that she might have been a little scared about her impending delivery and perhaps wanted to make sure I was still alive and supportive of her. I remembered a paper by Heather Craige (2009) I had seen recently. It caught my eye because of its title, "Terminating without Fatality." Many authors have written on how, after a good-enough analysis, the image of the analyst lives on in the mind of the analysand as a sustaining and helpful new internal object. I believe that a successful analysis depends in part on the formation of a positive bond between the analyst and the patient in which the child feels he or she matters to the analyst and that the analyst is trying to be helpful.

NEW OPTIONS FOR ENDING

It is extremely important for the analyst to help the child or adolescent end in a way that will foster and not undermine the internal relationship and will preserve the feelings of loving and being loved. The analyst's own discomfort with feelings related to loss and disappointment may interfere with her participating in the separation in a respectful, sensitive, and flexible manner. Recent writers (Craige, 2009; Frank, 2009) have commented on the fact that a rigid adherence to certain psychoanalytic ideals regarding the correct handling of termination may interfere with empathic and respectful conduct during and following termination. For example, many of us were taught that analysis should be conducted four times per week to the very end. This may be ideal, but many children would prefer a gradual reduction in the number of sessions per week. Understanding the desire for an attenuated schedule may lead to the analyst being more compassionate with her patient's needs and negotiating a more supportive ending. Ideally the child or adolescent should feel that he has left the analyst in his own way and with the agreement and confidence of the analyst. This is a model of separating that can be used by the patient when he or she ultimately leaves home.

The analytic journey begins with the knowledge that this special relationship will end one day. For children and adolescents this ending may occur sooner than is desirable. No matter how much preparation is accomplished, the ending of an analysis can be quite disregulating. Hopefully, the child will maintain a positive internalized image of the analyst. Identification with the analyst and the analyzing function of the analyst is probably one of the most mutative aspects of the treatment. The analyst's availability after termination is crucial if the termination has set off feelings of abandonment. Post-termination contact with the analyst can help to solidify a positive internal image of the analyst. After a good-enough analysis and the successful negotiation of the mourning process, an internal image of the analyst lives on in the patient, providing a helpful new internal object. We hope that once the patient has mourned the loss she may feel enriched rather than impoverished by the loss. During the young analysand's journey through the next developmental stages, he may use what he has learned to negotiate the new challenges or may feel the need to return to his analyst for further help. The quality of the post-termination contact, responsive and respectful, will continue to shape the positive internal image of the analyst.

BIBLIOGRAPHY

ABRAMS, S. (1978). Termination in Child Analysis. In *Child Analysis and Therapy*, ed. J. Glenn. New York: Aronson, 451–469.
BERGMANN, M. S. (1997). Termination: The Achilles Heel of Psychoanalytic Technique. *Psychoanalytic Psychology* 14:163–174.
CRAIGE, H.(2009). Terminating without Fatality. *Psychoanalytic Inquiry* 29: 101–116.
FRANK, K. A. (2009). Ending with Options. *Psychoanalytic Inquiry* 29:136–156.

LYONS-RUTH, K. (1991). Rapprochement or Approchement: Mahler's Theory Reconsidered from the Vantage Point of Recent Research on Early Attachment Relationships. *Psychoanalytic Psychology* 8:1–14.

NOVICK, J., AND NOVICK, K. K. (2000). Love in the Therapeutic Alliance. *Journal of the American Psychoanalytic Association* 48:189–218.

_____. (2006), *Good Goodbyes*, Lanham, MD: Jason Aronson.

SANDLER, J., KENNEDY, H., TYSON. R. L. (1980). *The Technique of Child Psychoanalysis: Discussions with Anna Freud.* Cambridge, MA: Harvard University Press.

SCHMUKLER, A. G., ED. (1991). *Saying Goodbye: A Casebook of Termination in Child and Adolescent Analysis and Therapy.* Hillsdale, NJ: Analytic Press.

APPLIED PSYCHOANALYSIS

The Transformation of Achilles in *The Iliad*

A Reading from the Views of Sibling Narratives and Nonlinear Growth

CLAUDIA LAMENT, Ph.D.

I wish to showcase the importance of plasticity of narrative in fantasy formations, as exemplified in Achilles' psychological trajectory in The Iliad. *Applying conceptual formulations concerning the psychoanalytic developmental process to Achilles' growth piques my reflections about the sibling experience and its unique position in the mental life of children and adolescents. With developmental advance and the capacity for measured fluidity of self and other structures, the original sibling experience— whether it be tilted toward aggressiveness or toward loving concern or a place in between—may acquire new meanings.*

By locating it within this contextual framework, Achilles' story line can be seen as a metaphorical description of the continuous and discontinuous patterns in growth. This poses intriguing questions: What contexts are useful in pondering Achilles' psychological shifts? Might the domain of disposition prove useful? Is birth order another? Is his gradual empathic concern for the enemy a demonstration of an elasticity of imaginative capacity that reassembles murderous potential? Child and adult analysts alike may find a rich trove in Homer's masterpiece for

Claudia Lament, Ph.D., is a Training and Supervising Analyst at the Institute for Psychoanalytic Education, an affiliate of the New York University Langone School of Medicine. She is Assistant Clinical Professor in the Department of Child and Adolescent Psychiatry, the Child Study Center, New York University Langone Medical Center. She is also Senior Managing Editor of *The Psychoanalytic Study of the Child*.
The Psychoanalytic Study of the Child 68, ed. Claudia Lament, Robert A. King, Samuel Abrams, Paul M. Brinich, and Rona Knight (Yale University Press, copyright © 2015 by Claudia Lament, Robert A. King, Samuel Abrams, Paul M. Brinich, and Rona Knight).

contemplating potential sources within their patients that spur forward movement.

IN FULL KNOWLEDGE THAT I AM EXAMINING FICTIVE CHARACTERS, I follow Juliet Mitchell's guidance (Mitchell, 2003. p. x) that a wide array of sources, including literary works, can throw light on subjects that target aspects of the sociocultural and psychological domains. The character of Achilles in Homer's epic poem *The Iliad*[1] has been etched in our minds as the quintessential Greek ideal of the tragic hero. His story launches from his position as a ruthless, hypersensitive Greek warrior who is blisteringly reactive to perceived and real slights with rage. He is the eternal bad boy who will not submit to the Greek elder, Agamemnon, a ruthless autocrat and self-involved older man, or metaphorically, an elder brother. But over the course of the poem, Achilles undergoes a psychological metamorphosis that allows him to put aside his own pain and reach out to an enemy—another older man / elder brother figure—who has experienced a wrenching loss. In this way, the reader has been made witness to Achilles' experience of a grief-borne entry into human connections that opens the door to civilization.

I wish to focus my reflections using the lens of the nonlinear aspect of the developmental process that Sigmund Freud outlined in 1905. In particular, I wish to showcase the importance of plasticity of narrative in fantasy life as one facilitating aspect that assists children in forward movement to new levels. With developmental advance, the original sibling experience—whether it be tilted toward aggressiveness or toward loving concern or a place in between—will acquire new meanings, including more adaptive forms, when we consider the inevitable progression of psychological organizations (Abrams, 2001; Abrams and Solnit, 1998; Neubauer, 1984; Hartmann and Kris, 1945; A. Freud, 1965, 1974, 1976).

By locating it within this contextual framework, Achilles' story line can be seen as a metaphorical description of discontinuous growth. In this light, how are we to understand the role of Achilles' caring attitudes toward Patroclus in the sea change that occurs at its close? What are some contexts within which we can position this trajectory? Might the domain of disposition prove useful? Is birth order another? Is his profound shift of feeling a demonstration of his capacity for the reassembling of murderous potential?

---

1. From THE ILIAD by Homer, translated by Robert Fagles, translation copyright © 1990 by Robert Fagles. Used by permission of Viking Penguin, a division of Penguin Group (USA) Inc.

What I also wish to illuminate is an interpretation of the dramatis personae of *The Iliad* as sibling stand-ins for Achilles, which interweaves with the perspective of nonlinear growth. Achilles, Patroclus (Achilles' cousin and foster brother), Hector, Agamemnon, and Priam can be viewed as operating within the bonds of brothers. The presiding aspects of Homer's creation bluntly exposes one set of formulations (Mitchell, 2003) concerning a sibling's grandiose and narcissistic self-interests, murderousness, and cold-blooded hatred, which are directed toward Hector and the elder statesman, Agamemnon. However, at the same time, Achilles expresses a whole set of opposing strains of feeling—of profound love and comradeship—toward his beloved foster brother, Patroclus. The tensions that pull Achilles along these vertices are raised to high relief until they culminate in a human self who reaches across this divide and grasps the pain of his enemy's blasted internal landscape. This transformation, a discontinuous shift, reflects his monumental achievement of deep empathic caring.

THE STORY

There is no want for sibling themes in *The Iliad*. In fact, it is the backdrop of Patroclus's childhood that sets up the reader for the enduring drama of murder and punishment that will run like Ariadne's thread throughout the epic poem. It is late in the narrative that Homer informs us of this critical data. In Book 23, we learn of Patroclus's admission of his unintended killing of a boyhood friend. Achilles' father, Peleus, takes pity upon the homeless boy and brings him into his own family's fold, where the cousins' kinship takes the form of brothers. The story of these cousins, or what I contend is its likening to a fraternal relationship, contains and thinly veils multiple references to both vertical and lateral positions, the seeds of oedipal lust and hatred, rivalries on both vertical and horizontal axes, desires for gender-swapping, death wishes and murderous rage, grandiose imaginings, and omnipotent yearnings. Yet these two men also share a brotherly connection that is more than the sum of these parts. The strong bonds of fealty, comradeship, and love are prominently on view as the two "brothers" pit themselves against their archenemy, Hector, who slips easily into place as the "bad" brother. His personage may be viewed as the *locum tenens* for their collective rivalry and hatred aimed toward one another.

The Iliad begins nine years into the Trojan War. The Greeks have defeated a town under Troy's rule, and Agamemnon takes the fair maiden Chryseis as his booty; Achilles takes the other maiden, Briseis. The father of Chryseis prays to Apollo for help against this injustice, who sends a plague that overcomes the Greek warriors. Agamemnon releases his prize maiden to recompense the bereft father, but Agamemnon is outraged at this loss and insists that Achilles overturn Briseis to him. Now, it is Achilles' turn at rage; insulted by Agamemnon's theft, he unleashes his mighty wrath: he refuses to fight for the Achaeans, knowing full well that they will feel the sting of his loss. Only in this way does he feel that they will realize his worth. Indeed, the Greeks are crippled by the absence of Achilles, and, as a result, they are driven back to their beached ships by Troy's valiant leader, Hector, son of Priam. All seems lost until Patroclus, Achilles' beloved friend, finds Achilles and begs him to reenter the war and finally bring an end to his punishment against Agamemnon and the Achaeans. Achilles refuses to enter the battle himself, but he strikes a compromise: he allows Patroclus to wear his armor as he enters the fight. The Trojans are pushed back from the ships, but Patroclus is killed by Hector, who has stripped Achilles' armor from him and wears it himself. Achilles is wracked by grief for the loss of his dear friend and in a blind rage throws himself into the battle hungry with bloodlust, savagely intent on avenging Patroclus's death. The Gods have forecast that Achilles will find Hector and murder him; but in so doing, Achilles' own demise will soon follow. After Hector is slain by Achilles, he lashes Hector's body to his chariot and circles Patroclus's grave. Funeral games follow as a magnificent tribute to the fallen hero. For nine days, Achilles degrades the body of Hector by dragging the corpse through the festivities.

In agreement with the gods' desire that Hector receive a burial, Priam, accompanied and protected by Hermes, bravely risks his own death by stealing into the Greeks' camp late at night. He finds Achilles and implores him to return his son's body to him. In his anguish, he conjures up Achilles' own father, Peleus—alone and apart from his son—drawing a parallel between both fathers' yearning to see their sons again. Achilles is struck by the imagined picture of his own lamenting father and reaches out to Priam with compassion for his profound loss. Achilles achieves a deep emotional understanding of his enemy and returns Hector's body to him. Finally, a temporary truce is called between the warring factions to permit a peaceful funeral for Hector, the breaker of horses.

ACHILLES' BROTHERHOOD AND ITS INFORMING CONTEXTS

Homer's text provided several story lines for Achilles (Abrams, 2011). They are structured either in live interaction with other characters or within Achilles' own silent imaginings. These correspond to a retinue of underlying fantasy configurations—some even demonstrating a mash-up of reversals and paradox—which live cheek by jowl within him.

The first narrative that comes to life in the poem accesses the most popular interpretation of Achilles' personality: Achilles' reaction as an enraged *victim* to cruel Agamemnon—a father–elder brother figure. In Book 1, Achilles indicts Agamemnon for his abandonment of his duties as general of the Argives, of greed and timidity:

> "Shameless—
> armored in shamelessness—always shrewd with greed!
> How could any Argive soldier obey your orders,
> Freely and gladly do your sailing for you
> Or fight your enemies, full force? Not I, no. . . .
> "No, you colossal, shameless—we all followed you,
> to please you, to fight for you, to win your honor
> back from the Trojans—Menelaus and you, you dog-face!
> What do *you* care? Nothing. You don't look right or left. . . ."

> "My honors never equal yours,
> Whenever we sack some wealthy Trojan stronghold—
> . . . the lion's share is yours, and back I go to my ships,
> clutching some scrap, some pittance that I love,
> when I have fought to exhaustion." (Homer, 1990, pp. 82–83)

Finally, Achilles creates an imaginary schema of one who humiliates and dishonors versus one who submits. Agamemnon says of Achilles:

> "What if the everlasting gods have made a spearman of him?
> Have they entitled him to hurl abuse at *me?*"

> "Yes!"—blazing Achilles broke in quickly—
> "What a worthless, burnt-out coward I'd be called
> if I would submit to you and all your orders,
> whatever you blurt out. Fling them at others,
> don't give me commands!
> Never again, *I* trust, will Achilles yield to *you.*" (p. 87)

An amalgam of vertical and horizontal axes could be summoned up in these passages: what is of special interest in this sequence is the slow-burn one-upmanship in a zero-sum game. The phallocentrism of the tale highlights the elder and younger siblings' mutual rage and feelings of injustice. Achilles' sonar for such surges of inequality, which Agamemnon tosses off as his righteous due, comes at the reader full force. Achilles' signature trope cannot easily be explained, but introducing a contextual framework of dispositional variants may prove useful. Is this hypersensitivity some dispositional feature, as Anna Freud might have wondered? Did the boundary between himself and Patroclus, his scorned and beloved older foster brother, only partially congeal so as to make for a psychic skin that enveloped them together as a unit? Was it elastic enough to allow for a separateness at other moments? Might this feature have promoted an identification in fantasy with the outcast, humiliated Patroclus, who was mistreated by his community, thus priming him for the intensity of his experience of Agamemnon's assaults? Did Achilles use Patroclus' role as the elder brother as a figure who facilitated and assisted this developmental forward thrust? If Patroclus was paladin and victor in play, might Achilles have rivaled this bigger boy, envied his strength, or found himself jealous of his place, despite his not being within the blood tie? If so, might we imagine him as serving the role of spur to the younger Achilles? Did he also identify with his own father's benevolent role as taking in the homeless boy Patroclus—a point of contrast to the repeating reproofs of Agamemnon?

In a moment of reverie, Achilles slips into an imagining of himself as the loving protectorate sibling of Patroclus, another narrative. This appears at the beginning of Book 16, when the Greeks have been routed by the Trojans. In the following brief but perceptively elaborated passage, Achilles spins an imagining of Patroclus as the needy child to the parent-Achilles. Achilles keenly observes Patroclus's despairing countenance as he watches him approach and swiftly creates a deeply felt scenelet. It brings the reader fast-forward style into modern life. Filmic and immediate in its quick cuts from feeling to feeling, it captures pitch-perfect a toddler aswarm in an overload of passion:

> And the brilliant runner Achilles saw him coming,
> filled with pity and spoke out winging words:
> "Why in tears, Patroclus?
> like a girl, a baby running after her mother,
> begging to be picked up, and she tugs her skirts,
> holding her back as she tries to hurry off—all tears,
> fawning up at her, til she takes her in her arms . . .
> That's how you look, Patroclus, streaming live tears." (p. 142)

The hero takes the role of comforting mother to Patroclus's tearful child and, fascinatingly, exchanges Patroclus's gender for a girl, then reduces the age of this girl to an infant. Of course, it is open for interpretation how one views this imaginary scene: Is it a castrated, degraded image of Patroclus, and of Achilles himself as a mother, that is conjured up? Or is this a complex portraiture of a wounded, hapless baby, yes—but who is willful too, who demands—insists, even—upon extracting her preoccupied mother's loving caress. This scene bears the stamp of a fluid, biomorphic habitat of the imagination, where Achilles flows comfortably among selves that are inclusive of gender and generational swings. He is a natural shape-shifter. And on another level still, we must not forget that Achilles is the baby, too, still smarting from Agamemnon's humiliation. Here is a man whose dispositional makeup sets him in the direction of transforming external stimuli into psychic meanings. What has also occurred is that the lateral axis has morphed into a vertical one.

In Book 18, Achilles mourns Patroclus's death. The evocation of the vertical plane comes into view here, too, but this time it is the role of a lion-father that Achilles takes on:

> but all night long the Argives raised Patroclus' dirge.
> And Achilles led them now in a throbbing chant of sorrow,
> laying his man-killing hands on his great friend's chest,
> convulsed with bursts of grief. Like a bearded lion
> whose pride of cubs a deer-hunter has snatched away,
> out of some thick woods, and back he comes, too late,
> and his heart breaks but he courses after the hunter,
> hot on his tracks down glen on twisting glen—
> where can he find him?—gripped by piercing rage . . . (p. 478)

Achilles is overtaken by convulsive sobs of grief. Homer provides him with a way of managing these overwhelming and intolerable feeling states by turning him into a raging beast. In this interpretation, which places a dispositional variant in relief, an attempt at affect regulation surfaces to curb the tidal surge of emotion: the bellwether of grief is reversed into the animal-father's searing, bloodthirsty, blind rage. What then drives Achilles is a riotous take-no-prisoners vengeance against his "son's" murderer.

And in another passage that follows the death of Patroclus, Achilles' paternal feeling takes human form: he imagines himself a father who faces his son's death on his wedding day:

> All night long they hurled the flames—massed on the pyre,
> blast on screaming blast—and all night long the swift Achilles,
> lifting a two-handled cup, dipped wine from a golden bowl
> and poured it down on the ground and drenched the earth,
> calling out to the ghost of stricken, gaunt Patroclus.
> As a father weeps when he burns his son's bones,
> dead on his wedding day,
> and his death has plunged his parents in despair . . .
> so Achilles wept as he burned his dear friend's bones,
> dragging himself around the pyre, choked with sobs. (p. 566)

This spectrum of selves—from victim of an elder father/brother, to one who loves and honors the sibling other, to an imagined protectorate of that sibling in human and bestial forms—demonstrates Achilles' ever-changing roles in narrative and self-structures. It shows nothing if not a prodigious creative capacity to place himself into the fully felt experience of others, an elasticity of the boundary between self and others, which engages empathy and caring via fantasy creations. Might this capaciousness have been fed (not necessarily spawned) by his position as an only child—despite Patroclus's role in his life? Patroclus was brother, but yet not brother at all. Putting aside dispositional leanings and inventive proclivities, are we observing something that Achilles experiences as an only child?

CLIMAX: ACHILLES' MEETING WITH PRIAM

Achilles' fluid embodiments of son, father, and brother take hold near the close of the poem upon his fateful meeting with Hector's father. With Hermes as his escort, Priam has stolen into the Greeks' camp to ask Achilles to return his son's body to him.

With an arresting poignancy, Priam imagines an image of Achilles' father, Peleus, alone, frightened of forces beyond his control, grasping at an illusion that his only son will return home to him. He then returns to his own feelings:

> "But I—dear god, my life so cursed by fate . . .
> I fathered hero sons in the wide realm of Troy
> And now not a single one is left, I tell you." (p. 604)

Priam draws a sharp distinction between Peleus and himself: Peleus, a father whose son is very much living and sits before him and himself, a father who has lost every son, the last at Achilles' own hand. Then, in what may be the most profoundly moving moment of the entire poem, Priam makes an unthinkable gesture:

> "Revere the god, Achilles! Pity me in my own right,
> remember your own father! I deserve more pity . . .
> I have endured what no one on earth has ever done before—
> I put to my lips the hands of the man who killed my son." (pp. 604–605)

Priam pleads to Achilles to see him as separate, "in his own right"; yet, paradoxically, in the same breath, he insists that he "remember his own father."

> Those words stirred within Achilles a deep desire
> to grieve for his own father. Taking the old man's hand

he gently moved him back. And overpowered by memory
both men gave way to grief. Priam wept freely
for man-killing Hector, throbbing, crouching
before Achilles' feet as Achilles wept himself,
now for his father, now for Patroclus once again,
and their sobbing rose and fell throughout the house. (p. 605)

Indeed, just as Achilles sees the old man on his own terms he feels the urgency to "gently move him back" from the foreground of his consciousness. He must make way for an experience of being "overpowered by memory," which now takes center stage in this psychic drama. The extraordinary images that Homer paints contain the transparencies of father, son, beloved friend–foster brother that overwhelm him with intense grief as these take precedence in Achilles' imagination. The parent-child dimension overlaps and interlaces with the sibling one as he and Priam "give way to grief" and free-fall down the deep well of loss.

And on another level still, Achilles appears to assume the very voice of his benevolent father to the suffering Priam, who begs Achilles for the body of his dead child so that he may give him a final resting place. Opening wider to further unexpected ways of seeing through Priam's eyes, Achilles achieves a surprising insight as he realizes that he has been a perpetrator of terrible wounds and unbearable sorrow to the old man. He speaks first of his own father's adversities:

"Yes, but even on him [his father] the Father [Zeus] piled hardships,
no powerful race of princes born in his royal halls,
only a single son he fathered, doomed at birth,
cut off in the spring of life—
and I, I give the man no care as he grows old
since here I sit in Troy, far from my fatherland,
a grief to you, a grief to all your children . . ." (p. 606)

And then offers words of kindness and advice to the sonless father:

"You must bear up now. Enough of endless tears,
the pain that breaks the spirit.
Grief for your son will do no good at all.
You will never bring him back to life—
Sooner you must suffer something worse." (ibid.)

Almost immediately, Achilles becomes mindful of Hector's lashed corpse and desires that it be treated honorably; he wishes to avoid what he fears may be Priam's angry response and his own dispositional proclivities to react in rage. Achilles' earlier abilities to see the other is brought to an even greater depth of concern for the other, as well as a cognizance of his own vulnerability to fatally lash out. In deference to Socrates' admonishment, he knows himself: he brings an acute self-awareness to this moment, which privileges and protects his desire to heal and make amends.

> Then Achilles called the serving-women out:
> "Bathe and anoint the body—
> bear it aside first. Priam must not see his son."
> He feared that, overwhelmed by the sight of Hector,
> wild with grief, Priam might let his anger flare
> and Achilles might fly into fresh rage himself,
> cut the old man down and break the laws of Zeus. (p. 607)

It is as though the bountiful heart of Peleus, who took in the homeless child, finds itself renewed in its reach as Achilles lends himself as a harbor, if only briefly, to the bereft old man.

Suddenly, Achilles is caught off guard by an old feeling that is out of kilter with his newfound growth. As he lifts up Hector's body in his own arms and places him on a bier, he imagines the possibility that Patroclus might be angry for his compassion toward his killer's father.

> "Feel no anger at me, Patroclus, if you learn—
> even there in the House of Death—I let his father
> have Prince Hector back. He gave me worthy ransom
> and you shall have your share from me, as always,
> your fitting, lordly share." (p. 608)

Achilles answers this ghostly revenant with a voice of maturity that will not bend to the ancient ties of sibling connectedness that insist on possessiveness and a lockdown on the existence of encroaching others. He shatters the mistaken belief of childhood that love is finite and subservient to the laws of the material world: there is enough love to go around to Priam as well as Patroclus—even in death. We as readers have been witness to the building of a bridge of empathy: it has become Achilles' own to cross over.

This shift that occurs could be interpreted as a *transformational* one wherein Achilles has advanced into a new hierarchical organization that introduces a fresh capacity for object relationships. As stated previously, more sophisticated mental processes in maturational capacities and an increased ability to list away from a narcissistic and murderous frame of mind lift the individual into a new psychological organization wherein giving takes on a new meaning and is valued in its own right. By implication, the connection to others and the wider surround becomes incorporated into a new, reconstituted personal value system.

On the other hand, a related but different proposition could be advanced. Might the change in Achilles be the result of the liberation of repressed or muted potential for caring for others? Did the exchange with Priam provide an opportunity for a reassembly of feelings and ways of relating that yielded an outcome that was largely unpredictable? What occurred for Achilles might be described as a transformation that did not occur as the result of the ushering in of a new hierarchical order, but rather a fresh way of putting together features that until this moment have been out of awareness.

The experience tapped potential that was an inherent feature of Achilles' personality, as evidenced in his fantasy life earlier in the story. Such potential could be cataloged as innate, pointing to sensitivities to the feelings of others. Perhaps too Achilles' inherent capacity toward self-reflection—even when *in extremis*—led him to protect Priam against his own impulsivity to lash out.

A final perspective could be put forward. Despite a phallocentric leaning in psychoanalytic theory, boys have degrees of empathic and caring potential that societal attitudes may overlook (Balsam, 2008). Does this tale demonstrate the limitations in such phallocentric views of siblingship wherein the spectrum of bellicosity holds sway? Did Priam's approach to Achilles and the vulnerabilities, remembrances, and emotions that were evoked in that concluding interlude create propitious conditions for the flowering of Achilles' deeply felt empathic response, one that is traditionally perceived as embracing feminine trends? The psychological journey Achilles makes in this poem opens up a way of listening to metaphors of gender-based rhetorical devices. It envelops strategies with which a man dealt with conflict: those that were built upon hate and those that were built upon love.

DISCUSSION

As Achilles moved through *The Iliad*, he experimented with increasingly sophisticated theories of mind that permitted empathic awareness of others (Aragno, 2008; Fonagy and Target, 2007; Gergely and Watson, 1996). Whether Achilles fantasizes becoming a father-lion, on the hunt to avenge the murder of his cubs, or a very human mother who is caught between fulfilling her own desires or tending to her baby's distress, one may propose that he was becoming aware of earlier repressed attitudes and dispositional features that were components of what will become the eventual reassembling of the self.

In sum, these story lines that are a part of Achilles' psychic frame prior to his transformational dialogue with Priam are the green buds of transformational change that have not yet blossomed into a new form until the closure of the poem. Even Achilles' dispositional penchant toward narcissistic slights may prepare the path that eventuates in his exquisite sensitivity to another's wound, another's anguish. This achievement also serves to liberate him from a phallocentric mind-set of defiance and violence. The freshness and breakaway creativity of the final section of the poem, which embraces the customarily held feminine features of nurturance, capaciousness, and connection, sever the gender-specific codes typically associated with the strong masculine ideal.

Achilles' ability to perceive father–elder brother Priam freshly humanizes him and brings him into the fold of community and connectedness with others. What happens in the course of Homer's poem is the formation of structures that culminate in "new forms" (Mitchell, 2003) that have been transmogrified from one domain into another. Dispositional and constitutional aspects that encompass caring and cooperativeness and a sufficiently pliant elasticity in self and other boundaries would be contributing features to this growth. In this way, these facilitate the strengthening of social bonds and the sociocultural contracts that forge the world of others.

It is in the failures in the expectable discontinuous changes over the course of development that dispositional variants and male-oriented proclivities both are brought into full view. In their continuous press within the individual as development progresses into adulthood, they may cripple the promotion of healthy and caring relationships as they begin within the family structure of parent and child and brother and sister.

REFERENCES

ABRAMS, S. (2001). Summation—unrealized possibilities: Comments on Anna Freud's *Normality and Pathology in Childhood. Psychoanalytic Study of the Child* 56:105–119.

———. (2011). Historiography 101 for psychoanalysts. *Psychoanalytic Study of the Child* 65:103–128.

ABRAMS, S., AND NEUBAUER, P. B. (1976). Object orientedness: The person or the thing. *Psychoanalytic Quarterly* 45:73–99.

ABRAMS, S., AND SOLNIT, A. (1998). Coordinating developmental and psychoanalytic processes. *Journal of the American Psychoanalytic Association* 46:85–104.

ARAGNO, A. (2008). The language of empathy. *Journal of the American Psychoanalytic Association* 56:713–740.

BALSAM, R. (2008). Fathers and the bodily care of their infant daughters. *Psychoanalytic Inquiry* 28:60–75.

FONAGY, P., AND M. TARGET (2007). Playing with reality: IV. A theory of external reality rooted in intersubjectivity. *International Journal of Psychoanalysis* 81:917–37.

FREUD, A. (1965). Normality and pathology in childhood: Assessments of development. In *The Writings of Anna Freud*, vol. 6. New York: International Universities Press.

———. (1974). A psychoanalytic view of developmental psychopathology. In *The Writings of Anna Freud*, vol. 8, pp. 57–74. New York: International Universities Press.

———. (1976). Psychopathology seen against the background of normal development. In *The Writings of Anna Freud*, vol. 8, pp. 82–95. New York: International Universities Press.

GERGELY, G. AND WATSON (1996). The social biofeedback model of parental affect-mirroring. *International Journal of Psychoanalysis* 77:1181–1212.

HARTMANN, H., AND KRIS, E. (1945). The genetic approach to psychoanalysis. *Psychoanalysis of the Child* 1:11–30.

HOMER (1990). *The Iliad.* Translated by Robert Fagles. New York: Penguin Books.

MITCHELL, J. (2003). *Siblings.* Cambridge, UK: Polity Press.

NEUBAUER, P. (1984). Anna Freud's concept of developmental lines. *Psychoanalytic Study of the Child* 39:15–27.

The Role of Sports in the Development of the Superego of the Male Latency Child

MOISY SHOPPER, M.D.

Psychoanalytic literature has often overlooked the child's participation in organized sports, which often can facilitate or impede not only expression of aggression and narcissism, but enhance or skew the growth of the child's superego and ego ideal. Specific outcomes are largely determined by the experience and knowledge of the parents, the coaches, and sports organizations for latency-aged youth. Sports participation facilitates a major step forward in psychic development, that is, an agreed-upon adherence to a set of rules and regulations, monitored by an official embodying the final word regarding rules and their infractions.

This paper is an attempt to delineate the role of sports in the life of the latency child, the parents who become involved, the coaches who teach and supervise, and the social and individual milieu within which sports take place. All these contribute to common goals: the engendering of good sportsmanship and the encouragement of psychic growth, particularly regarding how aggression and narcissism contribute to the development of superego and ego ideals.

The fate of aggression and narcissism in superego and ego ideal development is influenced to a large degree by the nature, orientation, and motivations of all involved in sports for the latency-aged.

Dr. Shopper is Clinical Professor Emeritus of Pediatrics and Child Psychiatry, St. Louis University School of Medicine, and Supervising and Training Analyst (Adult and Child), St. Louis Psychoanalytic Institute.

The Psychoanalytic Study of the Child 68, ed. Claudia Lament, Robert A. King, Samuel Abrams, Paul M. Brinich, and Rona Knight (Yale University Press, copyright © 2015 by Claudia Lament, Robert A. King, Samuel Abrams, Paul M. Brinich, and Rona Knight).

INTRODUCTION

AS A PROFESSION WE HAVE IGNORED SPORTS AS THOUGH WE WERE never very good at it, or as if, being akin to play, it is a pastime of little psychological importance. Yet it is incumbent on child analysts to view sports as an important sector of child development. Those of us who see latency-aged children cannot help but be impressed at the amount of time, affect, and money that children and parents invest in sports. In addition, in many analyses of latency-aged children, sports often is the "playing field" of inhibitions, of parental conflict, as well as symptoms of intrapsychic conflict. In this paper I will review the literature on superego development in latency and emphasize not only the role of sports in superego maturation but also the important roles of parents, coaches, umpires, and sports organizations in this process.

It is my thesis that sports, typically initiated in latency, is often a crucible for the instillation of ethical, legal, and sportsmanship-like behavior and its accompanying values. Although the latency age child's participation in organized sports and its contribution to superego development may be apparent to many, this topic remains neglected in our literature and our thinking. Latency represents the stage in development during which superego issues are not just a family matter but expand into the social, interpersonal, and group realm. At the high school and college levels additional factors come into play, namely the huge financial and narcissistic rewards possible in sports, which may at times overwhelm both individual and group superegos. However high school and college sports require their own extended discussion (Hirsch and Blumberg, 2010).

In most practices, as well as mine, there is a preponderance of boys in latency compared to latency girls. Since there are many significant gender differences in sports participation and significant gender differences in the approach and meaning of sports to latency girls, this paper is based predominantly on my experience with latency boys. Several women analysts have written about their personal history of sports involvement: Jean Petrucelli (2010), who started tennis at age 13, and Adrienne Harris (2010), who was taught to hit a baseball by her father when he returned from World War II. While gender differences are distinct and everpresent in latency, female involvement in latency sports is often modeled on existing male models and established customs. Accordingly, while many aspects of this paper may or may not have applicability to latency girls, there will be the tendency to develop along their own unique gender lines, especially as more girls participate in sports. Another distinction needs to be made between those sports that are more individualistic, such as diving, swimming, figure skating, equestrian events, gymnastics, archery, and so on. While being part of a swim "team" is viewed as a team sport, it lacks the face-to-face contact with opponents that characterize soccer, baseball, or football.

REVIEW OF LITERATURE

This review will not focus solely on superego nor ego ideal development, but rather the degree to which sports are correlated with the development of these two important developmental advances.

Peller (1954) states, "An analytic study of various board and card games, such old favorites as chess, checkers, dominoes, etc., and also of the team sports could provide important clues for our understanding of ego and superego development in latency and maturity" (p. 191 footnote). Unfortunately her understanding was not further elaborated.

Anna Freud's developmental lines (1965) move from "the ability to play to the ability to work," and she mentions the use of toys, building materials, movable toys, as well as gender-specific toys and the pleasures of achievement. In progressing from play to work, daydreaming, games, and hobbies are mentioned. While "games" are an all-inclusive category, I would suggest augmenting her developmental line to specifically include sports.

Sarnoff (1976) in his classic treatise "Latency," notes that in mid-latency, the child's increased abilities may also be used to lie, cheat, steal, and otherwise break accepted rules of behavior. He notes that increased access to peers and group influences often undermines parentally established ethical behaviors. Sarnoff emphasizes the regression from the oedipal conflict to the anal-sadistic phase and its defenses against the direct expression of those impulses. He then states, "The latency age child is too small physically to express his aggressive drives effectively in reality" (p. 153).

However, I would take exception. Size is seldom an impairment to aggressive expression. The latency-aged child can and does express aggressive drives effectively. One has only to recall one's own latency age sibling relationships or, as a parent, having to restrain and redirect siblings from actually injuring each other. Latency age children cannot only inflict hurts physically but also verbally, through name-calling, taunts, bullying, as well as their open delight at the misfortune of others. Despite many latency children's involvement in Little League–type sports, the terms "athletics," "baseball," "coach," "sports," "sportsmanship" are not to be found in Sarnoff's index. In an otherwise thorough discussion, Sarnoff ignores sports and games from his discussion of superego development.

Shapiro and Perry (1976) "revisit" latency, focusing on the significance of "age 7 plus or minus 1." This age is accorded great educational, social, religious, and legal significance in most cultures. The authors emphasize the cognitive and neurological development, especially the ability to enter into social relationships with peers, to understand concepts of time and arbitrary rules, an increased capacity to learn, not only experientially but to learn what is taught—all accompanied by an abeyance and/or diminution of direct aggressive and sexual impulses and behavior. I would add that these qualities make the latency child both interested in and capable of participation as player, spectator, and fan, that is, the child is now ready to go from games to organized sports.

Arlow (1982) emphasizes that superego development continues throughout the life cycle. He believes the superego is seldom to be considered a finished product, even in mature adulthood. Since much of parental authority and superego development of the latency child is now shared and transferred to others (teachers, coaches, relatives, and society at large), we should not ignore latency's contribution to the superego.

Ablon (1988) treated a stuttering youngster, age five, who was inattentive in school and had angry outbursts at friends and family. Reporting material from the last two and a half years of the analysis, Ablon highlighted progress in terms of his patient being enthusiastically involved in sports and capable of playing "aggressive games." However, little is said about the role of sports in this improvement. Similarly, Babatzanis (1997) documents his treatment of a latency child who was enabled to participate in sports only after the analysis started. It is as though both these analysts regard involvement in sports as normative behavior.

In his discussion of mass culture, Kernberg (1989) wishes to explore psychoanalytically some of its characteristics and the basis of its appeal. He includes TV and films and notes that they seem to have the morality of the latency-aged child, but he makes no mention of sports, which occupies a large place in mass culture. However, it can be argued that sport is the latency child's entrée into mass culture.

Finkelstein (1991) noted the many areas of neglect of the superego and points to the loss "of the unity and power of the superego as Freud described it" (p. 531). Despite his extensive discussion and a survey of articles on the superego and the contributions of the preoedipal child observers and theorists, nothing is said about latency and its contribution to the superego.

Etchegoyen (1993) notes that Freud regarded the latency phase as the product of the solution of the oedipal conflict but wrote little about the concept thereafter. It was Anna Freud who brought the concept of continuity of the latency period into other periods of development, a theme echoed by Emde (1988) and the Tysons (1990). "The notion of a developmental continuum represents a departure from Freud's original formation, that the latency period is a consequence of the resolution of the Oedipus complex." Rather it is to be seen as a "process of progressive and more complex elaboration throughout latency"(Etchegoyen, 1993, p. 349).

Frenkel (1996), in her evaluation of a latency boy, noted, "With a weak ego and superego he was unable to adequately sublimate his drives, had diminished academic achievements, avoided sports, and had infantile interactions with his family and peers" (p. 332). She notes that good motor activity is helpful in discharging aggression that cannot otherwise be bound.

Novick and Novick (2004) posit a "two-system model" for superego development. Their "closed system" is an omnipotent sadomasochistic one that avoids and denies reality. The "open system . . . because it is attuned to inner and outer reality; constantly expands and changes; and is characterized by joy, competence and creativity in self-regulation, problem solving, and conflict resolution" (p. 238). Open-system functioning is "bolstered by the pleasure . . . from playing by the rules, expanding their competencies, forging empathic friendships with peers, and gaining approval from teachers and other important adults" (p. 248).

Free (2008) has an extensive review of a large number of sports. While lacking a developmental viewpoint, he examines how authors of varying analytic orientations view sports from the symbolic and dynamic viewpoints. Free views soccer in terms of the intrapsychic dynamics, deeming them universal. While Free focuses on sports and analytic thinking, his focus is limited to adulthood.

Hirsch and Blumberg (2010) co-edited an issue of *Contemporary Psychoanalysis* entirely devoted to "Intense Involvement with Sports." While many of the contributors trace their interest in sports to the latency period, and recall their early involvement with sports, the emphasis is on the significant role of sports in their own lives, their patients', and in American culture. Many of the articles illustrate the continuity between childhood sports involvement and adult emotional involvement and participation.

More recently, Sherick (2012) proposed a developmental line that leads "to an emerging athleticism and participation in sports" with a "focus on the importance of the body in the origins of ego development" (p. 700). He also notes that this is a neglected topic in our literature.

This paper will focus on an overlooked aspect of superego development, namely, the value of sports participation in the extrafamilial socialization of the latency boy. Sports do not offer simply an ego ability or pastime, but they exert an adverse or beneficial effect on the superego and ego ideal and the development of values of the latency child.

LATENCY-AGED CHILDREN AND SPORTS

While the parents of latency girls may be pleased by the broadening of their daughter's opportunities for individual and team sports, often paralleling male participation in softball, track and field, basketball, and so on, only some aspects of this paper may apply to girl athletes. I have had insufficient experience with latency girls to state any generalizations. However, I'm sure that some aspects of the athletic scene may apply to girl athletes as well as the boy athletes.

Intuitively, latency-aged children and their parents "know" that sports are good for them, physically, emotionally, socially, and morally. Often the major impetus for involvement comes from the latency-aged child. Analysts of an older generation may remember when, absent any organized sports programs or parental input, punchball, stickball,[1] stoopball, and so on were played in city streets and schoolyards, unsupervised and unprogrammed. No leagues, no win/loss records, no spectators, no uniforms, no coaches, and no overwhelming desire to win at all costs. We played because it was "fun" and we needed the physical activity.

Currently, there is an organizing social structure to latency sports. Many parents finance and encourage their children's involvement. Consciously parents are motivated by (a) the social aspects of team sports, (b) the acquisition of skills and competences, which will likely last a lifetime, and (c) the realization that their child needs an expenditure of physical energy amid a day of sitting in school, sitting for homework, sitting for dinner, and so on. On another level they intuitively understand that their child will learn how, when, and to what degree one can be aggressive and assertive. While not overtly stated, many parents want their child to know how and when to compete and when and how to cooperate, albeit the emphasis is often on the competition. Some parents find a welcome relief in enrolling the child in still another "outside the

---

1. *The New York Times* (July 9, 2012, p. A12) had a three-quarter-page article on an old timers' league that gathers together on Sundays to play stickball, with the traditional broom handle as the bat.

home" activity. Sports educators speak of the children learning about teamwork, discipline, functioning under pressure, learning athletic skills, as well as gaining a sense of personal responsibility. Academic sports educators speak of the benefits of healthy competition combined with the virtues of "sportsmanship," often adding the historical concept of "moral education."

Parental motivations vaguely articulated or outside immediate awareness are that their child is more likely to submit to a coach in an athletic milieu than to parents or to school teachers. Parents who have had moderate to outstanding success in sports want their child to have a similar experience, particularly when the parents feel that their success in sports made a significant contribution to their character and personal attributes. For other parents it is an opportunity not to relive past successes, but rather to undo past failures, lost opportunities, and to live vicariously through their child. Intuitively, many parents recognize that even the modulated aggression expressed in competition is far better than overt aggression expressed to siblings and/or parents. Some parents hope that their son's sports participation will create or solidify a somewhat shaky sense of masculinity. While sports per se can no longer be equated with masculinity, nevertheless, for many it is an accepted symbol of masculinity.[2] For the parents of girls, sports may represent an area of gender equal opportunity, especially since the passage of Title IX, mandating that colleges and high schools provide athletic opportunities and funding for women equal to that provided for men.

Parents often contribute to the idea that latency-aged sports participation should lead to victories and wins, as though caught up in the ethos of college and professional sports, and uncritically apply them to latency sports. While at the high school and college levels, winning teams are highly desirable for all sorts of reasons, this is not necessarily so at the latency level. Parents who want their child to be the star may engender a "win at all costs" atmosphere, little realizing the potential harm to the team and to their child's emotional growth. Other parents, wishing to create a "winner," may place undue emphasis on training,

2. In actuality we see many professional athletes whose masculinity is arrested at the adolescent level in the sense that masculinity is measured by how much alcohol is consumed and how many women they have had sex with or physically overpowered. In college recruitment practices, sex and alcohol parties as inducements for prospective male athletes are an accepted routine, despite being roundly criticized by the administration. "Sports = masculinity" is being vigorously challenged by the success in sports of individual women and women's teams and the mandated opportunities in those institutions abiding by Title IX.

not just for competence but for excellence, sometimes to the point of exploitation, physical injury, and reparative surgery. Children, male or female, in a single sport with year-round training and year-round competition are especially vulnerable.

"Win at all costs" or "winning is the only thing" expresses the mindset of many professional sports gurus. At the professional and even amateur college levels, the cheating, rule breaking, and the use of illegal drugs and doping have been well documented. In some instances these methods are utilized even at the high school level. This prevailing cultural ethos may and often has a "trickle-down effect" to latency sports. At the latency level this translates into playing when injured, using a good pitcher for more pitches than is recommended for that age child, playing only one's best players instead of giving everyone a chance to play, lying about a child's age or place of residence, and encouraging players to cheat and lie.[3] While this ethos may be seen as a microcosm of our society, the latency-aged child and the sports they play should be, if possible, insulated from the more noxious areas of our society until such time as they are able to understand and maneuver safely within it. At its best, latency sports participation offers the opportunity to be taught and to experience the multivaried pleasures of sportsmanship and fair play.

Sportsmanship and its values can be seen as the goal of age-adequate superego development in latency boys. This is a goal that players strive to attain in the exercise of their sport skills and attitudes toward teammates and opponents. However, the attainment of that goal needs knowledgeable support from umpire, coach, and parents. Their efforts, together with the rules of the game and the social milieu, all engrave the concept of sportsmanship and fair play into psychic structure. In brief, while parents support, encourage, give time and money to their child's sports participation, what is also crucial is the nature of their motivation, conscious and unconscious, and the degree to which it supports or undermines the values of sportsmanship, which in turn will influence the child's ego mastery, emotional growth, and the development of the superego.

---

3. These attitudes have generated several popular sports books (Hyman, 2009; McMahon 2007; Engh 1999) decrying coaches' lack of training, their lack of knowledge, or even concern about injuries, and how a coach or parent's desire to win creates untenable pressure to the point that many children are traumatized and/or lose their desire to participate further in a sport that for them has more pressure than enjoyment. Hyman (2009), a reporter for *The New York Times*, documents (regretfully) how he pushed his son to excellence, entailing the overuse of his son's pitching arm and necessitated "Tommy John" reparative surgery (replacing an elbow tendon).

WIN OR LOSE

A healthy psyche should be able to deal "maturely" with winning and with losing. When a team loses, there are many possible reactions. One player may be scapegoated and may passively accept the blame and the team's hostility. At other times it is not a single player who makes a crucial misplay; the entire team plays poorly. Do they blame themselves and walk out depressed, angry with each other, or focus on the referee's "bad calls" against them and the many uncalled fouls of the other team? Much depends on the coach and the degree to which "winning was everything." When winning is *the* goal, there is not only the discomfort of shame (for a bad show) but also the aggression that accompanies the public humiliation of self and team. When loss engenders shame, the question is often where and to whom hostility will be vented.

When a coach's emphasis is on playing well, working as a team, and developing one's skills, then a loss is not a tragedy but can be used as a learning experience. Can a coach convey the concepts that "perhaps the other team might have been a better team"? Or "we had a lot of fun and we will do better next game." When the standards of judgment differ from "winning is everything," the team is under less pressure to win, less pressure to play dirty, less pressure to hurt an opponent. "Less pressure" psychoanalytically means less aggression and less narcissism invested in winning, and thus less shame and humiliation in losing. It does not mean less effort or less desire to excel. In a sportsmanship-motivated game, the ego ideal and the narcissistic investment in winning are different. The narcissistic investment in winning gets subsumed under playing hard, playing well together, learning more about the game, and having a good time. Unlike a "winning is everything" approach, sportsmanship is infused with a sense of satisfaction and enjoyment of a game played hard and fairly. That the coach and the parents can accept the team's loss reduces children's own punitive impulses toward their own team, toward themselves, and toward their coach. Win or lose, the game was worthwhile and fun. There is ample praise (from self and others) in a game played hard and well, albeit lost.

THE CONCEPT OF FAIR PLAY, SPORTSMANSHIP, AND THE ROLE OF UMPIRES

For many, the very word "sportsmanship," rooted in the hierarchal class structure of British society, may invoke images of upper-class morality, that is, not being overly concerned with winning in sports since, in a sense, participants have already won on the economic and social playing fields. In nineteenth-century England certain of the public schools "forged the cult of athleticism" (Arnold, 1997), which linked the playing of games to the forming of character, with "character" being defined in terms of "an ideal of a muscular-Christian gentleman" (p. 45), a concept strongly related to training those who would conquer and administer the far-flung realms of the British Empire. The "English gentleman" concept gradually migrated to others in the Commonwealth and to the United States. The phallocentric bias also comes from that era in Britain when females did not participate in competitive sports.

Before the beginning of the twentieth century, British school children of the lower classes had physical exercise as a means of teaching sacrifice of personal desires for the common good, which translated into the intended purpose of creating an obedient work force (Theodoulides and Armour, 2001). This remained the goal of physical education until the 1920s, when physical education in all (public and private) schools viewed the playing of games as a pathway to character development, that is, sportsmanship and fair play. Some disciplines introduced the additional concept of "spiritual development," while others saw benefits in what they labeled as "greater body awareness." In 1926, the "Sportsmanship Brotherhood" promulgated the concept of sportsmanship as a "form of social and moral well-being," adopting the slogan "Not that you won or lost—but that you played the game" (Arnold, 2003, p. 97). The underlying concept was that of a social union that esteemed fellowship rather than the more specific win/lose criteria. The dean of sportswriters, Grantland Rice (1880–1954), stated the issue even more elegantly: "For when the One Great Scorer comes to mark against your name, He writes—Not that you won or lost—but how you played the Game" (Fountain, 1993).

While much rhetoric is given to sportsmanship as a concept and ideal, in actuality it can be easily forgotten and/or superseded by the narcissistic and aggressive needs of players and coaches. Considerable superego maturation is required to attain and practice sportsmanship: refrain from cheating even when one can "get away with it"; curb one's aggression so as not to cause deliberate harm or injury to an opposing player; accept an official's call even when you are certain that it is in error; and maintain a proper balance between your own narcissistic wishes to excel and/or dominate and the teamwork essential for a well played game.

Only after looking at sports from an analytic perspective does one realize the degree of superego development necessary for a child's effective and enjoyable sports participation. It requires a commitment and relationship not just to the sport, but to coach, teammates, and parents, which ultimately becomes internalized. It is to oneself: to participate, to learn the sport, to follow instructions, and to learn to cooperate strategically with teammates. To the extent that this is an obligation entered into not only with others but with oneself, it represents a significant hallmark of the maturing internalization and superego development in the latency child.

A sport requires learning the rules of engagement, that is, what is permissible and what is not. Rules clarify the areas and opportunities for cheating, modifying, and otherwise "bending" the rules to your team's advantage. The concept of sportsmanship entails the clear proviso that even if there is the opportunity to cheat, even when coupled with the likelihood of not getting caught, "it is not the way the game is played."[4] When there is a strong incentive to win (as in a sports league as opposed to a casual pickup game), abiding by the rules, calls of boundary issues, (strike zones, offsides, fouls, safe at first base, and so on) are not to be decided by prolonged discussion or arbitration. Thus the umpire, the referee, the official line caller, and the like are brought into the game. With an impartial person making decisions, the game speeds up and fairness is insured, at least theoretically.

The umpire, judge, referee, or linesman needs to be accepted by all as the final arbiter, even though many calls are equivocal or even incorrect. Professional sports may have a video replay, or several officials might consult with each other. At the latency level, there is usually one official. The latency age child expands his development from the intrafamilial issues to the rules of the game, and by the acceptance of the judgment calls of an official. Nevertheless, whatever the outcome of a game, there is the opportunity for ego ideal growth and satisfaction in the sense that he/she is a "good sport" demonstrating a high level of "sportsmanship."

These social and psychological advances can be undone by the antics of parents who confront the umpire nose-to-nose and publicly disparage and demean the official. These parents seem more concerned with their own narcissistic issues and less about teaching their child that sometimes good people may make poor calls but without malevolent intent, or even that it was an accurate call but against their child.

I was treating a highly narcissistic professional man who came from an uneducated, argumentative family. Their poverty led to his placement in an orphanage for several years preschool. Inwardly he felt himself to be a fool, a "nobody," and could not imagine that his sons felt differently. Despite their seeming lack of interest, he enrolled them in a sports program. He made sure to give

---

4. To go back to the British roots of sportsmanship, "It is not cricket."

them additional lessons and attended their games. On one occasion he stormed out onto the field, stood nose-to-nose with the umpire, and argued his son's called third strike. He ignored his wife's and son's pleas to return to the stands. Only when threatened with a call to the police did he desist and return to his seat. In our sessions, it was difficult for him to see that he embarrassed his son and that he acted inappropriately as a parent.

Few people consider the difficulty for an official, even an experienced professional, to call a game totally accurately. In most instances a questionable call is accepted by both sides and the game proceeds. In some instances even an erroneous call is accepted as a final decision. This may be a critical point in a child's development, namely the ability to see that a grown-up may be wrong, even inept, but if it is not personally motivated, it needs to be given due respect. The umpire, in addition to his or her on-field presence and as an expert on the rules and regulations of the game, may also have a symbolic internalized function.

A ten-year-old patient, with lots of rage at his father and two subsequent stepfathers, loved to play ice hockey and particularly enjoyed slamming an opposing player into the boards. He often reassured himself that the referee would make sure he really did not hurt anyone since he had no animosity against the opposing players, but he acknowledged that he had a great deal of rage, anger, and hate inside him.

A well-trained umpire or referee with knowledge and experience has the final word in disputed or ambiguous situations. While the umpire is often "invisible" or in the background, a well-umpired game is appreciated by all, except by fans who wanted their team to win and view the umpire as a biased participant who ruled "unfairly" against their team. All the controlled and sublimated aggression on the playing field may exacerbate spectators' preexisting aggressions, leading to shouts of "kill the umpire," and the like. Spectator rowdiness and violence have become serious problems in many parts of the world. Some of the violence is fan against fan; other times it is against players, necessitating police escorts of the players at the end of a game. It is as if the sublimated aggression on the playing field exacerbates existing inner hostilities of the spectators so much that the aim of inhibited aggression modeled by the athletes is no longer relevant or determinative, perhaps because there is no comparable physical outlet available to spectators. In highly contested events, spectator aggression moves quickly from ideation and impulse to overt action. More pointedly, the latency children who witness this regression in adult behavior may have their own recent psychic achievements and sublimations rapidly undone. Unfortunately there is often a "trickle down" effect from adult sports fans' behavior to the latency sports field. In response, some communities in the United States are considering or have adopted some form of "spectator training" and the signing of pledges for proper behavior as a prerequisite for parental and spectator attendance at their children's sporting events. These communities readily use the police to control parental "misbehavior" and to serve as backup for a beleaguered umpire. I believe that parental and spectator abusive and violent behavior needs to be controlled quickly and definitively lest the adult behavior provoke a regression in the latency child and undoes the child's efforts to channel, control, and modulate one's aggression and narcissism. It is hard for a latency child to maintain recently attained psychological advances when witness to uncontrolled regressive parental behavior.

EXTRAFAMILIAL IDEALIZATION AND SUPEREGO GROWTH

Anna Freud (1981) noted that de-idealization of the parents is not a characteristic of adolescence but that it is latency where the process begins. To the degree that the latency child needs an object to idealize, sports figures are readily available. Hopefully they will not disappoint the latency child's need for a hero or heroine. Latency age children are intent on finding a person, present or past, to idolize as an awesome athlete. In my days of growing up we knew little and cared little to know of the foibles, alcoholism, adultery, and so on of our athletic heroes. We thought of them as living in their uniform now and forever more. Sadly, things are different now. We see professional athletes arrested or indicted for drug crimes, barroom brawls, drunk driving, even shooting themselves in the leg. Hardly models for the latency child. Fortunately, the need for the fantasied identification is strong and present. The latency child looks for the untarnished player and proudly wears that name on his or her T-shirt as an identification with an idealized professional athlete.

Being a "team player" is a recognized compliment that is not easily earned. Psychologically this entails placing one's individual aspirations and ego ideal into a social context. Teamwork, team spirit, team cheers, team shirts and emblems, while having a distinct narcissistic flavor, contribute to the beginnings of belonging to a group, separate from the immediate and extended family. While individual team members may stand out as superior players, it does not negate the group psychology involved. Team photographs are a permanent record of a team of which you are only one among others.

On a theoretical level, the latency age male child emerges from the oedipal conflict with a superego and values that preserve his father's life as well as his own. "Society," at the oedipal level, is the immediate family. In latency the superego broadens in scope to embody rules and practices defining the how and when of using socially approved, highly modified aggression against another. All players survive. Skill and competence in sports become a means of rank ordering, both of individuals and of teams. In addition, team sports provide children with a voluntary decision (unlike school, which is mandatory) to enter into a social network and a social organization, a team, with each child having assigned tasks and cooperating for the common good of themselves and their team. The team and the playing field to some degree replace the family as the stage for the further taming and socialization of primitive narcissism and aggression. The child is not only a member of a family but expands membership status to include his or her teammates and coach. Hopefully, sports participation can become more inclusive, as children with special needs are given the special tools for their participation.

SPORTSMANSHIP AT THE EXTREMES

Sportsmanship entails being a "good winner," that is, treating the losing team with respect with an absence of belittlement and insult. The importance and significance of winning is the issue that divides the athletic and sports community. Working hard, practicing a sport, learning to work with your teammates are the concepts we try to help the latency child internalize as values in their ego ideal. To take an example, to pass the soccer ball to a teammate who is not guarded as closely as you are and who probably has a better chance to score the goal is not just obedience to what the coach has taught the players, but also involves shedding personal narcissism for the benefit of your team. This entails getting narcissistic pleasure from the collective narcissism of the team's effort as opposed to the individual narcissism of having scored that goal.

I attempted to treat an excellent early adolescent lacrosse player who knew he could score the goal without passing to teammates, and often did so, unassisted. Despite repeated warnings and explanations, he could not understand why the coach kicked him off the team even though he was the highest scorer and in his mind the best player. Lacking was the ability to work as a member of the team. Instead he acted as though his teammates were there to set up his scoring all the goals. While his team enjoyed winning, they did not enjoy playing with him or, as they experienced it, "playing for him." The coach had tried to imbue him with "team spirit" and team play, but to no avail.

In contrast is a late-latency-aged girl and her two-years-younger sister, the latter being an award-winning soccer player as a "striker" and who played soccer all year. The father earned three letters in sports in high school and currently coaches soccer teams. The older sister was referred to me because the parents felt that she was a loner who avoided friendships. She told me that she was neither lonely nor in need of friends since she enjoyed doing all sorts of things totally alone. However, in her own soccer play as a fullback (a totally defensive position), she decided that she would try her best to become a center halfback (a less defensive position and one closer to midfield). Despite strenuous and concerted efforts in daily practices for over a year, she remained a fullback. She acknowledged no sense of disappointment, claiming ample satisfaction from having tried. Interestingly, she and her sisters are the best of friends and there is no history of sibling rivalry that she can see. However she described her sister as very pretty and relatively slim, while she is twenty pounds overweight with a history of asthma and headaches. I believe that much of the anger, aggression, and competition that one customarily sees in siblings close in age is operative here but defended against, denied, and somatized. Not having access to her aggression, she could only play a defensive position well, as opposed to a position calling for more overt aggressive actions. As a "striker" (a forward attack and scoring position) the sister had no such inhibitions and could make full use of her physical abilities.

While a glaring example, the way a person plays the game often mirrors the intrapsychic processes and may become fruitful sources for understanding the latency child's psychic development and at times become a focus for therapeutic work.

Win or lose, at the end of the game there is the ritual handshake between winners and losers, as though to say, "Glad I did not kill you; glad I defeated you, and I will again. But I can pretend to be a generous victor, and you can pretend to be a forgiving nonvengeful loser." Whatever the unspoken thoughts of the handshakers, a social ritual has developed that seems to say that "This is only a game; we all played hard" and both winner and loser can be "good sports" because it is the game and the sport that is more important than the win or lose issue. Or at least that is implied. The "return of the repressed" can be seen in the recent report of a high school football player, who, although ineligible to play in the game against McClain High School (Ohio), put a tack in his gloved hand as he shook hands with each member of the other team (who had lost 28–0), which necessitated tetanus shots of the "tacked" players (*USA Today*, 2011).

THE COACH AS SURROGATE PARENT AND SUPEREGO REPRESENTATIVE

At the early stages of sports indoctrination and training, parents often serve as coaches or assistant coaches. Some parents will read a book on coaching; others recall their own playing experiences under various coaches. Knowing the strategy and rules of the game is only one basic ingredient of psychologically effective and intelligent coaching. More critical is attitude. Does the coach recognize (consciously or intuitively) that sport, enjoyable in itself, is also the vehicle for teaching more than athletic skills and rules? Does the coach recognize their role in building "character" (read: superego values and ego ideal as psychic structures) and that the coach also serves as a surrogate and representative for parents and society at large? Many sporting organizations recognize the coach's importance, by requiring training, testing, and certification, even at the latency level of play.

Parents who coach a team in which their own child is a member may be in a difficult psychic position. Parent-coaches must neither favor nor disfavor their own child but treat their child as just another member of the team. Even if approaching this ideal of neutrality, the child's perceptions and those of the other team members will see it from their own unique perspective. For the parent-coach the specialness of the parent-child relationship has to be denied as the coach walks the narrow line between neither favoring nor holding his or her child to a higher standard. Parent and child each have the potential to embarrass the other. For some children it is again an exercise in restraining one's aggression. To act up, not listen, mess up on a play, and so on may be especially embarrassing to a parent-coach who may expect the child to be a model to all. Will the child pay dearly for it when both are at home? Some parent-coaches counterreact and are unduly harsh toward their own child as though more is expected, or the child has to set a "good example" for teammates. If the coach is actually or is perceived as favoring his or her own child, the hostility and envy of teammates is often a high price to pay for being the "coach's pet." While a parent-coach may be a suitable transition for some five-to-seven-year-old players, the parent-coach becomes more problematic with the older child who may neither need nor want such continued parental "supervision."

Ideally coaches want players to control their tempers on the field, yet some coaches will scream at a player as though unaware that teammates, opposing players, and the player's parents all hear the critical remarks directed at that player. A coach is a poor model for superego identification if continually arguing with officials about an adverse call, or if attempting to blame the team's loss on the biased refereeing. A coach's disrespect for officials, especially when compounded by inaccurate or incomplete knowledge of the rules, is not a good model for identification. Coaches who run up the score against inferior teams are teaching their team "humiliate or be humiliated; that is the nature of the sport."

Such a coach fosters taking pleasure in the humiliation of others, a far cry from the ideals of sportsmanship. Sometimes the need to win may involve using a good pitcher for more innings than are advisable for a player of that age, thus exposing him to the risk of injury. Coaches who urge a player to play even though hurt and/or injured may expose a player to more serious injury. The coach walks a fine line because not every hurt represents an injury. Nevertheless, many coaches have been known to disparage injuries, as though playing when injured is a mark of "manliness" and dedication to the team and coach. This disregard of health issues at times has been carried to the extreme by coaches at the high school and college levels, who work their players strenuously, regardless of the heat of the summer, and at times with deadly results. While at the college level, a coach's salary or even continuance may hinge on the success or failure of the team, this is less so at the high school level and even less at the latency level. Yet if personal narcissism is at stake, coaches at the latency level may push for a winning team to the point that players feel themselves to be pawns of a narcissistic coach rather than able to enjoy the sport and the competition. Playing only the best players while teammates spend most of the season on the bench is replacing the values of sportsmanship with a "winning is everything" attitude. A recent Pop Warner pee-wee football game between ten-year-olds unfortunately provides a glaring example of thoughtless narcissistic coaches. Within the first six plays between Southbridge and Tantasqua, in Massachusetts, two of the latter's players were taken off the field with possible concussions. At halftime the score was 28–0, but the game continued even though the Tantasqua team had an insufficient number of players to field a team. The final score was 58–0 with five concussions (Belson, 2012).

How a coach helps the team deal with loss is again an exercise in the control of aggression and the restoration of narcissistic equilibrium. Some coaches may single out a particular player as responsible for the loss, and vent on that player. Or the aggression can be aimed at the other coach or accusations that the other team played unfairly, or that the officials were prejudiced, and so on. On the other hand, even a psychologically unsophisticated coach should be expected to soothe a particular child or other children who hold him- or herself to blame for the team's loss, even if the pop-up, easy-catch ball was dropped, allowing the winning run to score. A coach has a psychological task, similar to that of parents and teachers, to channel, modify, and regulate excessive and/or inappropriate narcissism and aggression, especially when they are self-directed.

An angry, harsh, yelling coach is in a sense aggressing against his play-ers, by either frightening them before the game, lest they play poorly, or after the game, berating them for not playing well enough to have won. This aggressive stance by the coach is thought to serve two func-tions: first to unite the team in their hatred and/or fear of the coach, and second, to arouse pregame aggression that will be vented on the opposing team. Whatever the stated motive, the coach ceases to be a model for the sublimated use of aggression and narcissism.

For some professional and amateur coaches, "Winning isn't every-thing, it's the only thing" (Vince Lombardi, 2010), while others feel that playing their best and trying hard is all one should ask. My own belief from the analytic sidelines is that all too often many a younger player's emotional development is placed secondary to the team's winning the game. It is as though professional goals are frequently accepted unmod-ified by many coaches despite their coaching at the latency level.[5]

In St. Louis, the Catholic Youth Council requires coaches to take a course, "Coaching to Make a Positive Difference," a course that ten thousand coaches have already completed. They emphasize several is-sues: (1) think of yourself as a teacher, not just in the skills and strat-egies of the game but in team effort and cohesiveness; (2) provide opportunities for all players. The "opportunity to strike out" needs to be balanced by being part of the team. The statistics of the game take second place to the emotional growth of the child, that is, being ac-cepted as part of a team effort and cohesiveness. Coaches are advised "not to yell" (thus modeling emotional self-control over ego regres-sion). "Don't berate the officials." "Know the rules of the game." These concepts serve as models for the values embodied in sportsmanship and facilitate superego growth and the modeling that embodies good coaching.[6] Other nations have addressed these issues on a governmen-tal level, as they attempt to make sports, similar to the educational system, an activity that enhances the emotional and ethical growth of their youngsters.[7]

5. McCloskey and Bailes (2005) in their chapter "When Winning Costs Too Much" col-lected several typical and/or outlandish incidents of parent rage and spectator rage at *chil-dren's* athletic events. They note that despite much awareness and discussion, the situation has deteriorated. They list "at least six unacceptable mistakes committed by parents and coaches who use inappropriately aggressive approaches to youth sports, thereby eroding the pleasure of sports for kids and fans" (p. 182).

6. Joe Holleman, "Coaching Coaches," *St. Louis Post-Dispatch*, sec. E, April 22, 2008.

7. The British have recognized the enormous impact and importance of the coach in amateur and professional teams both. In 1989 the British Institute of Sports Coaches

Moisy Shopper

THE PARENTS

Some parents think of sports as normative, thus therapeutic for their child's emotional problems. Often parents hope that sports participation will create social skills and friendships where none existed before. It is as though the enforced social contact in the framework of a sport will help the child mature. Hope often exceeds actuality, since many latency boys and girls have problems whose extent or intensity precludes sports participation. For others, sports participation fosters an emotional maturation in areas untouched by academic education.

There are fathers who for either personal shortcomings or work or training obligations[8] had little involvement in the raising of their children early on. However, once the child reaches the age where he or she can participate in a sport, the father becomes energized and uses the sport as a bridge for a relationship to the child. This may be even more so with fathers who had a successful athletic career in high school and college. The father feels knowledgeable, qualified, and eager to engage the child in a sport but may become disappointed and angry when his well-intentioned efforts are rejected. In some instances, the boy has already made significant identifications with either the mother or with her (nonathletic) interests. For other boys, it almost seems as though the father has thankfully rescued them from a feminine identification. Some fathers turn their athleticism into encouragement and interest in their daughter's athletic pursuits: gymnastics, tennis, swimming, diving, soccer, and track. Sports now becomes an added and comfortable medium of exchange and contact.

Many parents, lacking coaching skills, still participate by unfailing attendance at their child's games. This is not only an act of loyalty and support but also an appreciation of the child's maturation, growth, ability, and participation in sports. Often unrecognized is that sports participation can be a measure of emotional growth, much like math or English skills are a measure of intellectual progress. In my work with children, sports and its vicissitudes occupy a significant role in the initial history taking and often in the ensuing treatment.

---

published a Code of Ethics, with revisions in 1992 and 1998. Section headings are as follows: "Humanity," "Relationship," "Commitment," "Co-operation," "Integrity," "Advertising," "Confidentiality," "Abuse of Privileges," "Safety," and "Competence."

8. This is changing, as many women work outside the home or are getting advanced degrees and their husbands stay at home to care for the young preschoolers.

LATENCY CHILDREN NOT INVOLVED IN SPORTS:
CHOICE AND/OR PSYCHOPATHOLOGY

Many latency-aged children who identify with non–sports-interested parents do not participate in sports, which is consistent with their family orientation. Other parents are ideologically opposed to what they perceive as organized sports' ideology of "winning at any cost," as well as a perception of inadequate concern by coaches for childhood injury. Some parents are ideologically opposed to the emphasis on the competitive nature of sports and prefer physical activities that foster cooperation and common good. Other families have talents and interests in music, art, nature study, and so on. Sports, advocated by many, is nevertheless not the only path to psychological maturity in latency.

On the other hand, many latency age children are uninvolved in sports as a result of psychological impairments that preclude participation. Of the more debilitating conditions is the child with serious issues concerning body image and body integrity and the belief that his or her body is so weak, so vulnerable, and so fragile as to preclude emerging intact after sports participation.

For example, a former quarterback of his high school team and a sports enthusiast pushed his ten-year-old son into sports only to have the son push back, drop out, invent excuses, and so on. Over many years his son developed an intense closeness to his mother, whose interests were more in the music and drama realms. It was the last straw for the father, when on Christmas break, vacationing in sunny Florida, his son insisted on wearing a long-sleeved shirt on the beach, fearing that the sun would severely burn him. Seeing his son that fearful overcame the father's prejudice against psychiatry, and the son was brought for consultation. When I asked him about his medical history (which I do for all children, even when I have taken this history from the parents), he told me that when he was young, his "intestines fell out" and he needed surgery to put them back in, but that they could fall out again. He was referring to a hydrocele and an inguinal hernia. This sense of bodily vulnerability and his feminine identification led him to view bodily contact as a danger he would not survive intact. Tackling or being tackled was dreaded. He avoided wrestling, but "loved track."[9]

A nine-year-old boy was brought for consultation. He "worried too much." He felt himself to be very short compared to his age peers (accurate), and had two older sisters, both achieving academically and athletically. His father developed

---

9. This patient is similar to the boy described by A. Freud (1981) who was so afraid of bodily hurt that he was unable to play any sport and simply avoided them.

"asthma" at the time of his birth, which disabled him from mowing the lawn or even carrying his son. The nine-year-old wanted to be a major league baseball player but wanted to play third base, shortstop, or left field, "because the ball does not come at you hard, and nobody throws it hard at you." He then imagined that his fingers or nose would be broken if a ball were to be thrown at him "hard." It seemed to me that it was not only the aggression coming at him (the fastball) but his own sense of vulnerability stemming from his identification with a damaged, weak father.

Another nine-year-old boy was brought for consultation because of "erratic school performance." His brother, age twelve, was born with a cardiac defect, transposition of the great vessels, and required surgery as an infant. Despite a scarred-up chest, he is on the swim team. When I asked for figure drawings, the nine-year-old drew a "little boy who only liked girls and doesn't play with boys. He does not play baseball or soccer and tries to dress up like girls. He plays with dolls and has a girl's bike. He doesn't like rough stuff or getting dirty, playing baseball, and sliding into the dirt." His mother was aware and somewhat amused by his use of tennis balls to indicate "boobs" and his prancing about in feminine ways. She believes it will pass in time. In the boy's earlier years, the father was quite depressed, out of the home for long periods and then, when home, immersed himself in his professional work. In the absence of his father's involvement with him, his overwhelming feminine identification excluded athletics from his physical life. His brother, on the other hand, may have chosen a sport compatible with his physical capabilities.

Other children, though in the early grades of school, are in a latency mode intellectually but not socially, in the sense that they are often home-oriented, still conflictually close to their parents, and have either not been encouraged to enter the social realm of latency group life or regard it as too dangerous, hostile, and aggressive.

A twelve-year-old boy was pressured by his father to achieve both academically and athletically, but according to the mother (and corroborated by my own observation), the father saw his son as identified with the father's younger brother, whose schizophrenia severely impaired his academic and vocational attainments. The twelve-year-old lacked ambition, lacked interest in most things, and was chronically depressed. Pushed to play soccer, he would play only defensively and often lost interest in the game while playing. His teammates rejected him, and his tenure on the team was brief. The father himself did poorly in school, dropped out of college because of his grades, but later was able to discipline himself to become a very organized workaholic and successful businessman. I believe that the father's re-creation of this brother into his son effectively limited his son's academic and athletic success.

Other children are precluded from sports participation because of the demands of academics and the attraction of musical, artistic, and dramatic extracurricular activities. Some children are so overwhelmed with such activities, whether of their own choosing or of their parents', that they often have little time for an after-school snack and bathroom stop.

All of the above instances represent children who could not or chose not to enter into the athletically oriented life of the latency child. In the course of their development, they often find other nonfamily adults, such as teachers and coaches in music, art, drama, dance, and so on, who present skills to be learned, the rules and techniques to learn them, and often capped with the public display of their attainments. The standards for proficiency in these nonathletic fields are well established and laden with opportunities to live up to expectations or to fall short. In addition, the opportunity for scholarships and future employment exist for the nonathlete. I do not in any way want to convey that sports participation per se is essential for psychological development in latency. There are many pathways to maturity.

THE NATIONAL SCENE

Most of us would recognize that the fans watching sporting events at whatever level are emotionally involved and vicariously living through the athlete. However, for some participants being a fan and spectator is insufficient to contain the emotional surges of contested play. Umpires are the logical recipients, as when spectators become so unstrung as to verbally and physically attack an umpire. As of 2001 sixteen states have laws prohibiting assault of an official or a child player. Often the incidents are small and receive little national or even local attention. However, the child athletes who are witness to these adult outbursts are exposed to experiences antithetical to their emotional growth to harness, control, and channel strong emotions into motivated hard-played sportsmanship. Every sport has rules that clearly define what constitutes breaking those rules and the penalties thereof. For the child athlete, these superego functions are in the formative stages, and incidents of adult "misbehavior" (that is, not abiding by the rules of spectatorship) present the latency athlete with a regressive pull and a negative example.

ATHLETICS, SOCIETY, AND CHEATING

Before the Columbine massacre, the student assailants had earlier complained of the exalted and privileged status of the football team, allowing them to harass, bully, and demean other students. The failure of faculty and parents to acknowledge and correct this situation was viewed by the assailants as tacit approval of this behavior. It is almost axiomatic that schools, students, and parents support the football team. Of all sports, football, despite its huge expense, seems to represent a school more than other school sports. American life is infused with sports at all levels of competence and organization (sandlot, school-yard games, to soccer leagues, little league baseball, and so on) and certainly by the dominant position of professional sports. It is a matter of pride to have a professional team in one's city, even if costly to the city financially. Sports, with its emphasis on monetary rewards and win-ning, often engages, encourages, and/or conceals cheating and other rule infractions. The illegalities of the college basketball and college football recruitment practices would necessitate a book in itself. Even at the high school level, bending and/or concealing residence require-ments, academic deficiencies, and financial (illegal) rewards are almost standard operating procedures in some school districts. In addition, for those unable to afford the costs of a college education, excellence in sports appears to be the only road open to them. Even achieving an athletic scholarship may not provide the education needed for reason-able employment. Once graduated, only a small percentage get the call from professional teams. It is a common perception that these athletes have been exploited by their educational institutions and often end up injured, without a degree or a marketable skill, and despairing for their futures. The argument can and often is made that these college athletes were knowledgeable as they made their choices to play. This cannot be said for the latency child. To the extent that superego attitudes filter down from high school, college, and professional sports to the latency age child and to their parents, coaches, and organizations, considerable harm may occur to those participating in latency age sports.

CONCLUSIONS

Psychoanalysts need to give greater attention to the role of latency sports in the interaction between child and parent and the child's interaction with teammates, coaches, and referees. While school problems usually get early parental attention, sports problems should not be overlooked. Sports, unlike school, are voluntary and physical, necessitating a differ-ent arena of ego abilities, particularly those involving overt aggressive discharge, self-esteem regulation, and establishing a superego and value system in harmony with social groups.

Sports play an essential role in the latency child's developing super-ego, as they introduce them to parents/surrogate adults representing societal as well as their own personal conceptual superego functions. When the surrogates' views are not in unison with those of the parents, the latency child has the added task of attempting to reconcile the disparate views.

Sports participants, engaged in both the discharge and the inhibition of aggression, should follow the values of sportsmanship and fair play, which define allowable outlets of aggression and narcissism. The rules of the sport, combined with the imbued spirit and techniques of teamwork, temper the allure of unitary individual achievement.

Parental involvement in latency sports offers a discharge route for unresolved narcissistic and superego conflicts of the parent, which, if counter to acceptable spectator behavior, undermines the basic psychological advantages of organized latency sports for their child. Just as parents wish their child to go to the best available school with the best available teachers, so too parents should review the credentials of the sports program and the training and orientation of the coaching.

Children who have physical or emotional impediments to sports participation, or simply a disinclination or lack of interest in sports, need to find other group activities, led by knowledgeable adults, that will provide the opportunities and advantages of sports, that is, working with others under a system of appropriate rules, such as musical performance, drama, and art productions and projects.

Sports, like it or not, are part of our popular culture that idealize part objects, for example, singers, movie and TV stars, celebrities of all breeds, and finally the sports superstar. Many are worthy and outstanding people; others are cardboard figures loosely attached to a skill. While sports heroes appeal to the latency child, parental help may be needed when the hero betrays the child: "Say it ain't so, Joe."[10]

BIBLIOGRAPHY

ABLON, S. (1988). Psychoanalysis of a Stuttering Boy. *International Review of Psychoanalysis* 15:83.
ARLOW, J. (1982). Problems of the Superego Concept. *Psychoanalytic Study of the Child* 37: 229–244.

10. This is attributed to "Shoeless" Joe Jackson's interaction with a child at the time of the Chicago Black Sox scandal. He was an outstanding player for the Chicago team, which was so superior to its opponent in the World Series that gamblers bribed several players of the Chicago team to lose the Series. All players involved were banned from professional baseball for life.

288 *Moisy Shopper*

ARNOLD, P. J. (1997). *Sport, Ethics and Education.* London and New York: Cassell.
_____. (2003). Three Approaches Toward an Understanding of Sportsmanship. In *Sports Ethics: An Anthology,* ed. Jan Boxhill. Malden, MA: Wiley-Blackwell.

BABATZANIS, G. (1997). The Analysis of a Pre-homosexual Child with a Twelve-Year Developmental Follow-up. *Psychoanalytic Study of the Child* 52:159–189.

BELSON, K. (2012). A 5-Concussion Pee Wee Game Leads to Penalties for the Adults. *New York Times,* Oct 23, 2012.

BERNSTEIN, D. (1983). The Female Superego: A Different Perspective. *International Journal of Psychoanalysis* 64:187–201.

EMDE, R. (1988). Development Terminable and Interminable II. Recent Psychoanalytic Theory and Therapeutic Considerations. *International Journal of Psychoanalysis* 66:311–320.

ENGH, F. (1999). *Why Johnny Hates Sports: Why Organized Youth Sports Are Failing Our Children and What We Can Do about It.* Garden City Park, NY: Avery Publishing Group.

ETCHEGOYEN, A. (1993). Latency—A Reappraisal. *International Journal of Psychoanalysis* 74:347–357.

FINKELSTEIN (1991). Neglected Aspects of the Superego. *Journal of the American Academy of Psychoanalysis and Dynamic Psychiatry* 19:530–554.

FOUNTAIN, C. (1993). *Sportswriter: The Life and Times of Grantland Rice.* New York: Oxford University Press.

FREE, M. (2008). Psychoanalytic Perspective on Sports: A Critical Review. *International Journal of Applied Psychoanalytic Studies* 5 (4): 273–296.

FRENKEL, R. S. (1996). Oedipal and Preoedipal Transference Transformations: Comments on the Analysis of a Latency-Age Boy. *Psychoanalytic Study of the Child* 51:326–347.

FREUD, A. (1965). Diagnostic Skills and their Growth in Psychoanalysis. *International Journal of Psychoanalysis* 46:31–38.
_____. (1981). The Concept of Developmental Lines—Their Diagnostic Significance. *Psychoanalytic Study of the Child* 36:129–136.

HARRIS, A. (2010). Baseball's Bisexuality. *Contemporary Psychoanalysis* 46:480–503.

HIRSCH, I., AND BLUMBERG, P., ISSUE EDS. (2010). Introduction to the Special Issue on Intense Involvement with Sports. *Contemporary Psychoanalysis* 46 (4): 475–479.

HYMAN, M. (2009). *Until It Hurts: America's Obsession with Youth Sports and How It Harms Our Kids.* Boston: Beacon Press.

KERNBERG, O. (1989). The Temptations of Conventionality. *International Review of Psycho-analysis* 16:191–204.

LEDERER, W. (1964). Oedipus and the Serpent. *Psychoanalytic Review* 51:79–104.

LOMBARDI, V. (2010). "Famous Quotes by Vince Lombardi." Official Web site of Vince Lombardi, http://www.vincelombardi.com/quotes.html.

McCLOSKEY, J., AND BAILES, J. (2005). *When Winning Costs Too Much: Steroids, Supplements and Scandals in Today's Sports.* Taylor Trade Publishing.

McMahon, R. (2007). *Revolution in the Bleachers: How Parents Can Take Back Family Life in a World Gone Crazy over Youth Sports*. New York: Gotham Books (Penguin Group).

Novick, J., and Novick, K. K. (2004). The Superego and the Two-System Model. *Psychoanalytic Inquiry* 24:232–256.

Peller, L. E. (1954). Libidinal Phases, Ego Development, and Play. *Psychoanalytic Study of the Child* 9: 178–198.

Petrucelli, J. (2010). Serve, Smash, and Self-States: Tennis on the Couch and Courting Steve Mitchell. *Contemporary Psychoanalysis* 46:578–588.

Sarnoff, C. (1976). *Latency*. New York: Aronson.

Shapiro, T., and Perry, R. (1976). Latency Revisited: The Age of 7 Plus or Minus 1. *Psychoanalytic Study of the Child* 31:79–105.

Sherick, I. (2012). The Emergence of Athleticism and Participation in Athletics: A Proposed Line of Development. *Psychoanalytic Review* 99 (5): 697–716.

Theodoulides, A., and Armour, K. M. (2001). Personal, Social and Moral Development Through Team Games: Some Critical Questions. *European Physical Education Review* 7 (1): 5–23.

Tyson, P., and Tyson, R. (1990). *Psychoanalytic Theories of Development: An Integration*. New Haven, CT: Yale University Press.

USA Today (2011). Ohio Player Arrested for Using Thumbtack in Handshake Line. *USA Today*, Oct. 25.

Index